Studien zur Migrations- und Integrationspolitik

Herausgegeben von
Uwe Hunger, Münster, Deutschland
Roswitha Pioch, Kiel, Deutschland
Stefan Rother, Freiburg, Deutschland

Weitere Bände in dieser Reihe
http://www.springer.com/series/11808

Migration ist einer der zentralen Globalisierungsphänomene des 21. Jahrhunderts. Entsprechend groß ist das Interesse an Fragen der politischen Regulierung und Gestaltung der weltweiten Migration, den Rechten von Migrantinnen und Migranten und der Integration von der lokalen bis zur globalen Ebene. Die Buchreihe ist interdisziplinär ausgerichtet und umfasst Monographien und Sammelwerke, die sich theoretisch und empirisch mit den Inhalten, Strukturen und Prozessen lokaler, regionaler, nationaler und internationaler Migrations- und Integrationspolitik befassen. Die Reihe richtet sich an Wissenschaftlerinnen und Wissenschaftler, Studierende der Geistes-, Sozial-, Wirtschafts- und Rechtswissenschaften sowie an Praktikerinnen und Praktiker aus Medien, Politik und Bildung.

Herausgeber der Reihe sind die Sprecherinnen und Sprecher des Arbeitskreises ‚Migrationspolitik' in der Deutschen Vereinigung für Politische Wissenschaft (DVPW): PD Dr. Uwe Hunger, Universität Münster, Prof. Dr. Roswitha Pioch, Fachhochschule Kiel, Dr. Stefan Rother, Universität Freiburg. Der wissenschaftlichen Beirat setzt sich aus ehemaligen Sprecherinnen und Sprechern des Arbeitskreises ‚Migrationspolitik' zusammen: Prof. Dr. Sigrid Baringhorst, Universität Siegen, Prof. Dr. Thomas Faist, Universität Bielefeld, Prof. Dr. Karen Schönwälder, Max-Planck-Institut zur Erforschung multireligiöser und multi-ethnischer Gesellschaften, Göttingen, Apl. Prof. Dr. Axel Schulte i. R., Leibniz Universität Hannover, Prof. em. Dr. Dietrich Thränhardt, Universität Münster.

Laura Block

Policy Frames on Spousal Migration in Germany

Regulating Membership, Regulating the Family

Laura Block
Berlin, Deutschland

Dissertation European University Institute Florence, 2012

Studien zur Migrations- und Integrationspolitik
ISBN 978-3-658-13295-8   ISBN 978-3-658-13296-5 (eBook)
DOI 10.1007/978-3-658-13296-5

Library of Congress Control Number: 2016934428

Springer VS
© Springer Fachmedien Wiesbaden 2016
This work is subject to copyright. All rights are reserved by the Publisher, whether the whole or part of the material is concerned, specifically the rights of translation, reprinting, reuse of illustrations, recitation, broadcasting, reproduction on microfilms or in any other physical way, and transmission or information storage and retrieval, electronic adaptation, computer software, or by similar or dissimilar methodology now known or hereafter developed.
The use of general descriptive names, registered names, trademarks, service marks, etc. in this publication does not imply, even in the absence of a specific statement, that such names are exempt from the relevant protective laws and regulations and therefore free for general use.
The publisher, the authors and the editors are safe to assume that the advice and information in this book are believed to be true and accurate at the date of publication. Neither the publisher nor the authors or the editors give a warranty, express or implied, with respect to the material contained herein or for any errors or omissions that may have been made.

Printed on acid-free paper

This Springer VS imprint is published by Springer Nature
The registered company is Springer Fachmedien Wiesbaden GmbH

Acknowledgements

This book is based on my PhD research carried out in the years 2007-2012 at the European University Institute in Florence. Many thanks to Rainer Bauböck, Kees Groenendijk, Martin Kohli, Anne Phillips, Saskia Bonjour, Betty de Hart and René Gabriëls for their comments and inspiration and to all my interview partners for taking the time to speak to me.

Table of contents

Tables and figures 11

List of abbreviations 13

1 Introduction 15
1.1 "Marriage migration" literature meets migration
   policy analysis 16
   1.1.1 Literature on "marriage migration" 16
   1.1.2 Migration policy in theory 20
1.2 Research problem and research design 33

**2 A theoretical framework for the analysis of spousal
migration policies** 41

2.1 Analysing family migration policies 43
   2.1.1 The right to family and the power of social
      membership 43
   2.1.2 Ideas on family and membership within
      family migration policies 47
   2.1.3 An analytical framework for family migration policies:
      Regulating membership and regulating the family 51
2.2 Marriage-of-convenience policies: Preventing the
   state from being duped? 61
   2.2.1 How to justify marriage-of-convenience policies 63
   2.2.2 How to criticise marriage-of-convenience policies 64
   2.2.3 The European preoccupation with
      marriages of convenience 70
2.3 Fighting forced marriages: Defending liberal norms? 72
   2.3.1 Forced marriages and the rationale for state action 74
   2.3.2 Forced marriages as a minority practice? 78
   2.3.3 Forced marriage policies within migration law 82

3 Empirical and legal realities of spousal migration to Germany 87

3.1 The evolution of German family migration policy 88
   3.1.1 1950-2000: Political negligence and judicial activism ... 88
   3.1.2 2000-2005: Reforming migration law
      in a protracted process 102

3.1.3 Language skills as a pre-migration requirement:
   The Aussiedler-Nexus 108
3.2 The legislative framework of spousal migration 112
3.3 The demographics of spousal migration to Germany 116

4 2005-2010: Spousal migration comes into focus **127**

4.1 Institutional and conceptual shifts enabling the
   "restrictive turn" 127
4.2 Spousal migration law changes after 2007 134
4.3 Immediate effects of the reform on spousal migration inflows 146

5 The European dimension of family migration policies **157**

5.1 The supranational dimension 157
   5.1.1 Family migration rights within international
      and European law 157
   5.1.2 The 2003 Family Reunification Directive 161
   5.1.3 The Free Movement Directive 167
   5.1.4 Turkish citizens' rights under association law 171
5.2 Spousal migration policy developments in other
   European states 2005-2010 176
   5.2.1 The Netherlands 176
   5.2.2 France 180
   5.2.3 Denmark 183
   5.2.4 The United Kingdom 186
   5.2.5 Austria 190
   5.2.6 Switzerland 191

6 Political and institutional frames on spousal migration **197**

6.1 Framing spousal migration in the *Bundestag* 2005-2010 207
   6.1.1 Forced marriages 209
   6.1.2 Integration 213
   6.1.3 The language requirement 220
   6.1.4 The EU and other European states 229
   6.1.5 Minister Schäuble's framing 231
6.2 Framing spousal migration in the legislative
   and the executive branches 234
   6.2.1 The protection of female victims 236
   6.2.2 Breaking up parallel societies 240
   6.2.3 The "devaluation" of German citizenship 243

6.2.4 The protection of the public budget 249
6.2.5 The differentiation of migration flows 250
6.2.6 Fighting abuse of spousal migration 256
6.2.7 The role of Europe and other institutional dynamics 258

7 The "other" side: Transnational couples' and migrant advocates' perspectives 265

7.1 Spousal migration framed by migrant advocates 269
   7.1.1 General framing of spousal migration 269
   7.1.2 Ethnic minority Germans 271
   7.1.3 Forced marriages 272
   7.1.4 Integration 273
   7.1.5 Language requirement 274
   7.1.6 Marriage patterns and marriage norms 276
   7.1.7 Institutional dynamics 277
7.2 Transnational couples' difficulties 280
   7.2.1 Language requirement 281
   7.2.2 Marriage-of-convenience suspicions
        and intimacy inquiries 283
   7.2.3 Minimum income and required documents 285
   7.2.4 Interaction with public authorities
        and procedural difficulties 287
   7.2.5 Emotional and relational difficulties 290
7.3 Transnational couples' reactions to restrictions 291
   7.3.1 Transnational couples' agency: Creating pressure 291
   7.3.2 How do transnational couples frame their claims? 295
   7.3.3 What are the transnational couples' coping strategies? 301

8 Conclusions 309

Bibliography 325

Annex – Overview primary material 345

Tables and figures

Table 1: Examples of policy approaches regulating membership and family ties 54
Table 2: Number of total visa granted to spouses 1996-2006 119
Figure 1: Percentage of spousal migration visas granted by citizen and foreign sponsors 120
Figure 2: Spousal residence permits granted in 2006 by gender and legal status of sponsor 122
Figure 3: Gender breakdown of spousal residence permits granted in 2006, in per cent 123
Table 3: Spousal residence permits granted in 2006, by incoming spouses' most common countries of origin 125
Table 4: Spousal visas granted 2005-2010 and relative change to previous year 147
Table 5: Spousal residence permits granted 2005-2010 and relative change to previous year 147
Table 6: Absolute (relative change compared to amount in 2006) and relative amount of spousal residence permits granted in 2010, by incoming spouses' most common countries of origin 149
Table 7: Spousal residence permits granted in 2006 (% of total), by gender and legal status of sponsor 152
Table 8: Spousal residence permits granted in 2010 (% of total), by gender and legal status of sponsor 152
Table 9: Absolute and relative numbers of residence permits granted to parents of minors in Germany, 2006-2010 153
Table 10: Political parties in the German Bundestag in the 16th legislative period (2005-2009) 201

List of abbreviations

AA	Auswärtiges Amt (German Foreign Office)
Abs.	Absatz (paragraph)
AufenthG	Aufenthaltsgesetz (Residence Act)
AuslG	Ausländergesetz (Foreigner's Law)
BGB	Bürgerliches Gesetzbuch (Civil Code)
BMI	Bundesministerium des Inneren (Federal Interior Ministry)
BVerfG	Bundesverfassungsgericht (Federal Constitutional Court)
BVerwG	Bundesverwaltungsgericht (Federal Administrative Court)
BVFG	Bundesvertriebenengesetz (Federal Law on Expelled Persons)
CEFR	Common European Frame of Reference for Languages
CDU	Christlich Demokratische Union Deutschlands
CSU	Christlich Soziale Union in Bayern
ECHR	European Convention on Human Rights
ECtHR	European Court of Human Rights
ECJ	European Court of Justice
EU	European Union
FCN	First-country national (non-moving EU citizen)
FDP	Freie Demokratische Partei
FR	family reunification
GDR	German Democratic Republic
GG	Grundgesetz (Basic Constitutional Law)
IAF	Verband binationaler Familien und Partnerschaften (Association of Binational Families and Partnerships)
MP	Member of Parliament
OECD	Organisation for Economic Co-operation and Development
SCN	Second-country national (intra-EU migrant)
SPD	Sozialdemokratische Partei Deutschlands
StGB	Strafgesetzbuch (Criminal Code)
TCN	Third-country national (non-EU citizen)
UDHR	Universal Declaration of Human Rights
VG	Verwaltungsgericht (Administrative Court)

1 Introduction

No analysis regarding migration in contemporary Europe can afford to ignore the phenomenon of family migration. In 2007, 13 out of 17 European countries listed indicated that "family reunion" was their most extensive category of long-term migration.[1] It was only in the remaining four cases[2] that "work" qualified as the main category (Niessen et al. 2007). In these states, family-related migration makes up between 40 and 63 per cent of all long-term migration inflows. Family-related migration, which includes the admission of foreign family members of citizens, long-term resident foreigners and new migrants, made up approximately 44 per cent of all legal immigration to OECD countries in 2006, thereby constituting both the single largest category of entry and the category with the largest increase (OECD 2008: 36). This development is not new; for the past three decades family migration has been the principal way of legally migrating to Europe (Kofman 2004: 243). This pattern, which has been established in most of Western Europe since the mid-1970s, is intrinsically connected to the decrease of other legal immigration possibilities. When large-scale (low-skilled) labour migration was halted all over Europe after the economic downturn following the oil crisis in 1973, family migration grew in proportion to other types of migration inflows in most European states.

More recently, family-related migration[3] has also become the target of restrictive policy reforms in various European polities. In the context of the 2015 refugee crisis, family reunification rights of refugees were controversially debated, including proposals to curtail these rights in order to halt refugee inflows. The increasing political and public attention directed at controlling family-related migration, and especially spousal migration, has not yet been met with a similar degree of academic con-

---

[1] Austria, Belgium, Denmark, Finland, France, Germany, Italy, Latvia, Lithuania, the Netherlands, Norway, Sweden and Switzerland.
[2] Hungary, Portugal, Slovenia and the United Kingdom.
[3] Intra-EU migrants are governed by EU legislation and not directly affected by national (family) migration policies across Europe due to their free movement rights. Therefore, in the European context within this thesis, the concepts "migrants" and "migration" generally refer to third-country nationals, i.e. non-EU citizens.

sideration. While some work, mostly sociological and anthropological, has explored the trajectories and perspectivesof family migrants themselves (see Williams 2010 for an overview) and many research endeavours have attempted to theorise and explain the general direction migration policies take (see Boswell 2007 for an overview), less work exists that analyses policy-making directed specifically at family-related migration, an empirical gap that this work partly aims to fill. On a theoretical level, it explores the ways in which liberal democracies, despite being under pressure to protect individual rights, nonetheless manage to implement restrictive policies.

1.1 "Marriage migration" literature meets migration policy analysis

In the following, two bodies of literature are reviewed. First, research on spousal migration flows is considered (1.1.1). Most of the studies discussed focus largely on the perspectives of the individuals involved with sociological and anthropological questions and methods. While no profound analysis of migration policies takes place in these investigations, the migration flows they document are nevertheless relevant, as they inform policy framings of decision-makers explored later. The theoretical literature on immigration policy is reviewed in a further section (1.1.2). Most of the work considered here contends that despite most immigration policies having restrictive goals, they often lead to liberal outcomes because of various economic, judicial and political "liberal constraints."

1.1.1 Literature on "marriage migration"

In the last two decades, scholars have increasingly investigated phenomena associated broadly with the migration of spouses. Initially coined as "marriage migration" by Thadani and Todaro (1984), it typically referred to a marriage between a woman from an underdeveloped country and a Western man, implying female upward economic mobility (Waldis 2006: 8). Even semantically, the term "marriage migration" conveys a notion of the marriage's (sole?) purpose being the goal of migration – which is why I will use the more neutral term "spousal migration" in the following. Indeed, economic incentives to marry (in order to migrate) have featured prominently in many studies, even if the neoclassical model of rational choice was soon expanded to include structural aspects such as historical, institutional and socio-cultural factors as well as individual agency into the picture (Fan & Huang 1998).

Most of the literature dealing with spousal migration, which has also been conceptualised as "cross-border marriages" (Constable 2004) or "transnational marriages" (Charsley 2005), is based on anthropological and sociological research often focusing on the spousal migrants' perspectives. Much of the work explores the dynamics of migrants' motivations to engage in this process in the first place as well as outcomes resulting from it. Attention is paid both to the structural (demographic, economic, legal, social, cultural) conditions in the countries of origin and destination propelling and/or constraining both spouses to engage in the process, as well as to the agency developed and employed by individuals within these structures.

Perhaps unsurprisingly, gender dynamics feature very prominently in nearly all studies on spousal migration. They are used as an explanatory variable of decisions and/or as a site of individual contestation between the spouses and their families. Attention is also paid to the business structures surrounding spousal migration, such as agencies and brokers (e.g. Wang & Chang 2002), alongside the changes in communication technologies facilitating cross-border acquaintances (Constable 2003a; Robinson 2007). In general, the overwhelming focus of all this research is on the perspective of female movers, even though some work consciously addresses this bias and incorporates the perspectives of men as sponsors (Constable 2003a: 6; Ruenkaew 2003) or even focuses primarily on experiences of incoming male spouses (Charsley 2005; Gallo 2006; Fleischer 2008). The research methods employed are mainly qualitative, often consisting of in-depth interviews with the individuals involved concerning their life-stories and other types of ethnographic fieldwork. However, quantitative analyses do also exist. Based on survey data, they explore the interconnections between socio-economic factors (e.g. income, education) and other individual background characteristics (e.g. age, gender, children, urban/rural provenance) and spousal migration decisions and outcomes (Ortiz 1996; Fan & Huang 1998; Lievens 1999; González-Ferrer 2006).

Much literature has concentrated extensively on migration of spouses within and from Asia, again especially on Asian women moving in the context of marriage (Piper & Roces 2003; Constable 2004a; Palriwala & Uberoi 2008; Lu & Yang 2010). The authors often question stereotyped ideas that regard female spousal migrants as either passive victims of trafficking or desperate gold-diggers seeking to escape poverty and hardship by marrying upwards. Instead, the diversity of experiences is explored, as are the (often deeply gendered) instances of agency displayed by the individuals involved.

In this context, the "paradoxes of global hypergamy" (Constable 2004: 10) are revealed, rejecting a simplified notion of exclusively economic motivations propelling women from poorer countries into marriages with men from richer ones. The socio-economic status of both the brides and grooms are shown to vary; scholars have documented well-educated, middle class female movers who even risk stepping down the social ladder through their cross-border migration. For example, Thai (2003) describes the case of highly-educated female professionals in Vietnam who are considered "too successful" to be desirable in their home country, and therefore turn towards low-wage Vietnamese migrants living in the USA instead of staying single or marrying "down" in Vietnam. Non-material desires or love are shown to play important motivational roles as well. For example, the wish to (re-) marry, as an important life course goal, can in itself propel migration, especially if structural constraints to marriage (such as restrictive divorce laws) are present in the home country, which can lead to "migration in order to marry" (Constable 2003b; Lauser 2008).

Real or imagined gender constructions are variously demonstrated to be of importance for both spouses. Constable (2004b: 7) suggests that "cartographies of desire" (Pflugfelder 1999) manage spousal migration flows as "marriage-scapes both reflect and are propelled by fantasies and imaginings about gender, sexuality, tradition and modernity." Accordingly, it is often reported that (Western) men associate traditional moral and (exotic) sexual ideas with foreign women, frequently implying more conservative gender roles than are predominant in domestic societies or possible in a relationship with native women. Ironically, research on female Asian marriage migrants (e.g. Freeman 2004) reveals that they often imagine their marriage to a "modern husband," either from the West but also from Japan, South Korea or India, as a way to escape patriarchal gender roles in their home countries (Constable 2004b: 7). Some scholars also examine the connections between cross-border marriages, domestic work and sex work (e.g. Mix & Piper 2003), while others warn of conflating these different types of gendered migrations with "human trafficking" (Constable 2006).

The family-migration nexus long remained under-theorised and under-researched in Europe, which stands in contrast to the more extensive research done in the North American and Asian-Pacific contexts (Kofman 2004: 244). However, many studies have emerged in recent years. When turning to this body of literature on European cases, a strong (though not exclusive) focus on the phenomena of second or third-generation ethnic minorities engaging in spousal migration with partners from their parents' home countries is discernible.

This research "often departs from the idea that marrying a partner from the country of origin is symbolic of a lack of integration" (Eeckhaut et al. 2011: 273). Interestingly, here the research often focuses on the sponsoring spouse, regarding what motivates second-generation minorities to choose a partner from abroad (e.g. Timmerman & Wets 2011), though some scholars have also started to explore the perspectives of incoming spouses too, such as Charsley (2005), Gallo (2006) and Fleischer (2008), who all concentrate on incoming husbands.

Different structural and individual reasons have been put forward to explain what drives ethnic minorities in Europe to search for spouses abroad (Beck-Gernsheim 2007). Some authors have shown how a significant degree of loyalty towards, or pressure from, family and kin can influence the decision to marry a partner from abroad (Ballard 1990; Straßburger 1999; Shaw 2001). Other work focuses on the dynamics of the transnational marriage market. Since emigration into Europe is sought after in many sending countries, the "market value" of sponsor spouses can increase. This bargaining advantage can enable sponsors to find a spouse with a higher social status or prestige (e.g. in terms of education or income, but also attractiveness or youthfulness) when marrying a partner from abroad than would have been possible on the domestic marriage market. Sponsoring marriage migration can thus result in upward social mobility, as is the case with marriages of highly educated professionals to low-income ethnic minority women documented by Charsley (2005: 94), for ethnic Pakistanis in the UK, and by Hooghiemstra (2001), for ethnic Turks in the Netherlands. However, in this context strong "de-skilling" and a connected decrease of socio-economic position can be a consequence of migration as well. Contrary to the "ethnic loyalty" factor, this "higher market value" dynamic holds for inter-ethnic couples as well, as has been shown by Glowsky (2007: 299). The foreign wives of the German sponsors he studied were on average younger, thinner and more educated vis-à-vis their husbands than in German-German marriages. These two factors (familial pressure and better bargaining position) can interact, as the larger dowry accompanying the immigration of incoming grooms might induce parents to arrange their daughter's marriage with a spouse from abroad (González-Ferrer 2006: 173).

Finally, (real or imagined) gender dynamics have been mentioned in several European studies as motivation for individuals to engage in spousal migration. Ethnic minority male sponsors, for example, have been shown to prefer brides from abroad since they consider them to be more traditional and docile than the "spoiled" women in Europe (Shaw 2001). This finding is similar to the dynamic mentioned above of gendered imaginings concerning "traditional" Asian women and "modern" Western men (Constable 2004b). Other research has contested the popular notion of ethnic minority spousal migration to be a display of archaic traditional values or an indicator of deficient integration. It has been repeatedly established that ethnic minority female sponsors in Europe consciously opt for a husband from their parents' country of origin because they expect their skills and experience in the host country will lead to an enhanced (gendered) power position in the relationship vis-à-vis their newly incoming migrant husband and less familial control due to the absence of the in-laws (Autant 1995; Lievens 1999; Timmerman 2008).

All of the work reviewed here provides fascinating insights into individual and structural factors propelling spouses to engage in spousal migration. However, the relevant state policies on admission, if considered at all, mostly figure as external variables influencing the migrants' opportunity structures.[4] The corresponding policy processes, thus the formulation, implementation and discursive framing of policies, which are partly informed by the (actual and/or stereotyped) dynamics of the flows outlined above, have more rarely been subject to an extensive analysis. Since the present research aims to bridge this gap, I will now turn to the body of literature dealing with the analysis of migration policies.

1.1.2 Migration policy in theory

As is the case with analyses of other policy fields, most of the literature on migration policy-making analyses both policy processes and policy outcomes, often aiming at establishing theoretical models that account for particular dynamics within this policy area. While comparative analyses across countries are rather common, the general regional focus lies strongly on Western liberal states.[5]

What exactly is meant by migration policies? In earlier work on the topic, Hammar (1985) distinguishes between policies of "immigration control," which relate to the admission and residence of foreigners, and

---

[4] However, see ter Wal et al. (2008) for an examination of the effects that the Dutch legislative restriction of 2004 had on Turkish spousal migrants' decisions and experiences.
[5] Exceptions that analyse migration policies of non-Western states include Russell (1989) writing on Kuwait, Cornelius (1994) on Japan and Seol & Skrenty (2004) on South Korea. See also Massey (1999: 315-316), who theorises that migration-receiving states' capacity to implement restrictive policies depends, among other factors, on the respective strength of constitutional protections and the independence of the judiciary.

"immigrant policies" dealing with the incorporation (or integration) of foreigners into the host society. However, the two areas are highly intertwined: the expansion or curtailment of foreigners' rights, although related to immigrant policy, often has a direct impact on new migration inflows, and can thus be seen to influence immigration control too (Lahav & Guiraudon 2006: 208). Therefore, while the main aspects associated with immigration control, such as laws on admission and residence, remain central to most studies referred to here,[6] questions about the consolidation of foreigners' basic rights and their claims to membership in the polity are also crucial in much of the literature. In the case of family migration policies, this intertwining is especially pronounced, as family migration is situated at the crossroads between migration policy and foreigners' rights. Whereas family migration itself constitutes a new inflow and its regulation can thus be classified as migration control, the rights granted to foreign residents to sponsor the admission of their family members relate to their incorporation and are thus instances of immigrant policy. Recently, elements relating to integration, especially host language proficiency, have been introduced into the control of residence and even initial admission of (family) migrants, blurring the distinction between the two areas even more.

Theorising the acceptance of unwanted migration: The "gap" debate and liberal constraints

The above-mentioned near exclusive empirical focus on migration policies of liberal democracies in Western Europe and North America also explains the main questions dealt with by researchers. One of the most-discussed empirical puzzles within the scholarly debate of migration policy asks why, despite strong anti-immigration positions on the part of the public and the government, large-scale legal immigration continued into Western countries, especially after the economic downturn of the mid-1970s. The main empirical evidence informing this puzzle is the (mainly European) "spectacular instance of cross-national policy failure" (Hansen 1999: 417). This refers to the phenomenon of guest workers

---

[6] A parallel body of literature (comparatively) analysing incorporation policies towards migrants and ethnic minorities also exists (e.g. Joppke 1996; Freeman 2004) but will be largely disregarded here, since initial spousal admission policies constitute the later main research focus.

transforming their temporary sojourn into a permanent one by remaining in their host states and bringing in their family members.

Since this puzzle deals with an apparent gap between the proclaimed policy goals of preventing migration and the policy outcome of significant legal inflows, Cornelius, Martin and Hollifield famously summarised the idea in their "gap hypothesis" in 1994: a gap between proclaimed goals and actual outcomes of migration were "wide and growing wider in all major industrialized democracies" (1994: 3). The notion that this gap might be caused by inefficiency or lack of enforcement has largely been rejected (Hollifield 1992: 94; Boswell 2007: 75). While irregular migration and its impact should not be underestimated, the overwhelming majority of post-war migrants have entered and settled in Europe via legal channels (Bonjour 2011: 92). Therefore, the far more significant and theoretically interesting question is what factors actually lead to policies that allow immigration inflows officially considered detrimental for overall societal welfare, or in other words, "why liberal states accept unwanted migration" (Joppke 1998a).

In an attempt to explain this disparity between officially stated restrictive policy objectives and expansive policy outcomes in the field of migration control, academics have put forward various ideas relating to the impact of different domestic and international forces within the policy process. In early work on this issue, Hollifield (1992: 27) adopts Ruggie's notion (1982) of "embedded liberalism" to demonstrate that liberalism is the dominant framework of the post-war international (economic) order affecting migration policies (see also Cornelius et al. 1994: 31). Hollifield basically considers two variants of "liberal constraints" influencing migration control policies in Western democracies. The constraints, which are intrinsic to liberal democracies themselves, confront politicians and policy-makers with a "liberal dilemma." First, within an increasingly international (neoliberal) economic system with large global inequalities, pressure is created for a relatively free flow of labour next to the free flow of capital and goods in order to sustain domestic economic growth. The second and most important factor concerns the growing importance of rights-based liberalism within the political process. As an integral part of their identity, liberal democracies are not only democratic (and accordingly might tend to give in to public pressure for restriction) but are also liberal; respect for individual rights is therefore an important part of their identity and legitimacy. As these rights have been increasingly extended to foreigners and minorities, the liberal state's autonomy to expel migrants at will, for example, or prohibit family migration, is inherently diminished.

Accordingly, I propose to distinguish these two variants as an "economic liberal constraint" on the one hand, and a "liberal rights constraint" on the other. Some authors see these constraints mainly emanating from globalisation and suggest that the explanation for the control gap lies in the generally decreasing autonomy of the nation-state in an ever-globalising world. For example, Sassen (1999) presents a combination of economic and political arguments to support her contention that the nation-state is being transformed. She posits that the economic pressures and institutional changes emanating from globalisation limit nation-states' capacity to restrict migration as much as they might like to. Such factors include the market's structural need for free movement of labour and the handing over of sovereign national powers to international organisations, such as the WTO and the EU. She further argues that a privatisation of government functions within migration control, itself pertaining to a neoliberal economic logic, transforms the ability of states to influence migration. However, Sassen refers to the liberal rights constraint too, by stating that international human rights codes are growing in importance, thereby increasing the pressure upon nation-states to grant individual rights to all persons on their territory, and not only their citizens.

The two variants can be assumed to play out differently for the policies controlling distinct inflows, a point which Hollifield partly takes up in his later work (2004). While the economic liberal constraint presumably strongly influences labour migration policies, the liberal rights constraint is more important in the context of humanitarian inflows, such as asylum and family migration, and the expansion of basic rights to resident foreigners. Moreover, whereas the economic liberal constraint can have an impact on illiberal states' migration policies as well, the liberal rights constraint is probably truly unique to liberal democracies. As the family migration policies of European liberal democracies are the focus of this research, the following will further explore the different ways researchers have dealt with the liberal rights constraint.

Judicial liberal constraints

One way liberal rights constraints have been theorised to restrict the amount of control governments have over migration is by way of codified (human) rights, which are ensured by international and domestic courts. As mentioned above, Sassen points to the growing importance of international human rights codes, which force nation-states to respect the rights not only of their citizens, but all residents on their territory as well.

Authors such as Jacobson (1996) and Soysal (1994) have made similar points. Soysal argues that after World War II, a post-national normative world order emerged, where international and European charters bind nation-states to respect human rights of all individuals, regardless of their nationality. In this view, the protection of individual rights is increasingly guaranteed beyond the nation-state and the formal citizenship status loses importance, leading Soysal (1994: 3) to speak of "post-national citizenship." To Soysal, the main explanation for inclusionary migration policies is the expansion of individual rights to former guest workers and other foreigners in Europe. She associates these "changes in the parameters of membership" directly with the "institutional rules of the global system," especially respect for human rights, which shape nation-states' "interests and self-definition" (Soysal 1994: 33).

Other authors however, are more sceptical of the actual power emanating from international human rights norms. For example, authors such as Joppke (1998) or Guiraudon and Lahav (2000) contest these "globalist" arguments. They point out how, instead of international human rights, liberal domestic legal norms have been crucial in the expansion of foreigners' rights. Interestingly, they concur with the globalists (e.g. Jacobson 1996: 13; Sassen 1999: 194) concerning the importance of the judiciary within a democratic state that embraces the rule of law and separation of powers. Nonetheless, their explanations differ. While for Sassen, Jacobson and Soysal, international human rights conventions and globally institutionalised norms push European and domestic courts towards liberal judgements on migration control, in Joppke's mind, "[n]ot globally limited, but self-limited sovereignty explains why states accept unwanted immigrants" (1998: 270). In Europe, in particular, this self-limitation emanates mainly from an "activist judiciary" (Joppke 1998a: 284), which mainly defends the rights enshrined in domestic constitutions rather than being forced to adhere to international obligations. Guiraudon and Lahav (2000: 189) further sustain this claim empirically by tracing the influence of the European Convention on Human Rights (ECHR) on migration policies in Germany, France and the Netherlands. They conclude that while some norm diffusion from the international to the national level can be observed (mainly regarding expulsion), the predominant factors limiting restrictive migration control are national human rights obligations emanating from domestic constitutions and jurisprudence.

Nonetheless, the European Court of Justice (ECJ) has certainly played an important role in expanding the rights of intra-EU migrants (Kostakopoulou 2007; Carrera & Merlino 2009), while the European Court of Human Rights (ECtHR) has, especially recently, pronounced various judgements establishing (family) migration and residence rights of third-country nationals (TCNs) in Europe under the guise of the ECHR (Thym 2008; de Hart 2009; van Walsum 2009). In any case, whether international, European or domestic in their outlook, all these approaches are united by their strong emphasis on the judiciary, which, by challenging political decisions and overturning restrictive migration policies, is conceptualised as a main source of the liberal rights constraint. I propose to speak of "judicial liberal constraints" in this context. Of course, judicial liberal constraints do not only manifest themselves in corrective judgements, but can influence political decisions *a priori* too, as the possibility of being condemned by the courts later on might also have a "preemptive" effect. This can lead policy-makers to refrain from devising policies they assume will be later overruled by the courts to be incompatible with basic constitutional or human rights.

Political liberal constraints

Scholars have also established other kinds of liberal rights constraints, which are not directly linked to court judgements, but rather concern liberal dynamics emanating from within political systems and processes themselves. In the following, I will refer to these factors as "political liberal constraints." While different authors have proposed various approaches and explanations in this context, they all focus on liberal tendencies emanating in one way or another from within the political system. Of course, the political and judicial aspects of liberal constraints interact; for instance, when policy-makers appropriate their behaviour to real or expected reactions from courts, or when judges refer to political goals in their judgements. It is nevertheless useful to conceptually disentangle these different actors and sources of liberal rights constraints.

One of the first approaches to explain migration policy outcomes with dynamics stemming from the domestic political process was that of Freeman (1995). In a similar manner to what Joppke or Guiraudon and Lahav find, Freeman rejects the notion of the state losing sovereignty in the field of migration control. Instead, he explains expansive migration policies with a model of "client politics" by zooming in on the distribution of interests among different societal groups. Contrary to other authors, he largely ignores the role of courts in ensuring the individual rights of foreigners. According to Freeman, migration inflows result in concentrated benefits and diffuse costs in the host society. Those benefiting immediately from liberal migration policies, such as employers and migrants, organise into interest groups and manage to make their voices heard to policy-makers. He claims that the immediate costs of migration affect only those segments of society competing directly with migrants for education, housing and jobs, but being highly disenfranchised, their opinion is not heard. More importantly, migration also has costs for society as a whole, but these perceived problems are often not immediately apparent (Freeman 1995: 885). Another part of his analysis concerns the reasons for an apolitical public opinion on migration. He posits that reliable information on migration is scarce to the public and a "constrained discourse" inhibits anti-immigration voices in the public realm as these are quickly charged with racism in liberal democracies. Furthermore, he proposes that an "antipopulist norm" exists among political leaders to not exploit immigration-related fears (1995: 883-885). To him, the resulting public opinion that is favourable or indifferent to migration allows pro-migration "client politics" to be endorsed by politicians. Therefore, the impetus for liberal migration policies emanate from various factors, which are all situated within the political process.

Freeman has been criticised for ignoring the judicial realm altogether (Joppke 1998a: 271) and for overestimating the neutrality of the state as an independent broker between different interests (Boswell 2007: 79). His notion of a "constrained discourse" has been put into question as being by no means intrinsic to liberal democracies at all times but rather a "historically specific and contingent feature of public discussion at certain times and places" (Brubaker 1995: 905). Guiraudon (1998: 288) similarly emphasises that a "constrained discourse" might adequately describe the situation of early guest worker recruitment in Europe, but becomes untenable regarding the empirical realities of clear politicisation of migration issues from the 1980s onwards, while Perlmutter (1996: 384) points to the autonomy of political parties in exploiting migration issues for political gain, especially in Europe.

Nevertheless, Freeman's strong emphasis on the policy process, which locates the explanations for migration policy outcomes within the decision-making structures of states, has found many adherents who have expanded and modified his ideas. For example, Guiraudon (1998; 2000a; 2002) has adopted Freeman's emphasis on the political process (which she terms the "institutional trajectory") of migration policy-making. She especially stresses the importance of the relevant institutional sites ("venues") of decision-making and their specific *modus operandi*: "In sum, the 'why' of reform depends on the 'where' of reform" (Guiraudon 1998: 287). In her work on the expansion of rights to foreigners in Europe from the 1970s onwards (Guiraudon 1998; 2002), she asserts that liberal policy outcomes are the result of migration-related decisions taking place behind "closed doors," mainly in high courts and public welfare agencies. Contrary to Freeman, she assumes that public opinion leans strongly towards restriction, and thus liberal migration and incorporation policies are most likely to occur when they are least politicised and shielded from public discussion (1998: 290). According to this view, judges and bureaucrats are only able to implement liberal reforms due to their insulation from electoral pressure. While for Freeman the answer to the gap puzzle lies in interest distribution across societal groups and political agreements to depoliticise migration issues, Guiraudon's explanation is situated within liberal democratic institutions. She assumes high courts and social bureaucracies to be inherently biased towards the expansion of rights due to institutional logic. For courts, applying due process and equal treatment in a consistent manner is crucial to maintain their own legitimacy, while welfare bureaucracies tend to standardise operations in order to save costs and thus incorporate foreigners into existing schemes instead of developing new ones (2002: 140). Next to a judicial liberal constraint originating from high courts, she therefore theorises a political liberal constraint to emanate from domestic bureaucratic actors as well.

Another approach focusing on political rather than judicial liberal constraints is presented by Boswell (2007), who argues that the state and its interest in securing its own legitimacy and capacity to govern vis-à-vis the public must remain central to any migration policy analysis. She thus rejects the idea that the source of any liberal constraints are "exogenous" factors (such as liberal institutions or a powerful business lobby), but emphasises that the state will only be receptive to calls for inclusionary migration policies (or any policies for that matter) if they resonate with the state's own interests in keeping up legitimacy ("functional imperatives") (2007: 91). She considers security, fairness, accumulation and institutional legitimacy to be the four conditions that states strive to achieve for their members in order to be considered legitimate and proposes a typology of migration policies along these criteria. While fulfilling goals related to security and fairness tends to produce restrictive migration policies, successfully improving accumulation and institutional legitimacy can lead to inclusive migration policies (2007: 89). To Boswell, the state expanding foreigners' rights is not simply due to the objective power of courts constraining the state, but rather emanates from the state's desire to ensure its own legitimacy as a liberal democracy that respects its independent institutions, its constitution and the rule of law. The state thus cannot just "roll back" the judiciary when it pronounces liberal and thus inconvenient judgements. In this view, any liberal constraint influencing migration policies can ultimately be traced back to political interests of decision-makers to ensure their own legitimacy.

Bonjour (2011) also places a lot of emphasis on political liberal constraints emanating from within the political process. In her historical analysis of Dutch post-war (1955-2005) family migration policies, she critically deconstructs various earlier strongholds of the "gap" debate. Bonjour questions both the notion of a unitary state actor, as well as the idea that states always want to restrict migration but are hampered in this undertaking by external liberal forces. Instead, she shows firstly how opinions on family migration diverged among various actors within the state, and secondly how some of these actors, such as Catholic parliamentarians and civil servants from the Ministry of Social Affairs, were strongly in favour of family migrant admission. Most pertinently, Bonjour shows that "values matter," as in her case the pro-migration attitudes of policy-makers neither emanated solely from judicial constraints nor from economic interests. By contrast, they were formed by individual ethical considerations rather than through liberal norms "imposed" from forces external to the political process. Without reaching the depth of Bonjour's analysis, Joppke (1998: 287) makes a similar point when repeatedly referring to the "independent workings of moral obligations" of political decision-makers, especially towards the first generation of guest workers, in the case of German family migration policies.

Theorising restriction: Escaping liberal constraints by venue-shopping and strategic framing

The empirical reality of increasing restriction is considered in work analysing more recent migration policy initiatives in Europe. For example, Guiraudon extends her focus on domestic actors and the importance of decision venues to work on the development of migration and asylum policies at the EU level (e.g. Guiraudon 2000a). Here, she theorises that at the national level various actors, especially courts, national migrant organisations and migration-friendly parts of the executive, in combination with abstract constitutional and legal principles, protect liberal migration policies. In order to circumvent these liberal constraints, restrictive-minded executives engage in "venue-shopping" by transferring decision responsibilities from the national arena downwards to the local level and outwards to private actors (Guiraudon & Lahav 2000). Most significantly, however, her contention is that a shift upwards to the EU is also occurring, with domestic liberal actors virtually "disappearing," making EU venues highly amenable to restrictive reform (Guiraudon 2000a: 268).

Some writers also argue that the implementation of migration policy has been partly externalised, with "remote control" instruments

(Zolberg 2003), to escape liberal rights constraints. Operating at both the domestic and the EU level, examples of such "remote control" policies include carrier sanctions (i.e. making transport companies liable for controlling their passengers), strict visa requirements, establishing international zones at airports that amount to "juridical no man's lands" (Guiraudon & Lahav 2000: 185) and migration control agreements with sending and transit states. Put bluntly, with "remote control" instruments, policy-makers can dodge liberal rights constraints by selecting and deterring (irregular) migrants and asylum seekers before they even enter liberal democratic territories where they would be entitled to human rights protection and could not easily be expelled (Guiraudon 2000a: 259; Lahav 1998: 683; Lavenex 2006a: 334).

Lavenex (2001; 2006a) has also explored the phenomenon of domestic actors using the EU arena in order to achieve restrictive migration objectives. In a compelling analysis, Lavenex (2001) shows how restrictive national actors, such as the Member States' interior ministries, have strategically influenced the way asylum is framed at the EU level. She shows how domestic actors, instead of focusing on human rights, mainly presented asylum as a side issue of the single market project and thus as a security issue, thereby establishing a sense of urgency for restriction. This is further sustained by the opaque nature of intergovernmental EU negotiations (Guiraudon's "closed venues") alongside the possibilities to use the normative power of the supranational EU framework to convince (liberal) political and institutional opponents of the necessity for migration policy reform. In this way, the EU presents an "autonomy-generating" escape route to the liberal rights constraints emanating from liberal institutions and actors at the domestic level for restrictive-minded executives, mainly from national interior ministries.

In later work, Lavenex (2006a) expands this idea to policy-making within the EU: After having successfully escaped liberal constraints at the domestic level by shifting policy-making to the EU and framing asylum as a security threat, restrictive executives were increasingly confronted with a replication of previously domestic "political, normative, institutional constraints" at EU level (Lavenex 2006a: 346), especially from the Commission and the European Parliament (EP). Therefore, "venue-shopping" continued to flourish and, by framing migration as an issue of external affairs, certain migration decision-making responsibilities again shifted away from the partly supranational Justice and Home Affairs (JHA) pillar, which included the Commission and the EP in its procedures, to the strictly intergovernmental external affairs pillar. In this way, restrictive-minded actors were able to maximise their autonomy vis-à-vis liberal actors at both domestic and EU level. In addition to her focus on institutional constraints and opportunities, which both relate to Guiraudon's analysis, Lavenex illustrates how policy-makers strategically employ certain framings of migration and asylum issues in order to "escape" judicial and political liberal rights constraints and justify restrictive policies.

A similar focus on framing is echoed by other authors focusing more explicitly on the "securitisation" of migration. Building on critical security literature, including Waever et al. (1993) and Buzan et al. (1998), scholars such as Kostakopoulou (2000), Huysmans (2000) and Ibrahim (2005) illustrate how migration and asylum are politically framed as threats to security in order to justify "exceptional" policies that aim to restrict migration. Specifically, (certain) migration inflows are framed by politicians, policy-makers and the media as endangering internal security by linking them principally to criminality and a general loss of control, but also to threats to national cultural identity and economic security by an overburdening of the welfare state. The literature on security framing, therefore, basically also assumes the presence of political liberal constraints. In this view, restrictive-minded policy-makers are conscious of liberal tendencies emanating from within the societal system, be it from political parties, the executive or civil society, as well as from abstract norms of individual rights and equal treatment. As a reaction, policy-makers legitimise their restrictive policies by framing migration as a danger. Put differently, if no political liberal constraint existed, security framing would be largely obsolete as well. The fact that policy-makers choose to go out of their way to construct migration as a security threat in order to justify restrictive policies is indicative of the presence and stature of such political liberal constraints. The securitisation literature thus basically engages in a kind of frame analysis without necessarily labelling it explicitly so: Migration is constructed to be a threat to security, and the resultant (security) policy solutions are implicit in the depiction of the problem.

Recently, several Dutch scholars have extended the range of issues connected to migration by applying "policy frame analysis," as developed by Verloo (2005). Policy frame analysis focuses on the various meanings and interpretations multiple stakeholders in the field give to an issue in order to explain policy outcomes, and will be the epistemological approach that is also applied in the subsequent research. Roggeband and Verloo (2007), for instance, critically examine the conflation of the two issues of gender equality and migration in the Dutch political discourse. They show how gender equality policies increasingly focus on migrant women and minority policies concentrate on gender relations among minorities as an obstacle to integration. As a result of both processes, the allegedly "oppressed migrant woman" appears as a problem at the top of the political agenda necessitating policy solutions. In an attempt to explain increasingly restrictive migration policies in the Netherlands, Roggeband and Vliegenthart (2007) analyse and compare the framings relating to migration in the Dutch parliament with those that dominated the Dutch media landscape from 1995-2004. They find that, especially after 9/11, the threat of Islam is the dominant frame in both spheres. Interestingly, the authors point out that, contrary to the rather hegemonic media landscape, the framings in parliament are much more diverse and the notion of Islam as a threat is contested.

Over the last two decades, the research agenda has thus changed significantly. In the years of the "gap" debate in the 1990s, researchers were puzzled by expansionary policy outcomes in spite of restrictive policy goals. Different types of liberal constraints were put forward to explain these results. From roughly 2000 onwards, in part inspired by EU involvement in the field, scholars turned towards increasingly restrictive policy outcomes despite previously established liberal constraints, explaining them by highlighting government strategies of institutional escapism and discursive framing.

Analysing family migration policies?

Finally, among the authors analysing migration policy-making, few have differentiated between specific types of migration inflows. This is rather surprising as the treatment of groups as diverse as high-skilled labour migrants, family migrants and asylum-seekers are bound to be subject to very different political considerations, and in practice the policies usually differ significantly. A few instances exist within the literature on migration policy analysis that focus on specific inflows such as family migration (Joppke 1998a; Bonjour 2009; 2011), asylum (Joppke 1998b; Lavenex 2001) or irregular migration (Joppke 1998a). However, the majority of authors try to cover all migration policies with their theories and usually cite specific policy instruments as examples to support their particular line of argument. Therefore, "there is a critical need to explain the multiple dimensions of immigration policies" (Lahav & Guiraudon 2006: 205-206), in the sense of disaggregating the policy processes behind instruments aimed at different migration inflows, when analysing policies.

Other insightful work on family migration laws and policies in Europe is not directly related to the theoretical debate presented above. For instance, legal sociologists de Hart and van Walsum have both written extensively on the evolution of Dutch family migration legislation. De

Hart predominantly focuses on bi-national unions involving one (ethnic) Dutch partner and the presence of institutional discrimination on the basis of gender and ethnicity within policy formulation (de Hart 2003) and implementation (de Hart 2000; 2001). By analysing legislation, case law and political debates on the issue of Dutch-foreign couples as well as immigration dossiers, she shows how a strong norm of the dependent female following her husband continues to prevail throughout the years. This notion can discriminate against couples involving a Dutch woman and a foreign man, as they frequently are suspected of leading a marriage of convenience. Van Walsum (2004; 2008) critically reflects on how dominant societal norms on gender, marriage and family influence family migration policies. She asserts that while within general family law (triggered mainly by female emancipation), an increase in individual liberties and a tolerance for diverse family models has emerged, this development is not mirrored within family migration law. Here, strong normative ideas on family and marriage tend to lead to discrimination and exclusion. As also shown by de Hart, Dutch migration and citizenship law lagged significantly behind the emancipative achievements in general gender relations until the late 1980s, and gave preference to male-led spousal migration, while from the 1990s onwards, strong notions of gender equality norms have served to exclude the supposedly extremely patriarchal Muslim families.

Wray (2006; 2009) raises comparable points of family and marriage norms that serve to exclude certain groups and to control migration inflows in the UK. Furthermore, authors such as Dustin and Phillips (2008) and Wilson (2007) have focused on the specific role of the issue of forced marriage within the (spousal) migration debate in the UK. Another important project has been a cross-national study comparing spousal migration policies and particularly their effects upon migrants across Europe (Kraler 2010). Overall however, a research gap exists regarding the analysis of the political process surrounding spousal migration policies in Europe, and in Germany especially. This is all the more astounding considering the quantitative significance of spousal migration within the overall migration inflow nowadays. This analysis on political framing of spousal migration in Germany is thus one attempt to fill parts of the gaps in the literature highlighted above.

1.2 Research problem and research design

Research problem and research questions

The puzzle of liberal democracies opening up extensive legal channels for migrants despite apparent public and political opposition has occupied scholars trying to answer "why liberal states accept unwanted migration" (Joppke 1998a). Notwithstanding different emphases on the exact mechanisms of this process, one of the main factors identified by previous research has been liberal states' commitment to individual rights, taking the shape of judicial or political liberal constraints. In the specific case of a humanitarian inflow such as family migration, this "liberal rights constraint" can be assumed to be especially strong, since the entrance claims are directly based on an individual right, the protection of marriage and family. Furthermore, this fundamental right in question is not that of the incoming migrant, but that of an established member of the receiving state's community (either a citizen or a foreign resident). The individual right to the protection of marriage and family is not only enshrined in international declarations, as well as more binding legal texts such as the ECHR and different national constitutions, but also has a powerful abstract moral value for policy-makers as it is difficult to entirely dismiss the importance of family unity for individual well-being (Bonjour 2011: 116). At the same time, the past decade has witnessed increasing restrictions being placed on family migration across Europe.

Hence, in a field where, theoretically, the liberal rights constraint could be assumed to be strongest, empirical analyses demonstrate increasing restriction instead, making spousal migration policies the ideal test case for a distinct research problem: How do liberal democratic states manage to restrict migration *in spite of* liberal constraints? An easy answer to the puzzle might be to say: There is no liberal constraint impacting upon migration policies (anymore). However, the answer is not that simple. Liberal norms indeed continue to influence policy-making in the field of migration in Europe. Governments and policy-makers are highly conscious of their obligations to protect individual rights, and thus legitimise restrictions within the logic of rights-based liberalism. While not dealing specifically with family migration, researchers, including Lavenex (2001), have pointed to strategic framing as a way in which governments resist liberal forces. An underlying assumption here is that "framing matters" – or, put differently, the way an issue is spoken about is linked to what policy decisions are taken. Strategic framing can therefore be a way to circumvent or at least diminish the power emanating from the liberal constraint: By depicting an issue in a specific way, liberal rights considerations can be overridden. For instance, by framing asylum seekers or irregular migrants as serious threats to national security, exceptional measures can be justified that would be mitigated by the liberal rights constraint protecting individual rights under other circumstances.

Applying these ideas to family migration policies, we can ask: Does the government employ specific framings in order to introduce and justify restrictive family migration policies? Within the epistemological approach of policy frame analysis (Verloo 2005), specific research questions emerge, such as: How do the relevant institutional actors frame spousal migration policies? Which issues are associated with spousal migration and which policies are presented to deal with them? By uncovering the explicit and implicit policy frames of relevant stakeholders, the institutional strategies of reconciling the liberal constraint with restrictive spousal migration policies are explored. Additionally, a migrant perspective is added to the institutional one by addressing the questions: How do affected transnational couples perceive spousal migration policies? How do they react to them? What frames do they employ in order to strengthen their case?

Modifying Freeman's (1995) notion of a "constrained discourse" regarding migration policies, I suggest that a "liberal discursive constraint" is at work, which compels liberal democratic governments to frame restrictive migration policy instruments in such ways that the general commitment to fundamental individual rights is not put into question. I hypothesise that policies potentially violating individual rights are framed to either achieve other much more pressing goals (including the protection of other human rights), or to actually not infringe rights by demarcating the right itself or those entitled to lay claim to it. The alternative, open disrespect for individuals' rights, is difficult to reconcile with the self-definition as a liberal democracy.

Research design

How are the research questions outlined above empirically dealt with in the following? First, "frame analysis" was identified as a particularly useful epistemological device to explore the research problem. The idea behind this constructivist approach is that any issue can have various meanings, because significant stakeholders interpret (implicitly and explicitly) them in specific, and also contested, ways (Verloo & Lombardo 2007: 31). The theory, first developed within social movement theory (e.g. Snow & Benford 1992), was expanded to the field of policy analysis by introducing the concept of "policy frame," defined by Verloo as an "organising principle that transforms fragmentary or incidental information into a structured and meaningful problem, in which a solution is implicitly or explicitly included" (Verloo 2005: 20). Policy frame analysis thus uncovers the different ways that political stakeholders interpret issues, causally explain them, and accordingly link them to reactions in the form of policy solutions (Rein & Schön 1996). For example, spousal migration can be conceived of as an integration problem, a human right under threat or a legal loophole prone to abuse. Accordingly, the policy recommendations made on the basis of these various explanations differ. The ways in which the concepts of frame analysis are applied to the case at hand will be further explored below.

Second, the spousal migration policies of a single country, Germany, are analysed in an in-depth study that focuses on the years 2005-2010 – a period of restrictive changes in this field. The rationale of a single case research design lies in the nature of the problem and questions under scrutiny. Instead of identifying and measuring independent variables that explain specific policy outcomes in a comparative design, this research aims at contributing to a theoretical debate. In order to advance general understanding of the role of human rights norms within migration policies of liberal democracies, some of the complex discursive mechanisms at work within the specific field of family migration policymaking are disentangled. With this goal, it can be assumed that an in-depth case study of a single polity will produce more relevant results than a comparative analysis could. Furthermore, as will be outlined below, significant instances of comparison are also given within the German case. The institutional framings relating to spousal migration are contrasted not only across the political party spectrum, but also by branches of power (legislative vs. executive). Moreover, transnational couples' views are compared with institutional perspectives.

What factors contributed to specifically choosing Germany as the case study? To begin with, Germany is one of the most important migration-receiving states in Europe. In 2006, an estimated 6.75 million foreign nationals were permanently residing in Germany, which is unmatched by any EU state in terms of size. The percentage of foreigners within the total population amounts to about 8.8 per cent (Maaßen 2007: 2). In contrast to more recent migration destination countries such as Spain, Italy or Ireland, immigration has seen a recent decline in Germany. Nonetheless, in 2005, 707,000 foreigners migrated to Germany, thus establishing it as the most important gross migration destination within the EU in absolute terms (BAMF 2007: 133). As will be outlined in more detail below, family migration constitutes a very significant share of total immigration to Germany. In 2006, 28 per cent of all residence permits granted to third-country nationals were based on family migration, and the largest part of these permits went to spouses[7] (BAMF 2007: 30). After spousal migration suddenly moved to the top of the political migration agenda in 2007, legislative changes were enacted to restrict certain conditions pertaining to spousal migration. Intense public discussions among members of government, parliament, political parties and civil society surrounded the formulation and adoption of these legislative changes, and therefore provide a rich contemporary insight into the issue when examining the time period 2005-2010.

Notwithstanding the quantitative significance of spousal migration to Germany and the recent political and legal dynamism in this field, little academic work on spousal migration policy-making in Germany exists. This research gap marks a contrast to the work produced on the Dutch (de Hart 2000; van Walsum 2008; Bonjour 2009), British (e.g. Wray 2011) and various Scandinavian cases (as Rytter 2010; Borevi 2015; Pellander 2015) well as the research carried out in relation to developments at the EU level (e.g. Groenendijk 2006).

Operationalisation of research questions

As outlined above, spousal migration claims are based on individual rights and are hence strongly "protected" by liberal constraints. I assume that the way decision-makers discursively approach the topic – that is the framings they employ – is crucial to explain restrictive policy shifts. Accordingly, for the empirical analysis, diverging framings of spousal migration across the German political and institutional spectrum are analysed, alongside the connected policy recommendations.

How these policy frames empirically explored? An extensive documentary review of both the historical development of family migration policies and the more recent laws and government practices pertaining to spousal migration, including the restrictive changes introduced in 2007 by the new *Zuwanderungsgesetz,* will first lay the basis for the remaining empirical work. Questions addressed in this documentary review are: What are the official policies on spousal migration? How have they developed over time? How are they framed in official documents? Additionally, available statistical data on the amount and characteristics

---

[7] In 2007, about 75 per cent of all residence permits granted for the purpose of family migration were granted to spouses, 22 per cent went to minor children and 3.5 per cent to "other" family members (BAMF 2009: 127).

of spousal migration into Germany is evaluated in order to contextualise the policies, and reflect upon the actual inflows.

Leaving the realm of official government documents and delving into the frames in more depth, a detailed analysis of all speeches held in the German parliament *Bundestag* surrounding the issue of spousal migration from 2005-2010 is presented in order to uncover the frames employed by the Members of Parliament (MPs) across the political spectrum to defend and attack spousal migration policies. How are the issues surrounding spousal migration and the relevant policies framed in the setting of the parliament? What differences and dynamisms can be discerned across and between parties?

In a second empirical step, the frames found in 19 in-depth interviews held with key stakeholders in this policy field were analysed in order to gain a more profound and differentiated view on the range of institutional approaches towards spousal migration. Semi-structured interviews, lasting on average around 90 minutes, were held with key stakeholders in the field, namely federal MPs of all parties and civil servants working at federal and regional ministries as well as municipal aliens authorities *(Ausländerbehörden)*. Therefore, another important aspect of the thesis concerns the internal differentiation of the state apparatus. While earlier analyses of migration policy often conceptualise the state as a unified actor with one certain set of preferences and strategies, this research at least partly tries to pry open this "black box" and explore the inner workings of the state as well. Apart from analysing the state by way of the laws and policies enacted in the field of spousal migration, a closer look is cast upon the divergent frames employed by actors across the political spectrum and institutional levels when formulating, defending, criticising and implementing spousal migration policies. How is spousal migration framed in the intimate setting of a personal interview? What issues are connected to spousal migration and how are they causally linked to policies? Which different positions can be discerned among the actors?

Finally, a great deal of what is fascinating about the study of migration has to do with the people involved, the migrants themselves. In order to investigate the "other side" of the spousal migration process, interviews were held with representatives of migrant organisations and lawyers working in the field of family migration. In addition, an archive of dossiers documenting single cases of transnational couples in the admission process was included in the analysis. Here, the impact of spousal migration polices on the transnational couples involved were explored, as were the alternative framings of spousal migration policies presented by actors serving migrants' interests.

Terminology

For clarity's sake, some remarks regarding the terms employed in this publication might be helpful. First, even though the terms "family reunification" and "family reunion" are widely used in political and academic contexts, the more generic and encompassing concepts "family migration/migrants" is applied to describe the admission and residence of individuals based on family links to legal residents in the following. Semantically, "family re-unification" implies a pre-existing family joining a primary migrant. This notion, however, is not applicable to certain situations, such as citizens or second-generation migrants forming families with foreigners (sometimes termed "family formation") or to the simultaneous migration of entire family units. However, "family reunification" will still be employed when referring to specific laws or quoting policymakers as it is still the main term used in those contexts.

As the following is mainly concerned with the family migration of spouses, the parallel terms "spousal migration/migrant" are employed as well, and are similarly meant to be encompassing and unbiased concepts describing the admission of individuals due to their marriage or partnership with a legal resident. As mentioned in section 1.1, the commonly employed term "marriage migration" often purports specific connotations I wish to avoid, i.e. marriages concluded primarily for the sake of achieving migration, stereotypically between a woman from a developing country and a man from a developed country. The couples engaging in spousal migration are accordingly labelled "transnational couples," again in order to conceptually include all possible constellations, regardless of nationality and legal status of either spouse. Regarding the distinction between the two spouses, the interchangeable denominations "migrating/incoming/migrant spouse are straightforward. The employed terms "sponsor" or "sponsoring spouse," which describe the citizens or resident foreigners who are joined by an incoming spouse, might be unusual for some readers but reflect the legal terminology in this field.

A last remark regarding the terminology used relating to different citizenship statuses within the European Union. Citizens from outside the EU are commonly described as "third-country nationals" (TCNs) and this idea has been expanded to distinguish between moving and non-moving EU citizens (Bauböck 2007: 468): non-moving EU citizens residing in their home country are termed "first-country nationals" (FCNs) and intra-EU movers "second-country nationals" (SCNs).

Structure

This chapter (1) introduced the state of the art informing the work and outlined the research problem, several research questions and the overall research design. The thesis is structured into seven further chapters. Chapter Two (2) explores the most important normative arguments behind family migration policies in liberal democracies and subsequently presents a tentative theoretical framework for the analysis of family migration policies. The chapter further explores different normative arguments relating to policies that address "marriages of convenience" and "forced marriages." The third chapter (3) turns to the case of Germany, introducing the historical post-war development of policies directed at family migration. In addition, the chapter presents an overview of the basic legal framework pertaining to spousal migration from 1990 up until 2005 and a statistical overview of the demographics of the phenomenon. Chapter Four (4) analyses policy developments from 2005 onwards, including an increasingly restrictive stance on spousal migration that resulted in the introduction of significant legal reform in 2007. Light is shed upon the political intricacies leading up to this decision, the exact legal changes as well as the immediate demographic repercussions on spousal migration inflows. The fifth chapter (5) situates Germany within the larger European landscape of family migration policies by sketching out relevant developments at the international and European levels. Furthermore, spousal migration policy developments in other European states, namely the Netherlands, France, Denmark, Great Britain, Austria and Switzerland, are reviewed. Chapter Six (6) explores how restrictive changes in the field of spousal migration were introduced in Germany. This is done through a frame analysis of parliamentary debates between 2005 and 2010. By exploring the ways in which MPs representing different political parties frame spousal migration and related issues in plenary debates, valuable insights are given into governmental and oppositional approaches within this policy-making field. The second part of this chapter contains an analysis of the frames regarding spousal migration employed by relevant members of the legislative and executive during a series of in-depth interviews. In the seventh chapter (7), the perspectives of transnational couples involved in spousal migration on the policies in Germany are dealt with. The material analysed consists of further in-depth interviews that took place with individuals representing migrant interests alongside an archive of dossiers documenting single cases of transnational couples in the admission process provided by the main family migration organisation in Germany. The migrant advocates' political assessment of German spousal migration policies is explored before turning to the main issues confronting transnational couples, as well as their reactions to these issues. The final chapter (8) summarises the central results of the thesis and outlines the contributions to the theoretical debate, provides recommendations for a possible further research agenda and gives a tentative outlook into the future of spousal migration policies.

2 A theoretical framework for the analysis of spousal migration policies

For more than four decades, family migration has constituted a considerable share of all legal immigration into Europe. Many European states' guest-worker-schemes ended in the 1970s; the economic crisis beginning in 1973 saw a rise in unemployment, and few new possibilities for large-scale labour migration. Family migration continued and grew disproportionately to become the most important mode of entry for third-country nationals (TCNs) into most European countries. In the majority of Western states, family-related migration provisions are in place, allowing the admission and residence of family members of domestic nationals, of legal permanent residents, and of certain categories of newly-arrived migrants (e.g. high-skilled migrants).

Scholars have mainly attributed the political impetus behind a toleration of family migration in the early post-war years to the economic interests of employers' organisations and labour ministries in creating favourable conditions for labour migrants (Triadafilopoulos & Schönwälder 2006; Bonjour 2011). However, even in this time period, normative considerations played a role: In the Netherlands, moral interests expressed by (Catholic) MPs in parliament were important in enabling family migration rights for foreign residents in the 1960s (Bonjour 2011: 102). In Germany, a 1963 proposal to strongly restrict Turkish guest workers' right to family migration was rejected by policy-makers, who worried that discriminatory policies would provoke international criticism and damage the young liberal democracy's image in the world (Triadafilopoulos & Schönwälder 2006: 8).

The continued toleration of family migration after the 1970s throughout Europe has been explained with an ever-increasing normative importance placed on universal human rights (Soysal 1994), or rather on an expansion of basic rights, especially the right to the protection of family and the right to equal treatment in the case of foreign residents. This expansion of rights was sometimes promoted by an "activist judiciary" (Joppke 1998: 283), but has also been shown to be important as a moral framework for policy-makers and civil society, independently from courts (Bonjour 2011).[8] For the entire post-war period, norms have arguably played a crucial role in European family migration policy-making processes. For the past decade, a restrictive turn in family migration policies has been observable in several European countries (the German turn provides the main field of investigation for this research), which itself is strongly embedded in the normative framework surrounding family migration policies that has emerged since the 1950s.

Kofman (2004: 243) claims that the proportion of family-based migration out of the total overall inflows has been growing steadily across Europe without being accompanied by adequate scholarly consideration. A parallel statement can be made regarding policies governing family migration, which are also growing in relevance, although this has not yet resulted in adequate academic analysis. Therefore, in the following three sections, a tentative theoretical framework for the analysis of family migration policies is presented. The initial section explores the most important normative arguments behind family migration policies in liberal democracies, including the role that family and marriage norms play in their formulation, and proceeds to outline a theoretical framework for the analysis of family migration policies. Thereafter, two further sections explore different normative arguments relating to policies aimed at "marriages of convenience" and "forced marriages"[9] in more depth.

The chapter thus provides an overview of the (partly conflicting) normative arguments regarding general family migration policies, as well as regarding the specific policy instruments aimed at marriages of convenience and forced marriages, situated within the wider framework of family migration. It also explores and analyses the political framing approaches employed by policy-makers in order to develop and justify

---

[8] At the same time, some authors point towards a continued need for flexible and cheap low-skilled migrant labour in Europe also (or even especially) after the economic slump in the 1970s, leading employers to turn to family migrants, especially in the construction and service sector (Hollifield 1992: 80-95; Messina 2007: 30). While this might have partly weakened political resistance against family migration behind the scenes, it is unlikely to have considerably influenced mainstream policy-making. Furthermore, the incorporation of family migrants into the labour market differed across Europe. For instance, in the Netherlands and France, incoming family members generally gained immediate access to the labour market, while in Germany, work permits were only hesitantly given out to family migrants (Hollifield 1992: 85).

[9] As the following analysis will show, "marriages of convenience" and "forced marriages" are both highly ambiguous concepts. This ambiguity would certainly justify a continuous placing of both terms in inverted commas. However, for sake of legibility, in the remainder of the thesis both terms will be largely employed without inverted commas; this does not imply that they refer to clear-cut, empirically observable phenomena.

family migration policies, which in most cases aim at restricting family migration.

2.1 Analysing family migration policies

2.1.1 The right to family and the power of social membership

The fundamental right to the protection of marriage and family life is enshrined in many important international human rights documents, the most crucial commitment for European states being the binding and enforceable obligations arising from Article 8 of the European Convention on Human Rights (ECHR).[10] Furthermore, various national constitutions in Europe, including the German one, contain similar articles concerning the special importance of the family as a societal unit that is entitled to state protection.[11] While this right to the protection of the family does not directly amount to a binding universal right to family migration, it does provide a strong "humanistic and moral basis for countries to allow family migration" (Lahav 1997: 354). This normative power of the right to family life is likely to constrain sovereign states' room for manoeuvre in formulating family migration policies. However, this right to the protection of family life is only the first aspect; membership completes the logic behind allowing family migration. We need to consider that next to the

---

[10] The Universal Declaration of Human Rights also protects the family in its Article 16. Similar articles exist in the American Convention on Human Rights, the International Covenant on Civil and Political Rights, the International Covenant on Economic, Social and Cultural Rights, the Convention on the Rights of the Child, the African Charter on Human and Peoples' Rights and the European Social Charter. See also section 5.1.1 on the enshrinement of the right to protection of family life in international and European law.

[11] In Germany, Article 6 Abs. 1 of the constitutional Basic Law (*Grundgesetz*, GG) states "Marriage and the family shall enjoy the special protection of the state." Other (mainly Southern) European constitutions that contain such a "strong" protection of family, that is, a special article concerning the importance of family within society and its protection through the state, are those of Greece (Art. 21), Ireland (Art. 41), Italy (Arts. 29-31), Portugal (Art. 67), Spain (Art. 39) and Switzerland (Art. 14). In France, the constitutional right to family life has been derived from paragraph 10 of the preamble of the 1946 Constitution protecting the conditions necessary for family development, and it is considered a *principe général du droit* since the 1978 GISTI case. In Belgium (Art. 22(1)) and Sweden (Art. 2(3)), constitutional articles protect the family life of individuals together with individuals' privacy, while in Luxemburg (Art. 11(3)), the "natural rights of the individual and the family" are constitutionally guaranteed by the state. In Austria, Denmark, Finland and the Netherlands, no mention at all is made of the family in the national constitutions, while in the United Kingdom, no constitution exists. However, all of these countries are bound by the ECHR.

43

vital interest any individual has in being able to lead a family life, all human beings can also be assumed to have a "right to remain," which is a strong interest in living in the society where they have settled and in which they participate. This "rootedness" is a crucial consideration; otherwise governments could suggest joining one's family abroad as an adequate means to satisfy the protection of family life. As Carens (2003: 97) puts it, "no one should be forced by the state to choose between home and family" – thus only when the legitimate and crucial interest of a society's members to remain in their country of origin is combined with the individual right to the protection of family, the case for family migration provisions emerges in the first place. The "right to remain" is thus also why it is primarily established members of society (citizens or legal residents) who can lay claim to a state protection of their right to marriage and family.

It is paramount to realize that this is one of the main distinguishing features characterizing family migration, in contrast to other types of migration and possibly the most powerful normative argument in its favour: family migration is based on an existing, meaningful relationship between an outsider (or nonmember) of society, that is, the incoming family member, and an insider (or member) of society, that is the sponsor.[12] By granting family migration, the state, at least in theory, recognizes not only the importance of the relationship between individuals in the microunit of the family (thus respecting the "right to the protection of family life") but also the importance of the relationship between individuals and the wider community they belong to (respecting the "right to remain"). Authors working on family migration have begun to explore the ways in which politics of belonging and issues of identity, especially gender and family norms, interrelate with the restriction of family migration policies in the last years (Bonjour & de Hart 2013; Eggebø 2010; Gedalof 2007; Muller Myrdahl 2010; Schmidt 2011; Wray 2009).

But who is considered to be a member of society? While the membership of citizens living in their home country is not questioned by normative theorists, the position of long-term resident foreigners, also termed "denizens" (Hammar 1990), is less clear. It has been forcefully argued that foreign residents acquire certain "rights of membership" after a certain period of legal residence; Carens suggests around five years as the threshold (Carens 2002: 101-106). This suggestion is largely

---

[12] However, see de Hart (2009) for a critical analysis of the gendered and ethnicizing ways the European Court of Human Rights fails to take the interests of "insiders" into due account in case law on family reunification appeals.

mirrored in empirical reality in liberal democracies. While extensive political rights are usually reserved for citizens,[13] typical rights awarded to foreign residents are residential rights, social, educational and employment rights, but also, the right to family reunion[14] (Kostakopoulou 2002: 444). However, tensions may still arise regarding the specificities. For instance, it can be argued that the five years Carens suggests that it takes to establish rights of membership is too long a period of time for family members to be separated from one another without this being considered to seriously harm their family life. The universal right to family life indeed can take effect earlier than the particular right to social membership, but in this interim period the state is consequently under fewer obligations to ensure the fulfilment of this right than later, when temporary migrants become permanent residents, and thus can lay claim to membership rights.

While Carens (2003) strongly rejects any differential treatment of citizen and foreign sponsors as morally indefensible, one can posit that a distinction nonetheless exists between the two groups, as their claims to membership in the community are not equally strong. One point that can be made that weakens the family migration claims of foreigners is that migration is an intentional act and, therefore, the possible separation from one's family is merely one of the costs it induces which can be expected to be borne by the voluntary[15] migrant (Honohan 2009: 776).

---

[13] The exclusion of foreign residents from political participation is the basis of a related normative discussion on the permissibility thereof and the boundaries of a just framework for the acquisition of citizenship (see Bauböck 2006).

[14] The fact that in some cases, even newly arriving migrants immediately have family migration rights or, put differently, can bring family members directly along with them when migrating, is less explicable from this vantage point. Why does the state assume this kind of responsibility also for the well-being of recent, possibly short-term, migrants? Here, probably a more economic rationale is at play which nevertheless displays the state's recognition of the importance of family. Sought-after migrants (e.g. high-skilled individuals or investing entrepreneurs) are given the opportunity to be with their family in order to enhance the attractiveness of the receiving state as a migration destiny in a global competititve environment for desirable migrants.

[15] The situation of refugees is different, since their migration is assumed to be involuntary and a return to their home countries in order to establish family unity cannot be plausibly demanded. In fact, Convention refugees (i.e. recognised according to the 1951 Geneva Convention) generally enjoy family migration rights across Europe under more favourable conditions than labour migrants (see ECRE 1999). Indeed, since 2003, the Family Reunification Directive obliges its signatories to treat its Convention refugees more favourably than "regular" TCN migrants regarding family reunification in its Chapter V, Art. 9-12. For example, according to Articles 7 and 8 of the directive, Convention refugees are regularly exempted from the minimum residence time, as well as income, housing and integration, requirements applicable in other cases of family migration (see Groenendijk et al. (2007: 41-

However, the picture is not that simple since not all foreign residents have migrated, nor have all citizens of a country been born and lived all their life there. For example, the position of second or third generations, born in a host country without acquiring the citizenship in question, is complicated. Never having themselves migrated voluntarily, but finding themselves as foreign residents in their parents' (or sometimes grandparents') migration destination, they lack the legal security of citizenship without ever having made any conscious choice to migrate. This condition of legal insecurity is obviously relevant far beyond the realm of family migration rights and is generally normatively difficult to defend. Naturalised immigrants or ethnic migrants with immediate citizenship rights, such as ethnic resettlers *(Aussiedler)* in the German case, by contrast, have made a voluntary migration decision but enjoy all the rights of citizens. Another argument in this context relates to a fundamental difference citizenship makes: Citizens, contrary to foreigners, always have an unconditional right to residence in their home country. Therefore, it is occasionally argued that citizens cannot easily be expected to leave their home country in order to unite with their foreign family members abroad, while this might be a more plausible demand to be posed towards foreign residents.

Even if the responsibility assumed and the subsequent details of the policies differ across polities, some kind of family migration provisions for both citizens and foreign residents are indeed in place in most Western liberal democracies, often with reference to human rights provisions. Direct access to one's spouse and family is thus in theory accepted as a fundamental right and therefore a crucial component to individual well-being, which should be ensured by the state towards its members.

---

45) on the implementation of the provisions on refugees' family reunification rights in the EU). However, the situation for non-Convention refugees enjoying some type of subsidiary protection is very diverse across Europe. While in some states subsidiary refugees enjoy roughly the same family migration rights as Convention refugees, in other polities, they are either treated similarly to regular migrants or they are not granted any family migration rights at all (John 2003: 38-40; Groenendijk et al. 2007: 42). During the asylum procedure, i.e. before (subsidiary or Convention) protection is granted, asylum seekers are generally not granted family migration (ECRE 1999).

2.1.2 Ideas on family and membership within family migration policies

Marriage and family norms within family migration policies

Marriage and family are far from being neutral, clearly defined concepts. Instead, notions of what "family" and "marriage" actually constitute, what societal and private purposes they serve, and ideas of how family and marriage should function, are in continual flux, both over time and across cultures. As is the case with most contested norms and values, even within one society there will be a plethora of different opinions on what constitutes a proper marriage and family. However, it is not individual marriage and family norms that are relevant for the present research, but rather institutional ones. What marriage and family norms does the state put forward by way of laws, policies and discourses? There are many fields in which institutional marriage and family norms are expressed. Most obviously, through marriage law, divorce law and family law the state establishes marriage and family norms. But also certain provisions in social, educational and fiscal policies reflect and establish institutional norms on marriage and family.

What is particularly relevant for the present research is the question of what kinds of norms the state puts forward within family migration policies. Which normative ideas regarding family, marriage and gender can be discerned within family migration policies? As will be shown later, proposing specific family and marriage norms can be instrumental for policy-makers when aiming at restricting family migration. For example, the definition of eligible family members within admission provisions is one of the ways marriage and family norms interact with migration policies. Mostly, only the nuclear family members, i.e. spouses and minor children, are admitted, which suggests that a norm of small family units is at work here. This has led to criticism that a narrow definition of the family might be biased culturally, as extended family ties are often more important in non-Western cultures. Furthermore, admitting extended family members might be crucial in order to ensure the supply of familial care (Honohan 2009: 781). Another example is the notion of familial dependency, which is a prominent feature of family migration provisions in most countries. Incoming family members, at least initially during a probationary period, derive their residence permit and often also their work permit from the sponsor's residence permit and status. Furthermore, certain family members, such as adult children or ascending relatives, are often only admitted if a (financial) dependency upon the sponsor is proven. By making dependency upon the sponsor such an important condition, states thus suggest that the family is, first, aimed at reproduction and, second, a unit of (economic) solidarity (Kraler 2010: 47).

In an historical analysis of institutional marriage norms, Ursula Vogel (2000) proposes three inter-related perspectives to analyse wider questions of the way marriage is institutionally given meaning, which can in turn be applied to analyse marriage norms in the context of family migration policies. The first perspective highlights the power struggle between religious institutions and the state over the authority to regulate marriages, which is connected with a claim to sovereignty. In the context of migration policies, different religious institutions and national authorities compete over the power to regulate and thus define marriages as an expression of their sovereignty. Secondly, one can focus on the "extensive regulatory involvement and coercive presence of the public power in the terrain of marriage" (Vogel 2000: 179). Here, the notion of a "tripartite contract" is crucial, implying that the spouses make vows not only to each other, but to a third party (such as the kinship community, God or the state) as well. It is mainly from this perspective that the issue of the public-private nexus is highlighted: To what extent may spouses define their marriages as private? Where and in what ways does the state have the authority to define and regulate marriages? The third important political dimension of marriage concerns the "constitution of gender as a political relationship of rule and subordination" (Vogel 2000: 179). Examining the (often asymmetrical) power relations between husband and wife as constituted and reinforced by the state in its regulation of marriage is crucial when analysing migration policies as well. These three perspectives on the larger political debates involved in marriage norms (regulatory power as an instance of sovereignty, the public-private nexus and gender power relations) are paramount to any analysis of institutional marriage norms put forward by political authorities in the context of family migration policies.

However, it would be naïve to assume that all state institutions have one set of family and marriage norms, which in turn are reflected across all policy fields. Actually, conflicting and contradictory family norms might be put forward in different contexts, depending on the actors involved and the different immediate policy goals at stake. For example, there seems to be a widening gap between increasingly liberal family norms, manifested in legislation and jurisprudence recognising and strengthening the rights of familial constellations beyond the traditional heterosexual married couple, such as same-sex relationships, non-married couples or single/divorced parents, and a continuing narrowing of conceptions of family within migration legislation, which results in restrictive family migration policies.

How can this gap be explained? Kraler (2010: 48) proposes the possibility that, despite the legal consolidation of alternative family and relationship models, which seem to imply a liberal shift, family norms in most European societies might not have actually changed that much. In reference to Turner (2008: 53) and his concept of "reproductive citizenship," he underlines the continuing importance of the family as a site of both biological reproduction of citizens and cultural reproduction of the nation, which explains the ongoing institutional protection of the family as well as its position as a "site of contestation and social engineering and subject of moralising political and public discourses" (Kraler 2010: 48). On the other hand, Kraler (2010: 48) also acknowledges that family migration policies, rather than reflecting (progressive) family norms emerging in other societal contexts, must mainly be regarded as policies controlling migration. He proposes that migration and citizenship policies tend to strongly favour individuals behaving in "proper" ways, that is, economically productive, law-abiding and civically engaged persons, which is why conditions testing and ensuring these criteria are part of family migration policies. Furthermore, van Walsum (2009: 299-300) has pointed out that discrepancies between family norms discernible within family law and those found in immigration law can be explained by racialised notions of the family, leading different family norms to be applied to different groups. She shows that while the state in the Netherlands largely accepts white Dutch single mothers or even regards them as emancipated when they successfully combine work and mothering, it considers ethnic minority single mothers to be irresponsible and incapable of parenting, and their inflow accordingly a threat to social cohesion.

Even within the policy field of migration law, different marriage and family norms are articulated in different contexts. For example, as will be elaborated in the following sections, the policies aimed at combating marriages of convenience implicitly propose an ideal marriage norm based on love and the desire for the couple to live a common life together, which strongly rejects the idea of a merely contractual marriage. In the practice of marriage-of-convenience policies, rather traditional norms, such as the cohabitation of spouses, minor age differences between them, or the purpose of having common children, are all endorsed as important features of "authentic" marriages. At the same time, political framings of forced marriages criticise the gendered and generational subordination and repression of the spouses in the marriage decision, and propose instead an ideal marriage norm based primarily on individual free will, thus rather supporting the notion of marriage as an autonomously concluded contract.

Membership and family migration

Migration policies have previously been analysed as instances of "politics of belonging," that is, policies involved in "the maintenance and reproduction of the boundaries of the community of belonging by the hegemonic political powers (Yuval-Davis 2006: 205). Notions of "who belongs (more)" to the national community influence national migration policies. These policies, in turn, create hierarchies of membership by allocating rights according to "strength" or "degree" of different dimensions of membership. Membership, in the simplest terms, is the state of belonging to or being part of a group. Understanding membership as socially constructed identity categories, this membership and belonging can be contested and politicized at virtually all sites and levels of individuals forming groups (e.g., cities, neighbourhoods, associations, churches, clubs), and the question "who belongs?" is especially pertinent at the level of the nation-state – even though postnational theorists might suggest otherwise (Brubaker 2010: 64). Also, in the following, since the focus is on the analysis of national (family migration) policies, it is not individuals' conceptions of identity and membership but the social construction of membership at the level of the nation-state that is of interest – and how notions of membership are constructed and politicised by state actors through their policies. When adopting a narrow understanding of citizenship as amounting mainly to full legal membership in a given polity, citizenship and membership are strongly interrelated concepts, but distinct. Citizens' membership can be contested, just as noncitizens can be constructed to possess some kind of membership in the political community in which they reside (and at the same time in the polity they originate from). Brubaker urges to distinguish the "politics of citizenship *in* the nation-state" from the "politics of belonging *to* the nation-state"; he suggests marginal or minority populations might undoubtedly be "formal state members", that is, citizens, but at the same time their "substantive membership," that is, their access to the rights citizenship entails and/or their acceptance as "full members" of the nation, might be very much contested (Brubaker 2010: 64). Also the membership of noncitizens, that is resident foreigners or new migrants, can be subject to scrutiny and contestation in the politics of belonging. Importantly, membership is not conceptualized here as a fixed entity that might be either present or absent but along a continuum from strong to weak (thus rather than thinking of an "us/them" dichotomy, individuals can be considered "more part of us" or "less part of us"). Also, different membership dimensions can be distinguished, operating on distinct axes of social inequality. These membership dimensions can obviously intersect and interact with one another, offsetting and/or enforcing the degree of perceived or constructed "otherness," as has been pointed out by scholars emphasizing intersectionality and belonging (Yuval-Davis 2007). In the following, we will turn to an analytical framework useful in coming to terms with family migration policies by systematically exploring them as instances of membership regulation and family regulation.

2.1.3 An analytical framework for family migration policies: Regulating membership and regulating the family

Since the late 1990s, somewhat of a policy trend has emerged across OECD countries towards an increased restriction of family migration[16] (OECD 2011: 115). In Europe, restrictions of family migration policy have been introduced at least in Austria, Belgium, Denmark, France, Germany, the Netherlands, Norway, Sweden, and the United Kingdom. Consequently, a decrease of family migration inflows can also be observed in many European countries (Pascouau & Labayle 2011: 107). Connected to this restrictive policy shift have been negative perceptions of family migration, mainly connected to two disputed issues. First, does family migration facilitate or harm immigrant integration? Second, are family migrants an asset for the economy or a burden on the welfare state?

Regarding integration,[17] two opposing arguments have been uttered. On the one hand, some scholars have claimed that family migrants integrate into host societies better than other migrants since they can make use of the established networks and support, that is, the social capital, of their sponsors. Furthermore, it has been argued that if sponsors themselves are recent migrants, being joined by their family members rather than being socially isolated is likely to enhance their capacity for integration in the host country, also since "families, especially children, themselves constitute channels for wider interaction through school and

---

[16] Contrastingly, Kofman and Meetoo (2008: 159) claim that Italy and Spain have facilitated family migration in the same period, for example, by the formal introduction of a right to family migration in Spanish immigration law in 1996. This divergent Southern European path might be explained by their rather recent experience with immigration flows compared to older migration-receiving states in Northern Europe. Most recently, however, Spain has put more emphasis on integration in its family migration policy too (Pascouau & Labayle 2011: 17).

[17] See Favell (2001) for a substantive critique of policy makers' and researchers' conceptualization of integration in Europe.

other activities" (Honohan 2009: 772). In this view, allowing resident migrants to be joined by their family members benefits both the sponsors and their receiving community (Cholewinski 2002: 274). This "integration-through-networks" argument thus posits that family migration has a positive impact on integration, and is also the official view of the European Union (Strik et al. 2013: 48) which is, for example, mentioned in the preamble of the Family Reunification Directive 2003/86/EC.[18] On the other hand, family migration, especially of spouses joining ethnic minority sponsors, is also claimed to contribute to self-reproducing, segregated minority communities, and is thus seen to hamper integration of both the sponsoring and the incoming spouses. This "ethnic-segregation" argument posits that family migration has a negative impact on minority integration. In recent years, in particular, the ethnic-segregation argument has become increasingly popular among policy-makers in various European countries who have been mainly influenced by observations regarding the marriage behaviour of second- and third-generation migrants opting for partners from their (grand) parents' country of origin (see Beck-Gernsheim 2007; Eeckhaut et al. 2011; Sterckx 2015).

A second set of arguments concerns the (economic) productivity of family migrants. Finding family migrants in the United States to be nearly as productive in the long term as employment migrants screened for their skills, Jasso and Rosenzweig (1995: 86) suggest that family-based support networks enhance the occupational upward mobility of spousal migrants. Hollifield (1992: 80-95) illustrates how, after the recruitment stop in the 1970s, German and French employers gladly turned to family migrants to fill continuing labour needs in the construction and service sector. Also, Honohan (2009: 772) claims that in many instances family migrants indirectly enhance overall societal welfare by providing unpaid care and household work or by contributing informally but significantly to family businesses. Contrastingly, it has been argued that family migrants tend to be unproductive. Contrary to the treatment of labour migrants, receiving states do not select family migrants according to their skills or other resources but rather admit them solely due to their link to the sponsor. The ensuing "non-selection" is thus often seen as likely to

---

[18] Recital 4 of the preamble of Directive 2003/86/EC reads "Family reunification is a necessary way of making family life possible. It helps to create sociocultural stability facilitating the integration of third country nationals in the Member State, which also serves to promote economic and social cohesion, a fundamental Community objective stated in the Treaty."

produce an inflow of economically unproductive migrants, who are potentially a burden on the welfare state.[19]

Summing up, when family migration is viewed as furthering integration and producing productive inflows, family migration rights might be readily granted. However, when subscribing to the negative arguments of family migration as leading to unproductive, burdensome inflows that also have a negative impact on integration, the admission of family migrants is deemed to be potentially detrimental to the overall interests of society. Significantly, it is this negative view of family migration that has acquired salience in recent years: family migration thus seems to be increasingly perceived as unwanted in many Western European states. At the same time, however, these same states, especially in their capacity as liberal democracies, are under pressure to protect the fundamental rights of their individual members to the protection of marriage and family life. How can the liberal state limit family migration to achieve its migration management goals without completely disregarding its human rights obligations?

In section 1.2, I suggested that a "liberal discursive constraint" exists that limits liberal democratic governments' possibilities to openly disrespect individual rights. This constraint compels governments to frame restrictive migration policy instruments in such a way that the general commitment to fundamental individual rights is not questioned. In other words, policies possibly harming individual rights need to be appropriately framed either to achieve other much more pressing goals (including protecting other human rights), or to actually not infringe any individual right by demarcating the right itself or those entitled to lay claim to it. The alternative, open disrespect for individuals' rights, is difficult to reconcile with a state's self-definition as a liberal democracy.

I propose that two policy approaches can be observed in Europe to control family migration, while at the same time keeping in line with the broad human rights discourse of the protection of family life. As out-

---

[19] Due to the general tendency toward social homogamy, especially regarding education level (see Blossfeld & Timm 2003), social and educational characteristics of incoming partners are likely to mirror those of their sponsors. This means that largely unskilled labour migration inflows—as have dominated many European countries in the past—would be accompanied or succeeded by similarly unskilled spousal migration. However, transnational and migratory dynamics can also alter this tendency toward homogamy, especially in the following generations and with ethnic majority partners. When immigration is sought after, the bargaining position in the marriage market can be enhanced for low-income or uneducated sponsors (Charsley 2005: 94; Glowsky 2007: 299; Hooghiemstra 2001).

lined above, family migration is based on liberal states' commitment to the protection of **family** and to an obligation to safeguard the rights of its society's **members**. The liberal discursive constraint compels any restrictions to be framed as changing the definition of social membership and family instead of questioning the respect for the protection of marriage and family as such. Accordingly, the following analytical framework categorises family migration policies into those instruments regulating social **membership**, and those instruments regulating the **family**. Within these two logics, regulation takes place, firstly, by circumscribing the eligible **categories** of societal members and family ties, and secondly, by scrutinising the **quality** of social membership and family ties respectively. The following will explore the two approaches and briefly outline some of the policy instruments that exemplify them.[20]

	Social **membership**	**Family** ties
By circumscribing **categories**	Requiring sponsor to have certain legal status	Legal proof of relationship; maximum age for children
By scrutinising **quality**	Income requirement; (pre-) integration conditions	Evaluation of whether marriages are based on love/consent; scrutinising of parental ties

Table 1: Examples of policy approaches regulating membership and family ties

Regulating membership

With regard to the **regulation of membership**, states control family migration by allocating family migration rights according to different membership categories. They do so by evaluating the legal status of the sponsor and the quality of this social membership. Both of these phenomena will be explored in turn. At the risk of stating the obvious, the sponsor is required to have some legal membership status in the community in order to claim family migration rights. The sponsor needs to be a citizen or

---

[20] The policy instruments mentioned in this section are mere examples of the approaches described. While the German case is dealt with extensively in chapters 3, 4, 6 and 7, a more comprehensive overview of recent legislative changes in selected other European countries is presented in chapter 5. See Kraler (2010: 29-49) and Groenendijk et al. (2007) for overviews of family migration policies across Europe.

a foreign resident in possession of a valid residence permit. Accordingly, irregular migrants who are not legal members of the community do not enjoy family migration rights in most polities. Furthermore, immigrants often need a minimum residence time and/or must have acquired a consolidated residence permit before family members can join them. Thus, apart from cases mentioned above where immediate or early family migration is granted to desired migrants, a basic social membership in the community of the sponsor must be present before being granted family migration. These conditions can be tightened: In France, the minimum period of legal residence for foreigners prior to being able to sponsor family migration was raised from 12 to 18 months in 2006 (Kofman & Meetoo 2008: 160).

Another manifestation of regulating membership through legal categories, which has already been mentioned above, is the preferential treatment of citizen sponsors vis-à-vis foreign resident sponsors. The rationale behind this is that only citizens' membership in the community includes an unconditional right to residence. It is also sustained by the notion of a presumed stronger "rootedness" of citizens in society and the connected comparably higher sacrifice placed on them if they had to migrate abroad to establish family unity. In practice, many policies award more favourable conditions of family migration to citizens than to foreign residents. For instance, in the USA, citizens are allowed to sponsor a broader range of their family than foreign residents, including siblings and parents (Demleitner 2003: 293). Also, spouses of foreigners are subjected to annual quotas leading to waiting periods of up to 5 years, while US citizens' spouses are immediately granted green cards and only subject to regular processing delays (Abrams 2007: 1636). In Germany, fewer requirements concerning income and housing are imposed on citizen sponsors than on foreign resident sponsors. This point is of relevance at the supranational level as well: According to the 2004 Free Movement Directive, EU citizens residing in other Member States have much more extensive family migration rights than what is enshrined as the minimum standard for TCNs in the Family Reunification Directive of 2003.

"Rootedness" also plays an increasingly important role in determining the "quality" or "intensity" of someone's membership to the society in question. This notion is also reflected in European jurisprudence on family migration, with courts regularly evaluating the bonds of the sponsors in the host country when determining whether an emigration to establish family unity abroad can be considered a viable option or not.[21] Regulating the quality of membership relates to the integration debate since the quality of social membership concerns not only foreign residents but also ethnic minority citizens. In case the sponsors' integration into the host society is considered insufficient, their membership might be questioned and, accordingly, spousal migration restricted on an individual or collective basis.

One policy instrument that very directly reflects this idea of scrutinising the quality of membership through an assessment of rootedness is the so-called "attachment requirement" in Danish spousal migration law.[22] Since 2002, this provision requires all transnational couples applying for spousal migration in Denmark, both with citizen and foreign sponsors, to prove that their "combined attachment" to Denmark is "significantly greater" than their attachment to any other state (Danish Immigration Service 2015a). A closer look at the membership definitions implicitly present in this policy is illuminating. The required attachment is measured by evaluating the length and continuance of the sponsor's (and possibly the incoming spouse's) prior residence in Denmark, the presence of other family members and acquaintances in Denmark, the level of the couple's Danish language skills and their education and/or labour market participation in Denmark. Extended visits to other countries as well as the presence of children and other family members abroad are (negatively) taken into consideration as well. If custody or visiting rights to a child living in Denmark exist, the requirement is usually waived entirely (Danish Immigration Service 2015a). Here, membership leading to family migration rights is thus defined by length of residence on the one hand, but also by other variables such as language skills and personal strong bonds to other members (especially children) of the host society. Participation in gainful employment and language skills are regarded as especially important factors enhancing social membership: The regular residence requirement of 15 years stipulated for sponsors is reduced to eight years if the sponsor is in continuous full-time employment and speaks Danish on the job. It can be even further reduced to five years if the sponsor's job is considered "particularly integration-furthering,"

---

[21] For example, in its *Sen v Netherlands* judgement, the ECtHR decided that the Dutch decision to refuse minor Sinem Sen a residence permit was in breach of Article 8 ECHR, partly due to the fact that Sinem's parents had had two further children in the Netherlands after their immigration. The family could thus not be expected to leave the Netherlands in order to reunite with their oldest daughter, Sinem, in Turkey and she was granted a residence permit. See van Walsum (2009: 302) and section 5.1.1.
[22] See section 5.2.3 on Danish spousal migration policies for a more detailed description of the provisions of the attachment requirement.

that is, requiring high levels of Danish skills (Danish Immigration Service 2015b).

This policy instrument suggests that acquiring a strong membership claim through long residence can be at least partly offset by personal rootedness in the country and especially through participation in the education and the labour market, and by having certain language skills. There were protests following the initial implementation by expat Danes, who were prevented from returning to Denmark with their foreign family members because they failed the attachment requirement. The policy was changed to exempt citizens who had held Danish citizenship for more than 28 years. While the policy now clearly discriminates between naturalised and Danish-born citizens (Ersbøll 2009: 3), as well as against young adults (under 28) vis-à-vis older citizens, it also hints at a rather ethnic conception of membership that is implicitly present within family migration policies. In July 2011, the UK government proposed the introduction of a similar attachment requirement into UK spousal migration laws, specifically citing the Danish policy as a model (UK Border Agency 2011: 19).

Despite this Danish policy being, at least up until now, rather unique, it shows that apart from evaluating legal membership status, the regulation of membership may also include an assessment of the quality of this social membership. Personal and emotional links to other members of society and language skills can be evaluated, it is presumed, in the same way as the socio-economic status can be assessed. This evaluation of socio-economic achievement is actually another very widespread instrument of family migration control and I propose that it can also be categorised as an instance of regulating social membership. Put bluntly, the better the socio-economic status, the "better a member" the sponsor is, and, accordingly, the more rights that are awarded to him/her in the field of family migration. For example, it is very common to oblige sponsors to fulfil certain socio-economic standards regarding employment, income, housing and independence from social welfare in order to sponsor family migration. While these instruments obviously also serve the policy goal of preventing family migrants from becoming a burden on the welfare state, I suggest that, implicitly, highly normative notions of "good members" of society are put forward by these policies. Sponsors are expected to be law-abiding, economically self-supporting individuals, who actively engage with society at large through their language skills and civic involvement (see also Kraler 2010: 49), in order to "earn" the right to sponsor family migration. Significantly, these conditions can be tightened: In 2004, the Netherlands increased the income that sponsors needed to earn in cases of "family formation" to 120 per cent of the minimum wage.[23] Nonetheless, more liberal examples also exist. Portugal, which is governed by the most favourable family migration conditions in Europe according to the most recent MIPEX report (Huddleston et al. 2011: 15), temporarily lowered the "means of subsistence" that immigrants needed to sponsor family migrants from 100 per cent to 50 per cent of the minimum wage in 2009.[24] The government stated that this reduction was due to the international economic crisis, which would temporarily leave many migrants in situations of involuntary unemployment and professional instability (Serviço de Estrangeiros e Fronteiras 2009: 36).

Furthermore, socio-economic assessments of membership are also intermingled with other membership criteria. As mentioned above, in some countries, such as Germany, while foreign sponsors need to provide proof of employment, income and housing, citizens do not. Here, the obligations to establish socio-economic membership are higher when directed towards foreigners than citizens. This is in line with the stronger legal membership claims of citizens outlined earlier. However, in 2007, German spousal migration law was changed, extending the income requirement that previously was only applicable to foreigners to citizen sponsors in cases where it can be "reasonably expected" that the couple could establish their union outside of Germany.[25] The commentary to the law mentioned naturalised and dual nationals as examples of such cases. This provision is strongly connected to the above-mentioned notion of "rootedness" in society as an indicator of the intensity of someone's membership in that society, but also exemplifies again an ethnic conception of membership, since mostly ethnic minority citizens were affected by the rule. Their membership claims are thus implicitly categorised to be weaker than those of ethnic German citizens, since in this point they are treated just as foreign sponsors and required to provide additional evidence for their membership through socio-economic achievements in order to sponsor family migration.

Thus, in Germany too, "[c]lass intersects with ethnicity in establishing who is to be most severely regulated" (Wray 2009: 593). Implicitly assessing the quality of someone's membership along ethnic lines, as occurs with the Danish attachment requirement or the income requirement for ethnic minority citizens in Germany, can be criticised for being

---

[23] This provision was, however, struck down by the ECJ in the 2010 *Chakroun* case (see section 5.2.1).
[24] Portaria No. 760/2009 of 16 July 2009. Diário da República, 1ª série, No. 136, p. 4509.
[25] This provision was overruled in 2012 by the BVerwG. See sections 4.2 and 6.2.3.

highly discriminatory. At the same time, some special foreign sponsors, especially if their migration is considered to be socio-economically favourable, such as highly-skilled migrants or entrepreneurs, are subjected to less stringent conditions in order to have their family join them than even citizens of the state in question. This exemplifies how socio-economic attainments can even override legal status membership claims.

The most recent emerging trend within the policy approach of regulating social membership is that of also imposing conditions on the incoming spouses. I propose that this new type of policy instrument can also be understood to constitute a form of membership regulation, as here the future membership qualities of the incoming spouses are evaluated. These provisions are mainly politically framed within the above-mentioned sceptical view concerning family migration's impact on minority integration. This notion of membership is intimately connected to the recently emerging perspective that "the lack of integration or the assumed unfitness to integrate are grounds for refusal of admission to the country" (Groenendijk 2004: 113). Obligations to prove language capacity and civic knowledge, often demanded prior to admission, have been introduced in order to emphasise both the fundamental necessity and current deficiency of family migrants' integration into the social, economic and cultural life of the host society. To date, the Netherlands, France, Germany, Denmark, Austria and the UK have already installed such integration requirements for family migrants.

Regulating family ties

I will now turn to policies that exercise family migration control by defining the boundaries of marriage and family, and in so doing, embrace specific family norms. Within this second approach – and analogously to that of regulating social membership – family migration control is exercised first by defining the categories of family members eligible to apply for family migration and, second, by assessing the quality of the familial relationships in question. Policy instruments regulating the family exemplify the power of the state as the bearer of sovereignty as proposed by Vogel (2000).

Regarding family categories, while overt gender and racial discriminatory measures are difficult to justify in liberal democracies nowadays, examples of the typical hurdles in place across Europe include maximum age limits for children, proof of dependency of adolescents and the exclusion of multiple spouses, of siblings and other extended relatives. This circumscription of the eligible family to spouses and minor children is strongly embedded within the Western cultural norm of the nuclear family as the main locus of affection, care and shared economic responsibility. The exclusion of multiple spouses also suggests a rejection of non-Western marriage norms. Also, minimum ages for both spouses (sponsoring and incoming) have been installed in various European countries, setting it at 24 years (in Denmark), 21 years (in Austria, Belgium, and the Netherlands) or 18 years (in France, Germany, Sweden, and the United Kingdom). Again, this implies a Western norm of marriage at a later stage within adulthood, at least in the migration context. All governments argued this measure would prevent young adults from arranged and forced marriages (Strik et al. 2013: 54). As these are mainly thought to be Muslim practices, the restriction can also be interpreted as contesting the cultural membership of Muslim minorities. It has, for instance, been shown how in the 2007 U.K. consultation on raising the minimum age, the government juxtaposed supposed White middle-class family values (e.g., marrying later) with ethnic minority transnational marriage practices, associating them with force and victims (Wray 2009: 607). Similar observations have been made within Dutch political discourse (Bonjour & de Hart 2013) and will be traced in the later analysis for Germany. However, defining different categories of family regulation need not always go in a restrictive direction. In the course of instituting same-sex civil partnerships in the course of the 2000s, various European states expanded family migration rights to include these, and thus enlarged the eligible family in this respect (e.g. in Germany since 2001, in the UK since 2005, in Switzerland since 2007). Thus, progressive family norms can also lead to more liberal family migration policies.

Just as is the case in relation to social membership, states can also assess the "quality" of family ties through policy instruments that scrutinise familial relationships. Even categories of family members clearly included in family migration provisions, such as minor dependent children, parents of minor citizens and legal spouses, can be disenfranchised from family migration rights if the nature of their relationship to the sponsor is deemed to be in some way inadequate. This can occur by scrutinising biological parental ties by means of DNA tests,[26] evaluating the extent and importance of social parenthood for the affected minor or by qualifying some marriages as "proper" and others as "improper", as is

---

[26] See Murdock (2008) on the French decision to introduce DNA tests in order to assess biological parent-child relationships in order to qualify for family migration and see Taitz et al. (2002) regarding the introduction of DNA testing to prove biological relationships in the context of family migration across various Western states.

the case with marriages of convenience and forced marriages. By disallowing family migration if the verdict is negative, the state does not only forcefully impose marriage and family norms in the context of migration, but also manages to justify measures that might otherwise be perceived as infringing on the individual right to marriage and family protection. This is similar to the framing of asylum seekers as "bogus" or "economic refugees" who accordingly are not protected by any international convention. The restriction of asylum policies can accordingly be framed to solve this "problem" of bogus asylum seekers, which diverts attention from other possible human rights infringements.

Another example of regulating family ties via quality is the probationary period enshrined in many policies tying the incoming spouse's residence permit to that of the sponsor. Only after this probationary period can the spouse obtain an independent residence permit making a separation or a divorce from the sponsor possible. This probationary period was recently increased from two to three years in both France (in 2006) and Germany (in 2011), while in the UK the government has proposed to increase it from the current two to five years (UK Border Agency 2011). These provisions articulate a marriage norm of dependency and long-lasting relationships. Furthermore, they are framed as instruments in the fight against marriages of convenience.

It is this last approach of regulating the family by scrutinising its quality that the following section will analyse in more depth from a normative point of view by exploring the notions of marriages of convenience and forced marriages and especially the policy initiatives that have emerged within spousal migration legislation across Europe with the pronounced aim of combating these marriages.

2.2 Marriage-of-convenience policies: Preventing the state from being duped?

Intrinsically connected to a growing concern and subsequent scrutiny of family migration outlined above is the worry about possible "abuses" of relevant provisions by way of so-called marriages of convenience, commonly conceptualised as marriages conducted for the sole reason of gaining a residence permit, against money or as a favour, between individuals not in any kind of "romantic" relationship. Thus, in a political climate sceptical of family migration, marriages of convenience are increasingly perceived as a way to illegitimately enter the labour markets and welfare systems that states are anxiously trying to close off for migrants. This anxiety reverberates in policy responses as well.[27] As de Hart (2006: 51) observes:

> Media stories about "odd couples" (the elderly woman with a 25-year old African male), high estimates of the number of marriages of convenience (up to 80% in the Netherlands), and gangs dealing in marriages of convenience not only appealed to the public imagination, but also to politicians who, in response, pleaded for legislation to prevent such marriages.

The following section will explore the conceptual and normative implications of state policies that aim to uncover and criminalise so-called marriages of convenience. Instead of trying to establish a normative argument regarding the ethics of immigration admission (see Carens 2003), or entering into a debate about how to morally weigh up different entrance claims (see Gibney 2004 on refugees and Honohan 2009 on family migration), this section sets out to critically analyse and evaluate the normative implications of policy instruments that aim to prevent marriages of convenience. These policy instruments, which regulate the family by scrutinising the quality of family ties, may take the form of general provisions applying to all couples engaging in spousal migration with the underlying goal of fighting marriages of convenience, such as the establishment or extension of probationary periods. Alternatively, such policies may be manifested in administrative measures that single out "suspicious" couples and specifically scrutinise their relationships, as will be explicated below. The perspective of the public-private nexus (Vogel 2000) is particularly salient within these latter policies. In general, this section thus explores two main, contrasting questions: How can policies on marriages of convenience be normatively justified? How can policies on marriages of convenience be normatively criticised?

---

[27] A parallel discourse regarding "adoptions/paternities of convenience" has emerged in some European states and partly led to several policy initiatives, but will be largely disregarded largely for the sake of space. One example of these developments involves the bizarre story of German expatriate Jürgen Hass. In in May 2006, it emerged in the media that Hass had over 300 children in Central Europe, India and Latin America that he had recognised as his own in order to enable them to claim German citizenship. Hass also stated that he planned on expanding his "brood" to 1000 children as a personal vendetta against German authorities (DER SPIEGEL 2006; Phillips & Harding 2006). The story caused an outcry about this "legal loophole" and eventually led to the drafting and adoption of a new law in 2008 (*Gesetz zur Ergänzung des Rechts zur Anfechtung der Vaterschaft* (VaAnfRErgG)), granting public authorities the right to appeal an acknowledgement of paternity (§ 1600 BGB Abs. 1 Nr. 5) if no social-familial relationship between the father and the child exist and residential rights for the child or the mother are derived from paternity (§ 1600 BGB Abs. 3).

2.2.1 How to justify marriage-of-convenience policies

The acceptance that states are entitled to control immigration into their territory as an integral part of their sovereignty and democratic self-determination[28] (Walzer 1983), as is also commonly recognised by international law, leads to the emergence of certain normative arguments supporting policies aimed at impeding marriages of convenience.

The main argument in favour of policies that specifically aim to impede marriages of convenience is that they can prevent the abuse of family migration policies. As outlined above, family migration provisions are essentially based on Western states' commitment to the protection of marriage and family of those under their legislation. This commitment of liberal states is especially strong vis-à-vis their own citizens, and somewhat less strong vis-à-vis foreign residents of their polities.

How does the rationale behind family migration policies relate to marriage-of-convenience policies? Marriages of convenience are interpreted as being an abuse of family migration policies, since the expected familial relationship is not present in these cases, thus offsetting the foundations on which the entrance claims are based in the first place. In other words, if the particular familial tie is not a given, the state is under no legal or ethical obligation to grant the foreign spouse admission; on the contrary, both spouses attempting to abuse the legislation in this way could be perceived as engaging in criminal behaviour. The illegitimacy of the abuse has two dimensions: Marriages of convenience constitute, firstly, a skipping of admission queues vis-à-vis other migrants or refugees and, secondly, an undermining of state sovereignty in migration control through fraud. Policies targeting marriages of convenience do not delegitimise family migration claims as such, but go one step further back and regulate the family ties by questioning the authenticity of the marriage, i.e. the particular familial relationship, which is indeed worthy of state protection.

Thus, in theory, restrictive marriage-of-convenience policies are not at odds with liberal family migration policies. On the contrary, they might be interpreted as a serious commitment of the state to the importance of family life for individual well-being by only attributing family migration rights to "genuine" families and denying these rights to illegitimate claimants. The backlash argument, as brought forward by Carens (1992), is crucial in this context as well. Not extending any control over the quality, i.e. "genuineness" of the alleged familial ties of migrants

---

[28] For a challenge of this claim, see Carens (1987; 1992).

might cause a disproportionate abuse of this mode of entry, leading in turn to a "swamping" of migrants under the family pretext. This would necessitate restrictive policy measures and lead states to clamp down on family migration altogether, affecting genuine families as well.

One might go even further and oppose granting family migration rights in the first place. One argument against (even "authentic") family migration is the more urgent and thus possibly normatively superior admission claims raised by refugees (Gibney 2004). Furthermore, a utilitarian argument can be made supporting the state's right to admit migrants exclusively according to their (expected) contribution to society instead of according to family ties. Lastly, the issue of the multiplier effect and inherited privilege that is associated with family migration can be interpreted as problematic from a (global) justice perspective (Honohan 2009). These arguments question the normative basis on which any family migration policy rests and could be interpreted to further justify any legislative attempts to keep family migration at a restrictive, minimum level, if it must be put in place at all.

2.2.2 How to criticise marriage-of-convenience policies

Two serious, interconnected problems can be discerned regarding policies on marriages of convenience. The first issue concerns the difficulty of defining a marriage of convenience and the second one the difficulty of measuring or "detecting" a marriage of convenience. I will discuss both issues in turn and then outline their normative implications regarding the seemingly conflicting goals at hand, i.e. the individual right to family protection and the collective right to restrict migration.

Defining a marriage of convenience

As outlined above, the main thrust behind policies aimed against marriages of convenience is the idea that this practice constitutes an abuse of family migration legislation. Recapitulating, while a sovereign state has the right to control, according to certain procedural constraints, who is allowed to settle in its territory, it is also recognised that family ties are crucial to individual well-being and that the state bears a certain responsibility to ensure the protection of its residents' family life, regardless of the origin of the family members. Therefore, the question of distinguishing a "genuine" marriage from a marriage of convenience is imperative, since the former is assumed to be crucial for the sponsor's wellbeing and thus needs to be protected, while the latter is not.

However, the difficult question that emerges is: How exactly should a marriage of convenience be distinguished from a "genuine" marriage? Nowadays in Europe, civil marriages are usually legally valid as long as the two spouses contractually agree to marry, which is by definition also the case with marriages of convenience.[29] However, since family migration claims are based on the notion of the importance of particular, intimate relations with immediate family members, the standards of a "genuine" marriage within the migration context are placed somewhat higher. Often, the idea of a marriage based mainly on love is contrasted with the notion of a marriage of convenience motivated only by material interests. Institutions thus establish marriage norms by defining the (im-)permissible motivations to conclude a marriage in the context of family migration and by evaluating the presence/absence of these norms and motivations with couples perceived to be "suspicious." Furthermore, policies of probationary periods of typically several years for the incoming spouses endorse a notion of marriage as a long-lasting commitment and also penalise divorces.

With regard to refugees, Carens (2001: 11; 2003: 102) has repeatedly pointed towards the difficulty of establishing a clear threshold in determining who is a "genuine" refugee with a strong moral claim to asylum, i.e. persons suffering (possibly life-threatening) persecution from an oppressive regime on the one hand, and "fake" refugees with no moral claim to asylum, i.e. persons who face no danger in their home country and who want to use the "asylum ticket" to gain admission and access to the receiving country purely for economic or hedonistic well-being on the other. In Carens' view, in reality most refugees will not fall into one of the above extreme cases but rather somewhere in between on a continuum between "genuine" and "fake," with "mixed motives for their flight and facing varying degrees of risk" (Carens 2003: 102).

A very similar analogy can be drawn with regard to "genuine/fake" marriages. Most marriages are situated somewhere along a continuum between the prototype "genuine" marriage, with love being the sole motivation for marrying and material considerations playing no role at all, and the prototype "fake" marriage of convenience, with no

---

[29] This is also the reason why Lumpp (2007: 22) questions the parallel German term "*Scheinehe*" (bogus marriage) since it implies a legally invalid marriage. Within marriages of convenience, the spouses intend to enter a legally valid marriage, though they do not intend to lead a marital life.

familial relationship existent or envisioned between the spouses and a desire to improve standard of living being the sole incentive to enter into the marriage. If few pure "genuine" or "fake" marriages exist, but most fall into the large grey zone between the two extremes, with mixed motivations and incentives,[30] how should the state draw a clear line between what is a marriage of convenience and what is not? How can it be morally justified that wherever the line is drawn, those cases falling just outside the definition will closely resemble those cases just inside the definition, much more than either case can resemble the extreme cases at the ends of the continuum?[31] To classify the former as "genuine" marriages and the latter as marriages of convenience would not be "true to moral realities" (Carens 2001: 11); establishing more categories does little to solve the problem. In addition, considering the temporal dimension, another possibility emerges: Apart from the marriage ceremony being a fixed, one time event, a marriage is also an institutionalised partnership which extends and changes over time. How should definitions surrounding marriage-of-convenience incorporate the possibility of changing motivations to sustain a marriage, once concluded? Can a marriage initially concluded out of convenience purposes develop into a "genuine" marriage if the spouses do fall in love and vice versa?

Obviously, in practice, some kind of line must be drawn. Often, laws and policy papers speak of marriages of convenience if the "sole purpose" of the marriage is access to a residence permit. How morally and practically defensible this definition is, is up for debate Carens reminds us that:

> ...it is important to be conscious of the discrepancies between legal categories and moral continua. (...) Since we need definitions, we should try and have good ones (...) not draw distinctions among claimants that are arbitrary or otherwise morally indefensible (Carens 2001: 11).

Furthermore, restrictive immigration policies and marriage-of-convenience policies can have a perverse combined effect, which could be termed the "paradox of convenience." Transnational couples wishing to live together in order to pursue their relationship can be pressed to marry comparatively early on in their relationship if no other possibilities of admission are viable for the incoming spouse. This leads to the para-

---

[30] Jelínková and Szczepaniková (2008) empirically sustain this hypothesis in their work on bi-national marriages in the Czech Republic.
[31] Carens (2003: 102) makes exactly this point for individuals who barely qualify as refugees and those who barely do not.

doxical situation of state policies pressuring individuals, who might not feel ready to commit to a marriage, into concluding one in order to be able to live in the same country together.[32] For many transnational couples lacking other possibilities, an incentive thus exists to conclude a marriage with a considerable amount of "convenience" involved, i.e. the convenience of being together as a couple. In a similar vein, Joppke (1999) speaks of "catch-22" situations in his analysis of the so-called primary-purpose rule[33] in Great Britain, a rule that was a unique example of an extreme institutionalisation of marriage-of-convenience policies:

> The primary-purpose rule puts applicants into a catch-22 situation, because the very application can be taken as evidence that the principal reason of the marriage is immigration to Britain. Gerald Kaufman of the Labour Party phrased the dilemma this way: 'How does one prove that one's application is not intended to achieve admission, when the success of one's application will, of course, result in one's admission?' (Joppke 1999: 126)

Detecting a marriage of convenience

Even ignoring the difficulties outlined above regarding attempts to establish a working definition of what actually constitutes a marriage of convenience and what does not, another interrelated problem remains: How should these marriages be measured regarding their degree of "authenticity"? As with most "criminal" activities, the individuals consciously engaging in a marriage of convenience are unlikely to come forward and declare themselves openly "guilty." Instead, it is up to the state to "detect" whether a marriage can be classified as one of convenience or not.

There are commonly two steps to this procedure. In the first step, "suspicious" couples are singled out by the responsible civil servants dealing with the case (pertaining to the civil registry, the aliens authorities or the representations abroad) according to a particular set of indicators, which differ from state to state, but often include the lack of communication possibilities, an only brief period of acquaintance prior to

---

[32] This effect is empirically confirmed by Kraler (2010: 68).
[33] From 1985 until 1997, the so-called primary-purpose rule was an integral part of British family migration policy. Spousal migration applicants had to prove that their marriage had not been primarily concluded in order to enter the UK. The burden of proof that reasons other than immigration were the main motive of the marriage lay on the applicant. Many spousal migration applicants, especially from the Indian sub-continent, were refused access on the grounds of the primary-purpose rule (see Wray 2006: 307-308; Joppke 1999: 114-128; Sachdeva 1993).

marriage, a large age difference between the spouses (especially when the wife is significantly older than the husband[34]), a history of prior marriages, separate domiciles and an impending expulsion of the incoming spouse (Council of Ministers 1997; de Hart 2001: 20; Keim 2010). In any case, a considerable amount of discretion is left to the civil servants in charge. After raising the suspicion that a marriage of convenience might have taken place, state authorities proceed in different ways; most commonly, they interview the spouses, both separately and jointly, and pose questions on the couples' history, future plans and everyday life, as well as specific traits of the respective other spouse. By observing the couple's interaction as well as controlling their intimate knowledge of one another, authorities seek to establish whether the marriage is one of convenience or not. Other measures are (surprise) house visits, the questioning of neighbours and the request of documents bearing proof of a long-standing and emotional relationship (e.g. bills addressed to both spouses, private correspondence, photographs). The entirety of these procedures will be labelled "intimacy inquiries" in the following. These intimacy inquiries bear on at least three interconnected normative issues: Cost-benefit balance, discrimination and privacy rights.

When state authorities attempt to measure the "genuineness/falseness" of marriages suspected of convenience, they are spending their time and thus public resources on this enterprise. Therefore, one might justifiably question the balance of costs and benefits. Even with a workable definition of what constitutes a marriage of convenience and with a catalogue of indicators, intentions and feelings are extremely volatile and very difficult to measure. The result is most probably a lengthy procedure to determine the authenticity of the marriage. Therefore, it is reasonable to ask whether the benefit (i.e. presumably fewer marriages of convenience) is worth the price (paying civil servants to conduct this task) for the taxpayers. Going a step further, one can also question the effectiveness of the measurements: Due to procedural difficulties, it may very well be that "fake" marriages pass the test and "genuine" ones do not, further casting doubt on the public benefit of the entire undertaking. Scale is an important consideration here. For example, in 2005, a mere 8 per cent of those marriages investigated in Vienna were determined to be of convenience (Digruber & Messinger 2006: 295). This leads de Hart to question "whether expansive legal measures are really required for a

---

[34] See the statements of a German aliens authority civil servant (Stuttgarter Zeitung 2011).

relatively small number of proven marriages of convenience" (de Hart 2006: 261).

The second issue is that of discrimination, which potentially occurs at two levels. First, transnational marriages are discriminated against vis-à-vis non-transnational marriages, since the policies, though varying in degree and scope, clearly also work as *de facto* deterrents for these marriages. The procedure to marry a person who does not gain any residence status improvement by the marriage is significantly less complicated than the procedure of marrying one that does. Secondly, in the course of the intimacy inquiries, there is a danger of discrimination of different groups of couples along nationality, religious, race or gender lines, which constitute just the arbitrary and morally indefensible lines Carens (2001: 11) warns against. Empirical evidence demonstrates that discrimination takes place both overtly and covertly, i.e. both institutionally and officially enshrined, as in Great Britain along gender and ethnic lines during the years of the "husband ban"[35] (Joppke 1998: 290), and more surreptitiously (possibly even unconsciously) under the discretion of the civil servants handling the cases, either when determining who is subject to an inquiry in the first place and/or when judging the evidence gathered thereafter.[36] Such practices might even be construed as constituting an "abuse of the abuse," i.e. an employment of the discourse on abuse, outlined earlier, to achieve another goal, namely closing down legal migration channels for certain groups even further.

Another issue that arises from these policies relates to the effects that can result from the violation of the privacy of the spouses. Since the condition to be evaluated (i.e. a marriage and its authenticity) is such a private and intimate matter, the procedure often breaches the spouses' privacy by conducting (separate) interviews on intimate matters, house visits, interviews with neighbours and the like. These proceedings are often perceived as extremely invasive and humiliating by the spouses and place a lot of strain both on the relationship and on the individuals. Therefore, marriage-of-convenience policies can also be considered to violate human rights provisions defending individual privacy.[37] Both the Universal Declaration of Human Rights (UDHR) and the ECHR include the right to privacy and the right to family in the same article, suggesting an intrinsic connection between the two. In the case of transnational mar-

---

[35] From 1969-1985, it was extremely difficult or even impossible to enter the UK for incoming male spouses, especially for black ones (Wray 2006: 306).
[36] See Verband binationaler Familien und Partnerschaften, iaf e.V. (2001) for various empirical accounts of discrimination along gender and racial lines.
[37] E.g. Article 12 of the UDHR and Article 8 of the ECHR.

riages involved in a family migration process, however, a certain trade-off seems to exist: Either the couples cooperate with the authorities and give up part of their privacy in order to (hopefully) be granted the right to reside together, or they protect their privacy but risk their family. Obviously, most cases are not as dramatic as this, but the two rights, which commonly are considered as sustaining one another, come into tension in the case of transnational marriages suspected of being "bogus." The issue of scale, as mentioned above, is crucial here as well. Can the existence of some (few) marriages of convenience justify the institutional violation of privacy for a large number of transnational marriages? Joppke (1999) also touches upon some of the questions that I have aimed to untangle:

> And immigration officers are asked to measure what cannot be measured: intention. Because immigration officers are nevertheless forced to make a decision, a second set of 'hidden' immigration rules has been built up to inform such decisions. One of these secret instructions recognizes that there are 'no absolute criteria' on which a decision can be based, and that 'if there is no clear evidence either way ... [an applicant] should no longer be given the benefit of the doubt' (quoted in CRE, 1985: 64). The most questionable component of the subjective science of intention-measuring is the separate consideration of the genuineness of marriage, which can be quasi-objectively assessed by the actual intention and practice of living together, and of primary-purpose proper, for which there is no such indicator. Splitting both components apart means that perfectly genuine marriages can still fail the primary-purpose test. (Joppke 1999: 125-126).

2.2.3 The European preoccupation with marriages of convenience

At the European level, several legislative steps were taken to consolidate policies specifically targeted at marriages of convenience.[38] As early as 1993, an EU resolution on the harmonisation of national family reunification policies contained a point stating that "Member States reserve the right to determine whether a marriage was contracted solely or principally for the purpose of enabling the spouse to enter and take up residence in a Member State, and to refuse permission to enter and stay accordingly."[39] In 1997, another Council resolution was agreed upon dealing exclu-

---

[38] See de Hart (2006) for an extensive presentation of these policy instruments and the various legislative processes leading up to their conclusion.
[39] Resolution on the Harmonization of national policies on family reunification, Ad Hoc Group Immigration, Copenhagen, 1 June 1993, [SN 2828/1/93 WGI REV 1], point 4 under the "Principles Governing Member States' Policies on Family Reunification" (see Guild & Niessen 1996: 254; de Hart 2006c: 252).

sively with marriages of convenience,[40] this time specifically addressing marriages of foreigners with both Union citizens and third-country nationals. Furthermore, marriages of convenience were similarly recognised to be present if "the sole aim" of the marriage is the circumvention of rules and the obtainment of a residence permit for the foreign spouse (Article 1). Moreover, as noted by de Hart (2006: 253), in contrast to initial drafts, the final resolution explicitly rejects any systematic checks of all marriages with third-country nationals, and instead aims to limit checks to those marriages with "well-founded suspicions" in its preamble. The remainder of the resolution lists an extensive catalogue of possible indicators of a marriage of convenience, including the lack of cohabitation, the "lack of an appropriate contribution to the responsibilities arising from marriage," the spouses not having met before marriage, inconsistencies in the spouses' accounts of their respective personal details, the spouses not speaking a common language, financial retribution having been part of the marriage contraction and a past history of marriages of convenience. In order to obtain this information, authorities may consider "statements by those concerned or by third parties," "information from written documentation," or "information obtained from inquiries carried out" (Article 2).

While both of these resolutions are non-binding instruments, in 2003 the issue was included into binding Community legislation as part of the Family Reunification Directive. Article 16(2b) of the directive enables Member States to reject family reunification entry and residence applications or refuse their renewal if it is shown that "the marriage, partnership or adoption was contracted for the sole purpose of enabling the person concerned to enter or reside in a Member State." In order to determine this, Member States' authorities can conduct "specific checks and inspections where there is reason to suspect that there is fraud or a marriage, partnership or adoption of convenience" (Article 16(4)).

It is important to note though, that the directive deals exclusively with family reunification sponsored by third-country nationals, thus the provision on marriages of convenience strictly also only applies to those marriages, just as is the case with the 1993 resolution mentioned earlier. Contrastingly, the 1997 resolution dealing exclusively with marriages of convenience does not differentiate between citizens and foreign residents; it explicitly applies to marriages "concluded between a national of a Member State or a third-country national legally resident in a Member

---

[40] Council Resolution of 4 December 1997 on measures to be adopted on the combating of marriages of convenience *Official Journal C 382, 16/12/1997*

State and a third-country national" (Article 1). In this vein, the 2004 Free Movement Directive, which concerns EU citizens and their family members, mentions in Article 35 that "Member States may adopt the necessary measures to refuse, terminate or withdraw any right conferred by this Directive in the case of abuse of rights or fraud, such as marriages of convenience." In practice, while many national policies do differentiate between their own citizens and their foreign residents when it comes to family migration rights, marriages of convenience are perceived as a problem in both cases. Accordingly, many European states have in recent years introduced articles into their migration law dealing with, and criminalising, marriages of convenience[41] – in fact, most new Member States have done so in the course of implementing EU law.[42]

In conclusion, the preoccupation about an abuse of spousal migration provisions in the form of so-called marriages of convenience have led most European states to institutionalise certain mechanisms to detect and prevent them, mostly in the form of intimacy inquiries. While state institutions might legitimately claim a right to counteract obvious abuses of family migration provisions, the procedural and normative difficulties connected to defining and measuring marriages of convenience need to be considered as well. Regardless of these difficulties, marriages of convenience are not only targeted directly in most European states, but policy-makers also frame this phenomenon as a reason for introducing other restrictive measures.

2.3 Fighting forced marriages: Defending liberal norms?

In Europe, heightened political sensitivity to the topic of forced marriages and connected demands for policy initiatives to fight them are rather recent. The discussion on forced marriages only gained real prominence in the late 1990s and especially post-9/11 when debates surrounding the perceived dangers of migration, relating to an alleged failure of multiculturalism and minority integration intensified. In many national public spheres, forced marriage debates were preceded by intensive press coverage of so-called "honour killings," which mostly involved cases of young girls of migrant Muslim origin who refused or escaped forced

---

[41] For example, in Austria this is regulated by § 117 Abs 1-2 Fremdenpolizeigesetz 2005, in Germany by § 27 Abs. 1a Nr. 1 Aufenthaltsgesetz and in Belgium by § 146*bis* Civil Code.
[42] See European Commission, DG Justice, Liberty and Security (2006) and European Commission, DG Justice, Freedom and Security (2007).

marriages and subsequently were killed by members of their family (Razack 2004: 150).

In the UK, it was the 1998 case of Rukhsana Naz, who was of Pakistani-origin, which sparked off a nation-wide debate. Naz was strangled by her brother and mother after wanting to divorce her husband, who she wed in an arranged marriage, and after she had refused to abort her baby that was conceived out-of-wedlock. The Swedish case of Fadime Sahindal, who was shot dead by her father in 2002, caused uproar throughout Scandinavia: Fadime had previously opposed her family's plans of forcing a marriage upon her, and had instead maintained a relationship with a Swede. She then fled her family with police help and widely publicised her plight by, amongst other things, giving a speech to the Swedish parliament before her murder (Williams 2002). In Germany, Hatun Sürücü, a young woman who was killed in 2005 at a Berlin bus stop by one or more of her brothers,[43] attracted widescale media coverage. Hatun had escaped a forced marriage and was living independently, raising her son, and completing her education (Lau 2005). In all cases, second-generation migrant Muslim women had broken with their families by rejecting the proscribed marriage and lifestyle patterns, and were subsequently – and supposedly as a direct consequence – murdered by members of their families.[44] While "honour killings" might be seen to

---

[43] The judicial aftermath of the Sürücü case exemplifies the complexities when dealing with crimes committed within families. A revision of the case is currently pending. In April 2006 the youngest of Hatun's three brothers, Ayhan Sürücü, who was 19 years old at the time of the act, was sentenced to nine years in prison as a minor in the first instance after pleading guilty as the sole perpetrator. The role of the two older brothers, who the prosecutors suspected of having assisted in the planning and execution of the murder was highly contentious throughout the trial. The Federal Court of Justice (*Bundesgerichtshof*, BGH) has overturned the acquittals of the two older brothers in August 2007 (BGH, 5 StR 31/07; see Pressestelle des Bundesgerichtshofs 2007) and thus reopened the case. However, this second hearing, burdened by difficulties of Ayhan acting as a witness and the two older brothers needing to be tracked down by international arrest warrants in Turkey, has not begun yet (Beikler 2008).

[44] However, scholars such as Schiffauer (2005) have warned against using the concept of honour killings/violence to denote any family-related drama in ethnic (especially Muslim) minorities. Ethnicising conflicts in this way can distract from other underlying structural (e.g. socio-economic) problems and prevent finding effective solutions and policies. As early as 1997, Lama Abu-Odeh has critically compared the concept of "honour killings" of the East to the "passion killings" of the West, with the former being attributed to "culture" and the latter merely representing a deviant, yet legally (semi-) tolerated behaviour. Volpp (2001: 1187), Razack (2004: 152), Phillips (2007: 95) and Dustin and Phillips (2008: 412) similarly question this binary distinction between Western free choice and capacity for moral action on the one side and Eastern culturally determined and internally condoned behav-

constitute the tip of the iceberg, or as the extreme cases where forced marriage "went wrong," the intensive debates related to these incidents generated the first calls for policy responses. Subsequently, policies aiming at specifically combating forced marriages (hereafter: forced marriage policies) were installed in most Western European countries, in the shape of preventive, criminalising and/or mitigating measures. This section discusses these rather recent policy measures and the rationale behind them from a normative point of view.

In an attempt to normatively "map" the field of forced marriage policies in Europe, a first part will shed light on the general concept of forced marriage, its international legal definition and the general rationale for states to devise policies against it. The second part addresses the aspect of cultural minority practices that is highly relevant for the treatment of the issue in Western European states, since the practice of forced marriages is seen to emanate mainly from within ethnic or religious minorities, and minority protection norms might come into conflict with forced marriage policies. In the third and last part, migration is included in the analysis. As in Europe, forced marriage is largely considered to be an ethnic minority practice, migration enters the picture as marriages can be either enforced abroad, with citizens or foreign residents emigrating, or spouses "imported" and forced into marriage in Europe. Since many of the policies that aim to curb forced marriages are situated within migration law, this nexus must be critically evaluated. It is also within this nexus that forced marriage polices appear to regulate family ties by scrutinising their quality.

2.3.1 Forced marriages and the rationale for state action

In order to begin any theoretical or normative exploration of state policies on forced marriages, it must be clarified what is actually understood by the concept of forced marriage and how and why this phenomenon necessitates government action: What is the rationale behind any public policy aimed at eliminating the practice of forced marriage?

A forced marriage is basically a marriage concluded without the full or free consent of one or both of the future spouses. This practice infringes fundamentally upon Article 16(2) of the UDHR, which states

---

iour on the other. These issues of cultural stereotyping, stigmatisation and agency denial will be further touched upon in the section on forced marriage as a minority practice.

"Marriage shall be entered into only with the free and full consent of the intending spouses." Similar articles can be found in the 1966 International Covenant on Economic, Social and Cultural Rights,[45] the 1966 Covenant on Civil and Political Rights,[46] as well as the 1962 Convention on Consent to Marriage, Minimum Age for Marriage and Registration of Marriages.[47] Forced marriage has even been conceptualised as a form of contemporary slavery by the relevant UN working groups and rapporteurs, thus breaching Article 4 UDHR which grants freedom from all forms of slavery (Bielefeldt 2005: 5).[48] Furthermore, a forced marriage often leads to other human rights violations in the ensuing (enforced) marital life, which frequently lacks crucial (sexual) self-determination. Sexual aggression and rape, as well as domestic violence, can seriously harm physical and mental integrity and in consequence pose serious health risks to individuals forced into marriages. The right to work and education might also be infringed as a consequence of marital dominance and virtual or actual imprisonment (Bielefeldt & Follmar-Otto 2007: 14). Potential violations of human rights to life, liberty and security (Art. 3 UDHR), freedom from cruel and degrading treatment (Art. 5 UDHR), free development of personality (Article 22 UDHR), freedom to work and employment (Art. 23 UDHR) and to the right to education (Art. 26 UDHR) are therefore possible consequences of forced marriages as well.[49]

However, even if a forced marriage constitutes an infringement of human rights, it is not immediately obvious why any state needs to design policies to actively contravene this practice. At this point it is thus important to conceptualise *who* is actually forcing one or both spouses into the unwanted marriage. In most empirical evidence on contemporary practices of forced marriages in Europe, individuals are mostly forced into an unwanted marriage by their own family members and/or those of their spouse. Stemming from the cultural practice of arranging marriages among families, forced marriages often occur when the mar-

---

[45] Article 10(1) reads "The States Parties to the present Covenant recognize that (...) Marriage must be entered into with the free consent of the intending spouses."
[46] Article 23(3) reads "No marriage shall be entered into without the free and full consent of the intending spouses."
[47] Article 1(1) reads "No marriage shall be legally entered into without the full and free consent of both parties, such consent to be expressed by them in person after due publicity and in the presence of the authority competent to solemnize the marriage and of witnesses, as prescribed by law."
[48] See for example the Report of the Working Group on Contemporary Forms of Slavery on its thirty-first session, A/HRC/Sub.1/58/25. 22 August 2006.
[49] See Schöpp-Schilling (2007: 205-208) for an analysis of the relevance of international human rights instruments for forced marriages.

riage arranged is imposed on one or both spouses against their will by means of psychological and physical threats and violence. Authoritarian and non-egalitarian family structures, which often position older generations above younger ones as well as male members above female ones, lead to a power asymmetry potentially enabling the stronger family members to force the weaker ones into marriage. The domestic nature of this phenomenon plays a crucial role in devising effective policies, since the practice is hidden in the private sphere and since the victim and perpetrator(s) are often closely related as well as emotionally and economically bound together. Accordingly, commonly cited reasons for individuals remaining within forced marriages are the fear of being rejected by (parts of) their families and/or the worry of exposing family members to criminal prosecution and conviction, leading to overall (sometimes unbearably) high "sociopsychological costs" of exit (Reitman 2005, as cited in Phillips & Dustin 2004: 533).

Originally however, human rights were conceived to demarcate the legitimate boundaries of government authority and violence vis-à-vis its citizens, without having much significance for the private sphere. It was only during recent decades, *inter alia* influenced by feminist literature, that a new consensus spread among Western liberal democracies. Human rights are increasingly conceived of as not only limiting state power, but also as prescribing a duty for the state to actively ensure that the human rights of all individuals are respected horizontally, that is, by third parties. Furthermore, the idea has gained prominence that, if necessary, states should create the infrastructure to enable individuals to claim the human rights that they are endowed with (Bielefeldt & Follmar-Otto 2007: 14). Regarding forced marriages, a practice that mostly occurs within the private sphere of the family without state involvement, this idea of horizontal human rights validity and enforcement is the main rationale behind state policies that aim at eliminating them. From a human-rights-based perspective it could be followed that policies should ideally aim at empowering potentially and actually affected individuals to more self-determination and enable them to actually enjoy the human rights awarded to them by international conventions.

Furthermore, apart from being signatories to international conventions, all Western liberal democracies have transposed most of the rights mentioned above into their national constitutions. Legal provisions relating to (physical) coercion, extortion, kidnapping, abduction, false imprisonment, (sexual) assault and rape criminalise these human rights violations. Therefore, next to having international human rights obligations, Western liberal states ought to combat criminal practices occurring in the context of forced marriages as part of maintaining the rule of law in their territories. Most European polities also contain a clause in their marriage laws that invalidate marriages where one or both spouses wed under duress[50] and some have even specifically introduced forced marriage into their criminal law[51] as well.

Thus far, I have been silent on gender in an attempt to systematically analyse the phenomenon and carefully evaluate the responses normatively without reproducing common stereotypes. Human rights provisions protect both men and women from being forced into marriage. Clearly however, the overwhelming focus of all political and legal endeavours is on women as victims of forced marriages, even though recently some attention has surfaced regarding male victims (Elger 2008); the British authorities even repeatedly mention a male victim rate of 15 per cent (Foreign and Commonwealth Office 2004: 2). Additionally, homosexual victims of both sexes are surfacing as a group to be considered by practitioners as well (Thiemann 2007; Forced Marriage Unit 2008).

Nevertheless, forced marriage is generally understood as a problem mainly affecting young women, as they are seen to a) be more sexually controlled than men and more likely to be forced into marriage in the first place, b) less able to resist familial pressure than young men when marriage arrangements are put on the table and c) experience the negative consequences of an enforced marriage to a much greater extent than men, as a plethora of other gender-based discriminations potentially reinforce and exacerbate the rights violations endured in the context of the forced marriage (Schöpp-Schilling 2007: 203). It is therefore no surprise that the most important international instrument focussing specifically on women's rights, the 1979 Convention on the Elimination of All Forms of Discrimination against Women (CEDAW), contains an article proscribing forced marriage as well.[52] Western liberal states have largely

---

[50] In the German case, § 1314 Abs. 2 Nr. 4 BGB (*Bundesgesetzbuch*) invalidates marriages concluded under threat.

[51] In 2005, forced marriage was introduced as an especially serious case of coercion into the German Criminal Code (*Strafgesetzbuch*, StGB) with the new § 240 Abs. 4 Satz 2 Nr. 1 (see Kalthegener (2007) for a detailed discussion of the German criminal prosecution of forced marriages). In 2011, a law was passed that made forced marriage a specific type of offense, moving the unchanged wording from § 240 to the newly created § 237 StGB. See section 4.2.5.

[52] Article 16 (1) reads "States Parties shall take all appropriate measures to eliminate discrimination against women in all matters relating to marriage and family relations and in particular shall ensure, on a basis of equality of men and women: (…) (b) The same right freely to choose a spouse and to enter into marriage only with their free and full consent (…)."

incorporated a doctrine of gender equality into their constitutions, policies and discourses. When thus conceptualising forced marriage as a form of gendered violence, an additional strong case for state policies to combat these practices emerges. Indeed, forced marriage is almost entirely interpreted to be an instance of intolerable gender subordination, as will be shown later. Therefore, within forced marriage policies the gender perspective mentioned by Vogel (2000) is paramount, though not in the sense of the state institutionally subordinating women. On the contrary, the dominant institutional framing is that of emancipating oppressed women and of enabling them to enjoy the equal rights they are entitled to.

Summing up, it is Western liberal democracies' commitment to horizontal human rights, maintenance of the rule of law and gender equality that provide the main rationale to devise forced marriage policies. At this theoretical level, the case for some kind of forced marriage policies is a strong one. It is when turning to the practical empirical contexts that possible difficulties emerge, as will be shown in the following sections.

2.3.2 Forced marriages as a minority practice?

Although arranged marriages were the crucial political and economic institution which organised nearly all aspects of society across Europe until the at least the nineteenth century (Coontz 2005) – which presumably led to a certain incidence of forced marriages as well[53] – modernisation processes have led to substantial shifts in the legal, political and social meaning of marriage with strong emphasis on romantic love (Giddens 1992), individual self-determination and mutual consent as the main legitimate basis of marriage within Western Europe. Against this backdrop, in Europe practices of arranged and forced marriages are seen to nearly exclusively occur within ethnic minority communities.[54] If the

---

[53] Since most literature on contemporary forced marriages assumes that a widespread practice of arranged marriages leads to a higher incidence of forced marriages, forced marriages can be presumed to have historically existed in Europe as well. However, few studies exist on forced marriages within European history and culture – though Strobl and Lobermeier (2007: 28) mention the phenomenon in reference to European aristocracy in passing.

[54] As to be expected, the presence of different minority communities across Europe has led to different focuses for research. In Great Britain the discourse mostly refers to "South Asians" and the Forced Marriage Unit cooperates directly with police forces in Pakistan, India and Bangladesh (Dustin & Phillips 2008: 410), while in Germany, the public discussion revolves nearly exclusively around the Muslim community in general and the Turkish

practice of forced marriage is situated among ethnic minorities, the question of minority group rights comes into play.

As articulated most prominently by Kymlicka, minority groups can be seen to have "societal cultures" which give meaning in essential ways to their members' lives. As living within the culture is so important, its survival is crucial for the individual autonomy of the groups' members (Kymlicka 1995: 76). As they do not belong to the majority culture, these societal cultures are under potential threat of extinction and their prevalence is not sufficiently guaranteed by the mere protection of the individual rights of their members. Accordingly, in order to contribute to individual wellbeing, societal cultures must be further protected by special group rights.[55] This kind of reasoning, coupled with individual human rights being awarded equally to members of minorities, such as the freedom to practice religion and the right to non-discriminatory equal treatment, have strongly influenced the development of multiculturalism as a political doctrine. As Bielefeldt (2005: 7) outlines, it is intrinsic to the nature of liberal democracies committed to human rights to be religiously, ideologically and culturally plural – we can thus speak of a positive relationship between human rights and multiculturalism. What additional issues arise when conceiving of forced marriage as a minority practice? Do minority group rights overrule the individual human rights considerations outlined earlier?

These questions are obviously connected to the perception of minority rights and the legitimacy of protecting them. What qualifies as a minority right, for example? And at what costs should they be defended? Okin (1999) was among the first to identify the problematic tendency of multiculturalism and the associated tolerance of cultural minority practices to legitimise or even protract cultural elements that discriminate or oppress certain (weaker) members of the minority group. By embracing the liberal idea of allowing cultural diversity and thereby reducing structural inequalities between groups, illiberal practices might flourish that could lead to inequalities within groups increasing. Okin is particularly

---

one in particular. However, some official German documents also stress the point that forced marriages are not an exclusively Muslim or Turkish problem, repeatedly citing cases from Buddhist-Hindu Sri Lanka or Christian Greece and Southern Italy (Justizministerium Baden-Württemberg 2006: 2).

[55] However, Kymlicka (1995: 95-101) clearly distinguishes between voluntary migrants and national minorities regarding the force of their claims, making the case that the latter can justifiably claim self-government rights while the former ought to settle for polyethnic rights.

preoccupied with gender equality and focuses on practices typically located within ethnic minorities considered oppressive to women, such as female genital mutilation, polygamy and forced marriage. She fiercely criticises the predisposition of liberal multiculturalists to regard cultural groups as homogenous and ignore the fundamental internal power discrepancies as well as the importance of the private sphere in shaping, transmitting and enacting these (gendered) power differences (Okin 1999: 12). If one follows Okin's reasoning and applies it to the case of forced marriages by conceptualising it as an unacceptable minority practice of gendered violence, a very strong case for forced marriage policies emerges. Tolerating forced marriages under the pretext of minority rights is likely to further aggravate the situation of the (female) victims.

The distinction between forced marriages and arranged marriages comes into play in this context. Reiterating both Okin's notion of gendered violence and certain ideals of multicultural accommodation, most political manifestos dealing with the issue denounce forced marriages as unacceptable infringements upon (minority women's) human rights, while arranged marriages are perceived as permissible expressions of minority cultural practices (e.g. Foreign and Commonwealth Office 2004: 2). This approach would thus seem to be a popular way of reconciling the two opposing principles: Western states can accept cultural practices of minorities that are different (or archaic) as in the case of arranged marriages, as long as human rights are respected. If and when, however, as in the case of forced marriages, this threshold of human rights is crossed, Western tolerance of minority cultures ends. This kind of reasoning could be seen as a normative prescription in favour of designing effective forced marriage policies, which do not conflict with the practice of arranging marriages.

In theory, this distinction might seem to constitute an adequate and comfortable way of resolving the conflict between minority protection and human rights. In practice however, this differentiation is itself loaded with problems. As it is fundamentally based on the notion of consent as the main marker distinguishing between an arranged, consensual marriage and a forced, non-consensual marriage, difficulties arise when looking closely at the concept of consent and its opposite, coercion. How are consent and coercion defined? How are they measured? In the present context of minority practices, the impact that certain (cultural) socialisations have on individuals' ability to freely consent or dissent is of paramount importance.[56] Put differently, the question is how the mere option of exit can become reality (Phillips & Dustin 2004).

Without being able to enter this entirely separate discussion, suffice it here to say that a clear-cut distinction between forced and arranged marriages is highly contentious. Straßburger is among the sociologists who regard arranged marriages as important and legitimate cultural practices, while acknowledging the obvious difficulties of the large grey zones that exist between different cases (Straßburger 2003; Straßburger 2007). Kelek, on the other hand, one of the most important public figures engaged in the German debate on the issue, has often vociferously asserted that both arranged and forced marriages are expressions of the same authoritarian family structures which truncate individual self-determination. As a result, she argues that the distinction ought to be abandoned altogether[57] (Kelek 2005).

However, even when leaving the controversial distinction between forced and arranged marriages aside, the strong focus on forced marriages as sites of gender oppression[58] is not straightforward either. Indeed, scholars such as Bhabha (1999), Volpp (2001) and Razack (2004) have questioned the binary contrasting of gender equality in the West with complete gender subordination within "Eastern" minority cultures. This binary distinction is not only asserted by Okin but also within many public debates and policy frames, seemingly obliging us to choose between feminism and human rights on the one hand and multiculturalism and group rights on the other (with the choice tending towards the former). Instead, these authors invite readers to consider the pitfalls related to such oppositional distinctions. Their common underlying concern is the peril of oversimplifying "cultural" traits and stigmatising entire minority groups in the process. For example, both Volpp (2001) and Razack

---

[56] An extensive discussion of the paradigm of liberal autonomy and the notions of choice and consent in the context of minority practices can be found in Deveaux (2006).

[57] The fact that Necla Kelek herself was a subject of a forced marriage in her youth as well as her own Muslim Turkish background are often perceived as factors adding to the authenticity of her claims, while her critics have accused her of essentialist representations of Islam as barbaric, patriarchal religion and Turkish "parallel societies" within German society as inherently gender oppressive. This discussion culminated in a heated media debate in 2006 between Kelek and her detractors, led by Yasemin Karakaşoğlu (for a detailed analysis of the controversy, see Rostock & Berghahn 2008: 354-356).

[58] A rather understudied perspective relating to forced marriages is the oppression exerted by the older generation upon the younger one since the core focus is always gender. Evidence on male victims of forced marriages (Foreign and Commonwealth Office 2004: 2) and on the pressure exerted by the older female generation within forced marriages (Samad & Eade 2002) point towards the significance of including the generation nexus into future analyses.

(2004) show how gender equality is far from being the norm in Western states either, and thus heavily criticise the double standard deployed in this context. Furthermore, they question the helpfulness of employing concepts such as "culture" as a determining factor in individuals' actions. To them, this has encouraged a common discourse that tends to portray the minority/migrant/Muslim/Black male as backward and dangerous and the minority/migrant/Muslim/Black female as a perpetual victim, thereby denying the latter any kind of agency in the process. From this point of view, policies aimed at curbing forced marriages might be perceived as being imperialistic and inherently stigmatising of minority cultures.

2.3.3 Forced marriage policies within migration law

In this last part, the connection between the issues of forced marriage and immigration in general, as well as the situation of forced marriage policies within immigration law, will be considered. How are forced marriages connected to immigration? As outlined above, in Europe forced marriages are generally situated within ethnic minorities, predominantly of non-Christian origin. Individuals from ethnic minorities have entered European states by way of immigration, originally mostly in the context of (former) colonial ties or guest worker programs. However, this migration has already spanned several generations and *ius soli* provisions, as well as naturalisation policies, have incorporated sizeable sections of the ethnic minorities into the citizenry. Thus, even if conceiving of forced marriages as an ethnic minority practice, there is no necessary link to migration. A marriage can be forced upon one or both potential spouses completely outside of the migration context, making the near exclusive location of forced marriage policies within (restrictive) migration law across most European states somewhat questionable.[59]

However, certain links between migration and forced marriages remain and, as just mentioned, these links have often prominently pro-

---

[59] A notable exception constitutes the UK Forced Marriage (Civil Protection) Bill, which was passed in July 2007. Dustin and Phillips laud both the preceding policy process, characterised by a "trend towards consultation and engagement with the voluntary sector" (2008: 419), as well as the problem-setting within the law as it "provides recourse for people coerced into marriage with domestic, not just overseas, partners, thereby shifting the focus of official activity away from its problematic association with immigration; and it places forced marriage within the wider context of domestic violence, thereby favouring generic over culture-specific legislation" (2008: 411).

vided some of the rationale behind restrictive family migration provisions across various European states. The most commonly debated phenomenon are so-called "import brides"/"import grooms." Here, one or both spouses are forced into a marriage that is subsequently located in Europe where one of the spouses has a regular residence, and the other spouse enters as a spousal migrant. In this context, two important mechanisms come into play. Firstly, the "migration ticket" might be perceived to enter dowry negotiations and actually lead to a higher incidence of forced marriages. Secondly, incoming spouses find themselves in a rather vulnerable situation, both socio-economically as well as legally. Lacking language skills, social contacts and knowledge of the workings of the host society and depending for their residence permit upon the sponsor – at least during an initial period – migrant victims of forced marriages can be seen to be much less likely to escape the situation than someone who has grown up in the host society. Put differently, migrants constitute more exposed victims. Within this logic, generous spousal migration policies can even be seen as being directly responsible for forced marriages. This is part of the argumentation behind curbing forced marriages by controlling spousal migration more extensively.

Another possible way in which migration law is crucial for forced marriages is in relation to emigration: A marriage might be enforced abroad between citizens or foreign residents of European states, for example during family vacations. In the case of foreign residents, migration laws in Europe often stipulate that after a certain period of time abroad, a permanent residence permit expires, impeding their return to Europe.[60]

In what constitutes a clear example of state attempts to regulate the family, recent policy initiatives across Europe claim to combat the practice of forced marriage by targeting spousal migration, e.g. by increasing the minimum age of spouses eligible to apply for spousal migration and by introducing integration requirements which must be provided prior to entry. The official discourse legitimating these policy changes refers to discouraging family members from forcing young migrants-to-be into an unwanted marriage, as well as to empowering the potential "victims" through education and enabling them to mature into adulthood. However, only restrictive measures in migration policy seem to be embraced in an attempt to fight forced marriages, while enough evidence

---

[60] In Germany, this is regulated by § 51 Abs. 1 Nr. 7 AufenthG. The regular period that a permanent resident can leave Germany without it having consequences for their residence permit is six months. See Freudenberg (2007: 247).

exists that liberalising certain aspects of (spousal) migration might have a preventive and empowering effect as well.

The analysis has mapped out the normative arguments surrounding state policies that aim to combat forced marriage by considering human rights, minority rights and the issue of migration. In addition to being an extremely complex issue, it is also highly politicised and different actors involved tend to exploit stereotypes on both sides of the debate, which is further enabled by the widespread lack of data on this hidden phenomenon. Policy-makers' depictions of forced marriages as a widespread problem located within spousal migration, an instance of official attempts to regulate the family, has developed into an important framing approach enabling the introduction of restrictive policy responses, as the exploration of the German case in the later chapters will show.

Conclusions

Even though no absolute right to family migration is enshrined in international law or any domestic constitution, family migration provisions are in place in most Western liberal democratic states because norms do matter. However, norms matter not only when allowing family migration, but also when restricting it. The chapter showed how the right to the protection of family and the power of social membership together form the normative basis for family migration policies in Western liberal democracies. At the same time, since both "family ties" and "social membership" are vague and contested concepts, by investing these notions with certain meanings, policy-makers may in turn create a legitimate basis to control family migration, while staying within the discursive realm of protecting the right to family of their members. At times when family migration is perceived to be undesirable and thus restricting it is one of the priorities of migration policy, policy-makers may make use of different approaches in order to justify instruments of migration control.

When regulating social membership, policies assess the legal, civic and socio-economic membership claims of sponsoring (and recently also of incoming) spouses, thereby suggesting specific norms of social membership, sometimes in discriminatory fashions. Policy instruments situated within the approach of family regulation, by contrast, employ specific, sometimes even contradictory norms of marriage and family in order to circumscribe the admissible family and assess the "quality" of the familial bonds claimed. The remaining two sections focused on the policy instruments relating to the notions of marriages of convenience and forced marriages, respectively, normatively assessing both the general thrust behind them as well as the (critical) issues arising through their implementation.

Chapter 3 will introduce the case under research, Germany, by exploring the historical post-war development of family migration policies. It will also provide an overview of the empirical reality of this phenomenon and of the basic legal framework relevant to spousal migration in Germany.

3 Empirical and legal realities of spousal migration to Germany

"*Deutschland ist kein Einwanderungsland*" – "Germany is not a country of immigration." Few statements have been repeated more often or have been more controversial in recent German debates on migration. It was chanted as a mantra by the conservatives during the 1990s on the one side, and gradually questioned, rejected, revised and ridiculed as an alleged "refusal of reality" by the increasingly more liberal political forces gaining voice after 1998 on the other. It was at this time that a red-green coalition led by Gerhard Schröder replaced the Christian Democrats who had led the government for the sixteen preceding years. As the social reality of ethnic minorities in Germany was gradually acknowledged, citizenship law was somewhat liberalised in 2000, and integration actually emerged as a desirable political goal. Nevertheless, the forty years of political negation of permanent immigration not only pose "the single most enduring puzzle in the German immigration debate" (Joppke 1999: 62), but also markedly coloured all further policy debates on immigration and integration.

In this context of complex political negotiations on the meaning of immigration for the past, present and future of the German society, the following chapter introduces the relevant case of this thesis. The first section (3.1) briefly outlines the historical development[61] of German post-war family migration policy.[62] In the second section (3.2), the general legal framework pertaining to spousal migration in Germany is introduced, differentiating

---

[61] For a more profound historical analysis of the development of post-war migration flows and policy as well as the intrinsically connected issue of citizenship in Germany see (among many others) Brubaker (1992), Joppke (1999) and Green (2004).
[62] Unless specified otherwise, the legal and practical conditions pertaining to family members of asylum seekers and refugees will be ignored, since rather different logics and laws apply to them.

between the conditions that apply to all transnational couples and those pertaining only to foreign sponsors. The particular changes introduced in 2007 are left aside, as they are dealt with extensively in chapter 4. A statistical overview of spousal migration flows into Germany, tentatively differentiated by the legal status of the sponsor, the country of origin and gender, constitutes the last section (3.3).

3.1 The evolution of German family migration policy

3.1.1 1950-2000: Political negligence and judicial activism

1950-1973: *Gastarbeiter*, then their families

In the 1950s, the recovery and expansion of the German economy after the war (dubbed the economic miracle, the *Wirtschaftswunder*) caused a massive demand for low-skilled labour that domestic workers could not fill. As a result, business and industry groups, in particular, lobbied for the recruitment of foreign labour.[63] After the first recruitment treaty with Italy was signed in 1955, further treaties were signed between 1960 and 1968 with Spain, Greece, Turkey, Morocco, Portugal, Tunisia and Yugoslavia. So-called guest workers *(Gastarbeiter)* started filling German factories and cities. This influx of labourers continued to grow through the 1960s and, in 1973, guest worker labour participation reached an all-time high with 2.6 million gainfully employed guest workers. At this point, a total of 4 million foreigners were residing in Germany, which amounted to 12 per cent of the total population (Münz & Ulrich 1997: 79).

In order to ensure that the guest workers would really work as flexible "buffers" for the labour market, the recruitment regime initially envisaged that the workers would be temporary and would rotate. Work permits were only issued for one year and then renewed for another year if the work-

---

[63] In addition to the widespread interpretation that foreign labour was exclusively recruited into Germany in the 1950s and 1960s due to labour market needs, some authors emphasise the often-underestimated role foreign trade interests and foreign policy considerations, such as consolidating new NATO partners or East-West détente, played in the formulation of the recruitment agreements (e.g. Steinert 1995; Knortz 2008).

er was deemed not to be harmful to the German economy (González-Ferrer 2007: 12). Accordingly, the government did not particularly encourage permanent settlement of guest workers or support the idea that their families might join them. Nevertheless, in the Italian recruitment agreement, Article 16 stipulated that the recruited workers, provided that they had enough living space, could file an application to be reunited with their family members, which the authorities would "benevolently consider as soon as possible." Similar articles were included in the agreements with Spain, Greece and Portugal, which were not EC Member States at the time yet. However, Bendix (1990) argues that the requirement to provide housing also deterred or least seriously delayed the admission of family members. Employers were responsible for providing housing to their guest workers, but unlike wages, which were monitored by the trade unions, no regulations about housing existed. The barracks and dormitories provided to the workers were primarily cheap and obviously did not fulfil the requirements to sponsor family migration (see González-Ferrer 2007: 13).

The later agreements with Turkey, Morocco, Tunisia and Yugoslavia focused even more on enforcing a strict rotation principle. The maximum time workers from these countries were allowed to stay was strictly limited to two years, and no family migration provisions at all were included in the agreements (Mattes 2005: 67). In the case of Turkey, however, the practice of rotation was not upheld for long, as employers were very unhappy with the idea of their newly trained foreign workforce constantly fluctuating. In 1964, before the first round of Turkish workers would have been sent back, the German ministries responsible for economics and labour, as well as the Foreign Office, managed to push through their interests vis-à-vis the more restrictive Interior Ministry. The Interior Ministry first tried to strike a compromise and suggested allowing stays over two years but continuing to uphold the ban on family migration. Not only did Turkish officials reject this idea, but also other German authorities were worried about the possible harm such a discriminatory and restrictive policy could cause to Germany's image in the international arena. It has been argued that these negotiations show that even in the 1960s, norms influenced policy-makers in the liberal direction (Triadafilopoulos & Schönwälder 2006: 8). In a renewed Turkish recruitment agreement, the two-year maximum stay was scrapped and a family migration provision was included (Knortz 2008: 126-129).

According to Pagenstecher (1995), this political toleration of family migration from the early stages of post-war migration was due to various factors. The general ideological importance of the family unit and the knowledge that the constitutional Article 6 protecting marriage and family also pertained to foreigners created an important normative impetus for policy-makers. Furthermore, utilitarian considerations played a role, as employers deemed that allowing family migration was useful to limit the fluctuation of workers and could even enhance their productivity. Finally, ensuring social stability was an important motive, as the presence of young married men without access to their wives was considered to be a possible endangerment to social peace, for instance, through children born out of wedlock to German women (Pagenstecher 1995: 725). At the same time, many wives of male guest workers entered Germany not only as spousal migrants, but also as guest workers themselves. Actually, from the early 1960s onward, female labour was sought after in certain sectors. Employers quickly realised the advantages of nominally recruiting the wives of their guest workers; not only was it faster than the standard anonymous procedure, but it also increased the chances of the trained male foreign workers staying (González-Ferrer 2007: 13).

In spite of this massive influx, no cohesive legal framework was in place concerning the admission or residence of foreign workers, nor that of their family members. Legally, all foreigners entering Germany were governed by a 1938 police ordinance (*Ausländerpolizeiverordnung*, APVO), itself a relic of Nazi times, which granted few rights to foreigners resident in Germany but rather tolerated them in case "their character and their reason for residence (...) guarantees that they are worthy of the hospitality" (Section 1 APVO, as quoted in Green 2004: 34). No family migration provisions were enshrined in the ordinance at all. Both the embarrassment of relying on a Nazi ordinance, which was rather hostile towards foreigners, as well as technical deficiencies of the APVO led the government to draft a new legal framework applying to foreigners in 1962.

In the policy-making process leading up to the 1965 introduction of the Foreigner Law[64] (*Ausländergesetz*, AuslG 1965), the comparable lack of

---

[64] See Bundesgesetzblatt, Teil I, Nr. 19, p. 353. The fact that German political and legal discourse continuously referred to foreigners (*Ausländer*) instead of "immigrants," as was the case, for

political controversy or discussion has been claimed to be illustrative of the high degree of cross-party elite normative consensus on the issue of immigration that dominated policy-making throughout the 1960s and 1970s (Green 2004: 35). However, even if certain aspects of immigration into Germany were more codified after 1965, the Foreigner Law remained far from liberalising migration or enshrining fundamental rights for foreigners. Instead, national interests replaced the "worthiness" criterion of the old APVO, with the law stipulating residence permits were to be granted only if "the presence of the foreigner does not encroach upon the interests of the Federal Republic of Germany."[65] Castles critically remarks that instead of granting any rights to migrants, the law only provided "the authorities the power to confer or to deny privileges, according to the labor market situation and the behavior of the migrants" (Castles 1985: 523). As the new law continued to conceptualise all migration into Germany as temporary, it still did not mention family migration. This does not mean that no family migration took place, but it depended on the discretion of the authorities whether applications for family migration were granted or disregarded.

1973-1990: Increasing restriction per decree after the recruitment stop

Ironically, it was the recruitment ban (*Anwerbestopp*) issued in the aftermath of the first oil crisis in November 1973 that led to a sharp increase in family migration. Contrary to the rule in previous years, TCN guest workers who left Germany were not free to return. Therefore, many opted to turn their stay into a long-term project after 1973 and bring their families into Germany to join them (Green 2004: 36). While in 1972 foreign spouses of German citizens gained an unconditional right of residence for the first time,[66] family migration of foreign residents remained unregulated at the federal level.

---

instance, in the USA, has in itself been interpreted to be emblematic of the highly restrictive stance towards non-ethnic immigrants in Germany (Joppke 1999: 76).

[65] § 2 Abs. 1 AuslG 1965.

[66] Parallel to developments in other European countries, this right was first granted in 1972 only to foreign wives of German husbands, following the historically institutionalised notion of wives following their husbands. In 1975, this provision was revoked because of gender discrimination

In the following years, various restrictive decrees regarding work permits and family migration were issued with a clear view to reducing the number of foreigners by inducing return migration. For instance, a decree was issued prohibiting the distribution of work permits to spouses joining second-generation migrants after 1 December 1974, with a view toward discouraging family migration and causing some foreigners to leave Germany (Castles 1985: 524). Another reform in 1975 increased child benefits *(Kindergeld)*, but refused its payment to TCN residents if their children were not residing in Germany, which led to a major influx of children and spouses of foreigners to Germany. In fact, this immediate economic incentive has been shown to have had a more decisive impact on migrant families' decision to finally reunite in Germany than the 1973 recruitment stop (González-Ferrer 2007).

Whereas from 1973 until 1978 more migrants left Germany than entered it, after 1979, the figures reversed; most of the increase was due to family migration. Although the number of employed foreigners sunk from about 2.6 million in 1973 to roughly 2 million in 1980, the total foreign population increased from ca. 4 million in 1973 to 4.45 million in 1980 (Herbert 1986: 188). This growth was coupled with the first major hostilities against foreigners reverberating in German society, which led the issue to becoming highly politicised (Joppke 1999: 78). In a 1981 survey, two thirds of the respondents indicated that were in support of return migration of foreigners, while in 1978, only 39 per cent had voiced this opinion (DER SPIEGEL 1982: 37).

Until the late 1970s, cross-party consensus, corporatist decision-making and an "antipopulist norm" (Freeman 1995: 885) dominated migration policy-making in Germany. From the 1980s onwards, however, political parties, mainly the Christian Democrats (CDU/CSU[67]), started to politicise the issue. Boswell and Hough state that this move was not only motivated by a desire to mobilise voters, but was also reflective of the parties' cultural conservatism: "CDU and CSU politicians chose this course not just for its hypothesized electoral expediency; they also did it out of (at least a degree of)

---

and spousal migration rights were granted to foreign husbands of German wives as well (Joppke 1999: 288).

[67] The Christian Democratic sister parties CDU/CSU will be referred to as CDU only for the rest of this thesis.

conviction" (Boswell & Hough 2008: 337). At the same time, an increasing focus was directed at the group of Turkish migrants seen as locus of the "foreigner problem." This was not only owing to the fact that Turks had grown to be the largest single immigrant group (1.4 million were living in Germany in 1981) and were the only group which was still increasing instead of decreasing in size (Joppke 1999: 78), but also, unlike their Italian or Greek counterparts they were considered culturally incapable of integrating into German society by conservative policy-makers due to their Muslim background (Boswell & Hough 2008: 337).

As mentioned above, family migration was not codified in any national law, but essentially governed by administrative decrees issued directly to the aliens authorities by the regional interior ministries of the *Länder*. Due to regional and party political differences, the conditions for family migration developed differently across the *Länder*. In Berlin, the "Lummer decree", issued by the city's restrictive Interior Senator Lummer (CDU) in November 1981, stipulated the deportation of unemployed migrant adolescents upon reaching majority age, if they had lived in Germany less than five years. In an attempt to harmonise the situation, the federal government issued a set of non-binding recommendations in December 1981.[68] This set of guidelines was one of the first formal acknowledgements at the federal level of the realities pertaining to family migration. The document recommended setting the age limit for incoming children at 16 and excluding those with only one parent living in Germany from family migration. Furthermore, the document advocated only admitting spouses of second-generation migrants if the sponsor had legally and continuously resided in Germany for at least eight years and the couple had been married for over one year.

As the recommendations were non-binding, differences continued to prevail among the various *Länder*. In Hessen, the first-ever SPD-Greens (red-green) coalition taking up its work in 1984 reduced the minimum residence time for second-generation sponsors to five years and increased the maximum age of children to 18, as did Bremen. Conversely, the conservative governments in Bavaria and Baden-Württemberg went even further than the federal government had recommended by extending the minimum marriage

---

[68] See *Empfehlungen der Bundesregierung über Sofortmaßnahmen zur sozialverantwortlichen Steuerung des Familiennachzugs*, 2 December 1981.

period for second-generation migrants to three years (Hunn 2005: 246). In "hyper-restrictionist" Baden-Württemberg, this three-year rule was even applied to the first generation (Joppke 1999: 74). Furthermore, the vague term "adequate housing" was interpreted differently across the *Länder*. While in Bremen, seven m^2 per family member sufficed to fulfil the requirement, in Baden-Württemberg sponsors needed to provide 12 m^2 per family member, and children theoretically entitled to join but still residing abroad were included into the calculation as well (Joppke 1999: 81).

In any case, the guidelines did not lead the issue to become any less politicised; on the contrary, the Christian Democrats, in particular, tightened their stance towards family migration. While campaigning in 1982, the CDU announced the goal of decreasing Germany's foreign population by one million within five years (Castles 1985: 528). In his government statement after coming into power in 1982, Helmut Kohl (CDU) reiterated that Germany was "not a country of immigration" and in order to reduce the number of foreigners in Germany, policies would be introduced to encourage return migration and put a stop to further inflows, thus also restricting family migration (Boswell & Hough 2008: 337). In late 1983, a law incentivising return migration passed parliament.[69] The law granted one-time "return aid" payments *(Rückkehrhilfe)* of 10,500 German Marks (DM) plus 1,500 DM per child and an immediate access to their pensions for unemployed guest workers who returned to their home countries in the course of the next year.

Subsequently, the Federal Ministry of the Interior under Zimmermann (CSU) issued two draft proposals for a reformed Foreigner Law in 1983 and 1988. Both proposals included a legal framework for family migration, which was missing from the 1965 Foreigner Law, but under much more restrictive conditions than the 1981 guidelines. The 1983 proposal included a complete ban on spousal migration rights for second-generation migrants as well as an upper age limit of six years for incoming children. It was argued that such a low age limit was important for integration aspects, as it would ensure the children would receive a German schooling (Castles 1985: 529). The proposal was rejected in its early stages by the junior coalition partner Free Democratic Party (FDP), *inter alia* for being so highly "family-hostile"

---

[69] Gesetz zur Förderung der Rückkehrbereitschaft von Ausländern (Rückkehrhilfegesetz – RückHG), Bundesgesetzblatt, I, Jahrgang 1983, Nr. 48, p. 1377.

("familienfeindlich") (Commissioner for Foreigner Affairs Lieselotte Funcke (FDP) as quoted by Joppke 1999: 82).

The 1988 draft law was even more restrictive. By strongly embracing the idea of guest worker recruitment as a one-time, finite event, it proposed rather generous integration provisions to the first generation of guest workers while at the same time limiting the residence of all other TCN foreigners not belonging to the first generation of guest workers to an absolute maximum of eight years. This total closure of Germany to long-term immigration was claimed to be necessary due to the unresolved question of German unity and a connected need to maintain "the national character" (Joppke 1999: 83). This time not only was the FDP appalled by hardliner Zimmermann's proposals; the draft law was harshly criticised by a spontaneous and wide coalition of parties, churches, unions and other public actors. Even the Catholic Bishops and more liberal voices within the CDU found the draft law untenable, leading the ministry to consequently withdraw it (Joppke 1999: 83).

It is interesting to note the contrast between a rather tough political stance towards second-generation migrants, and a "special moral obligation" (Joppke 1999: 80) towards the first generation, which had been directly recruited a few decades before. Most of the restrictive policy initiatives targeted spousal migration of the second generation onwards, which is in line with the notion of the guest worker inflow during the 1950s and 1960s being a one-time, historically unique event. From a normative point of view, as discussed in section 2.1, it is not immediately obvious why the state should feel fewer obligations to protect the fundamental rights of second-generation foreigners than those of first-generation migrants. After all, the first generation made a conscious decision to migrate, and in the case of guest workers even initially committed to temporary migration. The second generation, on the other hand, was born in the host country and thereby, even without acquiring the citizenship in question, can be seen to possess a far stronger claim to social membership than the first generation and one wonders why the German state would not feel an equally strong moral obligation to protect their fundamental rights. When viewing spousal migration not as a fundamental right to family but as a specific migration flow to be managed, granting spousal migration rights to second-generation migrants is more conflict-laden, as it implies a prevalence of chain migration, which stands in sharp contrast to the unique event of guest worker recruitment. The government made this stance repeatedly clear, as demonstrated by the Interior Ministry's statement in the context of the 1987 Constitutional Court hearing dealing with family migration policies:

> Because of its recruitment of foreign workers, the Federal Republic has accepted a special responsibility towards the recruited; but it has not obliged itself to accept a generation-spanning immigration of family members. The number of immigrating family members could be perpetually renewed by marriage and birth. The federal government does not see itself constitutionally obliged toward the children and grandchildren of recruited foreigners to accept family immigration that is exclusively determined by the personal decisions of the individuals, without consideration of the interests of the Federal Republic. (BVerfG, 2 BvR 1226/83 et al.: 33-34, translation by Joppke (1999: 80))

In later decades this kind of chain migration was increasingly associated with integration difficulties. While first-generation guest workers were granted family migration, as it implied a step towards their integration, in the case of their children it was classified as a step backwards in the integration process.

The importance of the *Bundesverfassungsgericht* in securing foreign residents' rights

In the entire period lasting from the 1950s until 1990, the major political forces were thus unwilling or unable to institutionalise and legally enshrine fundamental rights such as family protection for foreign residents. Into this legislative vacuum at the federal level and ensuing executive discretion at the regional level stepped "activist courts" that "expansively interpreted and defended the rights of foreigners" (Joppke 1999: 69). This crucial role of the judiciary in expanding foreigners' rights in Germany and thereby strongly influencing the development of migration policies has been one of the most emblematic cases in Europe of the "judicial liberal constraint," as theorised by authors such as Joppke (1998a) and Guiraudon (1998).

The German constitution, the Basic Law (*Grundgesetz*, GG), was conceived in the aftermath of Nazi rule and out of this historical experience, firmly enshrined both the primacy of individual rights above state power and the irrelevance of nationality for the most basic of these individual rights (Joppke 1999: 69). These constitutional specificities were crucial to the expansion of fundamental rights for foreigners through judicial constitutional reviews. In a series of landmark cases, the Federal Constitutional Court (*Bun-

desverfassungsgericht, BVerfG) established the applicability of the Basic Law's Article 2(1), which warrants the free development of the personality, to foreigners. The court has given this article the meaning of an *"Auffanggrundrecht,"* thus a "residuary basic right," which provides long-term resident foreigners with access to rights usually reserved for German citizens (Joppke 2001: 349). The court especially emphasised that the protection substantially increased with the foreigners' residence time in Germany, according to the legal principle of a *"Rechtsschicksal der Unentrinnbarkeit"* (Schwerdtfeger 1980), a "legal fate of inescapability" (Joppke 2001: 349). This principle implies that "because they have nowhere else to go, settled foreigners must be treated like Germans" (Joppke 1999: 85).

Accordingly, especially harsh migration laws impacting strongly on fundamental rights of foreign residents were ruled to be incompatible with the constitution and overturned by the BVerfG. First, the 1973 so-called Arab case[70] established that foreign residents enjoyed a certain constitutional rights that could, according to the legal principle of proportionality *(Verhältnismäßigkeit)*, outweigh the state's interest in achieving a certain public good. In the case, immediate deportation orders on the basis of minor offences were ruled to be unconstitutional, since they infringed too harshly upon the personal liberty rights foreigners enjoyed according to the Basic Law. In 1978, again citing Article 2(1) GG, the BVerfG dealt with the issue of residential security in the so-called Indian case.[71] According to the 1965 Foreigner Law, the first-time residence permit and its renewal were subject to the same terms and conditions, and renewal could accordingly be denied irrespective of the length of stay of the foreigner. The plaintiff, an Indian national, had had his residence permit routinely renewed for 12 years, when the local aliens authority decided to deny a further renewal, claiming that the man was possibly harming the interests of the Federal Republic. The BVerfG ruled that this practice was unconstitutional. The judges stated that previous renewals had created a "legitimate expectation" (*"Vertrauensschutz"*) of further renewal. This legitimate expectation is not only constitutionally protected, but also overruled the state's attempts to impose a zero-immigration policy.

---

[70] BVerfG, 1 BvR 23, 155/73, judgement of 18 July 1973.
[71] BVerfG, 1 BvR 525/77, judgement of 26 September 1978.

After having established the (at least partial) right to residence and protection from deportation in these two cases, in 1987 the Constitutional Court approached the issue of family migration, thus dealing with new admissions. In the so-called reunification decision[72] (Bast 2010: 11), the Turkish and Yugoslav plaintiffs challenged the restrictive family migration provisions in place in Germany, especially the long waiting periods (up to eight years of residence of the sponsors and one to three years of minimum marriage) by arguing that they were incompatible with the constitution's Article 6, which strongly protects marriage and family. In its judgement, the BVerfG stated that no absolute right to family migration arises from Article 6 GG. Nevertheless, the court also stated that Article 6 GG does pertain to foreigners residing in Germany. Therefore, the authorities and courts dealing with admission applications of family migrants must "consider the spousal and familial relationships towards persons living in the Federal territory in a way that corresponds with the great importance which the Basic Law evidently accords to the protection of marriage and family" (BVerfG, 2 BvR 1226/83 et al.: 49). The Court lengthily reflected on permissible periods of separation and also pointed to the especially precarious situation of young separated couples:

> The demand placed upon the marital couple to decide between accepting a lengthy separation or resettling abroad falls in the initial phase of the (intended) marital life, which is often characterized by the birth of children and in which the demands placed on the affected persons by the marital community and parenthood are for the first time experienced and must be overcome. It therefore normally represents a heavy burden and threat to a young marriage when the couple is forced to decide between only being able to live together for short intervals during visits over three years or having to resettle abroad and forego completely an economic and social position that had been built up over years. [The three-year requirement] is also able to lead to a threat to a young marriage in that young married couples are often not in a position to assess the consequences of a lengthy separation and in recognition of these dangers, to decide against the establishment of the marital community in the native country. (BVerfG, 2 BvR 1226/83 et al.: 69, translation Members of the Court 1992: 710)

In the end, while it upheld the eight-year residence requirement and the one-year minimum marriage period as necessary to further the integration of the sponsor and thwart marriages of convenience, the BVerfG ruled that the

---

[72] BVerfG, 2 BvR 1226/83, 101, 313/84, 12 May 1987.

waiting period of three years instituted by Bavaria and Baden-Württemberg was too great an infringement on the right to marriage and family and not proportionate to the presumably conflicting public interest.[73]

Family migration in the GDR

A short note is perhaps in order in relation to the corresponding developments in the other German state. In the German Democratic Republic (GDR), migration took place as well, albeit to a far lesser extent. Due to a significant need for workers, in part because of a continuous emigration outflow, the GDR also recruited guest workers coming from Communist states around the world. In 1989, 190,000 foreigners were living in the GDR, thus amounting to only 1.2 per cent of the total population – one third of these foreigners were from Vietnam and 12 per cent from Mozambique. However, the guest worker system was much more restrictive than its Western German counterpart, as the preferably young and single guest workers were subject to a strict rotation principle not just on paper but also in practice. As a result, these migrants were basically forced to return home after a certain period of time. Family migration was not permitted at all, and if a female guest worker became pregnant, she had to choose between an abortion and an immediate return to her home country. This provision was only changed shortly prior to 1989, by allowing pregnant female guest workers in exceptional cases to give birth in the GDR – if her employer agreed and she returned to work six weeks after the delivery (Bade & Oltmer 2004: 94). This very different developmental course of migration laws shows how, in the absence of a strong constitution protecting individual rights and an independent judiciary, liberal constraints are less pronounced. In the case of the authoritarian GDR, a restrictive migration regime that disrespected human rights was able to flourish.

---

[73] See Joppke (1999: 69-76) for a detailed discussion of all three cases.

Moving onwards in 1990

Wolfgang Schäuble (CDU), Zimmermann's more pragmatic successor as Interior Minister, was able to propose a reform in 1989 that not only gained support but was also passed in the record time of eight months from its first draft to the parliament's vote. In early 1991, the new Foreigner Law[74] came into effect, finally legally entrenching family migration in its §§ 17-23. It established in law what court instances had already ruled, namely that foreign residents, regardless of whether they belonged to the first or second generation, were indeed entitled to residence and family migration rights if they fulfilled certain conditions, mainly pertaining to housing and income. The age limit for reuniting children was set at 16 years. The one-year waiting period for marriages, which had been explicitly endorsed by the BVerfG in 1987, was scrapped. Moreover, residence rights were instituted for spouses and children independent of their sponsors. As some of these measures even went beyond the minimum standard established by the courts, Joppke argues that they "indicate the independent workings of moral obligations, not just of legal constraints." (1999: 84).

After German reunification in 1990, several parameters that had existed concerning citizenship and migration policy fundamentally changed. During the Cold War, a strictly ethnic conception of citizenship (*ius sanguinis*) that included all citizens of the GDR as well as ethnic German resettlers (*Aussiedler*) from Central and Eastern Europe, had been fervently upheld as an important source of political legitimacy. Including all GDR citizens in the (West) German nation defined German division as provisional, and the Federal Republic's assertion that it was speaking for all Germans also undermined the GDR's legitimacy (*Alleinvertretungsanspruch*). Furthermore, by welcoming resettlers from Central and Eastern Europe as Germans, it kept the question of the final German borders open (Mushaben 2010: 82). After reunification and the successful incorporation of the GDR's citizens in the Federal Republic, the continuous stream of resettlers from the East who were granted immediate citizenship upon arrival proved politically difficult in the long run both in the domestic as well as the international spheres. The crass

---

[74] Gesetz über die Einreise und den Aufenthalt von Ausländern in Bundesgebiet (Ausländergesetz, AuslG 1990), see Bundesgesetzblatt, I, Jahrgang 1990, Nr. 34, p. 1354.

distinction between the generous treatment of ethnic German resettlers and the exclusionist attitudes in citizenship matters displayed towards children and grandchildren of guest workers who had been born and grown up in Germany was increasingly difficult to maintain.

Another migration-related issue that had already dominated political and public attention from the 1980s onward, but increased in political relevance after 1990, was that of asylum. As a reaction to the horrifying experiences of the Third Reich, a unique provision had been included in the German Basic Law when it was conceived in 1949, granting a constitutionally protected right to asylum to the politically persecuted (Art. 16(2) GG). In the post-war years, therefore, the German asylum system was comparatively porous. This is not to suggest that it was necessarily easy being granted asylum as a political refugee, but once on German territory, the constitution granted not only the right to seek asylum, but also various options for legal recourse if the application was rejected. Due to court backlogs and the possibility of submitting follow-up applications, in many cases years passed from an initial asylum application to the final decision. In the case of a rejection, by then, deportation had become a difficult option to pursue because of the ties and rights these people had accrued in the interim period.

A first societal debate on asylum occurred in the early 1980s with a focus on "bogus asylum seekers" (*"Scheinasylanten"*), which led to a tightening of the social deterrence measures placed upon asylum-seekers alongside a restriction of who was classified as a political refugee (Joppke 1999: 89). Without changing the Basic Law, however, the asylum inflow was far from deterred. As a result of the crumbling of the communist regimes in Central and Eastern Europe, the number of asylum-seekers started to rise drastically in the late 1980s. Between 1987 and 1992, applications increased by more than 750 per cent, from 57,379 applications to 438,191 (Ausländerbeauftragte 2001: 37), leading Germany to shoulder 80 per cent of all asylum applications in Europe in 1992. Faced with these massive inflows, the ruling CDU-FDP coalition managed to win over the SPD's participation in a constitutional change that passed the *Bundestag* in December 1992, with the required majority of two thirds.[75] This *"Asylkompromiss"* inserted Article 16a into the Basic Law,

---

[75] For detailed accounts of the asylum debate in Germany and the compromise on asylum that followed see e.g. Faist (1994: 61-66), Joppke (1999: 85-94) and Bosswick (2000).

which introduced concepts such as "safe third countries" and "safe countries of origin."

If asylum seekers enter German territory today via a safe third country – such as all EU states or any other countries where the Geneva Convention and the ECHR are supposedly ensured – they can be returned to this country immediately. As all countries directly neighbouring Germany are classified as "safe third countries," nobody entering Germany via its land borders will theoretically be able to enter the asylum procedure (Ausländerbeauftragte 2001: 37). If the asylum seekers come from so-called "safe countries of origin," which are assumed not to politically persecute (anyone), the asylum application can be rejected as "obviously unfounded." Furthermore, a newly introduced "airport regulation" creates the possibility for officials to detain asylum seekers without papers or from safe countries of origin and subject them to an "accelerated" asylum assessment procedure in the transit zones of airports, before formally entering German territory.

As a result of these changes, the rather generous asylum procedure stayed in place but the possibilities to access it were severely limited. The new article came into force in July 1993 and immediately produced results: In 1993, the total number of asylum applications was reduced by a quarter to 322,599 and in 1994, the first entire year the new laws were in place, the number dropped significantly to 127,210 applications. It continued to decrease, and in 1998 the number went under the 100,000 mark for the first time in the 1990s (BAMF 2009: 99).

3.1.2 2000-2005: Reforming migration law in a protracted process

In 1998, when a red-green coalition came to power under Gerhard Schröder (SPD), the reform of citizenship law was put on the political agenda. In 2000, a new bill was passed that for the first time included *ius soli* provisions for children born in Germany to foreigners with the so-called "Optional Model" (*Optionsmodell*) as well as less restrictive conditions for naturalisation.[76] This paradigmatic shift in the conception of German-ness set the scene for a fur-

---

[76] However, it has been largely criticised that the new law did not go nearly as far as the Schröder government had envisioned, especially due to a populist xenophobic campaign of the CDU in the regional elections in Hessen during the negotiations on the law (see Howard 2008).

ther reform in immigration law. In the meantime, the view that Germany had both (especially high-skilled) labour shortages as well a demographic problem with its aging society was gaining widespread support, creating a functional impetus for immigration law reform. Furthermore, the issue of integration was becoming evermore salient, culminating in the 2000 controversy about a supposed German "dominant culture" ("*Leitkultur*")[77] that CDU politician Merz suggested all immigrants were obliged to adopt. This controversy created political pressure to include integration policy into a comprehensive new migration law (Green 2004: 111-120). Thus, the three issues of high-skilled labour shortages in the face of economic globalisation, (future) demographic changes, and the integration of new and current migrants were acknowledged by most political actors. However, the suggested solutions diverged markedly.

In 2000, Interior Minister Otto Schily (SPD) convened the Independent Commission on Immigration (*Unabhängige Kommission Zuwanderung*), also dubbed "Süssmuth Commission" as Schily had won over the senior CDU politician and former Bundestag president Rita Süssmuth to chair the commission, giving the entire endeavour an air of bipartisan authority. Nevertheless, the CDU convened its own commission chaired by Peter Müller (CDU) in 2000 as well. Despite Müller being one of the only leading figures in the CDU that did identify Germany as a country of immigration (Tietze 2008: 231), a claim fervently rejected by so many other prominent CDU members, both the party's initial position paper[78] from 2000 as well as the CDU Commission's final report issued in April 2001[79] (which was adopted in a slightly modified version by the party as a resolution on 7 June 2001[80]) were rather divergent from the Süssmuth Commission's report.

The CDU publications of this period strongly invoke the idea of a homogenous German *Leitkultur* based on a "system of values of our Christian-Occidental culture, shaped by Christianity, Judaism, ancient philosophy,

---

[77] The concept of "*Leitkultur*" has been translated in various ways, including "guiding culture" (Klusmeyer & Papademetriou 2009: 231) or "leading culture" (Thierse 2004: 188)
[78] Arbeitsgrundlage für die Zuwanderungs-Kommission der CDU Deutschlands, 6 November 2000.
[79] Abschlussbericht der Kommission "Zuwanderung und Integration" der CDU Deutschlands. 28 April 2001.
[80] Zuwanderung steuern und begrenzen. Integration fördern. Beschluss des Bundesausschusses der CDU Deutschlands vom 7. Juni 2001 in Berlin, 7 June 2001.

humanism, Roman law and the Enlightenment" (CDU 2000: 3, my translation) as the guiding principle to be applied to integration. Integration is directly linked to religion, culture and education, as the report states that the prospects of successful integration are "all the better the smaller the cultural and religious differences between immigrants and receiving society are, and the better the educational level and social situation of immigrants and receiving society are" (CDU 2001: 18, my translation).[81] Regarding immigration, the CDU Commission claims that "hitherto, immigration to Germany mainly takes place in the interests of the immigrants themselves" (Kommission Zuwanderung und Integration 2001: 42, my translation), which Germany is obliged to allow due to its humanitarian commitments. Asylum seekers, war refugees, ethnic resettlers, Jewish migrants from the former USSR and family migrants are all categorised in the report as migrants that are admitted primarily in their own interest and do not serve the goals of the German state. While demographic pressures and the need for skilled and high-skilled workers are acknowledged, the CDU Commission advocates finding solutions within family policies to increase the birth rates of Germans and solutions in education and training policies to fill labour shortages with domestic workers (CDU 2001: 5-6). The overall tone is thus clearly one of immigration restriction coupled with a rising focus on integration, as exemplified by the title of the final resolution: "Controlling and limiting immigration. Supporting integration."

Shortly after the CDU Commission published its report, the Süssmuth Commission presented comparatively liberal suggestions for immigration reform, including the introduction of a points-based system for skilled migration in its report published in July 2001 (Unabhängige Kommission Zuwanderung 2001). In addition to advocating a change in migration policy thinking by embracing the diversity created by immigration, the Süssmuth Report presents a less assimilationist integration concept than the one advocated by *Leitkultur*-proponents. It rather emphasises both the dual nature of any integration process (thus also including efforts by the host society) as well as the importance of equal socio-economic and political participation in spite of cultural diversity. While the acceptance of the constitutional liberal

---

[81] For a detailed discussion of the concept of *Leitkultur* in the 2000 CDU position paper see Klusmeyer and Papademetriou (2009: 229-237).

democratic norms alongside basic German language skills is mentioned as a basis for integration, liberal citizenship acquisition provisions, including an acceptance of multiple citizenship, are also explicitly stated to be important for the integration process, instead of viewing naturalisation as the final crown of a completed and successful integration. Thus, the report suggests state-financed integration courses, with a particular focus on the German language, just as a further liberalisation of citizenship law (Unabhängige Kommission Zuwanderung 2001: 249). However, the report is not liberal in all aspects; regarding irregular migration and asylum, the Süssmuth Commission advocated further restricting the polices in place.

While neither of the two reports focused extensively on family migration, what they do say is in marked contrast to each other. As mentioned earlier, the CDU authors divide migration into two dichotomous flows: First, migrants received owing to a "humanitarian commitment," which "benefit the migrants," primarily asylum and family migration, and second, those migrants who are deemed "beneficial for Germany," especially high-skilled migration. This dichotomy implies that family migration and other "humanitarian obligations" are necessarily not beneficial to or even detrimental to "Germany's national interests" (CDU 2001: 2-6). Family migration specifically is mentioned in two contexts. First, with reference to high-skilled migration, family migration is considered to be very important. Liberal family migration provisions are considered necessary for Germany to stand any serious chance in the "global run for the best heads" – in fact, the SPD's "Green Card Initiative" for the attraction of high-skilled migrants is deemed unsuccessful since no perspectives for long-term stays are provided and family migration was much too restrictive (CDU 2001: 6). Second, regarding the control of family migration outside the context of highly skilled migration, the CDU authors state that, while no one questions the right to family migration as such, abuse must be forestalled and it must be ensured that family migrants are willing, and especially concerning their language skills, able, to integrate (CDU 2000: 4). Here, family migration is thus explicitly linked to the two problem issues of abuse and integration deficits. A balance is thus advocated between (apparently conflicting) constitutional obligations arising from Article 6 GG and Germany's interests regarding socially acceptable immigration. The final CDU report states that the total number of TCN family migrants should definitely not be expanded and recommends rejecting the EU Draft Family Reunification Directive. The report further mentions that the entire family migration procedure can be pursued from the home country and waiting periods need to be accepted by the migrants. Also, policy differentiations should be made regarding the "degree of relationship, nationality and *integration perspective*" (CDU 2001: 9, emphasis added). The integrative capacity of family migrants is thus defined as a future policy focus: "The integration perspective will henceforth play a decisive role regarding the decision on family reunification" (CDU 2001: 13, my translation). Since the "chance of integration of children without German language skills is significantly higher at a younger age than is the case if migration happens at a later stage," it is recommended to lower the maximum age for children entering in the context of family migration *(Kindernachzug)* from the then current 16 years ("too high") ideally to six and certainly not to any more than ten years of age. In addition, German language skills are to be considered an advantage in the decision on family migration in the case of spouses and other relatives (CDU 2001: 13). Considering that the 2007 migration law reform introduced a basic language requirement for spousal migrants (see chapter 4), it is very interesting to note that the first traces of the idea of making family migration dependent on integrative capacities, and more specifically language skills, outside the context of *Aussiedler* policies,[82] can be found in these CDU publications from 2000/2001. Even though the formulations are still quite vague and not linked to concrete policies ("language skills are to be considered a privilege in the decision on family reunification," "integrative capacities will play a role"), they foreshadow the developments of the 2007 reform quite clearly. Possibly anticipating criticism, the authors also explicitly maintain all of these recommendations to be compatible with the constitutional obligations relating to family protection.

The overall tenor of the Süssmuth-Report regarding family migration is more positive. The constitutional protection of marriage and family is depicted in a positive light, and not as a burden. The specific policy recommendations also (critically) refer to the Draft EU Family Reunification Directive. While the general liberalisation of family migration proposed in the directive is welcomed, the Süssmuth Commission is sceptical of widening the scope of family members' eligibility too much – to include ascending relatives and adult children – but instead advocates confining the legal entitlement to mi-

---

[82] On policies towards *Aussiedler* and their families, see the following section.

gration to the core family. Another proposal of the directive, namely granting family migration rights to TCN foreigners without long-term residence prospects, is rejected as well. The phenomenon of "reverse discrimination" (see section 5.1.5) is mentioned, as German citizens can sponsor their foreign children until the age of 18, while EU citizens living in Germany can bring in their TCN children until the age of 21 as well as relatives in the ascending line. The report proposes a prohibition of any type of reverse discrimination in the field of migration law, effectively meaning a levelling-up of German citizens' rights to those of EU movers (Unabhängige Kommission Zuwanderung 2001: 195). Integration in the context of family migration is not seen as a difficulty in the same way as it is the CDU Report; a positive relationship between both is clearly postulated: "Families provide a fundamental contribution towards the success of integration processes." (Unabhängige Kommission Zuwanderung 2001: 194). As liberalising measures, the report advocates raising the maximum age for children to join TCN residents from 16 to 18 years and acknowledges the possibility of including the immigrating spouse's income when calculating whether the financial requirements of securing the family's livelihood is ensured (Unabhängige Kommission Zuwanderung 2001: 195; 250).

The entire reform process from the initial idea and set-up of expert commissions until the final passing of the law took five years, a period that was characterised by political blockade, party tactics, election campaigns and extensive rhetoric. As Angenendt and Kruse (2004: 180) point out, even though a broad consensus existed across political parties regarding both the necessity for reform and the basic direction policies should take, divisive political controversies over single aspects created seemingly unbridgeable differences. Also, procedural difficulties in the already cumbersome federal law-making process contributed to halting the reform even more. Without going into too much detail on the exact disputes and negotiations, suffice it here to mention that this piece of legislation involved multiple draft laws, various votes in the different chambers and even a constitutional court case.[83]

---

[83] Research dealing with the legislative process surrounding the *Zuwanderungsgesetz* in more depth includes Kruse et al. (2003), Green (2004: 121-132), Angenendt and Kruse (2004) and Klusmeyer and Papademetriou (2009: 251-260).

In July 2004, a compromise law passed through both federal chambers, and on 1 January 2005, the Immigration Act (*Zuwanderungsgesetz*[84]) finally came into force. The provisions applying to family migration did not dramatically change (yet at least), with the maximum age for *Kindernachzug*, the topic of so much fervent debate, left at 16 years, just as it was before the 2005 reform. If sufficient knowledge of the German language is demonstrated, admission is even possible until 18 years. This is also the age limit for children of German citizens, high-skilled migrants and refugees. The laws applying to regular spousal migration were left completely untouched. One interesting novelty was however introduced relating to the specific policies applying to families of ethnic resettlers, as will be illustrated below.

3.1.3 Language skills as a pre-migration requirement: The Aussiedler-*Nexus*

The development of policies regarding ethnic German resettlers (variously categorised as *Vertriebene*, *Aussiedler* or *Spätaussiedler*) is complex and cannot be dealt with in depth here. However, some of the policies that were first developed in the context of ethnic Germans and their families were later introduced into general (family) migration policies and should be briefly outlined here.

Ethnic German resettlement had traditionally been kept legally and politically apart from classical migration, as exemplified by a completely separate set of applicable laws and policies. As is the case with asylum flows and family migration, ethnic German resettlement policies are based on humanitarian obligations, even if on self-imposed ones arising out of historical responsibility and political contingencies during the German separation. After 1990 however, resettlement increased dramatically and accordingly more problems came to be associated with it. Furthermore, geo-political con-

---

[84] The full name of the bill is *Gesetz zur Steuerung und Begrenzung der Zuwanderung und zur Regelung des Aufenthalts und der Integration von Unionsbürgern und Ausländern* (Law to Regulate and Limit Immigration and to Regulate the Residence and Integration of Union Citizens and Foreigners). The law is a so-called article law that contains various amendments of existing laws and also introduces two entirely novel laws, the Residence Act (*Aufenthaltsgesetz*, AufenthG) which is basically the main item of the bill, and the Free Movement/EU Act (*Freizügigkeitsgesetz/EU*, FreizügG/EU).

ditions also shifted. The previous Cold War situation with relatively closed borders was altered with the establishment of liberal democracies in Central and Eastern Europe, which decreased the historical and moral obligations to admit ethnic Germans. Also, the political legitimacy derived from an ethnic conception of the German nation that included both GDR and ethnic Germans residing further east decreased after reunification in 1990. A more pragmatic and restrictive approach emerged and resettlement was increasingly treated in similar terms as regular migration.

The entire rationale for admitting and immediately granting German citizenship to ethnic German resettlers from Central and Eastern Europe and the former USSR is the fact that they are considered part of the German people (in many cases they were forced to resettle due to WWII) who furthermore have incurred substantive discrimination and persecution due to their German heritage in the post-war period. Traditionally, the treatment of resettlers was handled rather generously, as was the according treatment of their families. Article 116 GG defined that not only ethnic Germans, that is "German within the meaning of this Basic Law," would find entry, but also their spouses and descendants, regardless of their ethnic origin. Thus, the early resettler policies do not only indicate ethnic preferences in immigration and citizenship policies, but also display a very generous interpretation of the importance of family and marriage in the context of migration.

In 1953, the main law regulating policies towards resettlers, the BVFG,[85] was issued. In Article 6, the definition of ethnic Germans was further refined to include those individuals that "in their home country [sic] have avowed themselves to the German nationhood, provided that this avowal is confirmed by certain characteristics such as descent, language, education and culture" (my translation). Therefore, for ethnic resettlers, "German language skills, mediated by the family, are immanent to their status" (Hensen 2009: 56, my translation). However, the actual existence of German language skills was never systematically examined prior to the immense expansion of the resettlement inflow in the beginning of the 1990s. In the course of 1996, a (non-repeatable) basic language test in the countries of origin was gradually introduced for individuals applying for admission as ethnic Germans (but

---

[85] *Gesetz über die Angelegenheiten der Vertriebenen und Flüchtlinge* (*Bundesvertriebenengesetz*, BVFG). See Bundesgesetzblatt 1953, Teil I, Nr. 22, 201 ff.

not their family members), and since March 1997 every admission has been based on a positive language test.

These obligatory pre-entry language tests, albeit in the special context of the *Aussiedler*, were the first of their kind in the EU, institutionalising the notion of refusing admission in cases of (an assumed) lack of integration (Groenendijk 2004: 116). Additionally, language courses were organised and financed in the main regions of origin. Since then and up until today, more than 320,000 individuals have undergone such tests, with only 52 per cent of the total passing the tests (Hensen 2009: 57), while in earlier years, the quota was higher; in 1997, for example, 63 per cent of those tested passed (Unabhängige Kommission Zuwanderung 2001: 181).

This new requirement was among the factors that slowly led to a change in the ratio of ethnic resettlers to family members included in the admission. While in 1993, 75 per cent of the admitted resettlers were ethnic Germans and 25 per cent were their family members, in 2004 this relationship had inversed, with only 19 per cent being ethnic Germans and 81 per cent joining family members (BAMF 2009: 50), presumably without any significant knowledge of the German language. It is important to bear in mind that the admission as an ethnic German resettler or as a family member of a resettler, if successful, signified (and signifies to this day) not an entrance visa or residence permit, but instead immediate full German citizenship. Thus, as more and more resettlers were coming on the "family ticket," the legislators considered it opportune in the 2005 *Zuwanderungsgesetz*[86] to introduce a language requirement for spouses and descendants of ethnic German resettlers in order for them to be included in the admission.[87]

The requirement stipulates that either by taking a test at a German diplomatic representation abroad or by providing a certificate from a Goethe-Institute, language skills equivalent to level A1 of the Common European Frame of Reference for Languages (CEFR) have to be proven, while exceptions are provided for very young and very old people (Hensen 2009: 59). If unable to abide by these requirements, spouses and descendants can only choose the path of regular family migration. This requirement had actually

---

[86] The law governing resettlers, the BVFG, was incorporated into the larger immigration act *Zuwanderungsgesetz* in 2005. This is another clear sign of the political shift of viewing ethnic resettlement flows as a form of migration.
[87] See § 27 Abs. 1 Satz 2 BVFG.

been suggested by the Süssmuth-Commission in its report, too, since the great numbers of non-German speaking family members gaining immediate access to citizenship constituted a privilege difficult to justify. The commission therefore recommended bringing the rights of non-German family members of resettlers at least somewhat more in line with the naturalisation conditions for "regular" migrants, which demanded sufficient knowledge of the German language (Unabhängige Kommission Zuwanderung 2001: 183-184).

The change meant, first, that adult children (who can be included in the initial admission as family members of ethnic German resettlers, but not as regular family migrants) without language skills had no possibility of being admitted to Germany. Second, if embarking on the path of regular family migration, the resettler family would most probably undergo a period of separation and the family members would not immediately gain access to German citizenship, but later be able to undergo the normal naturalisation procedure for family members of German citizens.

As will be outlined in the analysis later, in 2007 the same language requirement (skills equivalent to A1 of the CEFR) was introduced for all spouses joining their German or TCN sponsors in Germany. Admittedly, it is difficult to make a direct link between this language requirement introduced for the family members of resettlers to that devised for spousal migrants, since the former is a condition for immediate citizenship and the latter only leads to admission and an initial residence permit. To make a family admission conditional on language skills is much more difficult to normatively justify than requiring language skills for naturalisation. However, from a more pragmatic viewpoint, it is fair to assume that both the language requirements introduced for *Aussiedler* in 1996 and their spouses in 2005 alongside the one introduced for all spousal migrants in 2007 had at least the implicit goal to reduce these migration flows under the guise of integration policies. Similar developments in other European countries that will later be illustrated in chapter 5 further reinforce the observation that integration requirements are increasingly being introduced as migration restriction tools in various "unwanted" fields of migration across Europe.

These shifting admission conditions have had an enormous influence on the numbers of *Aussiedler* entering Germany. In the three decades from 1950-1986, 1.34 million *Aussiedler* and their families were admitted into Germany, another 1.05 million came between 1987 and 1990 as a result of the gradual relaxation of border controls in the Eastern bloc, and another 1.5 million arrived between 1990 and 1995. After the introduction of the comprehensive examination of the language skills of resettlers the influx per year went down; in total 940,000 persons entered Germany as resettlers between 1996 and 2004. After language skills were also demanded of accompanying family members, the numbers declined much more decisively, in the four years 2005-2008 a mere 50,000 individuals entered Germany under the title of ethnic resettlement (Hensen 2009).

3.2 The legislative framework of spousal migration

In 2005, the first post-war immigration bill actually acknowledging and regulating migration and integration, the *Zuwanderungsgesetz* (hereafter: *Zuwanderungsgesetz* 2005), finally came into effect. In the field of spousal migration, though, no significant changes were introduced. Rather, the provisions concerning the admission of spouses were taken from the *Ausländergesetz* 1990 into the *Zuwanderungsgesetz* 2005. In 2007, however, in the course of the implementation of various EU directives on migration and asylum issues, the Immigration Act was further amended[88] and became more restrictive in some areas, including the conditions for spousal migration. As the 2007 reform is dealt with in depth in chapter 4, the following section outlines the legal provisions applying to spousal migration from 1990 to 2007, many of which also stayed in place after the reform.

§ 27 of the Residence Act (*Aufenthaltsgesetz*, AufenthG) states the basic principles upon which family migration policies and rights are based. It refers to Article 6 GG as the constitutional basis for granting and renewing residence permits to foreign family members in order to establish and preserve a family community in Germany. The law applies to family migration sponsored by German citizens and third-country nationals resident in Germany, referred to in the law as foreigners *(Ausländer)*. Contrastingly, family migration sponsored by EU citizens in Germany is governed by the Free

---

[88] The amending law came took effect on 28 August 2007 and is entitled *Gesetz zur Umsetzung aufenthalts- und asylrechtlicher Richtlinien der Europäischen Union* (EUAufhAsylRUG).

Movement Act, the German transposition of the EU Free Movement Directive.[89]

Generally, the conditions are more favourable for spouses of German citizens than for spouses of *Ausländer*, which is based on the legal principle that, while a foreigner could also leave Germany in order to live with his/her spouse, this cannot be expected of German citizens. Accordingly, the government's explanatory statement of the *Zuwanderungsgesetz* 2005 states that it "takes into account that German citizens are entitled to the basic right of free movement in the federal territory and their interest in establishing family unity in the federal territory is especially protected" (Bundesregierung 2003: 81). However, a few conditions exist that both German citizens and foreign residents must fulfil in order to be able to sponsor the migration of their TCN spouses.

Conditions applying to all cases of spousal migration

First and most obviously, a legal marriage must exist and this must be proven. It is not relevant where the marriage has taken place, as long as legal proof in the form of valid certificates exists. In practice, transnational couples often opt to get married abroad, since the paperwork required to marry in Germany is quite extensive. For example, German bureaucracy requires the production of a document called a "Certificate of Legal Capacity to Contract Marriage" *(Ehefähigkeitszeugnis)*, which is distinct from a simple non-marriage certificate, in order to marry in Germany. It testifies that no impediments exist for these individuals to contract a marriage with each other, and must be requested from the home country of the foreigner. In cases when the respective home country does not issue this type of document, which is quite frequently the case, an exemption must be requested from the local superior court of justice *(Kammergericht)*. This procedure can take several weeks or months, which causes many transnational couples to marry abroad. According to international private law, marriages legally entered into abroad must be recognized in Germany.

---

[89] See sections 4.2 and 5.1 for futher explorations on EU citizens sponsoring family migration.

It must be kept in mind that for all foreign spouses entering Germany from a third country that is not privileged regarding visa requirements (the so-called negative states, *Negativstaaten*; accordingly foreigners from these states are often termed *Negativstaatler* in the administration), must as a first step apply for a visa to enter Germany. The visas are applied for at German embassies abroad, which are subordinated to the Foreign Office. The Foreign Office is known to question the legitimacy of all documents, such as birth certificates, passports etc., in certain states or regions, internally dubbed "document rogue states" *("Dokumentenschurkenstaaten")*, and can deny visas on these grounds. If doubts exist, the embassies occasionally send lawyers to the local authorities in order to establish whether the provided documents are authentic or not.

For every spousal migration visa that is applied for, the respective embassy establishes contact with the local aliens authority in the hometown of the sponsoring spouse, as this will be the future authority responsible for the incoming spouse. The aliens authority must agree to grant the visa to the spouse abroad, and often invites the sponsor to the office for an appointment.

In this context, another important step that can occur at the stage of applying for the visa abroad is that of a "marriage-of-convenience inquiry" *(Scheinehenüberprüfung)*. Both the embassy abroad as well as the aliens authority in Germany can try to assess by speaking with the spouses whether their marriage is one of convenience, or whether the spouses genuinely (intend to) lead a marital community *(eheliche Lebensgemeinschaft)*. In most cases semi-formalised interviews with a specific catalogue of rather personal questions are held simultaneously with the respective spouses in the embassy and in the aliens authority. As will be elaborated later in chapters 6 and 7, these "intimacy inquiries" are actually quite common. It can be initiated either by the aliens authority in Germany or the representation abroad, but apparently it is more commonly instigated by the embassies abroad.

The decision to carry out an intimacy inquiry in the first place is usually taken according to a number of indicators that raise suspicion, such as a great age difference, no common language, a short period of acquaintance of the spouses, or a history of previous marriages of either of the spouses. In many cases, however, as the marital community cannot exist prior to spousal migration; therefore, authorities need to evaluate the marriage in a prognostic manner, with all the problems associated with this kind of suspicion-based evaluation (see Eisfeld 2005: 216). Some recent judgements have even introduced the concept of a "unilateral marriage of convenience" *("einseitige Scheinehe")*, claiming that the lack of will to lead a marital union in the case of only one of the spouses suspends the right to spousal migration.[90] This position is controversial, however, especially since the practical and ethical difficulties of definition and measurement related to marriages of convenience, outlined in chapter 2, are complicated even further.

Finally, as laid down in § 31 AufenthG, after two years of living in a lawful marriage within Germany, the residence permit of the spouse becomes independent of the sponsor, which means that he/she will continue to be able to remain in Germany in case of a divorce from the sponsor. In exceptional cases, an independent residence permit can also be granted before the two-year probationary period *(Ehebestandszeit)* is up in order to avoid particular hardship. Particular hardship is assumed if the obligation to return to the country of origin after leaving the marriage or remaining within the marriage would put essential interests of the incoming spouse (or their children) under threat and is thus unacceptable, for example in cases of extensive domestic violence. It must be kept in mind that these threats have to be proven to the authorities, however.

Conditions only applying to foreign sponsors

§ 29 AufenthG governs spousal migration sponsored by foreigner residents. The first condition that only foreign sponsors must fulfil[91] is the possession of a valid temporary residence permit *(Aufenthaltserlaubnis)*, a long-term residence permit *(Niederlassungserlaubnis)* or a long-term EC residence permit *(Erlaubnis zum Daueraufenthalt EG)*.[92] Furthermore, the sponsor must be able

---

[90] OVG Berlin-Brandenburg, 12 N 29.05, judgement of 15 August 2005, and 2 N 207.07, judgement of 18 July 2008. See Oestmann (2008: 17) and Jobs (2008: 295).

[91] However, according to § 28 Abs. 1 AufenthG, German citizens do have to have their regular residence in Germany, i.e. they must live and be registered in Germany in order to qualify as a sponsor for spousal migration. In practice this provision sometimes leads to practical difficulties and periods of separation when Germans who are living abroad wish to move back to Germany with their foreign family members since, strictly speaking, they have to be registered in Germany before their family members can apply to join them.

[92] § 29 Abs. 1 Nr. 1 AufenthG.

to provide sufficient housing space.[93] Another important requirement that only foreign sponsors have to fulfil is the securing of livelihood according to § 5 Abs. 1 Nr. 1 for the incoming spouse as well. In practice this means that the sponsor must earn enough to cover the expenses of the family (including health insurance) without recourse to public funds. In 2005, social security was reformed with the introduction of *Arbeitslosengeld II* (more commonly termed *Hartz IV*); the minimum income that must be proven in the context of spousal migration has risen accordingly. A judgement of the Federal Administrative Court (*Bundesverwaltungsgericht*, BVerwG) furthermore established in 2008 that the mere possibility of receiving any benefits in the framework of *Hartz IV*, not the actual use of these funds, is decisive.[94]

All these requirements are currently still in place, but have been supplemented by a set of further conditions through the law change in 2007, which will be elaborated upon in chapter 4.

3.3 The demographics of spousal migration to Germany

In 2007, 7.3 million foreigners were permanent residents of Germany, with the ratio of foreigners within the total population amounting to about 8.9 per cent (Statistisches Bundesamt 2009a: 7). In relation to current migration inflows, even if – in contrast to more recent migration destination countries such as Spain, Italy or Ireland – the amount of immigration has been declining lately, in 2007 a gross figure of about 575,000 foreigners immigrated into Germany, which thus continues to be the second most important gross migration destination (after Spain) within the EU in absolute terms (BAMF 2009a: 16; 147). In 2005, the population in Germany contained 15 million individuals "with a migration background,"[95] which amounted to one fifth of

---

[93] § 29 Abs. 1 Nr. 2 AufenthG. "Sufficient housing space" (*"ausreichender Wohnraum"*) is defined in § 4 Abs. 2 AufenthG to be equivalent to the space provided in publically funded social housing, thus 12 m² per person older than six and ten m² per child younger than six. Children younger than two years are not included in the calculation.
[94] BVerwG, 1 C 32.0, judgement of 26 August 2008.
[95] The Federal Statistical Office (*Statistisches Bundesamt*) has defined the concept (*"Personen mit Migrationshintergrund"*) for their purposes to include "all individuals who immigrated after 1949 into the present-day territory of the Federal Republic of Germany, as well as all foreigners born in Germany and all individuals born as German citizens in Germany with at least one parent

the total population. Around 8 million of these individuals were "Germans with a migration background." The foreign-born population amounted to 10.6 million individuals, half of these (5.6 million) being foreigners, and the other half (5 million) German. Of the total population with a migration background, the largest ethnic groups were resettlers, with approximately 4 million, and individuals of Turkish origin (approximately 3 million) (Woellert et al. 2009: 6).

Family migration continues to constitute a significant share of total immigration to Germany. In 2007, 29 per cent of all residence permits granted to third-country nationals were based on family-related claims (BAMF 2008: 32), three fourths of which was spousal migration. The following section will outline the general amount and make-up of spousal migration to Germany until the law change in 2007, thus referring only to the statistics up to and including 2006. The impact the legal changes introduced in 2007 have had on spousal migration flows will be separately analysed in section 4.2.

Determining both the exact quantity and quality of spousal migration of third-country nationals to Germany is not simple due to the lack of availability of data and the intertwined issue of definition difficulties. Two main data sets exist, each with their own caveats. The Federal Foreign Office (*Auswärtiges Amt*, AA) has been collecting statistics since 1996 on visas granted for the purpose of family migration, recording the gender of the applicants, the consulate where the visa was applied for,[96] whether the application was made for a spouse, a minor child or a parent, and whether the sponsor was a German citizen or a foreigner. Not recorded is the number of total visa applications, the age of the applicants, the nationality of the applicants, and any information pertaining to rejected visa applications.

Since 2005, the Central Aliens Register (*Ausländerzentralregister*, AZR) provides data on all residence permits granted to third-country nationals for the purpose of family migration. This data is more illuminating since not all third-country nationals even need a visa to enter Germany and are thus not included in the AA statistics. For example, US and Japanese citizens, who in

---

who either immigrated or was born as a foreigner in Germany" (Statistisches Bundesamt 2009a: 6; my translation).
[96] Kreienbrink and Rühl (2007: 38) stress the fact that the place where the application is filed might not necessarily coincide in all cases with the nationality of the applicant.

2006, according to the AZR, represented the fourth and ninth largest groups of foreign nationals granted family migration residence permits respectively, are exempted from the visa requirement and thus do not feature in the AA statistics.[97] Furthermore, the theoretical possibility exists for all TCNs to enter Germany on a tourist or other visa and apply for a residence permit from within the country. These individuals also do not feature in the AA data but do turn up in the AZR statistics. The AZR data is broken down by nationality, age and gender of applicants, and also records whether the application was made for a spouse, a child or a parent, and whether the sponsor was a German citizen or a foreigner. From these data sets, certain trends are discernible that will be outlined below in order to gain a general picture of the size and composition of spousal migration to Germany.

Diachronic development

When looking at the development of spousal migration to Germany over time, it makes sense to consult the data of the AA, since it has recorded statistics on visas granted for family migration since 1996. From 1996 until 2002, there was a steady increase in spousal visas granted, climbing from 44,293 visas in 1996 to 64,021 in 2002, which represented an augmentation of 44.5 per cent. After this peak in 2002, the number of spousal visas granted rapidly fell in the course of just three years to 40,933 in 2005, and dropped even further to 39,585 in 2006, so that in the space of four years, the number of visas being granted to spouses almost halved. The AZR figures, which only contain data after 2005, also suggest that there is a downward trend. The number of residence permits granted to TCN spouses dropped from 53,569 in 2005 to 43,159 in 2006, a decrease of 19.4 per cent. Some of this reduction can be traced back to EU enlargement in 2004, which led immigrants from the new Member States in Central and Eastern Europe to be exempted from visa and TCN residence requirements.

---

[97] The exemption from obtaining a visa prior to entering Germany is governed by § 41 *Aufenthaltsverordnung* (AufenthV) and applies to citizens from Andorra, Australia, Honduras, Israel, Japan, Canada, the Republic of Korea, Monaco, New Zealand, San Marino and the USA.

Year	Visa
1996	44293
1997	46872
1998	48289
1999	53858
2000	58189
2001	63078
2002	64021
2003	58169
2004	51552
2005	40933
2006	39585

Table 2: Number of total visa granted to spouses 1996-2006
Source: Auswärtiges Amt

German sponsors vs. foreign sponsors

As Kreienbrink and Rühl (2007: 39) point out, since 2000 the absolute number of German sponsors has exceeded TCN sponsors. According to the AA, of 39,585 visa granted to TCNs in 2006 for the purpose of spousal migration, 22,697 (57.3 per cent) were granted to spouses joining their German husbands or wives and only 16,888 (42.7 per cent) to spouses joining foreign residents (Auswärtiges Amt 2007). In diachronic comparison, this trend seems even more striking, as only in 1996, the share of spouses joining foreigners (64.9 per cent) still clearly dominated over those joining German citizens (35.1 per cent). Thus, the ratio between citizen and foreign sponsors has nearly been inverted in the course of ten years.

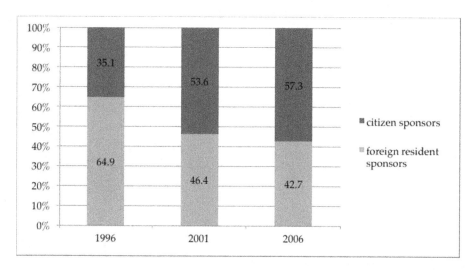

Figure 1: Percentage of spousal migration visas granted by citizen and foreign sponsors
Source: Auswärtiges Amt; own calculations

As noted above, though, not all spouses need to obtain a visa in order to enter Germany; some can apply for their residence permit from within Germany, if they come from a "visa-free" country. The AZR data on residence permits granted still strongly echoes this trend, with the tendency towards joining Germans being even stronger: in 2006, of a total 43,159 residence permits granted for the purpose of spousal migration, 27,368 (63.4 per cent) went to spouses joining German citizens and only 15,791 (36.6 per cent) to spouses joining foreign residents.

In this context it is important to realise that, contrary to earlier decades, the ethnic composition of the German citizenry has significantly diversified recently. Due to both the influx of ethnic German resettlers in the 1990s, who acquired citizenship immediately without a formal process of naturalisation, as well as the increased opportunities to acquire German citizenship (including a limited *ius soli* provision for children born to two foreigners in Germany) introduced in 2000, the newly-coined category of "Germans with a migration background" *(Deutsche mit Migrationshintergrund)* is growing.

In 2007, 15.4 million individuals with a migration background, both Germans and foreigners, were living in Germany, which amounts to 18.7 per cent of the total population. Within this group, slightly less than half, 7.3 million (8.9 per cent of the total population) are foreign nationals who have either immigrated themselves or were born to foreign parents in Germany. The other half of the group (8.1 million individuals, or 9.9 per cent of the total population) is made up of German citizens (Statistisches Bundesamt 2009: 7). This group consists of both individuals who migrated to Germany themselves, either acquiring citizenship immediately, as occurred in the case ethnic German resettlers, or who were later naturalised, as well as individuals born in Germany. Those born in Germany and possessing German citizenship were either born to foreign parents and later naturalised or acquired citizenship at birth but are nevertheless considered to have a migrant background since they were born to resettlers, to naturalised foreigners, to mixed migration-background/non-migration-background couples, or, most recently, as *ius soli* children to foreign residents (Statistisches Bundesamt 2009: 312). Accordingly, Kreienbrink and Rühl (2007: 40) attribute the increase of German citizen sponsors at least partially to higher naturalisation rates and the influx of *Aussiedler*. While it is not made explicit, these authors from the Federal Office for Migration and Refugees *(Bundesamt für Migration und Flüchtlinge,* BAMF) thus assume that significant parts of the naturalised migrant population and ethnic German resettlers choose spouses from their former home countries. However, as the data on sponsors are not broken down in any way by ethnicity, but only by citizenship, the exact impact of these developments on spousal migration dynamics is difficult to estimate.

Gender

Regarding gender, the first observation is that more women than men enter Germany as spousal migrants. In 2006, AA data show that the overall percentage of visas granted to women for spousal migration was 68.8 per cent (27,251 visas) while 31.2 per cent (12,334 visas) of the visas went to men. The AZR echoes these data surprisingly perfectly, with a total of 29,697 female (68.8 per cent) and 13,462 male (31.2 per cent) spouses being granted a residence permit in 2006, which means that the inclusion of spouses from visa-free countries does not alter the gender breakdown. Thus, even though women constitute two thirds of the overall inflow of spouses to Germany, male spousal migration is by no means a phenomenon to be neglected, even though political and also academic attention largely focuses on female movers. Connecting the gender breakdown with that of citizens/foreigners mentioned above, according to the AZR data the largest group within all spousal migrants are wives joining German citizens (39.4 per cent of all spousal migrants), followed by incoming wives joining foreign sponsors (29.4 per cent) and husbands joining German female sponsors. By far the smallest group are men joining female foreign residents (7.2 per cent).

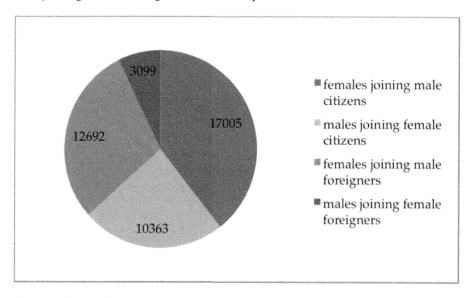

Figure 2: Spousal residence permits granted in 2006 by gender and legal status of sponsor
Source: Ausländerzentralregister; own calculations

When analysing the proportionate gender distribution, it is striking to note that the share of female spouses granted residence permits to join foreign residents (80.4 per cent of all spouses joining foreigners are women) is much higher than that of foreign wives joining citizens (62.1 per cent). Put differently, incoming husbands are much more likely to join a German citizen than a foreigner.

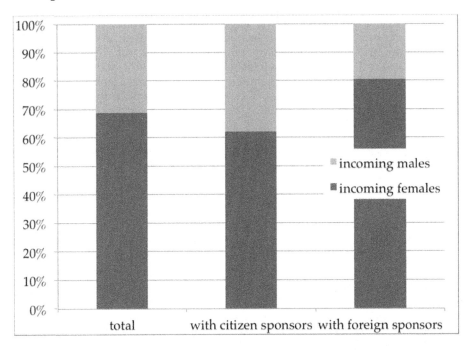

Figure 3: Gender breakdown of spousal residence permits granted in 2006, in per cent
Source: Ausländerzentralregister; own calculations

Countries of origin

By far the most common country of origin of spousal migrants to Germany is Turkey, with 8,489 residence permits (19.7 per cent of the total) issued on grounds of spousal migration in 2006. This is hardly surprising since the Turkish minority is also the largest group of foreigners in Germany in general. However, when considering all individuals with a migration background, whether German citizens or not, the group with an Aussiedler background amounts to almost 4 million, while individuals with a Turkish migration background make up the second largest group with 2.8 million. (Woellert et al. 2009: 26). At the same time, the 2005 Mikrozensus shows that the propensity to marry (native) Germans is particularly low among the Turkish minority. Only 5 per cent of the individuals with a Turkish migration background marry natives, while this proportion is much higher among other minorities in Germany, such as those with a former Yugoslav background (14.3 per cent) or Aussiedler (18.4 per cent). This trend also does not significantly change in the second generation (Woellert et al. 2009: 49). Of course, the propensity to not marry (ethnic) Germans does not immediately account for spousal migration, as ethnic minority partners can be found within Germany as well, but it does help to explain the large numbers of Turkish spousal migrants.

Besides Turkey, other important countries of origin are Serbia and Montenegro and the Russian Federation, both being the countries of origin of around 9 per cent of all spousal migrants receiving residence permits in 2006. Thailand, Ukraine, Morocco, the United States and India each provide around 3 per cent of spousal migrants. This means that around half of all spousal migrants are from one of these eight most common countries of origin, and the other half come from another part of the world. This suggests that spousal migration is a very heterogeneous and diversified process.

Country of origin	Residence permits	Per cent of total
Turkey	8489	19.7 %
Serbia and Montenegro	4037	9.35 %
Russian Federation	3798	8.8 %
Thailand	1436	3.3 %
Ukraine	1287	3 %
Morocco	1245	2.9 %
USA	1205	2.8 %
India	1127	2.6 %

Table 3: Spousal residence permits granted in 2006, by incoming spouses' most common countries of origin
Source: Ausländerzentralregister; own calculations

Some striking facts can be discerned when looking at the specific gender/citizen-foreigner breakdown of the different countries. In the case of Turkey, the general trend of more spousal migrants joining citizens than foreigners is not confirmed, as slightly more residence permits were granted to spouses joining foreigners than to those joining citizens. This is especially true for female spouses: Women made up 73.5 per cent of all Turkish spousal migrants joining foreign residents, but only 38.1 per cent of those joining German citizens. Overall, however, the proportion of male spouses from Turkey is remarkable, with men making up 43.1 per cent of all spousal migrants from Turkey, which is significantly above average (31.2 per cent). This fact belies the common image of Turkish spousal migrants as nearly exclusively being submissive "import wives." The only other country of origin with a similar high ratio of men mentioned in the AZR data available is Morocco, with a share of 42.6 per cent being male. Other exceptional cases are those of the Russian Federation and Thailand. The inflow of Russian spousal migrants is remarkable since a very large majority join citizens instead of foreigners: In 2006, 91.2 per cent of all Russian spousal migrants joined German citizens. This could indeed (in part) be due to spousal migrants joining ethnic German resettlers who are German citizens, as suggested earlier. Spousal migration from Thailand is exceptional since it is nearly exclusively made up of females joining German citizens (93.7 per cent).

Summing up

This chapter outlined the ways in which family migration policies developed in post-war Germany, from a neglected inflow that was barely legally monitored during the guest worker years, to a rapidly growing form of migration, especially after the recruitment stop. For years, however, legal uncertainty and regional differences dominated the policy field, with federal jurisdiction establishing the minimum criteria and local and regional politicians controlling the situation by decrees. Spousal migration sponsored by second-generation migrants was particularly viewed with much political scepticism. Only in 1990 was family migration officially recognised and federally regulated by law. This hesitancy is surely connected to an unwillingness on the part of the mainstream political class to accept the fact that Germany had become a country of immigration and the foreigners were going to stay.

Furthermore, the general laws and procedures applying to spousal migration were outlined. They include obtaining all documents to prove a legal marriage and the intimacy inquiries aimed at uncovering marriages of convenience. For foreign sponsors, additional residence, housing and income requirements apply. The chapter further provided an overview of the demographics of spousal migration, which constitutes the major inflow of TCNs into Germany, but which has also decreased in the last decade. The percentage of German citizen sponsors has substantially increased over the years and husbands constitute a considerable share of the incoming spouses, at around 30 per cent. Most spouses come from Turkey, but other important countries of origin include certain Eastern Europe states, as well as the USA and Thailand. The following chapter will now turn to the more recent developments in spousal migration policies in Germany from 2005 onwards, when increasingly restrictive instruments started to dominate the political and legal stages.

4 2005-2010: Spousal migration comes into focus

While the previous chapter sketched out the political developments and legal conditions vis-à-vis spousal migration in Germany in the post-war period up until 2005, this chapter explores the developments surrounding spousal migration policies in the time period 2005-2010. It explores the "restrictive turn" by zooming in on various institutional and conceptual shifts leading up to the law change (4.1), laying out the specific provisions introduced by the reform as well as the explanations brought forward by the government (4.2) and analysing the effect that the new provisions had on spousal migration inflows after their introduction (4.3).

4.1 Institutional and conceptual shifts enabling the "restrictive turn"

As elaborated in chapter 3, from 2000 to 2005 migration law was repeatedly discussed across party lines and reorganised in a protracted process in Germany. In the entire period, the issue of spousal migration had never been the subject of much debate. Accordingly, the respective provisions were transferred from the Ausländergesetz 1990 into the Zuwanderungsgesetz 2005 unchanged. Only two years later, in 2007, the issue of spousal migration suddenly took centre-stage, and new provisions restricting the admission of spouses were among the most important legal changes in the amendment of the Zuwanderungsgesetz. This seemingly sudden restrictive turn regarding spousal migration is puzzling. What factors can account for spousal migration changing from a rather ignored topic to one of the most controversial migration issues and the focus of restrictive control efforts in the course of only two years? Three important political (institutional and conceptual) shifts in the domestic and European realm can be hypothesised to have enabled such a restrictive turn in spousal migration policy in Germany. In chapter 6, the validity of these proposed explanatory factors will be subjected to further scrutiny.

The first important factor concerns a shift of political power in Germany. In September 2005, federal elections to the *Bundestag* took place. It was a snap election initiated by the Social Democrats (SPD) in government after the party had dramatically lost the prestigious regional election in the most populous *Land* North Rhine-Westphalia, traditionally a stronghold of the SPD. In this federal election, the Christian Democrats (CDU) scantily managed to establish themselves as the strongest party by gaining 35.2 per cent of the votes – the SPD secured a close 34.2 per cent. Thus, after eight years of rule, the red-green coalition under Chancellor Schröder was replaced by a grand coalition made up of the CDU as the senior partner and the SPD as the junior partner. Angela Merkel (CDU) was installed as the head of government. The grand coalition, the preferred governing solution of neither the CDU nor the SPD, was the only two-party-coalition able to achieve an absolute majority in parliament, and the other three-party-coalition talks were unsuccessful.[98] Succeeding Schily (SPD) in the position of Interior Minister was Wolfgang Schäuble (CDU), who had held this position before, from 1989 to 1991. This election result therefore not only eliminated the potentially migration-friendly Green Party from government power but also put a CDU politician at the head of the ministry in charge of migration policies. If, in the past eight years, the CDU had managed to indirectly influence migration policy by having a slight majority in the second chamber (*Bundesrat*), now it was in a major position to directly devise and decide upon migration policy. Furthermore, the constellation of a grand coalition implied a very comfortable government majority in both chambers. In practice this meant that if the ruling parliamentary groups of the SPD and CDU could find an agreement in the *Bundestag,* they could be sure that their proposals would pass all other legislative steps without further ado. Contrary to the complicated political constellation surrounding the conclusion of *Zuwanderungsgesetz* 2005, when a very strong CDU opposition made use of its position in the *Bundesrat* to protract and influence the reform process, from mid-2005 onwards, the circle of negotiating actors was thus rather limited, a situation potentially conducive to a swift change in policy.

---

[98] See Jesse and Sturm (2006) for an analysis of the German federal parliamentary elections in 2005.

The second important factor relates to the interplay between domestic executive and EU legislation. In her analysis of the impact of EU cooperation on asylum reform in Europe during the early 1990s, Lavenex shows how restrictive-minded domestic actors (mainly from the interior ministries) take advantage of cooperation at the EU level in two ways. On the one hand, decision-making at the EU level can essentially create autonomy for the executive branch. Liberal domestic actors (e.g. NGOs, political parties, parliaments) are silenced, as negotiations on binding EU legislation take place behind closed doors in far away Brussels and reforms can subsequently be presented as *faits accomplis* in the domestic realm. On the other hand, when later transposing EU legislation into national law, strong normative power can be derived from the EU in order to enhance the legitimacy of restrictive reform: "Whereas the impetus for restrictions clearly came from national constituencies, the legitimation of these restrictions with the 'need' to implement European agreements (...) provided the normative context for the consent of the pro-European opposition" (Lavenex 2001: 862). A parallel process can be observed in the context of the Family Reunification Directive (FR Directive) and the role of the Federal Ministry of the Interior (*Bundesministerium des Inneren*, BMI) in the context of spousal migration reform in Germany. Within the framework of the Council of Ministers deciding on directives, it is the relevant ministries that send their delegations to EU negotiations, not the national parliaments. During the negotiation on the FR Directive, this BMI delegation had pressed for the inclusion of a number of (at least potentially) restrictive provisions on integration measures, a minimum age for spouses and a maximum age for children (Groenendijk 2004: 119; see chapter 5). The German delegation had further lobbied towards the abolition of an article proposed by the Commission prohibiting reverse discrimination, i.e. putting German citizens in Germany on an equal footing with intra-EU movers concerning family migration rights as this would have meant an extension of German citizens' rights.

An important factor explaining the timing of the restrictive turn of spousal migration is thus that after German officials from the BMI had quite successfully "uploaded" German preferences to the final version of the FR

Directive in 2003, time had come to implement the directive.[99] Lavenex's notion of creating additional legitimacy for policies in the domestic realm by referring to the "need" to implement European legislation can also be found in the context of spousal migration restriction in Germany. Accordingly, the official title of the 2007 reform law is "Directive Implementation Act" *(Richtlinienumsetzungsgesetz)*, which refers not only to the implementation of the FR Directive but also to ten other EU directives in the field of asylum and migration. Even though the reform contains quite a few novelties in no way connected to any EU directive, for example concerning the migration of TCN spouses to German citizens, the references to the EU, both in the title of the law and in the parliamentary discourse, could thus be interpreted as a political strategy to create additional legitimacy and a sense of urgency regarding the policy process. This is also exemplified by the way Minister Schäuble's presented the draft law in parliament in March 2007: "I would like to ask the Bundestag already now to carry out the parliamentary deliberations rather speedily, since we are late in our implementation of a few EU directives" (Deutscher Bundestag, Plenarprotokoll 16/90: 9065).

A certain (restrictive) consistency can be distinguished in the BMI's strategies, regardless of party-political power constellations. All the restrictive preferences were negotiated and "uploaded" to the EU level by the BMI during the negotiation years of the FR Directive 2000-2003 under SPD rule and later implemented and "downloaded" from the EU level by the BMI under CDU rule after 2005. The BMI thus seems to maintain both a certain continuity of policy objectives and is assisted in the accomplishment of these objectives, regardless of the ruling political party, by the intricacies of the intergovernmental EU policy-making process. Admittedly, the mere negotiating position of pressing for the inclusion of an optional clause into a supranational directive does not amount to the actual formulation of a policy (not yet at least), but it certainly points towards particular policy preferences.

---

[99] Actually, the transposition deadline had already passed in October 2005. See Groenendijk et al. (2007) for details on the (late) implementation. The government has stated that due to the protraction of the final conclusion of the *Zuwanderungsgesetz* 2005, no time was left to negotiate on the inclusion of the directive into the law. The government had planned to bring an implementation bill into parliament in June 2005, but this endeavour was interrupted by the early elections, leaving the responsibility for implementation to the new CDU-SPD government (Bundesregierung 2007: 151).

A third factor which explains the restrictive turn is not related to changes in institutions but rather concerns a conceptual shift in the mindset of policy-makers regarding the importance of integration as political goal and part of migration policy. Novel policy instruments need inspiration to develop, and making the admission of spouses conditional upon language skills, and extending this condition to German sponsors, was certainly a new idea. While spousal migration had been restricted in the past, this had always taken the form of waiting periods or socio-economic conditions imposed upon the sponsor. Also, at least since the 1970s, German citizens had been very privileged in their spousal migration rights. In 2000, when negotiations on the *Zuwanderungsgesetz* 2005 started, the political goal of integration was not even enshrined in any German law, and a parallel requirement had not yet been introduced in any other European country. What inspired policy-makers to devise such an instrument? The *Zuwanderungsgesetz 2005* had, for the first time, legally enshrined integration to be an important aspect of migration and a desirable political goal. The introduction of publically financed "integration courses" for foreigners (principally teaching German, but also civic values), was the most direct expression of this paradigm shift. Furthermore, as elaborated in chapter 3, language tests for the spouses of resettlers were introduced in 2005, providing a further source of inspiration. Chancellor Merkel initiated a series of "integration summits" *(Integrationsgipfel)* from 2006 onwards, inviting representatives of "all societal groups relevant for integration" to discuss and find solutions to integration problems. At the second summit in 2007, representatives from migrant organisations, politics, media, trade unions, employers' associations and sports organisations presented the "National Integration Plan" containing over 400 (voluntary) commitments to further integration. Also, the belief slowly developed that any effort to restrict spousal migration needed to also include citizen sponsors. The yearly migration reports *(Migrationsberichte)* started reporting that more citizens than foreigners were sponsoring spousal migration, and explained this at least partly with higher naturalisation rates and spouses joining resettlers (BAMF 2007: 37).

In a parallel process, other European countries were developing similar policies, further inspiring and legitimising German efforts. The decision of the Dutch parliament in late 2005 to introduce a language requirement for incoming spouses provided a first real policy example in a neighbouring country for German decision-makers. Talks on introducing a language requirement started in France in 2007 as well. These parallel developments in the Netherlands and France, both bound by the FR Directive and by the European Convention of Human Rights (ECHR) just as Germany, further inspired German policy-makers and reassured them that they were on the right track (see Block & Bonjour 2013 and chapter 5).

A first glimpse of the direction taken by the ministry in the formulation of spousal migration policies can be extracted from the evaluation report of the Zuwanderungsgesetz 2005 that was published in July 2006 by the BMI. This evaluation assessed whether the intended goals of the Zuwanderungsgesetz 2005 had been accomplished and whether any improvements could be recommended. The fact that the implementation of the EU directives was imminent most probably led the evaluation report, containing many direct suggestions for further migration law reform, to be published so shortly after the law came into force. In the context of the evaluation, the Interior Ministries of the *Länder* compiled questionnaires dealing with the new law. In a two-day expert symposium in March 2006, practitioners from civil society and public administration further discussed their experiences with Members of Parliament (MPs) and BMI staff (BMI 2006a: 2).

The main issues regarding spousal migration put forward in the evaluation to require legislative action concern spousal migration to German citizens, marriages of convenience and forced marriages. Firstly, it is outlined (and underlined by statistics from the AZR) in the report that the proportion of spousal migration to Germans makes up a large part of total migration to Germany; it has grown to be quantitatively more important than spousal migration to foreigners. As mentioned in the previous chapter, spousal migration to Germans had never been dependent on an income requirement, and an extension of this income requirement to Germans was suggested in the framework of the evaluation for the first time. Tellingly, the report mentions integration to be the main objective behind such an extension. Thus, the implicit focus is on ethnic minority Germans, with report concluding that "especially for recently naturalized Germans (…) an income requirement will provide an extra incentive to integrate" and reduce the allegedly widespread "direct immigration into the social welfare system" (BMI 2006a: 108) and also make the conclusion of marriages of convenience more difficult (BMI 2006a: 109). In order to sustain this view, the ministry referred to former Berlin integration commissioner John's (CDU) statement at the expert symposium:

> The German sponsors who reunite with foreign spouses, regardless of whether it is a German marrying a Filipina or a naturalised Turk who brings in his wife from the outskirts of Izmir, do not have to provide a proof of income. I consider this wrong (...) for integration reasons. How will we create an incentive, and an incentive is also always pressure, how will we sustain an incentive to strive for qualification, to strive for employment, to be resourceful, to get trained, if [they] can become German at 16 years of age and have no perspective? Then [they are] German and get their wife from abroad. Everything is so easy, and obviously the social welfare system is responsible for these people. I do not consider this a wise integration policy, because they don't have any motivation to develop in the other direction." (BMI 2006b: 452)

Also, the practitioners believe marriages of convenience to be very common, a fact they sustain by pointing to the large number of divorces taking place right after the probationary period *(Ehebestandszeit)* of two years is over. On this basis, the BMI suggests in the evaluation to increase this period in order to fight marriages of convenience (BMI 2006a: 111). Regarding forced marriages, which are also classified as a pressing issue that requires policy answers, different actors within the evaluation outline two main policy paths. On the one hand, the *Land* Berlin, the parliamentary group of the Greens and human rights NGOs, advocate to extend the return possibilities of foreigners growing up in Germany who are forced to marry in their (parents') country of origin. According to the law in place, their residence permits expire after a certain time abroad. The BMI regards this suggestion to be legally difficult to implement and highly prone to abuse (BMI 2006a: 112). The other policy option, advocated by practitioners from the Foreign Office and the Aliens Authority Munich, is said to be "preventive," namely the introduction of a minimum age and/or a language requirement; the BMI clearly favours this latter option (2006a: 114).

The BMI had thus already prepared the possibilities to restrict policy in the sphere of spousal migration during the negotiations on the FR Directive and was additionally confronted with shifted political power constellations of a more conservative leaning when time came to implement the FR Directive in a revision of the Zuwanderungsgesetz in 2007. After the evaluation of Zuwanderungsgesetz took place in March 2006, in which first ideas regarding the restriction of spousal migration were uttered, the draft law for the amendment – officially the Directive Implementation Act (*Gesetz zur Um-*

setzung aufenthalts- und asylrechtlicher Richtlinien der Europäischen Union, EU-AufhAsylRUG) – was presented in 23 April 2007.100 A first parliamentary debate discussing the draft took place three days later.101 In May, the Permanent Committee on Internal Affairs (Innenausschuss) held public hearings with migration experts from administration and civil society (Innenausschuss 2007). On 14 June 2007, both a second parliamentary debate and the final vote were held on the draft law. Through a combination of the votes from all CDU MPs and most SPD MPs (n=398) the law was passed. 21 SPD MPs voted against the law while five abstained from voting. The Greens, the Left Party and the FDP unanimously voted against the law; the total number of no-votes measured 170.[102] Only four months after the first draft law was presented to the public, the law came into effect on 28 August 2007. The parliamentary discussions surrounding this law change are later analysed under the frame analysis presented in chapter 6, while the new provisions introduced into the law are presented in the next section.

4.2 Spousal migration law changes after 2007

This section provides an overview of the legal provisions introduced with the modification of the *Zuwanderungsgesetz* in 2007 concerning spousal migration. As well as summarising the law changes, the section very briefly sketches out the resultant government explanations as well as some of the critical points raised by the political opposition and civil society; an extensive analysis of the policy framings presented by the different actors relating to spousal migration law reform will be elaborated upon in chapters 6 and 7.

As outlined in chapter 3, the *Zuwanderungsgesetz* 2005 was devised, discussed and negotiated for five long years before coming into effect. Nevertheless, it contained no significant novelties regarding the conditions for family migration.[103] Initial traces of the 2007 changes can be found in two

---

[100] Deutscher Bundestag, Drucksache 16/5065.
[101] Deutscher Bundestag, Plenarprotokoll 16/94, pp. 9543-9567.
[102] Deutscher Bundestag, Plenarprotokoll 16/103, pp. 10584-10609.
[103] As mentioned in chapter 3 as well, one important novelty introduced in 2005 was a German language requirement for spouses of *Aussiedler*. Instead of being a condition for admission,

earlier documents. Firstly, Family Reunification Directive, which was heavily influenced by the German negotiators, contains provisions enabling signatory states to introduce minimum ages for spouses, demand minimum income and housing from sponsors, subject spouses to integration measures, and reject applications in cases of marriages of convenience. However, there is not a direct, necessary link between the FR Directive and all the novelties introduced in the *Zuwanderungsgesetz* 2007 since on the one hand, all the conditions of the directive formally only apply to TCN nationals residing in EU Member States, and not to FCNs, i.e. German citizens in Germany. On the other hand, more than 30 of the requirements, such as, for example, the provisions on integration measures and minimum age, are optional clauses (Hauschild 2003: 273), meaning that Member States are not forced to implement them. The second document foreboding the changes is the evaluation report of the *Zuwanderungsgesetz* 2005 discussed above, in which the BMI advocates introducing income requirements for German sponsors, an increase of the probationary period *(Ehebestandszeit)* to fight marriages of convenience and "preventive" measures vis-à-vis forced marriages such as a minimum age and a German language requirement. Four main changes were introduced into German spousal admission that will be discussed subsequently: A legally codified rejection of family migration rights in cases of "problematic" marriages, an income requirement for German sponsors in exceptional cases, a minimum age for both spouses and, most pertinently, a language requirement to be completed abroad by the incoming spouse.

Specific outlawing of "problematic" marriages

Two new basic provisions were introduced into the main paragraph enshrining the right to family migration, § 27 *Aufenthaltsgesetz* (AufenthG). These provisions refer explicitly to the problems of marriages of convenience and forced marriages. § 27 Abs. 1a states that family migration is not granted in cases that 1) it is certain that a marriage or another relationship was solely

---

however, this provision led to immediate acquisition of citizenship and is thus only indirectly classifiable as an example of migration policy.

concluded for the purpose of gaining an entry and/or residence permit in Germany or 2) actual indications substantiate the supposition that one of the spouses was forced to marry. However, at least in the case of marriages of convenience, case law[104] has clearly established since the 1980s that no family migration rights exist. The mere existence of a lawful marriage is not sufficient for Article 6 GG to be effective and spousal admission to be granted; the existence of a "marital community" (*"eheliche Lebensgemeinschaft"*) is additionally required. Why was an explicit inclusion into the law deemed necessary? In its official commentary on the new provisions, the government states that it wishes to explicitly standardise the rejection of family migration rights in cases of marriages (and adoptions) of convenience in order to inherently diminish the incentives to marry to facilitate migration in the first place (Bundesregierung 2007: 170). In order to create further legitimacy for the law change, the government also refers to Article 16(2b) of the FR Directive, which opens the avenue for Member States to reject an application for entry and residence for the purpose of family migration if "it is shown that (…) the marriage, partnership or adoption was contracted for the sole purpose of enabling the person concerned to enter or reside in a Member State." However, the government hinted at the fact that the main function of the newly introduced provision is a symbolic one, to increase both the sense of wrongdoing of the parties involved in such marriages as well as the awareness of those applying the law (Breitkreutz et al. 2007: 382). Even if these paragraphs introduce few practical changes, the explicit rejection is indicative of an increasing framing of marriages of convenience and forced marriages as serious problems that policies need to address.

Income requirement for German sponsors

§§ 28-31 subsequently deal with the specificities of spousal migration of third-country nationals joining German citizens (§ 28, § 31) and foreigners (§§ 29-31) respectively. In general, German citizens continue to be privileged and face less demanding requirements than foreign residents when sponsoring their spouses' migration. As elaborated earlier, this preferential treatment is

---

[104] E.g. BVerwG 65, 23 March 1982, p. 174

grounded in citizens' absolute right to residence in Germany and the principle that citizens should not be forced to choose between living in their country of citizenship or living with their foreign spouses. In other words, while foreigners can be expected to establish their family life abroad unless they are willing to fulfil certain conditions, this cannot be expected in the same way of German citizens. At least, this was the common political and judicial understanding until 2007.

However, as foreshadowed by the 2006 evaluation report, the *Zuwanderungsgesetz* 2007 introduced the first possibilities of demanding income requirements from German citizens as well. While prior to 2007, all German sponsors were exempted from the income requirement in place for foreign sponsors, the newly worded § 28 Abs. 1 Satz 3 AufenthG states that only "as a general rule," Germans being joined by spousal migrants should be exempted from the income requirement.

This is a restrictive shift since the expression "as a general rule" implies that exceptions to this rule exist. The government law commentary discloses what cases are regarded as exceptional: If it is deemed "reasonably acceptable" (*zumutbar*) that the marital community can be established outside of Germany, the sponsor can be required to provide a proof of income. Indications are given when this is thought to be the case, namely when the German spouse has dual citizenship, including the citizenship of his/her future spouse next to German citizenship or if the German spouse has lived and worked in and speaks the language of the country of origin of the foreign spouse (Bundesregierung 2007: 171). The government furthermore made explicit that this condition does not apply to ethnic resettlers.[105] Parallel considerations apply to Jewish immigrants with German citizenship (Bundesregierung 2009: 232). This condition is thus most likely to concern naturalised migrants or (non-resettler) second- or third-generation ethnic minorities who have acquired German citizenship. The commentary also explicitly states that this new provision is thought to be an "integration incentive" for naturalised immigrants.

---

[105] In the law commenttary, the government elaborates that following from the principle of primarily basing resettlers' admission to Germany on their special fate arising from the consequences of war (*"Kriegsfolgenschicksal"*), meaning discrimination in their areas of origin because of their German ethnicity, it cannot be deemed "acceptable" to require resettlers to transfer their marriage abroad (Bundestag 2009: 232).

While – contrary to the language requirement – this provision was met no public outcry to speak of, legal scholars were harshly critical of it at the time of its introduction: Markard and Truchseß (2007: 1028) condemn the provision to create second-class citizens based on their migratory background and claim it to be in breach of Article 3 GG, the constitutional article guaranteeing equality and non-discrimination. Weinzierl (2007) interprets the provision as seriously breaching Article 5(2) of the 1997 European Convention on Nationality, which prohibits discriminating between citizens by birth and naturalised citizens. The introduction of this provision thus blurred the clear distinction previously existing in the law between citizens' and resident foreigners' rights regarding spousal migration by reducing the rights of citizens in certain cases to those of foreigners. The phenomenon of naturalised or ethnic minority Germans marrying foreign spouses focused on the 2006 hearing was seemingly not only the incentive for including an income requirement for Germans but even inspired the policy-makers to find a legal solution that specifically targets this group. In 2012, the liberal judicial constraint struck once again, with the Federal Administrative Court basically invalidating this "exceptional" income requirement for citizens by ruling that Germans principally cannot be required to lead their marriage abroad and that dual citizenship cannot be a reason to impose an income requirement.[106] However, as the provision was in place during the time of the research, it is included in the subsequent analysis.

Minimum age and language requirement

Finally, two entirely new conditions were introduced in 2007 that need to be fulfilled by couples with citizen and foreign sponsors alike. First, a minimum age was introduced, requiring both spouses to be at least 18 years of age.[107]

---

[106] BVerwG 10 C 12.12, judgement of 4 September 2012, paras 26 and 30.

[107] § 30 Abs. 1 S. 1 Nr. 1 AufenthG and § 28 Abs. 1 S. 4 AufenthG. In the general German legislation, marriage is possible from 16 years of age onward, provided the other spouse is over 18 and the competent family court issues its permission. See § 1303 Abs. 2-4 *Bundesgesetzbuch* (BGB). Initially, the legislation proposal issued by the BMI aimed at establishing a minimum age at 21 years (Maaßen 2006: 163), even going to various lengths to confirm the constitutional conformity (Hillgruber 2006).

Second, a language requirement was introduced, stipulating that the incoming spouse must be able to communicate at least in simple German.[108] The language skills necessary amount to the level A1 of the Common European Framework of Reference for Languages (CEFR), including listening, speaking, reading and writing capacities. Usually, the skills need to be proven by a language certificate from an endorsed test institution, primarily the Goethe-Institutes abroad. In countries where no facilities exist to take such a German test, the representation abroad itself verifies the presence of German skills in the context of a personal interview. No certificate is needed if the necessary language skills are "evident" *("offenkundig")* beyond any reasonable doubt (Bundesregierung 2009: 247). Some categories of migrating spouses are exempted from the language requirement, namely spouses of refugees, spouses who are unable to learn basic German due to a mental or physical impairment (which does not include illiteracy, however), spouses who have "recognisably minor integration needs" *("erkennbar geringer Integrationsbedarf"),* meaning they have a university diploma and are likely and able to pursue a qualified employment in Germany which does not require German language skills (Breitkreutz et al. 2007: 383) and spouses of foreigners from countries who are not required to obtain a visa prior to entering Germany (hereafter: visa-free foreigners).[109] This last provision concerns spouses of citizens from Andorra, Australia, Honduras, Israel, Japan, Canada, the Republic of Korea, Monaco, New Zealand, San Marino and the USA, states to which Germany maintains close economic relations.[110] Entirely exempted from both the age and the language requirement are spouses joining foreigners who have been

---

[108] § 30 Abs. 1 S. 1 Nr. 2 AufenthG and § 28 Abs. 1 S. 4 AufenthG in reference to § 30 Abs. 1 S. 1 Nr. 2 AufenthG.

[109] All exemptions are listed in § 30 Abs. 1 S. 3 Nr. 1-4 AufenthG. The exemption from obtaining a visa prior to entering Germany is governed by § 41 *Aufenthaltsverordnung* (AufenthV).

[110] According to the wording of the law, it is the nationality of the sponsor that is decisive, not that of the incoming spouse. Accordingly, both a Japanese and a Congolese spouse of a Japanese sponsor would be exempted, while the Israeli or US spouse of a German or Turkish sponsor would not be. Of course, spouses coming from visa-free countries joining non-visa-free foreigners or German citizens have more elaborate opportunities to enter and remain in Germany in the short term, but formally need to prove their German skills in order to be granted a spousal residence permit. However, a certain degree of confusion regarding this intricate exemption seems to prevail even among politicians (MP Laurischk (FDP), for example, claimed: "Isn't it a two-class migration system if spouses of other nationalities – for instance from the USA or Australia – do not have to demonstrate German skills?" (Deutscher Bundestag, 16/94: 9556)).

granted admission to Germany as high-skilled migrants, researchers or entrepreneurs, or as long-term residents of other EU countries.[111] As mentioned above, these new conditions for spousal migration were introduced in reference to optional clauses of the FR Directive, and extended beyond the scope of the directive to include marriages with German citizens as well. Article 4(5) of the directive gives Member States the possibility to install a minimum age (though a maximum of 21 years) for both the sponsor and the spouse before admission is granted so as to "ensure better integration and prevent forced marriages." Article 7(2) allows Member States to require third-country nationals to comply with integration measures (see chapter 5 for further elaboration on the directive).

The government stated that the goal of both measures is to prevent forced marriages, since potential victims become less "controllable" with increasing age and education. It also stated that next to these preventive effects both measures would work integratively: not only learning German prior to entry but also the minimum age would enhance integration, since the chances of completing an education in the country of origin would be heightened with increasing age (Bundesregierung 2007: 172-174).

More than the minimum age, the language requirement was immediately met with a great deal of criticism and controversy from legal experts (e.g. Markard & Truchseß 2007), migrant NGOs (e.g. Verband binationaler Familien und Partnerschaften 2008a) and opposition parties, most notably the Left Party. The main points criticised were the effectiveness regarding its official aim of integration and forced marriage prevention, as well as the practical difficulties of the requirement related to the unavailability of German language courses abroad, the high costs to be carried by the couple and the additional separation time (at times amounting to months). Due to these burdens, the critics questioned the compatibility of the requirement with constitutional Article 6, which relates to the protection of the family. Furthermore, the exemption of spouses of visa-free foreigners has been criticised as being discriminatory as well as possibly unconstitutional. The most important Turkish associations in Germany took this provision, along with the other restrictive novelties introduced into spousal migration law as a motive

---

[111] § 30 Abs. 1 S. 2 AufenthG.

to boycott the "integration summit" in July 2007 (ZEIT online 2007). Even the centre-right FDP claimed this exception to create "first-class and second-class marriages" and thus potentially in breach of Article 6 GG when it was still in the opposition in early 2009 (Deutscher Bundestag, Drucksache 16/11753: 2). It was also criticised that, despite justifying restrictive measures with the goal of fighting forced marriages the AufenthG contains no provision on facilitating independent residential status for individuals seeking to escape forced marriages, thereby providing an incentive to remain in a forced marital situation and potentially aggravating the situation (Freudenberg 2007, Weinzierl 2007: 5). All these arguments will be extensively analysed in chapter 6.

A "Forced Marriage Law" in 2011

Three years after the 2007 changes, the government (now made up of a centre-right coalition among the CDU and the FDP) approved another migration-related bill in October 2010. It included various changes in the field of migration and integration law, but also specifically dealt with forced marriages, and was even named the "Forced Marriage Act."[112] It introduced, in addition to some other small modifications of migration and asylum laws, certain changes in the area of forced marriages and spousal migration, including an extended right of return to Germany for up to ten years for victims of forced marriages into the *Aufenthaltsgesetz*,[113] and a newly created specific paragraph in the Criminal Code relating to the practice.[114] Furthermore, the time period in which a marriage can be annulled in cases of forced marriages was prolonged to three years in the Civil Code.[115] Concerning spousal migration law proper, the probationary period *(Ehebestandszeit)* for spouses was increased from two to three years. The government's explanato-

---

[112] The law's full name is Law to Fight Forced Marriage and Better Protection of Forced Marriage Victims and to Change Further Residence and Asylum Provisions (*Gesetz zur Bekämpfung der Zwangsheirat und zum besseren Schutz der Opfer von Zwangsheirat sowie zur Änderung weiterer aufenthalts- und asylrechtlicher Vorschriften*).
[113] § 51, Abs. 4 S. 2 AufenthG.
[114] § 237 StGB is the newly created paragraph of the Criminal Code dealing specifically with forced marriages. However, the wording of the paragraph was taken over identically from § 240, changing nothing regarding the definition or punishment of the offence.
[115] § 1317 Abs. 1 S. 1 BGB.

ry note elaborates that in 2000, this period had been decreased from four to two years, and "evidence from the practice of aliens authorities suggest that hereby the incentive to enter into marriages of convenience was enhanced." (Bundesregierung 2010: 14). The bill entered into law in July 2011.[116]

A judicial liberal constraint?

The German judiciary has been evaluated as a crucial factor in the protection of family migration rights in the 1980s (Joppke 1998a), establishing a "judicial liberal constraint" that counterbalances restrictive policies, as outlined in chapter 3. How has this judicial liberal constraint influenced the new restrictions of 2007? After the introduction of the language requirement, many critics' most central argument was the provision's alleged incompatibility with the constitution. These critics thus uttered their hope that a high court, such as the *Bundesverfassungsgericht*, might overturn the language requirement (see chapters 6 and 7, e.g. on the well-publicised remarks in this regard by SPD MP Edathy). However, the German judiciary has, to date, not substantially overturned the political decisions of restricting spousal migration. Thus far, in all cases brought to courts on the language requirement, the judges ruled it to be in principle compatible with the German constitution.[117] However, concerning spousal migration to Germans, some tentative liberalisations were ordered by the courts.

In the first prominent case, involving two Turkish spouses trying to reunite in Germany, decided by the BVerwG in March 2010, the language requirement was judged compatible with both the German constitution and European law, specifically with Article 7 of the FR Directive and Article 8 ECHR as well as with the standstill clauses of EU-Turkey association law.[118] Since the instrument's compatibility with Article 6 GG depends upon it fulfilling the principle of proportionality *(Verhältnismäßigkeit)* between the pri-

---

[116] Bundesgesetzblatt, I, Jahrgang 2011, Nr. 33, p. 1266.
[117] E.g. OVG Berlin-Brandenburg, OVG 2B 6.08, judgement of 28 April 2009.
[118] BVerwG, 1 C 8.09, judgement of 30 March 2010. See paragraphs 18-20 and 30-34. The same plaintiffs later brought their case to the Constitutional Court. The court rejected the language requirement's infringement of the GG, and thus basically confirmed the BVerwG's decision, in March 2011. See BVerfG, 2 BVR 1413/10, judgement of 25 March 2011.

vate interests of individuals in relation to family unity and the "contrary public interests," the court assessed in great detail the government's goals of preventing forced marriages and enhancing integration with the language requirement in its decision.[119]

The arguments brought forward by the court are worth reviewing. The judges stated that integration and the prevention of forced marriages are generally "legitimate legislative goals" and whether the language requirement is a "sufficiently promising" instrument to achieve this goal lies in the "wide range of interpretation of the law-maker" (para. 38). The court also went into more detail, reiterating the government's rationale of the ways the language requirement achieves these goals to be a "justifiable assessment" and to "not raise objections" (para. 38). The court confirmed that speaking German prior to entry will enable spouses to "better participate in social life from the start" (para. 38) and that German skills complicate the abuse of a coercive situation in Germany, and thus the language requirement "at least indirectly" fights forced marriages. It also stated that fulfilling the language requirement abroad is necessary to fulfil these goals, since obliging incoming spouses to learn German once in Germany would not guarantee integration success in the same way. The court also found it "plausible" that spouses in forced marriages will be better able to turn to authorities and escape the dependency of the family-in-law if they speak German (para. 39).

Noteworthy also is how the BVerwG further substantiated the "public interests" of enhancing integration and fighting forced marriages as being of "special weight" (para. 41), especially in order to protect constitutional values. Swift integration is claimed to be important to protect the welfare system (Art. 20(1) GG) and for the free development of personality (Art. 2(1) GG). It is fair to argue that connecting integration to the "free development of personality" implicitly conjures up images of suppressed migrant women living in parallel societies. Therefore, this suggests that even the highest administrative judges seem to confirm stereotyped imaginings of spousal migration. Forced marriages on the other hand are stated to infringe upon the freedom to marry (Art. 6(1) GG) and indirectly upon sexual self-determination, personal freedom and physical integrity (Art. 2(1-2) GG). Consequently, infringing upon one individual constitutional right (Art. 6

---

[119] Paragraphs 37-41 of the judgement.

GG) is justified by protecting other constitutional values. As will become clearer in chapter 6, the Federal Administrative Court echoed the line of argumentation brought forward by the civil servants and CDU MPs in this judgement. It is remarkable how directly the court adopted the government's framing of the policy. Since the judges fundamentally only accepted a restrictive migration policy instrument due to its successful framing as protecting other (possibly more important) constitutional values, this judgement shows how important framing can be for legal evaluations. It also shows that the political and discursive liberal constraints leading policy-makers to frame restrictive policies as compatible with liberal values can be interconnected with later dynamics of judicial liberal constraints.

In the 2010 judgement, the fact that the husband could be expected to return to Turkey in order be with his family had played an important role (paras. 5, 48, 51). Therefore, when the BVerwG ruled on the language requirement in a case involving a German sponsor in September 2012,[120] the outcome was somewhat different. Here, while they once again upheld the general constitutional compatibility of the language requirement, the judges stated that contrary to foreign sponsors, German citizens (also those with dual citizenship) possess a constitutionally protected right to reside in Germany (Art. 11 GG) and thus principally cannot be expected to leave Germany to lead their marriage abroad. Therefore, their "private interests" in leading a marriage in Germany carry substantially more weight than those of foreign sponsors (para 26). The judges ruled that spouses of German citizens do not need to fulfil the language requirement if language acquisition is not possible, not reasonable (*zumutbar*) or has been unsuccessful for the period of one year (para 28), in practice installing a kind of a hardship clause for spouses of German citizens. However, it remains unclear how the authorities abroad are exactly implementing this judgement. In any case, here the judicial liberal constraint thus offset at least partly the approximation of spousal migration rights of German citizens to those of foreigners by reinstalling a slightly privileged treatment for spouses of Germans.

---

[120] BVerwG 10 C 12.12, judgement of 4 September 2012

EU citizens and their family members in Germany

Intra-EU movers in Germany derive their family migration rights from the Free Movement Directive (2004/83/EC), which was transposed into national legislation in the Free Movement Act (*Gesetz über die allgemeine Freizügigkeit von Unionsbürgern*, FreizügG/EU). Thus, while the AufenthG governs family migration sponsored by both German citizens and TCNs, a distinct set of laws applies to family migrants joining SCN sponsors. Overall, SCNs are granted more extensive family migration rights than Germans, which has led some commentators to speak of an *"Inländerdiskriminierung"* or "reverse discrimination" stemming from EU law (Walter 2008). This concerns, for example, the family members eligible to join the sponsor. While German citizens and TCNs in Germany can only sponsor the migration of their spouses and their children up to 16 (TCNs) and 18 (Germans), EU citizens are entitled to be joined by their spouses or registered partners, their children up to an age of 21, and even older children and ascending relatives if they are proven to be dependent upon their sponsor or spouse.[121]

In one paragraph,[122] the FreizügG/EU states that the conditions relating to the entry and residence of the spouses of Germans will equally apply to spousal migration with Union citizens in Germany. In this vein, it was initially practice to require German language skills prior to granting the residence permit to TCN spouses of SCNs in Germany as well. In July 2008 however, the ECJ ruled in the *Metock*[123] case that Member States are not permitted to impose further requirements on the reuniting spouses in order to ensure full free movement rights of the Union citizen. Subsequently, the language requirement was not demanded of SCNs' spouses anymore. Since the scope of reverse discrimination is actually further enhanced by the *Metock* ruling, some actors took the EU guidelines as an impetus for liberalisation and called for an abolishment of the language requirements for TCN spouses of Germans as well (Verband binationaler Familien und Partnerschaften 2008b; Bündnis 90/Die Grünen Bundestagsfraktion 2008). On the other hand, the government instead picked up the issue of reverse discrimination as an un-

---

[121] Directive 2004/38/EC, Article 2(2)
[122] § 3 Abs. 6 FreizügG/EU
[123] ECJ, Case C-127/08, Metock and others v. Minister for Justice, Equality and Law Reform, judgement of 13 September 2008.

fortunate disadvantaging of German nationals, which could be solved by downgrading SCNs' rights. On various occasions, conservative government members have called for more restrictive policies for the admission of EU citizens' family members by changing the Free Movement Directive in order to approximate the position of Germans to that of intra-EU movers again.

4.3 Immediate effects of the reform on spousal migration inflows

What immediate effects did the requirements introduced in 2007 have on the quantity and composition of spousal migration inflows until 2010? First, the amount of spousal migration was considerably reduced after the introduction of the new requirements. When comparing the visas issued for spousal migration, as documented by the Foreign Office (AA), in 2006 (n=39,585), with those issued in 2007 (n=32,466), we find a decrease of 18 per cent, which is all the more striking considering that the new conditions only came into force from August 2007 onwards. The number of visas issued declined in 2008 (n=30,766) by a further 5.2 per cent. When directly comparing the number of visas issued in 2006 and 2008, leaving aside the possibly ambivalent reform year of 2007, we observe a decrease of more than 22 per cent. In 2009, the spousal visas issued increased again by almost 8 per cent (n=33,194), which might be attributed to a more efficient enforcement of the new proceedings, clearing up backlogs from 2007 and 2008. The extreme drop in visas that occurred right after the introduction might also have been due to practical difficulties regarding the administrative procedure of the embassies, the availability of language courses and a lack of information among the concerned couples, all of which gradually improved. In 2010, a renewed slight decrease of spousal visas issued (n=31,649) was discernible. On the whole, the number of spousal visas issued seemed to have stabilised at around 30,000 per year by 2010, which amounts to an overall decrease of roughly a quarter compared to the spousal visas issued prior to the law change.

Year	2005	2006	2007	2008	2009	2010
Amount	40,933	39,585	32,466	30,767	33,194	31,649
Change		-3.3%	-18%	-5.2%	+7.9%	-4.65%

Table 4: Spousal visas granted 2005-2010 and relative change to previous year
Source: Auswärtiges Amt, own calculations

Also the figures provided by the *Ausländerzentralregister* (AZR) on spousal residence permits suggest a downward trend after the introduction of the restrictive provisions in 2007. The annual amount of residence permits granted to TCN spouses dropped from 43,159 in 2006 to 40,978 in 2007, and finally to 33,733 in 2009, a total decrease of 21.8 per cent in the course of three years. An increase is observable in 2010, which is presumably a time-lagged reflection of the above-mentioned increase in visas in 2009, since there is usually a time gap of several months between the granting of an admission visa abroad and the final issue of a residence permit in Germany.

Year	2005	2006	2007	2008	2009	2010
Amount	53,569	43,159	40,978	37,052	33,733	37,897
Change		-19.4%	-5.1%	-9.6%	-9%	+12.3%

Table 5: Spousal residence permits granted 2005-2010 and relative change to previous year
Source: Ausländerzentralregister, own calculations

However, regarding both the numbers of visas and residence permits, it must be kept in mind that a downward trend was already showing prior to 2007. As mentioned in chapter 3, the visa numbers had been declining since 2002. In the period since 2005 observable with the AZR data, the strongest decrease in annual spousal residence permits was not after the legal restriction of spousal migration in 2007, but actually from 2005 to 2006, by a whopping 19.4 per cent. One factor was surely the EU enlargement rounds in 2004 and 2007, exempting citizens from countries such as Poland, Bulgaria and Romania from visa requirements as well as easing up their residence conditions.

Who was affected most by the restrictive reforms? First, by comparing the data AA with the AZR data an interesting observation can be made. In 2006, 39,585 spousal visas were granted compared to 43,159 spousal residence permits; thus spouses from countries previously requiring visas constituted a share of around 92 per cent. In 2007, this share dropped to 79.2 per cent. Even if this comparison has its flaws (residence permits are not necessarily granted in the same year as the visas, or might not be granted at all, spouses from visa countries might enter on different pretexts and switch to spousal permits once in Germany), it does hint at spouses from visa-free countries being affected less by the policy changes. While the residence permits granted to spouses from Turkey decreased by 8.2 per cent, to spouses from Serbia and Montenegro by 12.4 per cent and to spouses from the Russian Federation by 13.8 per cent from 2006 to 2007, permits granted to spouses from the USA increased by 28 per cent and from Japan by 24.1 per cent during that same time. At least when they marry co-nationals, spouses from visa-free countries are exempted from the language requirement, making their immigration considerably easier.

Family migration from India and China also increased considerably, each by close to 30 per cent, making these two countries 5th and 9th, respectively, on the list of the most common countries of origin in 2007 (BAMF 2009: 128). In 2008, residence permits granted to spouses from the three main countries of origin Turkey (-12.9 per cent), the Russian Federation (-19 per cent) and Serbia and Montenegro (-51.6 per cent[124]) further decreased compared to the previous year. On the contrary, spousal inflows from China (+1.2 per cent) and especially India (+15 per cent) continued to grow, with India ranking 4th among incoming spouses' most common countries of origin from 2008-2010. Seemingly, spouses from India and China, while not visa-free as those from the USA and Japan, were having fewer problems with the new restrictive requirements than spouses from the classic countries of origin such as Turkey, the Russian Federation and those in the Balkans.

Important in this respect is again the fact that rather large proportions of spousal migrants from India and China get exempted from the lan-

---

[124] This extreme decrease is due to the fact that following the independence of Kosovo in February 2008, the data on spousal migration is listed separately. When taking the residence permits granted to spouses from Kosovo and Serbia and Montenegro in 2008 together (n=2,929), the decrease compared to 2007 shrinks to 17.2 per cent.

guage requirement, either due to having "recognisable minor integration needs" or since they are joining migrants admitted as highly-skilled workers, as researchers or who are self-employed. In 2009, an impressive 39 per cent of all Indian and 37 per cent of all Chinese applicants for a spousal visa were exempted from having to provide a language certificate. Another interesting case is that of Morocco, with the amount of residence permits dropping only very slightly after the law change from 1,245 in 2006 to 1,188 in 2007 and then hovering around that mark for the following two years, only to expand to 1,317 in 2010, with more spouses entering than prior to the restrictive reform.

Country of origin	Amount of residence permits	Per cent of total (n=37897)
Turkey	6,579 (-22.5%)	17.4%
Russian Federation	2,656 (-30.1%)	7%
Kosovo	2,233 (n.a.)	5.9%
India	1,720 (+52.6%)	4.5%
USA	1,691 (+40.3%)	4.5%
Morocco	1,317 (+5.8%)	3.5%
Thailand	1,249 (-13%)	3.3%
China	1,160 (+25.9%)	3.1%

Table 6: Absolute (relative change compared to amount in 2006) and relative amount of spousal residence permits granted in 2010, by incoming spouses' most common countries of origin
Source: Ausländerzentralregister, own calculations

When taking a closer look at Turkey, the main country of origin, a picture of strong decline emerges. While in the years 1998-2003 the total number of visas issued to Turkish citizens for family migration hovered between 21,000 and 27,000, constituting about a third of overall family migration to Germany, visas for spousal migrants from Turkey had already decreased to 10,208 in 2006. After the law change, the number of spousal visas issued to Turks dropped to 6,626 in 2007, climbing back to 6,886 in 2008 and 6,905 in 2009, making up only around a fifth of the total visas granted for family migration into Germany.

In 2010, at the request of the Left Party in an attempt to evaluate the mid-term consequences of the introduced language requirement, the government published an overview of the 20 countries of origin with the strongest decrease in spousal visas between 2006 and 2010. The list is headed by Romania, Bulgaria and Brazil, which however is due to the visa requirements being abolished for citizens from these countries. Next to these exceptional cases, the strongest relative decrease occurred in Kazakhstan (decrease of 73 per cent), Kirgizstan (65 per cent), Cuba (60 per cent) and Macedonia (58 per cent). In other main sending countries for spousal migrants, the relative decrease between 2006 and 2010 was less extreme, but still substantial, with visas issued in Bosnia and Herzegovina decreasing by 45 per cent, in Thailand by 38.5 per cent, and in Turkey and the Russian Federation by 36 per cent (see Deutscher Bundestag, Drucksache 17/5620: 24).

Evidence exists also regarding the pass rates of spouses taking the German exam abroad. In 2009, 64 per cent of all spouses taking the exam globally passed it. Of the spouses having prepared for the exam by following a course at a Goethe-Institute, 72 per cent passed. The pass rate among the "external examinees" lies lower; of all spouses not having followed a Goethe-course only 60 per cent were successful on the exam. However, the overall proportion of spouses taking the tests as external examinees without Goethe-course preparation was rather high, at 73 per cent (Deutscher Bundestag, Drucksache 17/1112: 2-3). This implies that even though a course at a Goethe-Institute is apparently the best preparation for the language exam, only a quarter of the spousal migrants in 2009 were willing or able to visit a course at the Goethe-Institute, be it due to time, prices, location or availability.

The pass rates also differed per country. While in the Russian Federation, Morocco (both 82 per cent), Ukraine (79 per cent) and China (78 per cent) the pass rates were exceptionally high, in India (73 per cent), Vietnam (69 per cent) and Turkey (68 per cent), they were considerably lower, while still above the global average. In Serbia (57 per cent), Kosovo (51 per cent) and Macedonia (33 per cent), the pass rates were among the worst, but in these countries, no proper Goethe-Institute preparation was available. Accordingly, in Serbia and Kosovo, not a single examinee was prepared by a Goethe-Institute, and in Macedonia, 99 per cent of the examinees were external (Deutscher Bundestag, Drucksache 17/1112: 10). The availability of adequate courses thus strongly correlates with the success rates of the incoming spouses in the language tests.

When comparing the gender composition of the spousal inflows and the legal status of the sponsors from 2006 with the values in 2010, two interesting trends can be observed. The relative numbers of both residence permits granted to incoming females and those granted to spouses joining foreign residents increased. Among the different groups, the strongest relative increase occurred among females joining foreign residents (+3.6 per cent) and the strongest decrease among males joining German citizens (-2.6 per cent). This is especially surprising, as since 2000, when spouses joining citizens outnumbered for the first time spouses joining foreigners, the share of citizen sponsors had been steadily rising. In 2010, though citizen sponsors still overall outnumbered foreign sponsors, the proportion had indeed shrunk.

Of course, the relative conditions for citizen sponsors had been tightened up through the partial introduction of an income requirement and their inclusion in the language requirement. Since the language requirement applies to spouses of foreign sponsors as well, it is not immediately obvious why this would not lead to an equivalent decline of foreign sponsors, leaving the proportion unchanged. Here it is important to remember that the restrictions do not affect spouses of all foreigners. Some of the spouses joining foreigners, especially from China and India, join high-skilled labour migrants and are thus treated favourably, e.g. exempted from the language requirement. Also the spouses joining visa-free citizens, e.g. from the USA and Japan, are exempted from the language requirement. In this way, the *"Inländerdiskriminierung"* treating spouses of some foreigners more favourably than spouses of German citizens seems to translate into a real shift in the inflows as well and could be one explanation for the relative increase in foreign sponsors. And lastly, the spouses from India and China (presumably joining high-skilled labour migrants) were predominantly female (BAMF 2011: 137). For instance, 85 per cent of all incoming Indian spouses in 2009 were wives joining foreign husbands.

	Female spouses	Male spouses	Total
Joining citizens	17,005 (39.4%)	10,363 (24%)	27,418 (63.5%)
Joining foreign residents	12,692 (29.4%)	3099 (7.2%)	15,791 (36.5%)
Total	29,697 (68.8%)	13462 (31.2%)	43,159 (100%)

Table 7: Spousal residence permits granted in 2006 (% of total), by gender and legal status of sponsor
Source: Ausländerzentralregister

	Female spouses	Male spouses	Total
Joining citizens	14,571 (38.4%)	8,121 (21.4%)	22,692 (59.9%)
Joining foreign residents	12,474 (33%)	2,731 (7.2%)	15,205 (40.1%)
Total	27,045 (71.4%)	10,852 (28.6%)	37,897 (100%)

Table 8: Spousal residence permits granted in 2010 (% of total), by gender and legal status of sponsor
Source: Ausländerzentralregister

Claiming admission as a parent to circumvent the language requirement?

Another observable trend is a strong increase in the residence permits granted to parents of minors since 2007. Individuals entering Germany as the parent of a minor German citizen do not have to fulfil the language or age requirements nor does their livelihood need to be secured by their sponsor (which is the minor German citizen). Since 2007, the conditions confronting spouses have thus considerably been tightened compared with the conditions to gain admission as a parent, which have remained unchanged. Put differently, the incentive to gain admission as a parent has increased.

Year	2006[125]	2007	2008	2009	2010
Residence permits	1,205	1,784	2,396	2,379	3,702
% of total family migration	2.1%	3.2%	4.7%	4.9%	6.7%

Table 9: Absolute and relative numbers of residence permits granted to parents of minors in Germany, 2006-2010
Source: Ausländerzentralregister, own calculations

This development can clearly be discerned from the data on residence permits. In 2006, 1,205 residence permits were granted to parents of minors in Germany, which amounted to 2.1 per cent of the overall family migration inflow. In 2007, the number of residence permits granted to parents of minors increased slightly to 1,784 permits, or 3.2 per cent of all residence permits granted to family migrants. In the following years, both the absolute and the relative numbers grew steadily, arriving at 3,702 permits in 2010, or 6.7 per cent of the total family migration inflow, and thus more than tripling the share of this type of family migration inflow in the course of only five years. The overwhelming majority (around 99 per cent) of these parental permits are issued to parents of minor German citizens, as gaining the right to admission as a parent of a foreign child in Germany is much more difficult.

It is safe to assume that most of the admitted parents are or were in a relationship or even married to citizens or foreign residents living in Germany and thus previously might have opted to enter as spousal migrants. Due to the new restrictions for spouses, most importantly the language requirement, entering as a parent of a German citizen becomes increasingly attractive. Whether this development is due to a mere change in admission strategies of individuals who qualify to enter both as spouses or as parents and

---

[125] Unfortunately, for the year 2006, the AZR only indicates the number of residence permits granted to parents of minor German citizens, while from 2007 onwards, it also specifies the number of residence permits that went to parents of foreign children (with a residence right). From 2007, I included these permits into my calculations (of residence permits granted to parents), but since they are overall rather negligible (9 permits in 2007, 22 permits in 2008, 17 permits in 2009, 43 permits in 2010) compared to the permits granted to parents of German children, taking the permits granted only to parents of German children as indicators for 2006 seems feasible.

now opt for the latter, or is attributable to children actually being conceived in order to circumvent the language requirement remains undisclosed.

Conclusions

This chapter explored the political and legal details surrounding the restrictive turn of spousal migration policies in Germany after 2005, as well as the observable quantitative and qualitative impacts of the reformed *Zuwanderungsgesetz* 2007 on spousal inflows into Germany until 2010. The first section placed special focus on why the issue of spousal migration arose when it did and was not discussed in the course of the wider migration policy debate in the years 2000 to 2004, when the initial *Zuwanderungsgesetz* had been debated and concluded.

Various shifts after 2005 presumably contributed to move the issue of spousal migration on the policy agenda. Perhaps most importantly, after the federal elections of 2005, Germany returned to a conservative government majority with the CDU leading the SPD in a grand coalition. A CDU minister, Schäuble, was installed as Interior Minister responsible for migration policies. Furthermore, time had come to implement the EU Family Reunification Directive which, due *inter alia* to successful negotiation results of the German delegation in Brussels, contained various possibilities to restrict spousal migration via age and integration requirements. Lastly, conceptual shifts concerning integration (policies) had an impact. Integration, as a buzzword and policy goal, had only really entered the German arena with the *Zuwanderungsgesetz* 2005, laying the ground for both critically evaluating spousal migration as a potential integration deterrent and thinking about enforcing integration via certain requirements. The language requirement introduced for spouses of *Aussiedler* in 2005 and the first EU-wide comprehensive "integration abroad" policy for all incoming spouses introduced in the Netherlands in 2006 served as source of inspiration and legitimisation for German migration policy-makers to toughen up on spousal migration too.

In 2007 then, the CDU-SPD coalition agreed on the reformed *Zuwanderungsgesetz* that introduced various restrictive provisions on spousal migration, resulting in a legally codified rejection of family migration rights in cases of marriages of convenience and forced marriages, an income requirement for German sponsors in exceptional cases, a minimum age for both spouses, and most pertinently, a language requirement to be completed abroad by the incoming spouse. The government justified the changes mainly with integration objectives and the intent to fight forced marriages. Critical voices from the political opposition, civil society and academia doubted the proportionality and effectiveness of the measures and pointed towards their partially discriminatory nature, leading the constitutional compatibility of the new restrictive provisions to be brought into question as well.

When assessing the impact the new provisions had, an ambivalent picture emerges. Immediately after the introduction, in 2007 and 2008, the numbers of spousal visas granted annually decreased by about a quarter. In 2009 however, perhaps due to improvements in the information provision and language course possibilities abroad, the initial strong dip was corrected upwards and annual visas increased again. Furthermore, it must be kept in mind that not all of the reduction in spousal migration is necessarily attributable to the new requirements, as the annual numbers were already steadily declining since 2002.

Evidence also exists as to which groups of spouses have been more or less affected by the law change. With substantially fewer spouses from traditionally popular areas of origin, such as Turkey, the Russian Federation, the Balkans and Thailand, the number of spouses from other countries remained stable or even increased after 2007. For instance, the inflow of spouses from the USA, traditionally a rather large group as well, increased after 2007. This is partly due to the exemption from the language requirement for spouses of US sponsors, since at least parts of the incoming US spouses are presumably married to US sponsors.

Also, there was a strong growth in residence permits granted to Chinese and especially Indian spouses, which in turn can be partially explained by a heightened admission of (high-skilled) migrants from these countries. This notion is further sustained by the fact that close to 40 per cent of Indian and Chinese spouses were exempt from the language requirement in 2010, as is regularly the case for spouses of high-skilled migrants. When evaluating the aggregate development, what stands out is that from 2006 to 2010, the proportion of incoming wives has grown, as has the relative proportion of spouses joining foreigners, while up until 2007 the share of male spouses and that of citizen sponsors had steadily grown. This shift might point towards a partial return to more "classical" spousal migration in the sense of wives accompanying primary (high-skilled) male migrants.

Finally, a marked increase in the number of residence permits granted to parents of minor German citizens could be noted after the 2007 reform. Since neither minimum income nor language or age requirements are applicable to incoming parents of German minors, the incentive to apply for a parental permit grows when spousal permits are restricted. Since the group of (potential) parental migrants is at least partially congruent with that of (potential) spousal migrants, this increase can be estimated to be the outcome of individual strategies adopted in order to avoid the new restrictions placed on incoming spouses.

5 The European dimension of family migration policies

This chapter will position the case of German family migration policy within the wider European context, by considering both the dynamics emanating from the supranational European level as well as domestic political developments in other states. It is not a comparative study, nor does it aspire to make empirically founded conclusions regarding policy convergence, divergence or other dynamics of Europeanisation. Instead, the chapter is meant to give the reader a general idea of the wider European context in which the case study of Germany is positioned. Also, German policy-makers, as is shown in the later frame analysis, repeatedly refer to both the European level and neighbouring states' policies when explaining and legitimising German policy decisions. The first section (5.1) deals with legislation and jurisprudence concerning family migration at the supranational level. Initially, the enshrinement of family migration rights in international law and European law is introduced (5.1.1). The remainder of the section concentrates on family migration policies at the EU level. It explores the dynamics surrounding the negotiations and results of the 2003 Family Reunification Directive (5.1.2), the family migration rights of European citizens (5.1.3) and the position of Turkish nationals according to the EU-Turkey Association Agreement and its subsidiary legislation (5.1.4). The second section (5.2) focuses on domestic developments in the field of spousal migration policies in recent years in selected European states, namely the Netherlands, France, Denmark, the United Kingdom, Austria and Switzerland.

5.1 The supranational dimension

5.1.1 Family migration rights within international and European law

As outlined in chapter 2, the individual right to protection and respect for family life is enshrined in various international human rights instruments.

However, a correlating universal claim to family migration cannot be deducted from this right. In her analysis of all international instruments containing references to family reunification of migrants,[126] Lahav (1997) stresses that most of these references remain at the non-binding level of recommendations. Even within these recommendations, the discretion of the nation-states to shape policies according to national interests remains strong – especially by establishing both vague definitions of "family" and "protection" and legitimising exceptions according to economic eligibility, security and welfare concerns. Furthermore, one of the international instruments most explicitly establishing a right to family reunification (in its Art. 44), the 1990 UN International Convention on the Protection of the Rights of All Migrant Workers and Members of Their Families, has not yet been ratified by any major developed destination country (Kofman & Meetoo 2008: 158). The 1989 UN Convention on the Rights of the Child, to which all UN member states except the USA are party, prohibits the separation of parents and minor children against their will (Art. 9) and recommends states to deal with family reunification applications from children or their parents in a "positive, humane and expeditous manner" (Art. 10 (1)). However, these provisions amount to recommendations rather than establishing a right to family migration, even if the convention is binding and widely regarded as authoritative (Lahav 1997: 359).

When leaving the international realm and turning towards Europe, more binding supranational treaties can be found that enshrine individuals with family migration rights. First, all forty-seven Council of Europe Member States are signatories to the European Convention on Human Rights (ECHR), which contains Article 8 protecting the right to family life. Individuals can call upon the corresponding European Court of Human Rights (ECtHR), and occasionally cases in Strasbourg concerning the right to family life have dealt with family migration issues. Until the late 1970s, the ECtHR upheld the dogma of state sovereignty over migration flows and regularly rejected the idea that restricting or denying family migration to foreign residents could

---

[126] Lahav (1997) examines the ILO Migration for Employment Convention No. 97, the ILO Migrant Worker 1975 Convention No. 143, the ILO Recommendation 86 Concerning Migration for Employment, the ILO Recommendation 151 Concerning Migrant Workers, the 1990 UN International Convention on the Protection of the Rights of All Migrant Workers and Members of Their Families and the 1989 UN Convention on the Rights of the Child.

be in breach of Article 8 ECHR, since family unity could also be established in the home country (Thym 2008). For example, in the 1985 *Abdulaziz* case[127] the ECtHR ruled that the UK's spousal migration policies were not in breach of Article 8 ECHR. However, the court ruled that the policies, which distinguished between male and female sponsors, constituted an intolerable discrimination on the basis of sex violating Article 14 ECHR. Famously, the British government reacted to the ruling with a downgrading of rights, as the more generous policies towards male sponsors were revised to match the more parsimonious rules applying to female sponsors. In 1991, the court limited state action in the field of migration for the first time by ruling an expulsion to be incompatible with the individuals' right to family life.[128] Ten years later in 2001, the *Sen* case[129] provided an important landmark in this field, as the ECtHR for the first time stipulated a positive obligation of the state to admit family members in those specific situations when it cannot be expected that family members go abroad to establish the unity of the family.[130] In 2006, the ECtHR ruled that an irregular migrant was to be granted a residence permit to the Netherlands in order to be able to be in contact with her baby daughter on the basis of Article 8 ECHR.[131] Thus, in recent years somewhat of an expansion of the ECtHR's scope in the field of family migration rules can be observed, with judgements increasingly ruling in favour of individuals' right to family life and thereby occasionally impinging upon state sovereignty in the field of migration control. Nevertheless, authors have also pointed towards the court's overall inconsistency in the application of Article 8 and its "default option" honouring state sovereignty rather than individual rights (Spijkerboer 2009) as well as its ethnicized and gendered applications of Article 8, e.g. judges being more likely to expect both ethnic minority citizen and women sponsors to follow their spouses abroad (de Hart 2009).

---

[127] ECtHR, Nos 9214/80, 9473/81 & 9474/81, *Abdulaziz, Cabales and Balkandali v The United Kingdom*, judgement of 28 May 1985.
[128] ECtHR, No 12313/86, *Moustaquim v Belgium*, judgement of 18 February 1991.
[129] ECtHR, No 31465/96, *Sen v the Netherlands*, judgement of 21 December 2001.
[130] The plaintiffs, the Turkish couple Sen, were requesting their daughter Sinem to join them in the Netherlands, but also had two further children while in Netherlands. See Spijkerboer (2009) for a detailed discussion of the case.
[131] ECtHR, No 50435/99, *Rodrigues Da Silva & Hoogkamer v the Netherlands*, judgement of 31 January 2006.

The other important supranational body granting family migration rights in Europe is the EU. Three important legal instruments exist granting family migration rights to different groups of individuals, which have been successively interpreted by the European Court of Justice (ECJ). First, since 1961 intra-EU migrants, or second-country nationals (SCNs), can rely on Community law granting them family migration rights. The very first regulation on free movement[132] specified that as part of their free movement rights, workers could bring along their spouses and children below the age of 21 to join them (Groenendijk 2006: 215). From 1968 onwards this was codified in Article 10 of Regulation 1612/68 EEC, and the only condition SCNs needed to fulfil to sponsor the migration of their spouses and children was to provide sufficient accommodation.[133] Since 2006 and until today, all SCNs can rely on the Free Movement Directive[134] containing even more extensive family migration rights, as here even the accommodation condition was scrapped and an automatic right to residence stipulated. The second group that is able to rely on EU legislation comprise Turkish nationals under the rights stipulated in EU-Turkey association law. While no direct family admission rights are codified in the different EU-Turkey association treaties, some rights can be derived by family members once admitted, such as a certain degree of residential security and access to education (Rogers 2000: 36). Furthermore, the standstill clauses included within association law have proved to be important legal instruments to contest restrictive immigration policies. Finally, the Family Reunification Directive[135] was adopted in 2003 and purportedly transposed into domestic law by 2005. Third-country nationals (TCNs) legally resident in any of the 24 signatory Member States can directly rely on the provisions of the directive enabling family migration vis-à-vis the domestic

---

[132] Regulation No. 15 of 12 June 1961, Art. 11-15, OJ 26 August 1961.
[133] Article 10(3), Regulation (EEC) No 1612/68 of the Council of 15 October 1968 on freedom of movement for workers within the Community, OJ L 257, 19 October 1968.
[134] Directive 2004/38/EC of the European Parliament and of the Council of 29 April 2004 on the right of citizens of the Union and their family members to move and reside freely within the territory of the Member States amending Regulation (EEC) No 1612/68 and repealing Directives 64/221/EEC, 68/360/EEC, 72/194/EEC, 73/148/EEC, 75/34/EEC, 75/35/EEC, 90/364/EEC, 90/365/EEC and 93/96/EEC, OJ L 158, 30 April 2004.
[135] Council Directive 2003/86/EC of 22 September 2003 on the right to family reunification, OJ L 251, 3 October 2003.

administration and judiciary. The following sections will take a closer look at the dynamics relating to these three legal instruments.

5.1.2 The 2003 Family Reunification Directive

The negotiations and Germany's position

The first impetus to devise a common European framework for family migration of TCNs can be found in the conclusions of the Tampere European Council in October 1999, where Member States agreed on and set out the principles for a harmonisation of migration policies and approximation of the status of TCNs to that of EU citizens.[136] In December 1999, very soon after the Tampere Council, the first proposal by the European Commission for a directive on family reunification emerged.[137] The entire procedure took place over an extended period; nearly four years passed from the first proposal to the final agreement by the Council of Ministers.

This first draft included rather generous family migration provisions, which has been attributed to a "liberal moment" surrounding Tampere and the opportunities seized by EU-level pro-migration NGOs to influence the content of the proposal (Kraler 2010: 37). It is important to remember that even though the Amsterdam Treaty had moved migration and asylum issues from the intergovernmental third pillar to the supranational first pillar under Title IV (Arts. 61-69) of the Treaty establishing the European Community (TEC), decision-making in large parts of the area remained intergovernmental. Article 63(3)a TEC stipulates that the Council should adopt "conditions of entry and residence, and standards on procedures for the issue by Member States of long-term visas and residence permits, including those for the purpose of family reunion." The according decision-making process is the "consultation procedure" (Art. 67 TEC). This means that legislative initiatives come from the Commission or the Member States, the European Parliament (EP) is merely consulted, and the Council takes a unanimous vote actually

---

[136] Tampere European Council 15 and 16 October 1999, Presidency Conclusions.
[137] COM (1999) 638 final, 1.12.1999, OJ 2000 C 116E/66

deciding the matter.[138] Various Member States, especially Germany, Austria and the Netherlands, considered the Commission's initial proposal to be much too liberal and requested the Commission to revise its proposal twice. The Commission's modified proposals were presented in October 2000[139] and in May 2002,[140] respectively, with the text of the directive becoming more restrictive in each version. As the United Kingdom and Ireland decided to opt out of the Family Reunification Directive, and Denmark generally does not participate in Community measures in the field of migration,[141] a total of twelve Member States were left to negotiate the intricacies of the directive.

Hauschild, who participated in the negotiations as part of the German delegation, describes the talks as primarily being divided between the German/Austrian camp on one side, and the French camp on the other (2003: 268). Rather than calling the German stance "restrictive," he describes it as being based on the highly regulated German law *("regelungsintensives deutsches Recht")*, which is only matched by Austria in its detailed differentiated position, which is why Germany and Austria find common ground. He concludes that the ability of Germany and Austria to argue for their position, on the basis of existing laws and implementation practices, in the end led these two countries to successfully push through their agenda (Hauschild 2003: 273). Hauschild further mentions two points as having been especially unacceptable for Germany in the Commission's first two proposals: First, the maximum age for incoming children (which the Commission had initially set at the age of majority of the Member States), and second, the abolition of "reverse discrimination" as envisaged by Article 4 of the first two directive proposals,[142] which would have given "static" citizens who had not made use

---

[138] With the Lisbon Treaty coming into force in December 2009, the TEC was amended and renamed the Treaty on the Functioning of the European Union (TFEU). Now, Art. 79 of the TFEU governs the conditions of immigration policy-making and stipulates that policies will be decided by the Council and the EP in accordance with "the ordinary legislative procedure." This procedure is set out in Art. 294 of the TFEU and was formerly known as the co-decision procedure, implying that decisions in the Council are made with qualified majority voting (QMV) instead of unanimity and that the EP is included in the decision-making procedure.

[139] COM (2000) 624 final, 10.10.2000, OJ 2001 C 62E/99

[140] COM (2002) 225 final, 2.05.2002, OJ 2002C 203E/136

[141] See Directive 2003/86/EC, preambles 17 and 18.

[142] COM (1999) 638 final, 1.12.1999, OJ 2000 C 116E/66. See Article 4: "The family reunification of Union citizens who do not exercise their right to free movement of persons has hitherto been subject solely to national rules. This situation generates an unwarranted difference in treatment

of their right to free movement (first-country-nationals, FCNs) exactly the same rights as intra-EU movers (SCNs). Government representative Hauschild comments: "For Germany this provision would have led to a considerable extension of reunification rights of family members of ethnic resettlers and naturalised third-country nationals" (2003: 269, my translation), underlining that the German government was especially worried about a possible liberalisation of family migration rights of German citizens with a migration background, either naturalised foreigners or ethnic resettlers. In other words, the reverse discrimination of German citizens vis-à-vis SCNs is tolerated mainly in order not to extend generous family migration provisions to ethnic minority Germans and resettlers.

The final directive

The final version of the Family Reunification Directive (FR Directive) was adopted in September 2003.[143] Compared to the ambitious first proposal made by the Commission, which would have provided a harmonised framework establishing a strong minimum standard for family migration, the final version is much more restrictive, "dealing as little as possible with legal obligations and, where necessary, introducing minimum standards below those existing in national legislation" (Lavenex 2006b: 1291). The final directive was watered down by the Council to include more than 30 optional clauses. Various national delegations wanted to ensure that their specific domestic practices would continue to be allowed, resulting in an "unintended harmonisation to the bottom" (Kraler 2010: 39).

---

between the family of Union citizens who have not exercised their right to free movement and have stayed in the country of their nationality and those who have exercised their right to free movement. National law in some circumstances regulates the family reunification of its own nationals more restrictively than Community law. As Union citizenship is indivisible, the gap must be filled. This Article accordingly allows the family members of Union citizens to enjoy the benefit of the relevant provisions of Community law in matters of family reunification."
[143] Directive 2003/86/EC of 22 September 2003, OJ 2003 L 251/12

The final directive generally grants legally resident TCN migrants[144] a right to sponsor family migration of their spouses and unmarried minor children. Children over 12 arriving independently from the remaining family may be required to fulfil an integration condition in order to be granted admission (Article 4(1)). Other family members such as dependent ascending relatives or adult children may be admitted (Article 4(2)), and in general, Member States are free to introduce or uphold more favourable provisions (Article 3(5)). Article 4(5) gives Member States the option to introduce minimum ages for both the sponsor and the incoming spouse in order to enhance integration and prevent forced marriages, but the maximum age for this is set at 21 years. The option to deny minor children over 15 years of age admission as family members is included in Article 4(6), leading Peers to comment that "while 20-year-olds could be considered too immature to get married, 15 year-olds could be considered too mature to enter as children" (Peers 2003: 403). Article 7(1) spells out the central conditions that may be required of the sponsor, that is normal accommodation, health insurance and stable and regular resources sufficient to maintain a family. Member States may also require family members to comply with integration measures according to Article 7(2), which will be further elaborated below. Moreover, an optional waiting period for the sponsor of two years (in exceptional cases even three) before granting admission to the family members is included in Article 8.

The European Parliament (EP) attempted to influence the directive in a liberal direction, but without much success since, as mentioned above, its role was more or less relegated to a consultative one. In its opinion on the final draft, the EP suggested to widen the scope of eligible family members and include individuals under subsidiary protection into the applicability of the directive.[145] More importantly, under influence of several migrant NGOs, EP members challenged three of the directive's provisions at the ECJ in December 2003. The EP argued that the optional clauses allowing integration conditions for children over 12 years, the maximum age of 16 years and the

---

[144] Article 3 states that the directive applies to TCN sponsors in possession of a residence document valid for at least one year with the prospect of permanent residence. This does not, however, apply to asylum seekers or individuals under subsidiary or temporary protection, while recognised refugees are governed by the more favourable Articles 9-12.
[145] European Parliament, Report on the amended proposal for a Council directive on the right to family reunification, FINAL A5-0086/2003, 24 March 2003.

minimum residence of sponsor, violated the right to family life and the principle of non-discrimination (see Groenendijk 2004: 120). While the ECJ rejected the EP's claim on all three points in 2006, it also used the judgement as a first important occasion to extensively interpret the FR Directive.[146] In the decision, the ECJ judges explicitly stated that the directive contains a directly enforceable subjective right to family migration for core family members, thereby providing the basis for later case law on the issue.

Article 7(2): Integration measures vs. integration conditions

Possibly the most controversial issue regarding the directive concerns the exact meaning of its Article 7(2), which in its final version states: "Member States may require third country nationals to comply with integration measures, in accordance with national law." As this paragraph was not included in any of the Commission's three proposals, it is clear that the main impetus came from the national delegations of some Member States, specifically from Germany, Austria and the Netherlands (Hauschild 2003: 271).

As elaborated by Groenendijk (2006: 224), in the negotiations on the FR Directive and also the Long-Term Residents Directive,[147] large disagreement arose among the Member States regarding the provisions on integration. As a compromise, a specific distinction was drawn between "integration measures" and "integration conditions," with an understanding that the latter include much higher burdens than the former. According to Groenendijk, the Member States agreed that "integration measures" mean that certain efforts can be expected from the migrant, who can also be obliged to participate in integration or language courses. However, "integration measures" do not imply passing tests or obtaining certain levels of test results as a condition for admission. This would come under the rubric of "integration conditions."

In this interpretation of Article 7(2), language requirements conditioning the admission of spouses, such as those introduced by the Netherlands and Germany, would be classified as being in breach of the FR Di-

---

[146] ECJ, Case C-540/03, *European Parliament v Council*, 27 June 2006.
[147] Council Directive 2003/109/EC of 25 November 2003 concerning the status of third-country nationals who are long-term residents, OJ L 16, 23 January 2004.

rective. However, another sentence was also introduced into Article 7(2) at the proposal of the Dutch delegation: "With regard to the refugees and/or family members of refugees referred to in Article 12 the integration measures referred to in the first subparagraph may only be applied once the persons concerned have been granted family reunification." This seems to imply that family members reuniting with sponsors other than refugees may very well be subject to participate in measures before admission. In any case, Groenendijk (2006: 225) has seriously questioned the lawfulness of basing the admission directly on a specific language level test result, considering the principles laid out in the FR Directive.

The European Commission has not been silent on this issue either. In a statement issued in 2011 in the context of the *Bibi Mohammed* case[148] concerning an Afghan woman requesting entry into the Netherlands, the Commission clearly stated that it considered the Dutch language requirement to be incompatible with the FR Directive's Article 7(2).[149] In particular, the Commission reiterated the difference between "integration conditions" and "integration measures." According to the Commission, only one case is specified in the FR Directive that allows Member States to make admission dependent upon the fulfilment of "integration conditions," namely Article 4(1) referring to children aged over 12. For all other family members, "integration measures" according to Article 7(2) may lead to certain obligations, but under no circumstances can the sole failure to fulfil an integration test abroad lead to the rejection of admission. In 2015, the ECJ finally evaluated the compatibility of integration abroad requirements with Article 7(2) in the *K and A* case,[150] ruling that in principle, such requirements are permissible, as long as they aim at facilitating integration and not "systemically prevent" family reunification or make it "impossible or excessively difficult." The court made clear that "special individual circumstances, such as age, illiteracy, level of education, economic situation or health" must be taken into consideration when evaluating whether incoming family members can be subjected to integration abroad requirements.

---

[148] ECJ, Case C-155/11 PPU, *Bibi Mohammad Imran v. Minister van Buitenlandse Zaken*, order of 10 June 2011.
[149] Document Sj.g (2011) 540657, 4 May 2011
[150] ECJ, Case C 153/14, *Minister van Buitenlandse Zaken v. K and A*, judgement of 9 July 2015.

Income requirements

In the *Chakroun* case in March 2010, the ECJ was asked to give a statement regarding both the income requirement set at 120 per cent of the minimum national wage and the distinction made in the law between family relationships arising before and after the sponsor's migration into the EU Member State.[151] The Moroccan plaintiff, Chakroun, had immigrated to the Netherlands in 1972 and married his wife two years later. When she decided to join him in 2006, the Dutch authorities had denied her a spousal residence permit since Mr. Chakroun did not earn an income equivalent to 120 per cent of the minimum wage. Since 2004, sponsors marrying after migrating ("family formation") needed to provide 120 per cent of the minimum income; in cases of "family reunification" the minimum income (100 per cent) was considered sufficient. Even though the Chakrouns had been married for 32 years before Ms. Chakroun applied for admission to the Netherlands, their application was considered one of family formation. The ECJ considered both aspects of the policy to run counter to the objectives of the FR Directive. The Dutch government was thus forced to revoke these two conditions of the law on family reunification. It was announced, however, that the government would continue to evaluate the possibilities for stricter measures in the field of family reunification, including a potential ban on marriages between cousins or a minimum education requirement (Van de Water 2010).

5.1.3 The Free Movement Directive

As mentioned earlier, the rights of EU citizens who legally reside in another Member State and wish to reunite with their TCN spouses are spelled out in Directive 2004/38/EC, the so-called Free Movement Directive. The Free Movement Directive bestows the right to free movement (that is, admission and residence) on Union citizens and their family members. The directive's Article 2 defines the family members falling under the scope of the directive to include spouses, registered partners, children of the sponsor or spouse under 21 and all dependent children or ascending relatives. The rights of

---

[151] ECJ, Case C-517/08, *Chakroun v. Ministerie van Buitenlandse Zaken*, judgement of 4 March 2010.

family members include a right to enter the Member State to which the Union citizen has moved (Art. 5(1)), and the right to reside with the Union citizen in that Member State for a period of up to three months without any conditions or formalities other than a valid passport (Art. 6(2)). Article 7(2) stipulates that family members are entitled to extended residence as long as the sponsor has the status of a worker, self-employed person or job seeker. They also qualify if they have sufficient resources to support the family.

These family migration rights are by far the most extensive rights awarded to any of the three groups mentioned earlier (SCNs, Turkish citizens and TCNs). In many cases, these rights also exceed what Member States grant to their own citizens (FCNs), leading to a situation of "reverse discrimination" (Walter 2008). While the Commission's initial proposal of the FR Directive contained an article prohibiting reverse discrimination, as elaborated earlier, it was soon met by resistance from Member States, including Germany, and was not included in the final version of the FR Directive. Thus, reverse discrimination, i.e. a better legal position for SCNs than FCNs in the field of family migration, continues to exist in most EU countries. Indeed, the question of how far EU citizen rights can be activated in "internal situations," involving no crossing of borders, has become especially salient in relation to intra-EU movers being in a more favourable legal position than non-movers.

In July 2008, the ECJ ruled in the *Metock* case[152] that the 2004 Free Movement Directive cannot be reconciled with the condition that the TCN spouse must have been legally resident in another Member State prior to joining the SCN spouse. This had been the specific question posed by the Irish courts submitting the case to the ECJ. In general, the ECJ underlines at various points throughout the ruling that Member States are not permitted to impose further requirements on incoming spouses in order to ensure full free movement rights of the Union citizen, meaning that demanding integration requirements abroad of spouses of these families is also not compatible with EU law (Dienelt 2008; Hofmann 2008). This ruling cemented the privileged position of SCNs in the field of family migration rights over non-moving FCNs: "The irony of *Metock* is that the more the Court invests in the en-

---

[152] ECJ, Case C-127/08, *Metock and others v. Minister for Justice, Equality and Law Reform*, judgement of 13 September 2008. See Lansbergen (2009) for an extensive overview of the case and its implications.

hancement of citizenship rights, the greater the gap between migrant and non-migrant citizens grows" (Lansbergen 2009: 295).

Member States reacted critically to the ECJ's ruling in *Metock*. The German government stated that the post-*Metock* interpretation of the directive is "likely to lead to abusive practices, such as marriages of convenience with EU citizens in order to bypass national provisions concerning family reunification" (Deutscher Bundestag, Drucksache 16/11821: 8). In Denmark, the government reaction was similarly negative. While the right-wing populist Danish People's Party suggested that the country should not implement the *Metock* ruling into Danish law at all, the government decided to transpose the consequences of the judgement but at the same time uphold Danish immigration policy principles and work towards amending the Free Movement Directive in order to fight the potential "negative consequences" that follow from *Metock* (Ersbøll 2010: 125). Lansbergen (2009: 292) suggests that as a reaction to *Metock*, countries such as Denmark and the UK have been tightening up measures in the field where the Free Movement Directive explicitly grants Member States the discretion to restrict the admission and residence to (the family members of) SCNs. This is the case when this is justifiable on the grounds of public policy, public security or public health (Art. 27), and in order to fight cases of fraud or marriages of convenience (Art. 35).

The ECJ has also touched upon the possibility of activating Union citizens' rights in purely internal situations. In the *Zambrano* case[153] the judges implied that Union citizens who had never exercised their right to free movement could also access EU citizenship rights. The case concerned a family from Colombia in Belgium. While the parents' residence status was precarious and they had difficulties regarding their access to the labour market and social welfare, two children were born into Belgian citizenship. The ECJ ruled that in this completely "internal situation," the minor children could rely on Article 20 of the TFEU, granting EU citizenship rights, to preclude "national measures which have the effect of depriving citizens of the Union of the genuine enjoyment of the substance of the rights conferred by virtue of their status as citizens of the Union" (*Zambrano*, paragraph 42). In other words, the parents were ruled to be issued residence and work permits, since otherwise the children would have been forced to leave the EU.

---

[153] ECJ, Case C-34/09, *Ruiz Zambrano v. Office national de l'emploi*, judgement of 8 March 2011.

This ruling caused huge commotion. Would *Zambrano* imply an end to reverse discrimination in the field of family migration, since all FCNs could rely on the rights granted to SCNs by the Free Movement Directive by similarly invoking Article 20 of the TFEU? Only two months later, the ECJ evaluated the case of Shirley McCarthy, a dual Irish-UK national living (and having lived all her life) in the UK.[154] She was trying to invoke the Free Movement Directive to have her Jamaican spouse join her in the UK. Here, the ECJ decided that in contrast to the children in *Zambrano*, Ms. McCarthy was not being deprived of any "genuine enjoyment of the substance of rights associated with her status as a Union citizen" by the national decision (to not grant her husband admission). While the Zambrano children would have had to leave the EU had their parents been forced out of Belgium, this did not hold for Ms. McCarthy, according to the ECJ. In other words, the needs and according rights of children to be with their parents were judged to be much stronger than those of spouses to be together. Accordingly, for the time being, reverse discrimination in the field of spousal migration persists.

Reverse discrimination has also led to the phenomenon of citizen sponsors moving (temporarily or permanently) to another EU Member State in order to gain access to the family migration rights of SCNs. Once the sponsors have lived in another EU state for a certain period, their EU citizenship is "activated" and they can also move back to their home country with their spouses without needing to fulfil more restrictive family migration conditions that normally apply to domestic citizens (Bundesregierung 2009: 220). Especially common is relocation to a neighbouring state, particularly from those states with restrictive family migration policies, such as the Netherlands and Denmark (see section 5.2). Accordingly, concepts such as the "Belgian route" or the "EU-Route," referring to Dutch sponsors relocating to Belgium, and the "love train," referring to Danish sponsors commuting across the Öresund Bridge from Malmö in Sweden to their jobs in Copenhagen (Rubin 2004: 319), have been established. In these two countries, media and even parliamentary attention has been devoted to the issue.[155] The ECJ has over the years issued a couple of rulings that affirm the possibilities of

---

[154] ECJ, Case C-434/09, Shirley McCarthy v. Secretary of State for the Home Department, judgement of 5 May 2011.
[155] See e.g. Spoeddebat over de zogenaamde "Europe-Route," Tweede Kamer, 46, pp. 4007-4026, 27 January 2009.

FCNs to avail themselves of EU legislation after returning home from another EU country. The 1992 *Singh* case[156] established that free movement rights applied to intra-EU workers returning to their home countries, while the 2003 *Akrich* ruling[157] stated that the intentional use of free movement in order to profit from EU legislation on family migration in itself is not relevant to the evaluation of the legal situation, as long as the marriage is a genuine one (Ersbøll 2010: 125).

5.1.4 Turkish citizens' rights under association law

Association law enshrining certain rights for Turkish workers is made up of various legal instruments. Next to the original (Ankara) Association Agreement of 1963,[158] there is an Additional Protocol from 1970[159] and three further decisions of the Association Council regarding the free movement of workers, namely Decision 2/76, Decision 1/80 and Decision 3/80. While no direct family admission rights are allocated within association law, some rights can be derived by family members once admitted, such as access to residential security and to education (Rogers 2000: 36). In recent years, the standstill clauses (Art. 41(1) of the Additional Protocol and Art. 13 of Association Decision 1/80), stating that no "new restrictions" regarding labour market access for Turkish nationals may be introduced in EU Member States than those in place when the agreements were signed, have particularly grown in importance as they offer "strong protection from new restrictive immigration policies" (Groenendijk 2006: 216).

For a long time, the rights conferred on Turkish nationals within association law were ignored, with Member States largely assuming "association law to be incomplete in the sense that no individual rights could be in-

---

[156] ECJ, Case C-370/90, The Queen v. Immigration Appeal Tribunal and Surinder Singh, judgement of 7 July 1992.
[157] ECJ, Case C-109/01, Secretary of state for the Home Department v. Hacene Akrich, judgement of 23 September 2003.
[158] Agreement establishing an Association between the European Economic Community and Turkey of 12 September 1963, approved by Council Decision 64/732/EEC of 23 December 1963, OJ 217, 29 December 1964.
[159] Additional Protocol and Financial Protocol signed on 23 November 1970, OJ L 293, 29 December 1972.

ferred from the Council's decisions" (Hailbronner & Katsantonis 1992: 57). Starting in the late 1980s however, an activist ECJ started to implement the provisions through its judgements (Guiraudon 2000b: 1110) by specifying and interpreting the rules laid down in association law in a total of 45 judgements between 1987 and 2010 (Groenendijk & Guild 2010: 51). Moreover, regarding the recent restrictive shift of family migration policies across Europe, certain judgements at both the EU and the domestic levels have had liberalising effects.

In the *Soysal* case[160] in February 2009, the ECJ ruled that Turkish citizens who want to either provide or make use of services could enter Germany without a prior visa according to the law in place at the time of the Turkey-EU Association Agreement in 1973. The full consequences of this ruling, especially for the implementation of the language requirement in cases involving Turkish spouses, were contested. In Germany, the Left Party (Dagdelen 2009), and even the police's migration law experts (Westphal & Stoppa 2009: 1), claimed that the ruling led to immediate "visa freedom" for Turkish citizens for sojourns up to three months. Importantly for spouses, this could allow them to attend a German language course in Germany. The Federal Ministry of the Interior however, claimed the ruling to only be relevant "for a very limited group of people" (Thieme 2009).

While earlier interpretations always regarded the standstill clause to only be applicable to labour market access once admission is granted, in April 2010, the ECJ ruled in the case *Commission v. Netherlands*[161] that initial admission policies are also subject to the standstill clause.[162] In late 2010, the ECJ decided on the standstill clause yet again in the *Toprak* case,[163] ruling that it must be interpreted in a dynamic way. This meant that restrictive changes to liberalisations introduced after 1980 also amount to "new restrictions" that are thus not compatible with the standstill clause. The ECJ also stated that not only new restrictions directly have an effect on the free movement of

---

[160] ECJ, Case C-228/06, Mehmet Soysal and others v. Bundesrepublik Deutschland, judgement of 19 February 2009.
[161] ECJ, Case C-92/07, European Commission v. Kingdom of the Netherlands, judgement of 29 April 2010.
[162] Paragraphs 49 and 50 of Case C-92/07
[163] ECJ, Joined Cases C-300/09 and C-301/09, *Staatssecretaris van Justitie v. F. Toprak and I. Oguz*, Judgement of the Court (Second Chamber), 9 December 2010

workers where incompatible with the standstill clause, but also measures indirectly affecting it.

The Left Party introduced this judgement into the German political debate by suggesting that various migration policy instruments might constitute "new restrictions" incompatible with the standstill clause.[164] Instruments such as the spousal language requirement, visa regulations and raised fees, and particularly the increased probationary period for spouses of three years (which had been lowered from four to two years in 2000, which meant that the minimum residence would thus not be more restrictive than it was in 1980) would therefore not be applicable to Turkish citizens. In its answers, the government affirmed that Turkish spouses (at least those gainfully employed at the time of the dissolution of their marriage to the sponsor) would be exempted from the increase from two to three years of minimum residence enshrined in § 31 AufenthG.[165] An according evaluation by the Scientific Service of the *Bundestag* also interpreted new restrictions on spousal migration, such as the language and age requirements, to be incompatible with the standstill clauses of association law (Schröder: 2011: 14). The German government, however, defended the viewpoint that, beyond § 31 AufenthG, no other implications of the *Toprak* decision were discernible.

In August 2011, the Dutch Administrative High Court (*Centrale Raad van Beroep,* CRvB), ruled that obliging Turkish migrants to participate in integration courses (*inburgeringsplicht*) was incompatible with the standstill clauses of association law.[166] Since a failure to pass a certain level could result in a revocation of residence permits, this policy constituted a new restriction regarding the security of residence, which is included in the standstill clause. Even though the decision did not directly touch upon the topic of spousal migration, it did affect it, since Article 16(1)h of the Dutch Foreigners Law *(Vreemdelingenwet)* states that the integration abroad requirement only holds for those TCNs that are obliged to follow an integration course in the Netherlands. Accordingly, in the declaration following the judgement, the Dutch

---

[164] Deutscher Bundestag, Drucksache 17/4317, 20 December 2010; Deutscher Bundestag, Drucksache 17/5539, 12 April 2011.
[165] Deutscher Bundestag, Drucksache 17/4623, 2 February 2011; Deutscher Bundestag, Drucksache 17/5884, 23 May 2011.
[166] Centrale Raad van Beroep, LJN: BR4959, 10/5248 INBURG + 10/5249 INBURG + 10/6123 INBURG + 10/6124 INBURG, 16 August 2011.

Interior Ministry stated that the integration abroad requirement was not applicable to Turkish citizens anymore either.[167]

In July 2014 then, the ECJ dealt with the compatibility of family migration restrictions, specifically with the German language requirement for spouses, with the standstill clause in the *Dogan* case.[168] The plaintiff was a Turkish woman seeking reunification with her husband, a Turkish entrepreneur with an unlimited residence permit in Germany. The embassy in Ankara had not granted her a reunification visa due to her lack of German skills. The judges did not argue that incoming family migrants themselves are protected by the standstill clause, but rather ruled that by restricting his family members from joining the economically active Turkish sponsor in Germany German policy infringed as "new restriction" upon his freedom of establishment, since he might have to choose between his economic activity in a EU state and living with his family in Turkey. The court further considered the German government's reasoning behind the language requirement, since it conceded new restrictions to indeed be allowed in order to achieve another objective of "overriding public interest." However, the ECJ considered the language requirement to "go beyond what is necessary" to achieve the goal of preventing forced marriages and promoting integration, at least if the "absence of evidence of sufficient linguistic knowledge automatically leads to the dismissal of the application for family reunification, without account being taken of the specific circumstances of each case." Also with this judgement, its exact consequences for implementation have been disputed. While the Left party claims the judgement to prohibit demanding language requirements from any spouses joining Turkish sponsors falling under association law, the government has announced to implement the judgement by merely establishing more generous hardship rules for these spouses.[169] Apparently, the European Commission has taken this (lack of) implementation

---

[167] Brief van de minister van Binnenlandse Zaken en Koninkrijksrelaties, mede namens de minister voor Immigratie en Asiel, over de gevolgen van de uitspraak van de Centrale Raad van Beroep (CRvB) van 16 augustus 2011 (LJN: BR4959), 23 September 2011. Available at http://www.rijksoverheid.nl/bestanden/documenten-en-publicaties/kamerstukken/2011/09/23/kamerbrief-wet-inburgering-buitenland/brief-wet-inburgering-buitenland.pdf
[168] ECJ, Case C-138/13, *Naime Dogan v. Bundesrepublik Deutschland*, judgement of 10 July 2014.
[169] Deutscher Bundestag, *Drucksache 18/4598*, p. 2; p. 11.

of the ruling as reason to initiative infringement proceedings against the German government[170].

In summary, three dynamics regarding family migration rights at the European level can be highlighted as particularly important. First, rather than the EU having established a strong catalogue of family migration rights upon which individuals living in the Union can rely, a tremendous stratification of rights is discernible. Depending on the legal status of the sponsor as FCN, SCN, TCN or Turkish citizen, different legal dynamics can unfold regarding family migration. Among the most paradoxical of these dynamics is surely the reverse discrimination of FCNs vis-à-vis SCNs regarding their family migration rights. Second, despite the ambitious proposals initially made by the Commission, the FR Directive has led to little harmonisation across the Member States, let alone liberalisation of family migration in Europe. Rather, the FR negotiations were marked by a race to the bottom and the ambition of various Member States, such as Austria, the Netherlands and Germany, to codify their national restrictive preferences at the EU level, albeit by way of optional clauses. Thirdly, a very significant judicial liberal constraint is observable regarding EU family migration law. While the Commission and the EP have been comparatively toothless in their fight for an expansion of family migration rights, the ECtHR and the ECJ have been instrumental in expansively interpreting the family migration rights as protected by the ECHR and Community law. The ECJ has ruled on the rights of SCNs (e.g. in *Metock)*, Turkish citizens (e.g. in *Dogan*), other TCNs (e.g. in *Chakroun*) and even, in the specific case of minor children, for FCNs (in *Zambrano*). Also, domestic courts, such as the CRvB in the Netherlands, have acted as a liberal corrective to restrictive family migration policies by applying EU law. The remainder of chapter 5 will focus on some of the specific developments in the field of spousal migration policies in different European states.

---

[170] Pilotverfahren Nummer 2012/3395, see Deutscher Bundestag, *Drucksache 18/4598*, p. 16.

5.2 Spousal migration policies in other European states 2005-2010

From the mid-2000s onwards, spousal migration was increasingly problematised and subject of heightened political and legislative attention in various European countries. In many places, policies grew more restrictive, partly also inspired by developments in other states. In the following, the most important spousal migration policy developments from about 2005-2010 in selected European countries are described so as to situate the German developments in this time period within a wider European picture.

5.2.1 The Netherlands

In many respects, the Netherlands can be described as having played a pioneering role regarding immigration and integration policies in Europe. Being heralded as an epitome of "multiculturalism" and famed for its tolerant policies regarding migration in the 1980s and 1990s, the past decade witnessed a retreat from these policies in part due to the rise of right-wing populist figures such as Pim Fortuyn and Geert Wilders. Nowadays, Dutch immigration and integration policies are among the toughest in Europe. These restrictive policies seem to have inspired other states to follow suit: "The Netherlands has set an example to other EU Member States in devising measures to integrate immigrants not as a goal in itself, but as part of a restrictive migration policy" (Besselink 2009: 241). In how far the Dutch policies functioned as a role model within the policy-making and framing processes in the case of Germany will be explored further in chapter 6.

In November 2004, in the course of the implementation of the FR Directive, the conditions for family migration were tightened. The law differentiated between "family formation" *(gezinsvorming)*, in which the family relationship (e.g. marriage) is formed while the sponsor is living in the Netherlands, and "family reunification" *(gezinshereniging)*, defined by a family relationship that existed before the sponsor entered the Netherlands. Since the criteria for family formation were established to be more restrictive than those for family reunification, the Dutch government indirectly gave preference to spouses of (new) migrants over spouses joining Dutch citizens or foreigners having lived all their life or a substantial part of it in the Netherlands. This is remarkable, since as outlined in chapter 2, from a normative point of view, the claim to the protection of marriage and family can be considered to be stronger in the case of established members of the community, such as long-term residents but also Dutch citizens. The minimum age for family formation was set at 21 years for both partners (family reunification: 18 years) and the income requirement set at 120 per cent of the minimum wage, amounting to € 1,441 net per month (family reunification: 100 per cent, € 1,201 net). Here, measures regulating social membership disproportionately affected more rooted members of Dutch society. This was a clear departure from the traditional preferential treatment of citizens regarding family migration.

In December 2005, on the initiative of the Minister of Foreigners' Matters and Integration Verdonk, the Act on Civic Integration Abroad[171] (*Wet inburgering in het buitenland,* WIB) was passed by the Dutch parliament and came into force in March 2006, making the Netherlands the first EU Member State to introduce a substantive integration abroad requirement. According to this act, which is an insertion of a new provision into the 2000 Aliens Act (*Vreemdelingenwet*), applicants for spousal migration joining both TCN foreign residents and Dutch citizens (not those joining asylum seekers however) have to pass an integration exam abroad in order to be granted clearance to enter the Netherlands. The integration exam tests oral language skills (listening and speaking skills) equivalent to level A1 (minus) according to the CEFR, and knowledge of Dutch society, including "elementary practical knowledge" on issues such as housing and education alongside "rights and duties of migrants and citizens in the Netherlands and the accepted norms in everyday life and in society" (Strik et al. 2010: 16). It is important to note that only migrants from countries who need a visa in order to enter the Netherlands have to pass the test. Accordingly, citizens from EU/EEA countries, Australia, Canada, Japan, Monaco, New Zealand, South Korea, Switzerland and the USA are exempted from successfully completing the test before being granted entry. As mentioned in chapter 4, a very similar exemption for TCNs from highly industrialised countries found entry into the German law in 2007 as well. The tests, which cost the applicant €350, are orchestrated by remote computer programmes which are accessed via a telephone in a Dutch

---

[171] Wet van 22 december 2005 tot wijziging van de Vreemdelingenwet 2000 in verband met het stellen van een inburgeringsvereiste bij het toelaten van bepaalde categoriëen vreemdelingen.

embassy or consulate general. Passing the test is an essential requirement in order to first obtain the visa and later the residence permit on family migration grounds (Besselink 2009: 246).

When comparing the framing employed by the Dutch government relating to their integration abroad policy with those dominant in other European settings, the strong emphasis on selection and restriction is striking. For instance, of the four reasons brought forward to justify integration abroad, only one really deals with the empowering potential of language skills. The government stated that integration abroad would firstly help spouses manage in the Netherlands immediately after arrival; secondly, enable them to make a more enlightened choice to migrate to the Netherlands; thirdly, improve the consciousness of migrants and their families of their responsibility to integrate; and fourthly, "work as a 'selection mechanism': [since] only those with the 'motivation and perseverance' necessary to integrate successfully in the Netherlands would be admitted" (Bonjour 2010: 304). The strong emphasis on the integration abroad requirement as a tool of migrant selection is striking. Responsible policy-makers explicitly stated that the restrictions to be indeed aimed at reducing low-educated spousal migration, especially from Muslim countries, as a solution to integration problems: "A reduction of the inflow of migrants whose integration in the Netherlands can be expected to lag behind will alleviate the problem of integration" (Dutch government as quoted in Bonjour 2010: 306). At the same time, spouses of high-skilled migrants were portrayed to be an asset for Dutch society, as exemplified by a letter sent by various ministers to the parliament in October 2009:[172]

One quarter of the spousal migrants that take the integration exam abroad is not sufficiently educated to be able to take part in Dutch society. The inflow of these low-educated migrants has detrimental consequences for their integration, and the upbringing and education of their children. (...) A part of spousal migration proceeds without huge problems. Those that come out of an environment with an international orientation, such as spouses of highly-skilled migrants, generally find their way without any difficulty and contribute to the dynamics of the Netherlands as a knowledge country. We

---

[172] Kamerstuk 32175, Nr. 1. Brief van de Minister voor Wonen, Wijken en Integratie, de Minister Van Justitie en de Staatssecretaris van Justitie. Kabinetsaanpak huwelijks- en gezinsmigratie, 2 October 2009.

instead see difficulties regarding the completely dependent and low-educated (spousal) partners from Southeast Asia, Morocco and Turkey, and with the follow-up migration from countries such as Iraq and Somalia.

Another aspect that distinguished the Dutch debate from that in France and Germany at the time was the large cross-party consensus regarding both the "diagnosis" of the integration problems emanating from the migration of spouses, especially low-skilled Muslim ones, and the proposed "therapy" in the form of the integration abroad requirement. Specifically, the Left opposition, which was outspoken against the language requirement in France and Germany, supported the government's plans in the Netherlands. Except for the green party *GroenLinks*, no party, not even the Socialist SP, opposed the introduction of the WIB in principle[173] (Bonjour 2010: 309).

After an evaluation report published in 2007 revealed that the pass rate of the integration exam abroad was as high as 90 per cent, the government decided to raise the pass limit from 15 March 2008 onwards. Additionally, the required language level was raised to A1 and literacy and reading tests were introduced from April 2011. Criticism was raised regarding the lack of Dutch learning facilities abroad, making the new exam standard especially difficult to fulfil for illiterates and spouses with a non-Latin alphabet. These criticisms were regularly rejected with an emphasis instead being placed on the responsibility of the migrant to take note of integration in this regard and the availability of special education packages (Strik et al. 2010: 25-27). In general, the test led to a significant reduction in applications for family migration visas. With the pass rates being quite high (88 per cent pass in their first attempt), the pre-selection could thus be assumed to have a marked effect. While in 2004, 29,000 long-term stay visas were applied for, in 2006 the number had halved to 14,500 (Besselink 2009: 246) further dropped further to 12,105 in 2007 (Strik et al. 2010: 28).

Since little controversy existed within the political class of the Netherlands on the necessity for these restrictive measures, the most important liberal constraint observable was a judicial one. As mentioned above, both domestic and European courts have constrained the Dutch lawmakers on

---

[173] However, the SP did withhold their final support of the WIB bill, but only since they were not convinced of the computer testing technology (Bonjour 2010: 309).

various occasions in their restrictive family migration policies. For instance, the distinction between family formation and family reunification and the particularly high income requirement were overruled by the ECJ in its *Chakroun* ruling. In March 2010, the Dutch council of ministers agreed to change the law in accordance with the ruling and eliminate the legal difference made between the groups. The income requirement was set to 100 per cent of the minimum wage for all cases of spousal migration (this had basically been mandated by the ECJ), thus levelling up transnational couples' rights. However, by setting the minimum age at 21, rights were also levelled down at the same time. In the accompanying press release, the government made it clear that it was dissatisfied with the court's decision and would only implement "the minimum necessary changes in order to obey the Court's judgement." (Rijksoverheid 2010, my translation). It worried that the lowered income requirement would lead to an expansion of spousal migration, which was the stated reason for increasing the age limit. Also, the minister announced that the requirements for the integration test abroad would be bolstered.

Additionally, domestic Dutch courts implemented Turkish' citizens rights according to association law. As mentioned above, in August 2011 the Administrative High Court ruled obliging Turkish citizens to participate in integration measures to be incompatible with the standstill clauses enshrined within association law, since their residence permit was made dependent upon successful participation. This also resulted in a parallel waiver of the integration abroad requirement for Turkish spouses, something that did not happen in a parallel way in Germany, regardless of the *Dogan* judgement.

5.2.2 France

With Interior Minister Nicolas Sarkozy famously calling for a shift away from endured migration *("immigration subie")* towards selected migration *("immigration choisie")* in 2006, several parameters changed in the previously comparatively generous French family migration policies. In 2006, a migration law change[174] restricted some of the conditions pertinent to foreign sponsors. All of these changes involved instances of regulating social member-

---

[174] Loi 2006-911 relative à l'immigration et à l'intégration, 24 July 2006.

ship, since the criteria that sponsors needed to fulfil in order to lay claim to their right to marriage and family were tightened. The law increased the minimum time period a foreign sponsor needed to reside in France prior to being able to sponsor spousal migration, from 12 to 18 months. Furthermore, it installed an income requirement for foreign sponsors (amounting to the minimum wage), alongside a new condition that sponsors needed to provide adequate housing. In addition, a separate law[175] was passed later that year with the purpose of fighting marriages of convenience by subjecting marriages concluded abroad to the same requirements as marriages in France.

Only one year later, another migration law amendment was agreed upon in late 2007 and entered into force on 1 January 2008.[176] This change further increased the income requirement by demanding that an income "proportional to the size of the family" must be proven. The minimum wage was considered sufficient for a family up to three, but for larger families more income had to be proven (Kofman et al. 2010: 20). Parents sponsoring the immigration of their children needed to sign a contract of reception and integration (*contrat d'accueil et d'integration pour la famille*, CAIF), ensuring that they will follow a course on "the rights and duties of parents in France" and take care of their children's schooling. Most pertinently, an integration requirement for family migrants prior to admission was introduced as well.

As Bonjour (2010) has shown, the parliamentary debates surrounding the campaigns to introduce such a requirement in the Netherlands and France were largely similar in the way they framed issues relating to migration, integration and social cohesion. In both countries parliamentarians "fear that, as a result of past and present immigration flows and failing immigrant integration, their societies are disintegrating into distinct, isolated, even hostile groups" (Bonjour 2010: 301). However, the policy instruments chosen differ in fundamental ways. In the French integration-abroad-policy, knowledge of basic French and knowledge of French Republican values in the applicant's own language are first evaluated. In case of insufficiency, the applicant must follow a pertinent course, which is organised and offered by a governmental agency and is free of charge. Final admission to France is not dependent on passing a certain test but only on sufficient participation in the

---

[175] Loi 2006-1376 relative au controle de la validité des marriages, 14 November 2006.
[176] Loi 2007-1631 relative à la maîtrise de l'immigration, à l'integration et à l'asile, 20 November 2007.

course (Bonjour 2010: 303). This model of integration abroad, which includes state-financed language courses on a worldwide scale, is somewhat different from the "privatisation of integration measures" (Michalowski 2009) with a significant emphasis being placed on the incoming migrants' own responsibility to develop their integrative capacities as enforced in countries as Germany and the Netherlands. It also lacks the restrictive and selective inclination, as no migrants are actually denied admission solely due to not passing an exam. Even though in the initial phases of the policy process in 2006, right-wing French policy-makers had suggested to introduce an integration test as a pre-condition for admission modelled on the Dutch, Danish and German policies, the final policy adopted was much more lenient as it proscribed participation and not the achievement of a certain result (Bonjour 2010: 312).

One possible explanation for the establishment of this rather moderate type of integration-abroad measure is the constitutional protection of the right to family migration in France. This protection was established in 1978 by the *Conseil d'Etat* declaring the right to lead a normal family life to be a general legal principle whilst repealing all-too harsh family migration provisions (Weil 1991). Accordingly, when MPs of the governing centre-right party UMP proposed amendments to include provisions into the law by requiring family migrants to not only pass a certain test level in order to be granted admission, but also pay for the courses and the evaluation themselves, the government advised against it. The government primarily cited the danger of the Constitutional Court "censoring" such a measure as infringing upon the right to family life as the explanation for following this course of action (Bonjour 2010: 313).

The importance of domestic legal principles for the expansion and maintenance of basic rights in the context of migration (Joppke 2001) is one factor explaining the divergent path taken by the French government. However, when analysing the impact of such "judicial liberal constraints," possibly not only the mere presence or absence of legal principles is important, but also their application. In her comparison of the policy processes instituting integration abroad instruments in France and the Netherlands, both equally bound by the legal norms established in the ECHR and the FR Directive, Bonjour (2010: 316) has pointed towards the importance of both the strength of judicial review – that is, how courts deal with politics, and the political judicial risk aversion – that is, how politics deal with courts. She shows that Dutch courts traditionally do not review the constitutional compatibility of legislation while this process is institutionalised in France. Furthermore, she argues that while the responsible policy-makers in the Netherlands publicly stated that they were consciously taking the risk of being overruled by European courts, the French government was much more cautious and preferred to pre-empt such judicial confrontation, possibly also due to the larger controversy and opposition surrounding the issue in France (Bonjour 2010: 317).

On a different note, in late 2009 the Minister for Immigration and National Identity, Eric Besson, launched a campaign against so-called *"mariages gris."* Contrary to the notion of consensual marriages of convenience *("mariages blancs")*, the minister defined *mariages gris* as "sentimental fraud with the goal of migration," which meant marriages where the sponsoring partner was unaware of the incoming spouse's true motivations (Fassin et al. 2009). However, apart from establishing a working group on the issue, no further legal or political steps were taken (Kofman et al. 2010: 25).

5.2.3 Denmark

As early as 2002, Denmark introduced an age requirement into spousal migration laws; both the incoming and sponsoring spouses must be at least 24 years of age.[177] Within Europe, this was both the earliest instance of such a policy and remains, today, the oldest minimum age for spousal migration legally installed. This is possible since Denmark opted out of EU cooperation on visa, asylum and migration issues since the 1992 Edinburgh Agreement; otherwise the age threshold of 24 years would be in breach of Article 4(5) of the FR Directive. This age requirement is a drastic type of family regulating, since it establishes that unions of individuals aged 18-23 are not full-fledged marriages that do not endow the spouses with all the rights granted to older spouses.

Another Danish policy instrument mentioned earlier is the so-called "attachment requirement." This is an example of regulating membership via quality, since sponsors and incoming spouses must actually demonstrate

---

[177] See § 9.1. Aliens (Consolidation) Act (Udlændingeloven), No. 808 of 8 July 2008.

their membership in the Danish community. Since 2002, in order to qualify for spousal migration, the (Danish or TCN) sponsor and the incoming spouse, together, must have a "greater combined attachment" to Denmark than to any other country. For the sponsor, this means that he/she must have legally resided in Denmark for at least 15 years (this was lowered to 12 years in 2012), and "made an effort to integrate into Danish society" (Danish Immigration Service 2015b). This minimum residence time can be lowered, where a "special effort to integrate" has been displayed by the sponsor, which basically means that the sponsor has continuously held a full-time job speaking Danish to colleagues and/or customers for 8-9 years. The residence requirement can be lowered in exceptional circumstances if the sponsor has been continuously employed in a position for 5-6 years that is considered to be "particularly integration-furthering," which basically relates to a job in which a high level of spoken or written Danish is required (2015b). Having completed an education lasting at least three years in Denmark and having subsequently worked in a job employing the acquired skills for 2-3 years can also reduce the residence requirement. The incoming spouses need to prove their attachment to Denmark by two prior visits to Denmark (lowered to one visit in 2012), or legal residence in Denmark. For a brief period from 2010 to 2012, additionally, a points system was in place for spousal migrants, with points awarded for language skills, residence, education and employment (for details see Wray 2013: 241).

This attachment requirement was met with a lot of criticism, especially when it prevented Danish expatriates from resettling with their foreign families in Denmark after working abroad. The criticism led the government to amend the law, since 2004 citizens holding Danish nationality for more than 28 years and TCN foreigners who were born or grew up in Denmark and have legally resided there for more than 28 years are exempted from fulfilling the attachment requirement. The threshold was lowered to 26 years in course of a slightly liberalising law reform in 2012. In general, this amendment however led to discrimination between Danish citizens, depending on the length of their citizenship possession (Ersbøll 2009: 3).

The age and attachment requirement had a strong impact on the amount of spousal migration to Denmark. While in 2001, about 6,500 spousal migrants had entered Denmark, this amount decreased by nearly 60 per cent to around 2,600 spouses in 2008. The most frequent reason couples were refused entry clearance to Denmark was that their "combined attachment" to

Denmark was not considered to be enough (Rytter 2010: 302). As mentioned earlier, many Danish sponsors decide to relocate to nearby southern Sweden in order to access the more favourable family migration rights available for intra-EU movers. Estimations suggest that between 2002 and 2010, 2,000-3,000 Danish sponsors relocated to Sweden or Germany in order to apply for spousal migration from there. Nearly 600 spousal migration applications were made by Danes with the Swedish authorities in 2005, more than 50 per cent concerned spouses younger than 24 (see Rytter 2010: 314), suggesting that this is indeed a common strategy for young transnational couples in Denmark to circumvent the restrictive domestic rules.

In 2007, the Danish government decided that it would follow the Dutch example and introduce a language requirement abroad for incoming spouses (the so-called "immigration test").[178] However, the immigration test for spouses actually came into force only three and a half years later, on 15 November 2010 (Ersbøll & Gravesen 2010: 19). As a working group had concluded that the establishment of a testing system abroad would be too costly, the law had been amended.[179] The immigration test, consisting of a computer-based oral exam with 40 questions assessing Danish language skills (equivalent to CEFR level "A1 minus") and 30 questions on Danish society, was taken in Denmark instead of abroad. The spouses, after having fulfilled all other requirements for spousal migration, were granted temporary visas for three months, during which they had to take and pass the immigration test, or else they would have to leave Denmark again. Citizens from Australia, Canada, Israel, Japan, New Zealand, Switzerland, South Korea and the USA were exempted from passing the test. Contrary to the Dutch government's emphasis on the selective function of the integration requirement, the Danish Integration Minister repeatedly stated that the intention behind the integration test was not to decrease spousal migration or deny entry to foreigners. In 2010, she commented that it was instead conceived of as a "taster," allowing incoming migrants to realise what life in Denmark would be like, and even remarked that the test might be adjusted to enable all participants to pass it (Ersbøll & Gravesen 2010: 23).

---

[178] Act No. 379 of 25 April 2007.
[179] Act No. 400 of 21 April 2010.

Only two years later, as part of the liberalising law reform of 2012 mentioned above, the immigration test was revoked and replaced by a Danish language test (level A1) to be completed within six months after arrival (Wray 2013). The exceptions of certain nationalities were scrapped, in a move towards greater equality between the different incoming spouses. If spouses fail the test, they have another three months to retake it; exceptions are granted in cases of maternity, sickness or "extraordinary unsuspected transportation difficulties (Danish Immigration Service 2015c).

In the course of introducing the language requirement, various references were made by the responsible minister and in parliament to the Dutch integration abroad policy (Ersbøll and Gravesen 2010: 22). The immigration test had not been invented by the Danish government but rather by the Dutch one, and it was pointed out that the successful implementation of this policy in the Netherlands had not been accused of violating any international treaty – even though the Danish government finally opted against an integration abroad policy. While for Denmark and various other EU states, the Dutch policies thus played an important symbolic and referential role in the field of restricting spousal migration, the Danish regime served as inspiration too, e.g. with various government representatives in the UK expressing interest in introducing an attachment requirement following the Danish model (Wray 2013: 139).

5.2.4 The United Kingdom

In the 1980s and 1990s, the UK was the first European country to have a largely restrictive stance on spousal migration with the "primary purpose rule," under which incoming spouses had to prove that the primary purpose of their marriage was not immigration into the UK. The rule was disproportionately applied to incoming South-Asian spouses, especially males. When the rule was abolished in June 1997 by the newly installed Labour government, a brief period of comparably liberal spousal migration policies followed and the amount of spouses granted settlement steadily increased (Wray 2009: 593). However, as other types of migration increased further, the proportion of spousal migration out of overall immigration into the UK actually decreased. While in 1995, spouses received 59 per cent of all settlement grants; in 2009 this proportion had dropped to 40 per cent, but still constituted the largest single category of settlement (Charsley et al. 2012: 4).

According to Wray (2006), public discourses on fraud and abuse have been particularly prominent in British discussions of spousal migration. Accordingly, policy initiatives were often aimed at tackling marriages of convenience and also often situated in marriage law rather than migration rules. For instance, in 2001, the government introduced so-called "Section 24 reports," referring to Section 24 of the Immigration and Asylum Act, which defined sham marriages as any marriage concluded in order to evade UK migration law. The Section 24 reports legally obliged marriage registrars to report any suspicious marriage to the authorities. Consequently, the amount of marriages reported increased from 752 in 2001 to 3,678 in 2004 (Wray 2006: 314). Whether this increase was due to an actual increase in sham marriages remains unclear as few further investigations were carried out on the suspicions reported. The media and politicians also singled out marriages of EU nationals in the UK (SCNs), making use of the "loophole" in EU law, as a main source of sham marriages (Wray 2006: 316). In any case, the numbers were used as evidence to justify another law change within marriage law, the Certificate of Approval scheme.

From 2005 onwards, the consent of the Home Office, in the form of a Certificate of Approval (CoA), cost the applicant £ 135, and was necessary for any marriage involving any TCN foreigner subject to immigration control. Such CoAs were denied to individuals without residence permits, but also to TCNs with permits for six months or less, or TCNs with permits due to expire in less than 3 months. No right of appeal was foreseen in case the Home Office decided to deny the CoA. The scheme was very controversial; first, because marriages concluded in the Church of England were not subject to the CoA, which was criticised as discriminatory, and secondly, in those cases where the CoA was refused, no marriage was possible, leading to serious human rights violations. Accordingly, the CoA was overturned only one year later by the High Court[180] on the grounds that it was a disproportionate interference with Article 12 of the ECHR enshrining the right to marry and Article 14 of the ECHR prohibiting discrimination (Kofman et al. 2008: 30). The CoA

---

[180] Queen's Bench Division, R (on the application of Baiai and others) v Secretary of State for the Home Department [2006] EWHC 823 (Admin), judgement of 10 April 2006.

scheme was rearranged after the judgement and overruled again in 2008 by the House of Lords due to the fees involved. Later, it was changed yet again, only to be subsequently finally abolished in May 2011 (see Charsley et al. 2012: 27).

At the same time, the issues of forced marriages and integration started to come up in the UK in connection with family migration as well. As a consequence, policy instruments situated more directly within migration law began to tackle spousal migration. In 2008, the idea came up to introduce a pre-admission language requirement for incoming partners as well, but this proposal was rejected by the Home Office due to "gaps in the provision of English language courses" (Ryan 2009: 293). A bit later, British policy-makers changed their views. From late 2010 onwards, spousal migrants entering Britain need a proof of oral English language skills (i.e. listening and speaking) equivalent to level A1 of the CEFR, unless they are nationals from one of the 16 countries considered to be "majority English-speaking" or have a bachelor's degree that was taught in English (UK Border Agency 2010). Next to OECD-states Australia, Canada, New Zealand and the USA, the 16 exempted states are mainly Caribbean former British colonies, while other large English-speaking states such as India and Pakistan are not exempted (Groenendijk 2011: 19) According to the government, the language requirement is "intended to help migrants integrate into British society – to open up more opportunities, help prevent exploitation, and allow them to benefit from, and contribute more to their communities, and it helps the UK economy" (UK Border Agency 2010: 2).

As a further measure, common in other European states, the minimum age for both sponsors and incoming spouses was increased from 18 to 21 years in 2008, with the intention of fighting forced marriages. However, here again, the domestic UK judiciary interfered. In October 2011, the Supreme Court ruled the minimum age of 21 years to be incompatible with Article 8 ECHR since it "disproportionately interfered" with the right to private and family life of genuine spouses.[181] From 28 November 2011 onwards,

---

[181] Supreme Court, [2011] UKSC45, R (on the application of Quila and another) (FC) v. Secretary of State for the Home Department and R (on the application of Bibi and another) (FC) v. Secretary of State for the Home Department, judgement of 12 October 2011.

the minimum age for both incoming and sponsoring spouses was reduced to 18 years.[182]

In mid-2011, the Home Office launched a large-scale policy initiative tackling family migration. The government proposals, which, according to the responsible Home Secretary May, aimed "to strike a proper balance between the individual's right to respect for family life and the broader public interest" (UK Border Agency 2011: 4). The reform package, focusing on "preventing and tackling abuse, promoting integration and reducing burdens on the taxpayer" (UK Border Agency 2011: 6), included a harsher policy stance on marriages of convenience and forced marriages. The proposed instruments included more explicitly defining what a genuine marriage is, a new minimum income threshold for sponsors, and an increase of the probationary period for incoming spouses and partners prior to gaining an independent residence permit ("settlement") from two to five years. A language requirement of level B1 for family migrants in order to qualify for settlement was put forward as well (UK Border Agency 2011). The consultation also suggested introducing an attachment requirement, following the Danish model, into UK spousal migration laws (UK Border Agency 2011: 19).

In November 2011, the government's "Migration Advisory Committee" (MAC) recommended to substantially increase the annual minimum income from the then-current £5,500 after taxes, in order to ensure that incoming family members do not "become a burden on the state." Since 2012, sponsors in the United Kingdom must prove they have an annual income of at least £18,600 (approximately € 23.000) to sponsor a spouse's immigration – about 140 per cent of the minimum wage. It has been estimated that about half of the employed British citizens could not meet this threshold. Due to income differences, certain population segments are especially affected: 58 per cent of jobholders between 20 and 30 years and 61 per cent of female employees in the United Kingdom did not earn enough in 2012 to bring a foreign family member into the country (Blinder et al. 2012: 18).

---

[182] House of Commons, Written Ministerial Statement by the Minister for Immigration Damian Green, Column 6WS-7WS, 7 November 2011.

5.2.5 Austria

For a long time, family migration to Austria was controlled in a way that is rather unique in Europe. With a quota system regulating TCN immigration, an annual maximum quota was also applied to family migration joining TCN sponsors, leading to waiting periods even if all criteria were fulfilled. The overall TCN immigration quota for 2010 and 2011 was 8,145; the largest part of this, around 60 per cent (4,905), went to family migrants. From 2012 onwards, a new points-based system *"Rot-Weiß-Rot-Card"* replaced the quota system (ORF 2010). However, Kraler (2010: 8) also points out that around 85 per cent of all family migration, that is TCN family members of Austrian citizens and EU citizens, are admitted outside of the quota system.

In early 2010, the Austrian government decided to introduce a language test for family migrants as well (Völker 2010). In February 2011, the Austrian Council of Ministers agreed upon a migration law reform package that included a language requirement for most TCN migrants aiming at a long-term residence in Austria, thus including family migrants. Contrary to the German law, the language requirement even needs to be fulfilled by TCN parents of Austrian minors. This provision was heavily criticised by Green MP Korun, who claimed it to be in breach of ECJ case law (Pressedienst des Parlaments 2011a).

In late April 2011, the migration law package was adopted by the Austrian parliament *(Nationalrat)* and approved on 15 May in the second chamber *(Bundesrat)*. In both instances, the law was passed with votes from the government SPÖ and ÖVP parties and met with considerable resistance from various opposition parties for diverging reasons. The far right party FPÖ considered the language requirement to be insufficient and too liberal a "chimera," while the Greens claimed it to be much too restrictive (Pressedienst des Parlaments 2011b). The language requirement in Germany and its political framing served as an example for Austrian policy-makers. For instance, Minister Fekter claimed that since 2007, "the groups with very patriarchal structures and from very uneducated strata, who in no case want to let their women learn German, do not migrate to Germany anymore, but to Austria," thus underlining the urgency of introducing a similar requirement in Austria as well (Bundesrat der Republik Österreich 2011: 153, my translation).

The new migration law came into force on 1 July 2011. It introduced a language requirement abroad *("Deutsch vor Zuwanderung")* that requires applicants to prove that had skills equivalent to A1 of the CEFR. It is required of most incoming TCN migrants applying for a permanent residence permit, including spousal migrants.[183] Other language-related restrictions were introduced as well. First, the time period to fulfil the integration agreement *(Integrationsvereinbarung)* was reduced from five to two years.[184] The integration agreement stipulates that immigrants need to reach German skills equivalent to level A2 of the CEFR. If new migrants fail to reach this level within two years, their residence permit may not be renewed and they could be expelled as a consequence. Second, new requirements to reach German skills equivalent to level B1 of the CEFR in order to be granted an unlimited residence permit[185] or Austrian citizenship[186] were introduced with the bill. Moreover, the state retained the final right to evaluate language skills. Even with a valid language certificate, it is possible for authorities to evaluate migrants' language skills as insufficient and accordingly deny, for example, the renewal of a residence permit.[187] Another novelty refers directly to spousal migration, as engaging in a marriage (or adoption) of convenience was added to the list of offences that can lead to not only an expulsion but also a prohibition of return valid for the entire EU for up to five years.[188] An NGO representative considered this novelty to considerably increase the pressure upon bi- or multi-national families and make the "common practice of denunciating marriages of convenience by neighbours or others even more dangerous" (Brickner 2011, my translation).

5.2.6 Switzerland

In 2008, the new Swiss Foreigners' Law *(Ausländergesetz, AuG)* came into force, with general conditions for spousal migration staying largely un-

---

[183] § 21a Niederlassungs- und Aufenthaltsgesetz NAG
[184] § 14a, Abs. 2 NAG
[185] § 14b NAG
[186] § 10a Abs 1 Z1 Staatsbürgerschaftsgesetz 1985
[187] § 14a Abs 7 NAG
[188] § 53 Abs 2 Z 8 NAG

changed vis-à-vis the prior foreigner's law that had been in place since 1931 (*Bundesgesetz über Aufenthalt und Niederlassung der Ausländer* (ANAG)). Spouses of Swiss citizens and of permanent residents (with a *"Niederlassungsbewilligung"*) have a legal claim to admission and stay in Switzerland.[189] The only new condition introduced in 2008 is an obligation for the spouses to live together, and even here exceptions are granted if important reasons for living apart are asserted and the familial unity continues.[190] For foreigners with a less consolidated residence permit (*Aufenthaltsbewilligung* or *Kurzaufenthaltsbewilligung*), spousal migration can be granted if the spouses live together, adequate accommodation is available and no recourse to social welfare is made.[191] It is important to note the difference in the legal wording; while Swiss sponsors and permanent residents have a legal claim to being granted spousal migration, in cases of less consolidated sponsors the state can grant admission to spouses, but the final discretion remains in the hands of civil servants. Thus, here there is a rather significant difference in the possibilities for spousal migration depending on the legal status of the sponsor. Another recent development is the introduction of a time limit with spousal migration being only granted within five years of either the marriage or the granting of the sponsor's residence permit.[192]

Contrary to the other European states examined above, in Switzerland no age limits or integration abroad requirements were introduced. However, historically and also recently, a considerable portion of legislative attention has focused on marriages of convenience. From 1952 to 1992, an article[193] in the Swiss Civil Code (*Zivilgesetzbuch*, ZGB) declared so-called "citizenship marriages" (*Bürgerrechtsehen*) null and void; that is marriages between Swiss men and foreign women concluded in order to circumvent the naturalisation procedure, as the wives had immediate access to Swiss citizenship. When the citizenship law was changed in 1992 and foreign women marrying Swiss men were immediately being granted Swiss citizenship anymore, the article was abolished as well. However, it was immediately reanimated in a modified version from 1992 onwards in the foreigner's

---

[189] Art. 42 AuG; Art. 43 AuG
[190] Art. 49 AuG
[191] Art. 44 AuG; Art. 45 AuG
[192] Art. 47 AuG
[193] Art. 120, Ziff. 4 ZGB

law ANAG, to which a paragraph was added stating explicitly that no spousal migration rights can be claimed when a marriage was concluded in order to circumvent the foreigner's law.[194] Despite case law and administrative instructions disallowing spousal migration in marriages of convenience in most European countries, explicit legal codification of such instances as early as 1992 is indicative of the strong stance Swiss legislation has towards marriages of convenience. The new 2008 AuG law went even further by additionally penalising not only any form of deception of the authorities leading to the issue of a residence permit, but specifically also the conclusion or even mediation of marriages of convenience, also for the sponsors, with up to three years of prison.[195] Thus, the sponsor spouse, as well as the "brokers" of marriages of convenience, can now be punished.

Next to these legislative changes within migration law, the Swiss government recently expanded the policy endeavours against marriages of convenience to the area of civil law, namely marriage law, as well. As part of the 2008 AuG law change, a clause was introduced into the civil code obliging the responsible registrar to deny the marriage ceremony, if one of the spouses obviously intends to conclude a marriage of convenience.[196] In order to evaluate the marriage, the registrar should meet the spouses but can also request information from other authorities or third parties. Since January 2011, a valid residence permit is a precondition for civil marriage,[197] which means that the approximately 100,000 irregular migrants (so-called *sans-papiers*) will no longer be able to marry in Switzerland (Keim 2010). If and when the civil registrars do come across migrants who are unable to prove their legal residence in Switzerland, the registrars are obliged to not only deny the marriage, but also immediately report the migrants' identities to the relevant authorities.[198] Conservative MP Schmidt (CVP) explicitly justified this measure in the fight against marriages of convenience: "We lose too much time determining what actually is a marriage of convenience. With this initiative, the parliament wants to inhibit many marriages that potentially could be marriages of convenience, without concretely certifying whether

---

[194] Art. 7, Ziff. 2 ANAG
[195] Art. 118 AuG
[196] Art. 97a ZGB
[197] Art. 98, Ziff. 4 ZGB
[198] Art. 99, Ziff. 4 ZGB

they actually are marriages of convenience or not" (as quoted in Keim 2010, my translation).

Forced marriages also entered into law recently, with the Swiss government issuing a bill for a "Federal Law of Measures against Forced Marriages" (*"Bundesgesetz über Massnahmen gegen Zwangsheiraten"*) in February 2011,[199] which passed parliament in 2012 and entered into law in July 2013.[200] The new law contains various changes in different fields of law. The most extensive changes were introduced into civil law:[201] registrars are not only obliged to verify if both spouses are voluntarily entering the marriage and deny the conclusion of any marriage they suspect to be a forced one, but must also report this to the responsible law enforcement agencies. Also, parliament amended the proposal issued by the government to include a provision immediately declaring a marriage void if it was contracted under force, even if the spouses express a wish to stay married. This "forced divorce" provision was strongly criticised by the responsible minister Sommaruga in parliament as disproportionate encroachment on the basic right to marry and potential matter for a ruling against Switzerland at the ECtHR in Strasbourg.[202] Furthermore, just as in Germany, forced marriage entered the Swiss Penal Code as a separate crime and can now be punished with up to five years in jail (previously: three years). International private law (Art. 44a IPRG) was amended to include an age requirement: both spouses must be 18 years old in order for a marriage to be valid in Switzerland, even if contracted abroad where domestic laws allow marriages of minors.

The concentration of restrictive spousal migration policies within civil law, instead of within migration law, and the allocation of resultant responsibilities with civil registrars, instead of aliens authorities, is almost unique to the Swiss case. However, a small journalistic investigation has indicated that civil registries only rarely make use of their new rights. In 2008 and 2009, of 1,139 marriage requests directed at the registry in the city of Basel, only 20 cases were further investigated as possible marriages of convenience and only in a mere three of these cases was the marriage denied

---

[199] Botschaft vom 23. Februar 2011 über die Massnahmen gegen Zwangsheiraten, BBl 2011 2185.
[200] Bundesgesetz über Massnahmen gegen Zwangsheiraten vom 15. Juli 2012, BBl 2012 5937.
[201] Art. 99 Abs. 1 Ziff. 3 ZGB; Art. 43a Abs. 3bis ZGB; Art. 105 Ziff. 5 und 6 ZGB; Art. 106 Abs. 1 ZGB.
[202] Ständerat, Sitzung vom 05. Juni 2012, Wortprotokoll AB 2012 S 449 / BO 2012 E 449.

(Keim 2010). The civil registrars' union has spoken out very critically regarding their new "investigative" duties, questioning its practical feasibility especially due to a complete lack of training of the registrars which, especially in cases of (supposed) forced marriages, could even put both the registrars and the victims at risk (Blumer 2011).

Conclusions

This chapter pursued two interrelated objectives. On the one hand, it explored the political and legal dynamics emanating from the international and, especially, the European level for spousal migration policy-making in order to fully grasp the developments in Germany. On the other hand, it situated the specific German case in the wider context of spousal migration policy-making across Europe by sketching some of the most important developments in this field in other European countries, some of which have inspired, or have been inspired by, German policies.

Regarding EU dynamics, a strong stratification of rights according to the legal status of the sponsor is prevalent, with SCNs enjoying the most extensive family migration rights. In contrast with the ambitious goals of the Tampere agenda, the FR Directive had little more effect than codifying the lowest common denominator of family migration rights present in the Member States. Additionally, it gave Member States the opportunity to justify restrictive measures back home with their European obligations after having successfully uploaded them within Council negotiations to the EU level. At the same time, the main actor expanding family migration rights at the EU level is surely the ECJ, as the Council has held the Commission and the EP on a short leash regarding (TCN) migration policy-making. SCNs are also the group which the ECJ has traditionally had the most competence to defend, which contrasts with their lack of responsibility for one of the largest groups engaging in family migration in Europe, namely citizens who have never left their home country (FCNs). This is because in "internal situations" the ECJ has had no competence to rule (though this might change if the *Zambrano* case proves to have a lasting effect in future cases).

Concerning developments in the different European states examined, a clear trend emerged towards the extension of restrictive measures pertaining both to the logic of the regulation of family and the regulation of membership. Regulating family ties has mainly taken the form of age requirements for spouses and increased measures aiming to combat marriages of convenience. The approach of regulating social membership was played out, on the one hand, in the establishment of (heightened) income and housing requirements in France, the Netherlands and the UK and, most pertinently, the "attachment requirement" in Denmark. At the same time, the introduction of integration requirements for incoming spouses in various European states pushes the logic of membership regulating even further, as (future) membership qualities of the incoming spouse are assessed as well. It is striking how the framing and policy instruments regarding spousal migration get disseminated from one country to the next. This is particularly observable with the integration requirements (abroad) for incoming spouses. As a policy instrument completely unheard of at the turn of the century, it managed to spread from the Netherlands in 2006 to five other states in the course of only five years. At the same time, many differences remain across countries. Domestic party politics, the strength of constitutional rights, processes of judicial review, and traditions of migration and migration policies are among the most important national factors that influence spousal migration policies.

6 Political and institutional frames on spousal migration

In the first chapter, different theories regarding migration policy-making in post-war European liberal democracies were explored. Driven by the puzzle of large-scale admission of migrants despite an assumed public and political bent for closure, scholars have searched extensively for answers to "why liberal states accept unwanted migration" (Joppke 1998a). Despite different emphases on the specific institutional and political mechanisms, one of the main factors identified by various authors are liberal states' commitments to individual rights.

Chapter 2 showed how, in the specific case of the humanitarian inflow of family migration, this "liberal rights constraint" can normatively be assumed to be especially strong. This is also because the state is committed to protect the marriage and family primarily of established members of the political community, who are either long-term legal residents or citizens. The individual right to the protection of marriage and family is not only enshrined in international human rights declarations, and in more binding legal texts such as the ECHR and various national constitutions, but also has a powerful abstract moral value for policy makers as it is difficult to entirely dismiss the fundamental importance of family for individual well-being (Bonjour 2011: 116).

Chapters 3-5 outlined how the past decade has witnessed increasing restriction of family migration, both in Germany and across other Europe countries. Thus, in a field where, theoretically, the liberal rights constraint could be assumed to be strongest, we can empirically chronicle an increasing turn towards restrictionism, which leads to a distinct research puzzle: How do liberal democratic states manage to restrict migration *in spite of* the liberal constraint? A straightforward answer would be to say that there is no liberal constraint impacting upon migration policies. However, the answer is not that simple. Liberal norms continue to be of great importance in Europe and also continue to influence policy-making in the field of migration. Governments and policy-makers are highly conscious of their obligations to protect individual rights, and thus legitimise restrictions within the logic of rights-based liberalism, as the following analysis will show. Modifying Freeman's

(1995) notion of a "constrained discourse" regarding migration policies, I suggest that a "liberal discursive constraint" is at work, which compels governments to frame restrictive migration policy instruments in such a way that general commitments to fundamental individual rights are not put into question. Violating individual rights is framed to either achieve other, more pressing goals (including protecting other human rights), or to actually not be an infringement by demarcating the right itself or those entitled to lay claim to it. The alternative – open disrespect for individuals' rights – is difficult to reconcile with any state's self-definition as a liberal democracy.

In section 2.1.3, I further proposed that in the field of family migration, the political approaches of the regulation of membership and of the family achieve re-definitions of both the social membership necessary to lay claim to the protection of the family and the family falling under this protection. The ways these mechanisms are actually played out will be further explored with the following frame analysis of policy-makers' arguments in Germany in the years 2005-2010. This chapter sets out to explore how restrictive changes in the field of spousal migration were introduced in Germany. An empirical analysis of the framings and dynamics present at the political and institutional level is guided by the following research questions: How do the relevant actors in the field of spousal migration policy-making and implementation frame the issue of spousal migration? Which phenomena and problems are associated with spousal migration (diagnosis)? How are they linked to resulting policy solutions (therapy)? In what ways are the approaches of family regulating and membership regulating employed by German policy-makers? What differences and which similarities can be detected across varying political orientations, and between the legislative and the executive?

In order to answer these questions, a frame analysis of parliament debates from 2005 to 2010 is presented in the first section (6.1). This time period was chosen because the Immigration Act (*Zuwanderungsgesetz*) was modified in 2007 to include significant restrictive changes in the conditions for spousal migration. Accordingly, spousal migration was much discussed in parliament both before and after the passage of the new law. By exploring the ways in which Members of Parliament (MPs) of all political parties frame spousal migration and related issues in plenary debates, valuable insights into governmental and oppositional approaches within this policy-making field can be gleaned. Furthermore, in order to substantially broaden the scope of inquiry, the frames employed by members of the legislative and executive involved in the development and implementation of spousal migration policies were analysed as well.

The second section (6.2) thus presents a frame analysis of a series of in-depth interviews led with both MPs responsible for migration issues (and potential opinion leaders on the topic from their parliamentary group) and civil servants working in relevant federal and regional ministries, and the implementing authorities at the local level.

Methodology: Critical Frame Analysis

The epistemological approach of frame analysis ideally lends itself to explore controversial policy-making. Frame analysis is based on the notion that any issue can have various meanings and is thus interpreted implicitly and explicitly in certain, often contesting ways by the multiple relevant actors or stakeholders (Verloo & Lombardo 2007: 31). While first applied in the context of social movements (Snow et al. 1986), it has proved its relevance within policy analysis as well (e.g. Triandafyllidou & Fotiou 1998; Bacchi 1999; Verloo 2007). The theory was further developed in the field of policy analysis by introducing the concept of "policy frames," defined by Verloo as "organising principle that transforms fragmentary or incidental information into a structured and meaningful problem, in which a solution is implicitly or explicitly included" (Verloo 2005: 20). This policy frame, in turn, is thought to have two main dimensions – the diagnosis (what is the issue or problem?) and the therapy (how should it be dealt with or solved?).[203]

Usually, arguments are presented that casually connect the diagnosis and the therapy ("xy is a problem and yz will solve this problem by mechanism abc"). For example, spousal migration can be framed as an integration problem, a human right under threat or a legal loophole prone to abuse, and the policy recommendations may differ accordingly. For the current case, diverging and even contrary framings of the issue of spousal migration across the political and institutional spectrum in Germany can be detected, and the connected policy recommendations differ accordingly. Of course, this mechanism works in both directions; if an actor wants to support, legitimise or also criticise a certain policy, this will strongly influence the initial framing of the issue as well. I want to emphasise the importance of understanding the elements of diagnosis and therapy not in a linear, unidirectional sense (e.g. "The CDU perceives

---

[203] In her work, Verloo uses the term "prognosis" to describe the solution presented by actors within the policy frame. However, I find the predictive connotation of the expression misleading and have replaced it with the term "therapy".

migration as a threat to the welfare state and therefore proposes to introduce an income requirement"), but rather as interconnected and reinforcing elements of the entire framing process.

Policy frame analysis thus starts from the premises that "policy problems are constructed, that there exist competing interpretations of what is the problem, and that policy solutions are in-built in the representation of the problem" (Verloo & Lombardo 2007: 38). For example, as I will show in the later analysis, the policy instrument of the language requirement was indeed presented as the solution to certain perceived problems connected to spousal migration, although at the same time, spousal migration was also framed in such terms that the language requirement could be justified as an ideal policy option. The question almost resembles the classic chicken-and-egg problem: Are restrictions introduced because spousal migration is perceived to lead to problems? Or do politicians want to justify restrictions and therefore portray spousal migration as leading to certain problems? I do not attempt to answer this question but rather I aim to uncover the complex and multidirectional dynamics of political discourse and framing with my following analysis.

Introducing the stage: The *Bundestag*

In the first decade and for the first two elections after reunification (1990-1998), the Christian Democratic parties CDU/CSU and the Liberal Democrats (FDP) were able to maintain their majority and thus continue the centre-right government that had been in place under Chancellor Kohl since 1982. In the elections of 1998, a leftward shift occurred when the Social Democrats (SPD) secured the majority, and then ruled in coalition with the Green Party *(BÜNDNIS 90/DIE GRÜNEN)* as junior partner for the following seven years (1998-2005) with Chancellor Schröder as the head of government. In the 2005 election, the Left Party *(DIE LINKE)* made a strong showing, although all other parties had *a priori* excluded them from coalition talks. Thus, neither the SPD nor the CDU managed to secure enough seats in the *Bundestag* to rule with their preferred junior partners – the Green Party and the FDP, respectively. Consequently, for the second time in German post-war history,[204] a so-called grand coali-

---

[204] From 1966 to 1969 the CDU and the SPD had already ruled together under Chancellor Kiesinger (CDU) after the FDP had left the coalition with the CDU. Brandt (SPD), who was

tion, a *große Koalition*, was formed between the CDU and the SPD. The Union parties, with their slight majority of four seats, laid claim to the position of the chancellor, which was filled by Angela Merkel. The 2009 election then firmly re-established an electoral shift towards the centre-right as the CDU and a strong junior partner, the FDP, managed to secure a majority of seats, with Merkel remaining as head of government.

For the present analysis of spousal migration policies in Germany, the legislative period of 2005-2009 is of special importance since during these years political attention shifted toward the issue of spousal migration and new policies were put in place. The special political constellation of the grand coalition in this period had an influence on the negotiations and policy outcomes in the field of migration policy. One of the main features of a grand coalition in regard to legal changes is that once the two big parties SPD and the CDU agree within the framework of the *Bundestag* on a proposed new policy, they do not only have a very comfortable majority within the *Bundestag* itself, but usually also subsequently in the second chamber made up of representatives of the *Länder*, the *Bundesrat*. This theoretically means that once CDU and SPD agree amongst each other, major reforms can be passed swiftly and with minimal debate. The following section will also analyse how this situation played out in the context of passing the reform of the *Zuwanderungsgesetz* in 2007.

Party	Orientation	Power Position
SPD	Centre-left	Government
CDU/CSU	Centre-right	Government
FDP	Centre-right/Liberal	Opposition
GRÜNE	Centre-left/Green	Opposition
LINKE	Left-wing	Opposition

Table 10: Political parties in the German Bundestag in the 16th legislative period (2005-2009)

Vice-Chancellor and Foreign Minister of this grand coalition, managed to take over as Chancellor and head of an SPD-FDP coalition after the elections in 1969.

Positioning the parties in the spousal migration policy process 2005-2010

CDU

The CDU entered into government in 2005 as senior partner of the grand coalition with the SPD after having been in opposition the preceding eight years, a period that had seen a certain paradigm shift of migration and minority issues under the SPD-Green government. The citizenship law had been liberalised to include *ius soli* provisions. The first *Zuwanderungsgesetz* passed in 2004 did not bring about a major liberalisation of migration law, but it did introduce integration courses, i.e. publically financed language and orientation courses, acknowledging that migrants was "here to stay" and that solutions to pressing socio-economic inequalities among the minority population needed to be found.

When taking over governmental power in late 2005, the CDU was thus confronted with this shifted reality of dealing with migration in Germany. To a certain degree, the party accepted it – by explicitly embracing the integration course policy, for example, and in large part acknowledging Germany was an immigration country. However, the Christian Democrats continued to be intent on controlling migration – with MP Mayer (CSU) stating in 2007 "Germany is not a country of immigration."[205] Regarding family migration, the CDU tended to portray it as an unwanted flow in need of control by discursively positioning it squarely between (unwanted) asylum and irregular migration: "The migration pressure is increasing: in former times, people came via the asylum track, nowadays by way of family reunification, and then there is also plenty of illegal immigration" (MP Uhl (CSU), Deutscher Bundestag, Plenarprotokoll 16/103: 10586[206])

The position of the Federal Interior Minister, in charge of migration issues, was filled by CDU representatives in this time period: From 2005-2009 it was Wolfgang Schäuble (CDU) and from 2009-2011 Thomas de Maizière (CDU) held the post. Another important CDU figure in the migration context of this time period was Maria Böhmer, Migration and

---

[205] This statement did not go uncommented upon. The parliament protocol of the session, for instance, documents large parts of the opposition breaking out into laughter and heckling Mayer as being completely out of touch with reality (Deutscher Bundestag, Plenarprotokoll 16/94: 9563).

[206] For the sake of simplicity, I will omit the cumbersome reference "Deutscher Bundestag, Plenarprotokoll" in the following. All subsequent references starting with "16/" or "17/" refer to the according plenary protocols of the *Bundestag*. All translations are my own.

Integration Commissioner from 2005-2013.[207] Chancellor Merkel in 2005 actually upgraded this position by relocating it to the Chancellor's office and giving the commissioner the rank of a "state minister."

SPD

The Social Democrats had a rather ambiguous position regarding migration issues between 2005 and 2010. As a junior partner of the grand coalition from 2005-2009 it needed to compromise with the CDU. In the case of the negotiations on the *Zuwanderungsgesetz* 2007, SPD delegates entered into a deal with CDU representatives. Some SPD representatives were very keen on granting "tolerated" individuals *(Geduldete)*, that is, rejected asylum seekers who cannot be deported, a right of residence *(Bleiberechtsregelung)*. The CDU made their endorsement of such a provision dependent on the SPD's support of the restrictions in the field of spousal migration. Even though large parts of the SPD parliamentary group were sceptical about the language requirement, in particular, it was finally decided that the *Bleiberechtsregelung* had priority: "Surely, there are critical issues from our side, also concerning the language acquisition. We led a constitutional debate concerning the topic of a [missing] hardship clause for reunification. But I am convinced that the advantages of a federal *Bleiberechtsregelung* weigh heavier. We can help 60,000 people." (MP Körper (SPD), 16/103: 10591).

While not a single MP from the CDU openly broached the issue of this compromise or even attempted to explain or justify it, many SPD MPs seemed to have been unhappy with this "deal." Many SPD members voiced weariness over the politicking in parliament either during their speeches, or by submitting a written statement stating their moral and personal difficulties with this compromise. In the final vote on the law, in contrast to the usual party discipline, 21 SPD MPs voted against the law while five abstained. Additionally, 12 declarations were issued – four by groups of SPD MPs and eight by individual SPD MPs – in which the legislators explained their objections to the act.[208] All of these declarations mentioned the restrictions of spousal migration as points of the law they did not support (16/103: 10639-10651).

---

[207] The official title in English is "Minister of State to the Federal Chancellor and Federal Government Commissioner for Migration, Refugees and Integration".
[208] According to § 31 of the *Bundestag*'s Rules of Procedure (*Geschäftsordnung des Deutschen Bundestages*, BTGO 1980), every MP can issue an oral or written personal statement on any vote taken in the *Bundestag*, which must be included in the protocol.

Some of the groups issuing declarations were rather large, and a total of 91 MPs (i.e. 41 per cent of the entire parliamentary group) issued declarations regarding the law. This demonstrates how uncomfortable a substantial part of the SPD MPs must have felt about the eventual compromise. Apparently, large parts of the SPD believed that their stake within the deal could soon be neutralised, if the Constitutional Court (*Bundesverfassungsgericht*, BVerfG) overruled the language requirement in the future (MP Beck (Grüne), 16/103: 10596). Accordingly, MP Edathy (SPD), the chairman of the Committee of Interior Affairs (*Innenausschuss*), stated during the debate leading up to the final vote on the law: "I am very curious to see how [the language requirement] will be judged in Karlsruhe [seat of the BVerfG] and I want to state clearly that I would not be sad to see this provision be overruled" (16/103: 10600). The fact that a prominent SPD parliamentarian publicly stated that he believed that the new law was possibly unconstitutional – a law that he and his party had voted for – is illustrative of the paradoxical situation that confronted large parts of the SPD in the context of the *Zuwanderungsgesetz* 2007. It also exemplifies the possible complexities regarding the interaction between migration policy-making and the "liberal judicial constraint." Migration-friendly politicians consented to a restrictive rule they did not support (and even considered possibly unconstitutional) in order to achieve a liberalising objective in another migration policy field. At the same time, they hoped that the Constitutional Court might step in and act as a liberal corrective. Put differently, the (future) liberal judicial constraint can already be factored into political considerations. Bonjour (2010: 317) makes a similar point when comparing the different approaches displayed by conservative governments in the Netherlands and France regarding the possibility of judicial review overturning an integration abroad requirement. While a Dutch minister boldly sought to "seek out the limits of the ECHR," the mere prospect of being overruled by the Constitutional Council led French policy-makers to adopt a moderated version of the integration requirement.

Their assessment of the judicial liberal constraints in Germany thus led many SPD MPs to agree to the language requirement even though they did not support it – instead, they aimed to achieve other political goals while hoping the measure would eventually be overruled by the courts. Unsurprisingly, after switching to the opposition bench in 2009, SPD MPs bluntly called to abolish all discriminatory provisions from spousal migration law (17/52: 5494).

FDP

The FDP, being a centre-right liberal party, had established itself firmly as the usual coalition partner of the CDU at the federal level from 1982-1998, after which the two parties spent eight years in opposition to the red-green government. In 2005, CDU and the FDP did not manage to secure a governing majority, and for the first time since 1982 the FDP parliamentary group found itself facing in opposition to the governing CDU, from 2005-2009.

On migration issues the FDP had traditionally played the role of a liberalising voice vis-à-vis its more restrictive coalition partner, the CDU (Tietze 2008: 141), as has been mentioned in chapter 3. In opposition, it continued to be a critical, liberal voice on migration issues, although not as strongly as two other opposition parties, the Greens and the Left. Within its profile as a liberal party, the FDP has generally focused on market-oriented policies and civil liberties. Accordingly, it has pushed for increased highly-skilled labour migration and a points system for immigration with a view to strengthening the economy. At the same time, however, FDP MPs in opposition viewed the language requirement critically, especially as it discriminates against German citizens. Thus, the FDP also put forward several critical motions regarding restrictive spousal migration policies between 2007 and 2009. These consisted of one minor interpellation[209] regarding the possible difficulties in the practical implementation of the language requirement, as well as two motions in early 2009. The first FDP motion suggested enhancing possibilities for migrants to learn German abroad, abolish the monopoly position of the Goethe-Institutes, and also proposed inserting a general hardship clause into the language requirement provision.[210] The second motion invited the government to completely transpose the *Metock* judgement[211] into German migration law to avoid a fragmentation of law and a disadvantaging of spouses of German citizens.[212]

Thus the position of the FDP from 2005 to 2009 in general was not as radically opposed to the government as the Greens and the Left when it comes to spousal migration. However, regarding practical difficulties and the disadvantages incurred by German citizens, it was critical. In 2009, when the FDP switched to the government coalition, its tone changed, with FDP MPs underlining the importance of controlling migra-

---

[209] Deutscher Bundestag, Drucksache 16/6856
[210] Deutscher Bundestag, Drucksache 16/11753.
[211] See section 5.1.3 for a summary and analysis of the *Metock* case.
[212] Deutscher Bundestag, Drucksache 16/12732.

tion in order to tackle growing burdens on the welfare state and xenophobia, thus accepting the general utility of the language requirement. However, as they still criticised the practical difficulties of the language requirement, the FDP continued to argue for the introduction of a hardship clause.

BÜNDNIS 90/DIE GRÜNEN
The Green Party, along with the parliamentary group of the Left Party, proved to be a harsh opponent on the issue of spousal migration for the grand coalition. The Green Party has traditionally been guided by a strong focus on strengthening minorities, as well as a more multicultural vision of society in their migration, asylum and integration policies (Tietze 2008: 190). Thus the party was strongly opposed to all restrictions in the field of spousal migration and severely attacked the government in all their discussion contributions on the issue. Various parliamentary initiatives on the issue of spousal migration were launched by the Greens. A total of nine motions were brought into parliament on the wider issue of spousal migration beginning in 2005, principally about forced marriages. Here, the Greens demanded an increase of help offers and a liberalising of migration law, such as instituting a right of return and an independent right of residence for forced marriage victims. The new restrictive spousal migration law was also criticised. In May 2010, the Green parliamentary group brought a legislative proposal[213] into the plenary that sought the abolishment of the language requirement for all spouses and the income requirement for spouses of German citizens as well as a guaranteed work permit for all spouses after 12 months of residence in Germany.

DIE LINKE
The parliamentary group of *DIE LINKE* was invariably the strongest critic of the government's policies on (spousal) migration and integration. Sevim Dagdelen, the group's speaker on migration and integration issues, consistently and bluntly attacked the coalition in her speeches and frequent minor interpellations and motions. While all other parties had at least two or three experts on migration issues regularly intervening in discussions, the Left Party seemed to leave most of the room in this field to MP Dagdelen. Between late 2007 and 2010, she posed a total of 13 mi-

---

[213] Deutscher Bundestag, Drucksache 17/1626.

nor interpellations,[214] grilling the federal government about the effects of the language requirement, which amounted to about one enquiry every three months. Other interpellations criticised the newly introduced possible income requirement for German spouses[215] and policies on forced marriages.[216] Additionally, in May 2010 the Left parliamentary group (in a similar manner to the Greens) brought forward a motion[217] to change the *Zuwanderungsgesetz* by abolishing the language requirement, a proposal that obviously found no majority in parliament.

6.1 Framing spousal migration in the *Bundestag* 2005-2010

This section explores the framing by German MPs in parliament of spousal migration and spousal migration policies, topic by topic. How is spousal migration framed by the MPs (diagnosis)? Which policies are accordingly suggested (therapy) and how are they causally linked to the diagnosis?

The analysis is based on a qualitative, in-depth study of all 31 plenary protocols touching upon the topic of family migration between 2005 and 2010.[218] As outlined in the previous chapters, in 2007, a reform of the German Immigration Act that included major changes in the field of spousal migration was adopted and came into effect. The documents from this time period give excellent insight into the framings in debates and discussions preceding the law's adoption as well as those succeeding it. The qualitative data analysis software "Atlas.Ti" was employed in order to categorise, label and analyse the frames presented by MPs during parliamentary debates.

Earlier research on the discourses within parliamentary debates on immigration includes the work of Wodak and van Dijk, in which the

---

[214] See the annex for an overview of all minor interpellations and other motions on the issue of spousal migration.
[215] Deutscher Bundestag, Drucksache 16/10254.
[216] Deutscher Bundestag, Drucksache 16/5202.
[217] Deutscher Bundestag, Drucksache 17/1577.
[218] All parliament documents from the 16th electoral term onwards, i.e. since 2005, are available online in a new version of the Parliamentary Material Information System (*Dokumentations- und Informationssystem*, DIP), which allows full text searches of all documents. The studied plenary protocols were those generated by full text searches of the terms "*Ehegattennachzug*" (spousal reunification) and "*Familienzusammenführung*" (family reunification), even though some protocols were later left out of the analysis if the reference to spousal or family migration was trivial or brief (n=5). See the annex for an overview of the protocols.

methodological approach of "Critical Discourse Analysis" was developed and employed (e.g. Krzyzanowski & Wodak 2009; Wodak & van Dijk 2000). In their analyses the theoretical concept of racism plays an important role when exploring how discourses in parliament produce and reproduce discrimination and disadvantages for migrants. The studies are also rather intricate regarding linguistics when they delve into the discursive strategies of MPs. For example, the entire analysis of public discourses of Krzyzanowski and Wodak (2009: 71-122) is based on only two plenary debates, which are explored in great detail.

Since my analysis is focused on one specific type of migration policy rather than on foreigners and discrimination in general, and since I aim to capture the general arguments presented in order to defend or attack contested policies, policy frame analysis seemed to present the most appropriate methodological approach. Recently, some authors have successfully applied critical frame analysis to political discussions on migration issues as well. Examples include Roggeband and Verloo (2007), who analyse policy documents and parliamentary debates on gender and migration over time in the Netherlands; Roggeband and Vliegenthart (2007), who compare framings of migration in the parliament with those presented in the media, and perhaps most pertinently, Bonjour (2010), who comparatively explores the frames presented in the Dutch and French parliaments surrounding the introduction of integration abroad policy instruments.

Parliament debates that are documented by plenary protocols can be conceptualised as the epitome of political discourse. It is in parliament where problems are defined, solutions discussed, and decisions taken – all in the public eye. Without wanting to understate the importance of other factors in the political decision-making process, parliamentary debates continue to be one of the most important avenues for producing and shaping political discourse. Speakers from all parties follow upon and reference one another, MPs both interpose official questions and interject with unofficial hecklings – all of which leads to a rather unique situation of publicly documented direct interaction and discussion across political camps on specific topics.

Which categories of analysis are presented? As the language requirement was the most far-reaching policy innovation introduced in 2007, a very large part of the discussions touching upon spousal migration revolved around the reasoning behind and the possible effects of the requirement. As the government's official motivations behind the introduction of the language requirement were to fight forced marriages and enhance integration, these two topics (forced marriages and integration)

– as well as their supposed connection to both spousal migration, and the language requirement – were prominent in discussions. The government approaches that were outlined in chapter 2.1 relating to the regulation of social membership and the regulation of family ties are both observable in these contexts, mainly among members of the ruling CDU. The first two sections thus focus on the framing of the problems (diagnosis) and the connected policy solutions (therapy) of forced marriages (6.1.1) and integration (6.1.2) by MPs of different political backgrounds. Building upon this, the third section (6.1.3) focuses entirely on the arguments presented by MPs in favour of and against the language requirement, as these controversial discussions also enable a telling insight into the framing of spousal migration in general. Another less dominant issue explored is the way MPs frame the roles played by the EU and other European states (6.1.4). A final section (6.1.5) explores the specific framing of spousal migration presented by Interior Minister Schäuble (CDU) in the *Bundestag*.

6.1.1 Forced marriages

As outlined in the theoretical framework, one approach for governments to legitimise restrictions in the field of family migration is by regulating family ties. This occurs by circumscribing the legal categories eligible to apply for family migration, but also by further assessing the "quality" of the relationships among family members. Excluding marriages made under threat and/or force from the scope of spousal migration provisions – since they do not correspond to the legal and moral definitions of marriages of the host society, but instead are classified as human rights violations and criminal activities – is a straightforward way of family regulating via quality. However, as is the case with many criminal activities in the private sphere, detecting and proving a forced marriage is close to impossible, especially when those involved are unwilling to cooperate with the authorities. Accordingly, another more indirect way of regulating family quality is the discursive connection of spousal migration with an unacceptable type of marriage, such as forced marriage, and the subsequent introduction of policy measures (presumably) fighting this phenomenon. In the German debate from 2005 onwards, this is exactly the type of regulation of family that was employed.

The issue of forced marriages was explicitly linked to spousal migration within parliament discussions only when the government justified restrictions in this area with the goal of fighting forced marriages in

2007. Generally, MPs of all parties agreed that forced marriages are intolerable human rights infringements that stem from atavistic and patriarchal gender norms inscribed in certain cultures – implicitly Muslim culture – that need to be inhibited. However, further notions of the dimension and character of the phenomenon, and especially the ideas on what constitute adequate and effective policies in this respect, differed considerably across the political parties. The rhetoric employed by the CDU MPs was rather dramatic, connecting forced marriages to rape, violence, humiliation, oppression and honour killings:

A forced marriage is a grave and severe violation of human rights and not excusable by anything, especially because cases of forced marriage often are connected with both brutal physical and psychic violence within the family, with humiliation, with oppression and with rape, and sometimes, as we have unfortunately had to realise in Germany as well, with so-called honour killings, which are unbearable and despicable crimes. (MP Mayer (CSU), 16/143: 15131)

In addition, forced marriages were more than once explicitly linked to the Turkish/Muslim minority population as the locus of the atavistic culture permitting or even fostering them, as well as to incoming women as victims ("import brides"), and to integration deficits (see the following section on integration). As to the dimension of the phenomenon in Germany, because no reliable data exists, some alternative sources of information are quoted; such as, for example this comment by MP Grindel (CDU): "We know through the aliens authorities, self-help-groups and our visa-offices abroad that forced marriages still exist to a significant degree" (17/43: 4372). In this way, family regulating that condemns forced marriages can only be expanded to general conditions applicable to all spousal migrants if the phenomenon is also framed to be significant within overall spousal migration. With an MP quoting aliens authorities and visa offices as authoritative informants on the issue, forced marriages are immediately situated within the migration process. Overall, by connecting forced marriages – a practice violating human rights standards and liberal Western norms – to spousal migration, the case for infringing upon the right to marriage and family within spousal migration policies can gain ground. Put differently, restricting individual rights in one field is justified with the goal of protecting them in another.

The SPD MPs, although they largely agreed with the CDU, nevertheless formulated their assessment a bit more cautiously, possibly in an attempt to mitigate some generalising statements made by their coalition partner:

> The free choice of the marriage or life partner is a matter of course for most of us. However, this is not the case for some people living in Germany. Victims of forced marriages are mostly young people with migration backgrounds, though not only of Turkish background. (...) I explicitly advise against putting all Muslim marriages under a general suspicion and saying: 'Every second Turkish family is affected by forced marriage.' This is definitely not the case. (MP Graf (SPD), 16/143: 15129)

Green and FDP MPs agree that forced marriages are appalling human rights violations affecting mostly (but not only) women and which stem from "archaic conceptions of society" (MP Laurischk (FDP)) and from "authoritarian and patriarchal ideas" (MP Schewe-Gerigk, (GRÜNE)). The Left, on the other hand, while admitting that "forced marriage constitutes maximised violence," saw socio-economic conditions as the decisive factor leading to forced marriages (MP Dagdelen (LINKE), 16/143: 15130). The opposition said little regarding the number of forced marriages.

Apart from the slightly different approaches as to how best to conceptualise the issue of forced marriages (diagnosis), the policy recommendations (therapy) differed as well, and this is also the arena where more harsh disputes on the issue across parties emerged. CDU MPs presented the age and language requirements as adequate policy instruments to prevent and fight forced marriages. According to them, potential victims who are older and have better education are less attractive for perpetrators (preventive effect). Furthermore, they claimed that German skills are necessary to bring attention to the situation of distress, thus empowering potential victims to escape a forced marriage once in Germany. The notion of the fundamental importance of German skills, in particular, as an indispensable tool to escape a forced marriage gained a lot of momentum in the course of the discussions, and it was increasingly portrayed as the only possible policy to effectively fight forced marriages:

> Forced marriages are integration-inhibiting human rights violations that we will not put up with, not tolerate and not accept in Germany. We will only stop campaigning for this when there are no forced marriages left in Germany (...) *How else* should a young woman who was forced into marriage defend herself here? *Only then*, with basic German skills, can she draw attention to her distress and say that she needs help. *It will not work any other way.* (MP Noll (CDU), 16/143: 15127, emphasis added)

This quote also illustrates the frequently employed analogy of a fight that is waged against forced marriages, which functions to frame forced marriage as an external threat that needs to be overcome and eliminated – as in, "no more forced marriages left in Germany." Overall, this argument not only positions forced marriages squarely within spousal migration, since it is within spousal admission policy that the solution is located, but it also largely concentrates on the constellation of forced marriages with incoming women by presenting a lack of German-language skills as the principal roadblock to escaping a forced marriage – as in, "Only then, with basic German skills…" By extension, the possibility of forced marriage victims growing up in Germany – and therefore being perfectly fluent in German – is ignored.

While the age requirement was not really disputed across party lines, probably since it was finally set at a relatively low 18 years, the logic pertaining to the causality of the language requirement was highly criticised by the opposition, especially by the Left and the Green MPs. They accused the government, above all the CDU, of hypocrisy and dishonesty regarding their policy goals through an instrumentalisation of the victims of forced marriages as justification to restrict immigration:

> We all agree in this High Chamber: Forced marriage constitutes maximised violence. But making this obvious over and over should not be an end in itself. Unfortunately, especially the [CDU] has not led this debate in a differentiated manner, but has been increasingly instrumentalising it. It is actually a manoeuvre to distract from the failure in integration and social policy of previous governments. (…) Forced marriage has been used as one more reason to generalise and stigmatise migrants, especially Muslim ones, as regressive or inferior. (…) In particular, those MPs that for years have consequently been inhibiting gender equality measures suddenly are worried about women's rights. The plights of women are instrumentalised and functionalised. This way the government restricts spousal reunification. Of course it is understood as a preventive measure to fight forced marriages, it is even spoken of preventive integration. However, the purported motive is more than hypocritical; since with this measure not one case of forced marriages is inhibited. What is camouflaged as victim protection simply aims at inhibiting immigration – and it seems to work: the numbers have gone down. (MP Dagdelen (LINKE), 16/143: 15130)

The policies suggested by the opposition went in the direction of a liberalisation of immigration law. One policy demand voiced repeatedly was the installation of a right of return for foreign women who grew up in Germany but were then forced into marriage abroad, since the current legal situation stipulates a loss of the residence permit when a foreign resident is abroad for more than six months.[219] MPs of all opposition parties demanded the adoption of such a right of return.

---

[219] However, an extended right of return for victims of forced marriages (up to ten years after leaving Germany) was included in the government's amendment of the Residence Act of 27 October 2010 (see section 4.2).

Another liberalising demand made by all opposition MPs is the creation of an independent residence permit for victims of forced marriages to enable incoming spouses forced into a marriage to be able to leave the marriage before the probationary period is up without risking the loss of their residence status. An exception to the rule was already enshrined in § 31 Abs. 2 AufenthG, but it is only applied if the victim can prove to have been subject to domestic violence; this hurdle was considered to be too high to effectively permit the leaving of a forced marriage. The objective authority of these demands was supported by referring to independent experts, such as counsellors who have pled for similar policy initiatives, *inter alia* in the context of the expert hearing for the *Zuwanderungsgesetz* within the Bundestag (16/103: 10592; 16/143: 15131). These two policy demands are supported by the governing SPD's MPs, who claimed to have tried to include both these aspects into the *Zuwanderungsgesetz* 2007 but failed to convince their senior coalition partner, the CDU (16/143: 15129).

Other policy suggestions included an expansion of social assistance, including the establishment of hotlines, consulting services and women's shelters, as well as awareness-raising campaigns within schools, youth facilities and with public authorities (16/143: 15128). CSU MP Mayer rebutted the opposition's demands for an independent right of residence for forced marriage victims. He pointed out that this kind of right already existed, and any further residential improvements for forced marriage victims would be "unconstitutional" and "perpetuate the victim role for a lifetime" (16/143: 15132).

6.1.2 Integration

Next to family regulation, the approach of membership regulation can be employed to control spousal migration. In this context, framing spousal migration as conducive to integration deficits (in other words, incomplete social membership) can justify policies that aim to assess the quality of (future) membership such as the language requirement. The notion of integration has indeed been extremely dominant in the framing of spousal migration and subsequent policy decisions. The following section explores the ways in which MPs frame issues surrounding integration to spousal migration.

Integration in general

For CDU MPs, the dominant focus when defining integration is the German language. The notion of German skills being the basis for integration, the necessary condition upon which logically all other integration steps can follow, is frequently invoked (e.g. 16/94: 9563). Turning the argument around, lacking language skills is defined as the "main integration obstacle" *("Hauptintegrationshindernis")* (16/103: 10588). This exemplifies a pattern rather symptomatic for the entire debate on integration. Integration is largely defined negatively by pointing out what it is not, by elaborating on integration deficits, and pointing to what can be classified as a lack of integration, instead of giving a clear idea what integration positively might mean or entail.

Language skills are framed as being important in two somewhat distinct contexts. On the one hand, language skills are presented as a precondition of a factual "hard" integration – which is deemed necessary to successfully participate in the educational sphere and/or the labour market. On the other hand, German skills are discursively connected to a more symbolic "soft" integration – which is understood to be necessary to participate in the everyday life of the society or to make friends. Since incoming spouses are typically assumed to be female, this soft integration is also implicitly framed as an emancipation project for oppressed migrant women:

> Ultimately, the basis of any integration is learning the language. It is the condition for any free development of an individual personality and incorporation into the society. (MP Mayer (CSU), 17/43: 4374)

Accordingly, two more arguments emerged. First, German skills were claimed to be necessary to emancipate women from oppressive family situations – i.e. to be able to call the police or other help services in order to get out of a forced marriage. Second, German is considered important since "women have a special responsibility in raising their children" (MP Bürsch (SPD), 16/88: 8941) and need to teach German to their children who otherwise will be stuck in a cycle of poverty and disintegration and robbed of opportunities for social mobility (e.g. 17/43: 4372). This argument thus places the responsibility for successful participation in the education and labour markets of minority youth on their parents, especially their mothers. Interior Minister Schäuble also mentioned that successful parenting, especially by women, depends on proficiency in German:

> Parents, especially mothers of children, need to speak German, so that we don't have to start all over for each generation. This is why we have said in the context of family reunification: it is better if at least a minimum of language skills is existent. (Minister Schäuble (CDU), 16/144: 16978)

Apart from German skills, integration was also defined as a commitment to German institutions, norms, customs, rule of law, or, as argued by MP Uhl (CSU), a kind of inner will. Who lacks this will to learn German and "take over our rule of law and system of norms" is not considered a member, since the suggested solution is to leave Germany:

> [Integration] is subject to the condition that immigrants *want* to feel at home here, that they *want* to learn the German language and that they *want* to take over our rule of law and system of norms. Who does *not want* this, has to understand that it is better to leave this country than to live in conflict with this country. (MP Uhl (CSU), 16/161: 16987, emphasis added)

Other parties' MPs agreed that language is important, but warned against reducing integration to language skills alone, though this warning was voiced and emphasised to varying degrees. An SPD MP, for example, while consenting to language being an important condition of integration, pointed out that education and participation were just as important (16/161: 16991). The FDP, on the other hand, completely concurred with the CDU, repeatedly conceptualising language as the "key competence in order to integrate here" (16/161: 16988).

The Left MPs warned most insistently not to equate language skills with integration, claiming this could even lead to language becoming a criteria of exclusion instead of an instrument of integration (16/161: 16984). Furthermore, they stated language skills, and even good education, by themselves to be no guarantee for integration in the sense of equal participation, as structural factors needed to be adjusted: "Integration is more than just language. Integration is a social issue." (MP Dagdelen (LINKE), 16/161: 16984). Thus, the Left Party defined integration as equal participation possibilities for everyone, with those possibilities being enabled by the government.

Framing integration policies

The CDU's motto regarding integration policy is *"Fordern und Fördern"* (roughly translating to "Demand and Assist," a concept first developed in the context of social welfare policies), while the element of "demanding" is clearly more emphasised by the MPs. A high degree of personal responsibility for successful integration is thus shifted toward the migrant, defining integration as a "duty," a "responsibility" and "not only the state's obligation to deliver *(Bringschuld)*, but also the foreigner's obligation to collect *(Holschuld)*" (MP Grindel (CDU), 16/94: 9555).

This maxim was portrayed as a paradigm shift *("Kurswechsel")*, (17/43: 4372) vis-à-vis the previous integration policy of the red-green coalition that was considered to have been too lax and was often framed as multiculturalism by the CDU. The notion of multiculturalism *("Multikulti")* is invariably used in a negative sense by CDU MPs (and interestingly, not at all by MPs of other parties). This was apparent in statements such as: "The Left has learned nothing from the mistakes of *Multikulti*-policies" (MP Grindel, 17/43: 4372) or *"Multikulti* is really just a big mess." *("Multikulti ist in Wahrheit Kuddelmuddel")* (MP Grindel (CDU), 16/94: 9555). It was largely overlooked that the red-green coalition was only in power for eight years and many of the integration issues also stemmed from the neglect of integration policies altogether in earlier decades when the CDU was in power.

The main instance of public support *(Fördern)* for integration was typified by the integration courses that were introduced in 2005. Both CDU and SPD MPs embraced these courses, while not failing to also underline their high costs, and defining them as a generous offer to the migrants by the state and taxpayer: "The integration courses are worth 155 million Euros per year to us. That is a considerable sum that we, the *Bund*, spend voluntarily for language training." (MP Bürsch (SPD), 16/161: 16990, see also 16/103: 10586 and 16/143: 15131).

Parallel to emphasising the personal responsibility of each migrant for his/her success in the integration process, CDU MPs also underlined the necessity of the state to enforce integration *("Integration durchsetzen")* (16/103: 10587). The main policy instruments are sanctions in cases of non-attendance of the integration courses; possibly sanctions are cuts in welfare benefits or even a non-extension of residence permits.[220] Another policy instrument is the enforcement of integration through the pre-entry language requirement for spouses. The idea, as presented, was that some migrants are either unwilling or (especially in the case of oppressed women) unable to fulfil their integration responsibilities by attending the integration courses and thus need to be directed or forced by the state to do so. These policies of integration enforcement were criticised by Green and Left MPs, with Left MPs employing the

---

[220] See § 8 Abs. 3 and § 44a Abs. 1 AufenthG. In the 2011 reform, these sanction possibilities were extended (see chapter 4.2).

most acrimonious descriptions such as "repressive integration policies," "policies of coercion" and "forced integration" *("repressive Integrationspolitik," "Politik des Zwangs," "Integrationszwang")* (16/94: 9561). Meanwhile, the Greens spoke of the state wanting to "enforce integration by threat of punishment" (16/103: 10593).

Framing integration deficits

As mentioned above, integration is generally framed negatively, by defining what it is not rather than what it is. In this context, the description and analysis of integration deficits are frequent and recurring features, with CDU MPs especially prevalent in making a case for more restrictive policies.

First, integration deficits were described by citing statistics of failed integration, primarily the low participation and success rates of migrants or ethnic minorities in schools and the workforce; juvenile crime rates were also cited. Some of these statistics refer to Germany-wide data, and some refer to Berlin alone, presumably since the data is more extreme and thus more impressive. Apart from this "objective proof" of failed integration, certain MPs told stories of failed integration that were hardly objective and instead relied on emotional and anecdotal evocations. Metropolitan areas as Berlin, or even specific districts such as Neukölln, were cast as "urban ghettos" where integration had utterly failed. In this context, two interconnected notions were especially prominent – a "parallel society" or even a "parallel world" *("Parallelgesellschaft"/ "Parallelwelt")* and an orchestrated "integration refusal" *("Integrationsverweigerung")* on the part of migrants. Using Muslim (and especially Turkish) migrants as examples, parallel societies were described as frequent phenomena, especially in big cities, and as a serious danger to the cohesion of society. The second and third generations of migrants were also frequently mentioned as being the main locus of integration difficulties:

> After the migrants of the first generation – they were very hard-working – integrated themselves into the working life and contributed significantly to our GDP, we made the false conclusion that integration would take care of itself. The exact opposite was the case: the problems did not develop with the first but with the second and third generation, and we have these problems today. A cultural disruption (*Kulturbruch*) can be observed. (MP Uhl (CSU), 16/161: 16986)

Furthermore, the implicit reproach is made vis-à-vis parts of the migrant population that they do not want to integrate, or "refuse" to integrate.

For example, MP Grindel (CDU) repeatedly speaks of "those migrant families that until now have steered clear of all integration offers made towards them" (16/94: 9554). This notion might be interpreted as the logical consequence of the emphasis on self-responsibility within the integration process mentioned above. If a migrant is not integrated, this means he/she did not try hard enough, or in other words, refused to integrate. By framing at least some migrants as unwilling to integrate, a stronger case can be made for adopting and enforcing more restrictive migration and integration policies:

> Preserving social peace also means to take more care of the foreigners living here and enforce their integration. Part of this is also that integration refusal is sanctioned more effectively than until now. Somebody receiving *Hartz IV* in Germany, who refuses to integrate and learn a minimum amount of German, but at the same time holds open the hand and receives social benefits, can in the future get these social benefits cut by up to 30 per cent. This is a good thing. (MP Uhl (CSU), 16/103: 10587)

The image thus evoked is that of a migrant population, especially those members of the second and third generations, often staying among themselves (parallel society) and not even trying or wanting to interact with the majority population (integration refusal), and taking advantage of the social welfare system.

It is against this backdrop that spousal migration comes into the picture. Next to being associated with arranged and forced marriages, and thus with types of spousal unions incompatible or at least difficult to reconcile with German or Western liberal norms, marrying a spouse from abroad is framed as both an outcome and a symptom of integration deficits and at the same time as an alleged cause of future integration issues. In other words, members of the disintegrated parallel societies have a preference for "importing" spouses the presence of whom only furthers the process of self-segregation in a sort of repetitive cycle:

> In our experience it is not correct to speak simple-mindedly of foreign fellow citizens, as if they were living with us. No, they are living partly next to us and without us in parallel worlds. Nowadays it is unfortunately easier than ever before to live in a parallel world – especially in a metropolitan area or in a large city – to continue living the familiar life of former times, that they know from their home country, to speak their old language instead of learning the German language, to not orient themselves along our customs and to not take over our norms and our lifestyle. Nowadays in Germany you can watch more than 40 Turkish TV stations and of course also get Turkish newspapers. It is correct like this; but this spreads out into the normal daily life as well: Turkish supermarkets, Turkish doctors, and even Turkish lawyers – all this can be found without any problem. They can live in Berlin as if they were in Turkey. (Heckling by Green MP: "The weather

> is not same!") And it even goes a step further: they can take care, by arranged and forced marriages – phenomena that all of us, also you, cannot tolerate – that this parallel world also continues to exist in the second generation. (MP Uhl (CSU), 16/161: 16987)

Apart from illustrating the above-described arguments connecting integration deficits defined as "parallel worlds" with spousal migration, this quote displays a strong We-Them dichotomy by clearly positioning foreigners, especially Turks, outside of the German community as living in a separate world. Since these individuals allegedly are not integrated into German society, their authentic membership in the community is questioned – and accordingly a case for restricting spousal migration via membership regulating is made. It also promotes a strong assimilationist concept of integration, since ideally integration would seem to imply "taking over [German] norms and lifestyle" as well as steering clear of any fellow citizens with Turkish heritage and services they might offer. Another important argument in this context takes the notion of a vicious cycle of disintegration a step further by outlining the negative impact spousal migration has on the offspring of these unions:

> It is an old experience within integration work that it is especially badly integrated families among whom, also after sometimes a decade-long residence, it is unfortunately still common, that young women and men do not look for a spouse in their personal living environment or circle of friends, but in the old home country of their parents. The joining spouses then usually come into a family where no German is spoken and where then the children grow up without any German skills whatsoever. Therefore they will from the outset not have good educational and professional perspectives. (MP Grindel (CDU), 17/43: 4372, emphasis added)

Again, sponsoring spousal migration is framed as being an outcome of not (yet) having reached a desired integration level. By framing spousal migration as both a symptom and a cause of integration deficits, a strong impetus for the introduction of restrictive policy instruments is constructed. Put differently, by engaging in spousal migration the (second-/third-generation) ethnic minority sponsors themselves deliver the best evidence that they are not sufficiently integrated and thus cannot be regarded as full members of German society. Implicitly, therefore, the membership of these sponsors is put into question and a justification emerges for policy measures aimed at regulating this membership.

While representatives of the SPD and the FDP did not really dwell on the CDU MPs' depictions of integration deficits, the Green and Left parliamentary groups opposed and explicitly rejected notions such as "parallel societies" and "integration refusal." They considered these approaches to be extreme generalisations, and thus stigmatising:

> General suspicions that people coming from rural regions cannot be integrated lead me to the question if someone that one might want to marry from a rural region in Germany, for you, also needs to be tested regarding his/her integration capabilities. (MP Dagdelen (LINKE), 16/209: 22637)

Framing "integration need"

Another topic that came up in the framing of integration in the context of spousal migration concerns a differentiation of migrants according to their "integration need" *("Integrationsbedarf")*. Of course, implicit differentiation also occurs by repeatedly using specific examples (e.g. referring to Turkish migrants as living in parallel societies) or also by condemning specific phenomena (e.g. the continuous references to forced marriages, which are typically associated with Muslim minorities) and thus classifying certain groups of migrants as being more in need of integration than others.

However, in the context of the language requirement policy, which includes exceptions for spouses of sponsors from visa-free countries such as the United States, Canada, Australia, New Zealand and Japan (see chapter 4.2), this idea of differentiation was taken beyond discourse and actually incorporated into law. In the discussions, the opposition frequently attacked this differentiation as being highly discriminatory. The CDU MPs, however, supported it as being legitimate since these visa-free immigrants and their spouses (who are often implicitly assumed to be highly-skilled) purportedly have less "need to be integrated" compared with migrants from other parts of the world: "If a business man comes to Germany with his Japanese wife, this provision does not hold, because no integration deficits exist in this context" (MP Uhl (CSU), 16/103: 10588).

6.1.3 The language requirement

Being such a controversial and far-reaching policy instrument, the language requirement was discussed intensively in parliament both prior to its introduction and thereafter. The various arguments presented, pro and contra, provide an excellent insight into the larger framing of spousal migration, while they also extensively refer back to the issues of forced marriage and integration presented above.

In a nutshell, the CDU's basic logic behind the introduction of the language requirement builds upon the arguments presented earlier. Forced marriages and integration deficits are serious problems among the migrant/minority population in Germany, especially and mainly among Muslim/Turkish communities. These issues do not only affect the individuals concerned, but endanger social cohesion and value systems in Germany. In the CDU's view, the liberal and generous spousal migration law existing in Germany is often "misused," which in turn exacerbates the problems of forced marriages and integration deficits. This was the diagnosis, the framing of the problem. In regard to the policy solution (therapy), the CDU MPs proposed the language requirement for incoming spouses. By obliging them to learn German and take a language test prior to migration, the state could fight forced marriages by empowering women with language skills, and at the same time enhance integration. This integration abroad measure was also dubbed "preventive integration:"

> By demanding the language requirement prior to family reunification we want to achieve preventive integration. Many migrants that come by means of family reunification are in reality objects of the events. They are married off, they are brought to Germany, they are held in apartments, some are victims of violence. In almost every integration course you will meet women that have been living in Germany for 17 or 20 years, but speak practically no German and do not leave their immediate surroundings because they are insecure or because they are not allowed to leave it. Family reunification has so far often been a relocation into a parallel society. By demanding a certificate of German skills, we see to it that the migrants become the subject of the proceedings. We do not leave them to their fate, but we ensure that they are finally taken care of. With the German skills they acquire their own capacity to act. Women, in particular, obtain the chance to more self-determination. (MP Grindel (CDU), 16/94: 9554)

As outlined above, CDU MPs also stated repeatedly that German skills are an indispensable condition to escape a forced marriage, framing it in a somewhat simplified manner as a situation similar to a kidnapping or hostage-taking where establishing contact with the outside world is the main (only?) practical issue in order to escape: "A basic condition to get help is that you at least are able to say on the telephone where you live and that the police should come in order to get you out of the threatening crisis situation." (MP Grindel (CDU), 16/169: 17862). After the introduction, the language courses at the Goethe-Institutes abroad[221] were addi-

---

[221] However, it should be kept in mind that it is not obligatory (and in some countries/regions also impossible) to follow a language course at a Goethe-Institute, or for that matter, any language course at all. The only legal requirement is to prove German skills

tionally framed as an important element of migration preparation, with the course instructors portrayed to function as integration aides. The specific emphasis in this context is again clearly on female spouses, which potentially fall victim to gendered oppression or even forced marriages:

> We stabilise these women with these courses. Not only language skills are provided. Something about our country is conveyed. It is brought across that women and men have equal rights and one can freely decide how to live. Very sensitive instructors work in the Goethe-Institutes and other language centres, who of course are aware that the women need to be strengthened, if they want to go to Germany. (MP Grindel (CDU), 16/169: 17862)

> From talks with the *'Stadtteilmütter'* [Neighbourhood-mothers] from [Berlin-] Neukölln we know – also if you continue to deny this, Ms. Dagdelen – that especially this information and the conveying of realities of life in the Goethe-Institutes prior to family reunification lead some fundamentalist families to refrain from forcing marriages upon their children. (MP Grindel (CDU), 16/209: 22635)

Thus, migration preparation is conceptualised as learning about German laws, customs and ways of life, but especially the liberal gender norms in Germany, which could in turn discourage forced marriages. In this line of thinking, language instructors can even fulfil the role of detecting forced marriages:

> Furthermore, in the preparatory language courses the trained employees of course will take a very careful look if they are maybe able to detect cases of forced marriages and get help prior to their emigration to Germany and offer consultation. (MP Grindel (CDU), 17/43: 4372)

Overall, the arguments brought forward by the CDU in its defence of the language requirement strongly referred to migrant women who experience difficulties due to being female, since their environment is characterised by antagonistic and patriarchal gender norms. As this environment potentially forces migrant women into marriages and/or inhibits them from fully integrating into German society (which could be resolved by

---

equivalent to A1 either in the form of a language certificate of an approved institution (in most cases this is a Goethe-Institute, but tests are possible without prior courses) or by means of an oral conversation at the German representation in cases of manifest (*offenkundig*) German skills. Thus, the argument of the importance of language courses as "migration preparation" is already somewhat flawed in that it is not at all ensured that all spouses take the courses.

taking part in integration courses, learning German or making German acquaintances), the language requirement would help these women. In this way, the language requirement was also presented as a "women-friendly" (*frauenfreundlich*) legal provision by the CDU (e.g. 16/143: 15131).

The opposition, especially the Left and Green parties, rejected this assessment as highly hypocritical. In their eyes, the CDU was not truly interested in gender equality but used this as an excuse to restrict migration:

> You claim that what you are suggesting here is good to fight forced marriages and good for women. I cannot help but notice that the CDU/CSU always becomes especially feministic when this can be instrumentalised against foreigners. (MP Beck (GRÜNE), 16/103: 10596)

> Those of you, in particular, who for years have consequently been inhibiting equal treatment measures in this house, are suddenly worried about women's rights. The plights of women are instrumentalised and functionalised. (MP Dagdelen (LINKE), 16/143: 15130)

Regardless of these criticisms of the CDU's so-called instrumentalised feminism, the opposition also ignored the fact that more than 30 per cent of spousal migrants entering Germany each year are men. Instead, MPs of all parties exclusively gave examples referring to female spouses entering Germany as wives (and mothers).

The CDU MPs' more specific lines of argument regarding the language requirement also were criticised by the opposition. The causal connection between the alleged goals and the suggested policy measure was rejected as unproven or implausible, and in any case, the measure was claimed to be disproportional (e.g. by a FDP MP 16/169: 17863; by Green MPs 16/169: 17862; 17/43: 4378; by an SPD MP after going into opposition 17/43: 4374). The Left MPs, in particular, maintained that the measure would even be counterproductive:

> The alleged goals of a supposed fight of forced marriages or an enhancement of integration cannot at all be fulfilled with language tests abroad, according to all professional organisations. On the contrary, the pressure upon those forced into marriages abroad would often even increase and the integration in Germany is obviously inhibited and postponed due to the hurdle of the language requirement abroad. (MP Dagdelen (LINKE), 17/43: 4377)

Regarding the issue of integration, other opposition MPs largely agreed that any kind of language training, also prior to migration, could indeed support the integration process, but they nevertheless considered the measure to be disproportional, as it infringed on the basic right to marriage and family. They argued that German could be more easily learned, and for far quicker and for far cheaper, in Germany:

> The infringement of the right to family in Germany is also not justified by the goal of integration, since there are milder means to achieve this intended goal. Languages are learnt best where they are spoken. Only then can it be guaranteed that the knowledge from the courses is practically employed and practiced, also with the support of family members and friends living here and by using the language in daily life. In short, learning the language in Germany is much easier, faster, cheaper and far less burdensome than doing it abroad. (MP Kilic (GRÜNE), 17/43: 4378)

By rejecting the inherent logic of the CDU's official policy goal, the opposition spurned the entire justification as hypocritical and claimed that the CDU was hiding its "real" political goal behind the fabricated talk of integration and women's rights. The real goal was claimed to be the widespread inhibition of low-skilled Muslim/Turkish immigration:

> You cynically claim that your law serves integration and the fight against forced marriages. In reality however you interfere with the basic right to family reunification and family life by restricting spousal reunification. (MP Dagdelen (LINKE), 16/103: 10592)

But the opposition MPs did not only criticise the CDU's framing. They also presented their own arguments for rejecting the language requirement. These arguments revolved around three main points. First, and most consistently, the language requirement was framed to be an intolerable infringement of the individual's right to the protection of marriage and family. Some MPs refer to the abstract value of marriage and family:

> All of these [consequences of the language requirement] are intolerable and have nothing to do with the protection of marriage and family. (MP Wieland (GRÜNE), 16/209: 22640)

> Why do employed individuals, in your opinion, have a right to marriage and family, while someone receiving *Hartz IV* [welfare benefits] does not? (MP Möller (LINKE), 16/90: 9071)

Other MPs make reference to the constitutional enshrinement of the protection of marriage and family in Article 6 GG:

> I would have expected the minister to explain how his ideas regarding spousal reunification can be reconciled with the special protection of marriage and family

> in Article 6 of the Basic Law. The suggestion you have made here is clearly unconstitutional. (MP Beck (GRÜNE), 16/103: 10596)

> What about the constitutional protection of marriage and family, when spouses and children are separated for years due to missing German skills? (MP Schewe-Gerigk (GRÜNE), 16/143: 15125)

> The Left Party continues to be firmly convinced that [the language requirement] is incompatible with the principle of proportionality and with Article 6 of the constitution. (MP Dagdelen (LINKE), 17/43: 4377)

Interestingly, the ECHR and other international human rights conventions were not mentioned at all in the context of the language requirement. However, in debates revolving around other initiatives to fight forced marriages, MPs of different parties and even the parliamentarian state secretary of justice pointed out that the practice of forced marriages was incompatible with European and international conventions (Green, FDP and SPD MPs 16/8: 545-550; State Secretary Stadler (FDP), 17/67: 7108). For spousal migration law, however, the German constitution seemed by far to be the most important and powerful point of reference for MPs. Sideswipes were made at the CDU's Christian party heritage by claiming that it had apparently forgotten its Christian values: "With this law you are the gravedigger of the constitutional Article 6, the special protection of marriage and family, and this as Christian Democrats. This is really a disgrace!" (MP Beck (GRÜNE), 16/94: 9562). All other arguments basically referred back to the importance of the protection of marriage as well as the disproportional infringement that the language requirement was seen to constitute.

The differentiation mentioned above was also a target for harsh criticism. The fact that spouses of EU citizens and visa-free citizens would not have to fulfil the language requirement – as opposed to spouses of German citizens and long-term residents – was framed by opposition MPs as a scandalous creation of first- and second-class marriages:

> The constitutionally protected right of spouses to live together will hereafter be limited to certain nationalities (...) Why does the Basic Law not apply anymore, or only partially to Turks, but when concerning the marriages of Japanese, Americans or Canadians it still holds? (MP Winkler (GRÜNE), 16/103: 10593)

The third strand of arguments concerned the practical difficulties and hardships experienced by individual couples. The issues brought forward to illustrate the disproportionate difficulties inflicted by the state included the local unavailability of German courses, the long travel distances, high costs connected to courses and tests, the monopoly position of the Goethe-Institute in the process, and the difficulties of lowly-educated or illiterate spouses in learning the language. Many examples of adverse individual situations were presented to illustrate these points. In this context, the lack of a hardship clause to account for extremely difficult individual situations was a source of criticism as well. Left MPs claimed that the language requirement would be particularly difficult for socio-economically weak individuals, and they framed this as both discriminatory and a hidden policy goal of the government:

> ...the goal of the new provision is the social selection within spousal reunification and the exclusion of so-called uneducated and socially rejected people. The government has more or less even confirmed the selection effect. Thus, it explicitly considers financial burdens of several thousand euros due to lengthy visa procedures to be acceptable. (MP Dagdelen (LINKE), 17/43: 4376)

Of course, the CDU reacted to these arguments. Regarding the rejection of the rationale behind the language requirement of fighting forced marriages and integration, two different responses were presented. First, CDU MPs simply insisted that forced marriages would be prevented by the language requirement. After the implementation in 2007, further "proof" was provided by pointing to the decreasing number of spousal migrants and authoritative information from the embassies:

> I have been told by the employees responsible for issuing family reunification visas in our embassies in Ankara and Istanbul that they believe – though they cannot always prove it – that 30 to 40 per cent of the visas that are issued involved forced marriages. In this context I'm telling you: if the numbers of family reunification go down now, this also means that we have successfully fought forced marriages; that we kept hundreds, probably thousands of women from having to live in a forced marriage here in Germany. This is a correct policy. (MP Grindel (CDU), 16/161: 16992)

MPs from the CDU tended to frame the language requirement not only as effective but also as an indispensable one in the fight against forced marriages. Consequently, they denounced bills brought forward by the Left and Green parties suggesting the abolition of the language requirement as not only "integration-hostile" *(integrationsfeindlich)* but also "hostile to women" *(frauenfeindlich)* (17/43: 4372, 17/52: 5497). According to this CDU logic, without the language requirement, forced marriages could not be inhibited or prevented:

> The decline in spousal reunification is due to the fact that significantly fewer requests for family reunification have been made. For me, this allows only one interpretation of the phenomenon: there are a certain number of families that actually refrain from bringing daughters-in-law to Germany via forced marriages if

> these women have German skills and thus would be able to get help in their struggle to escape this forced marriage. (...) I say in all clarity: who does not apply the law consistently in practice – by learning German prior to the family reunification the concerned women have the possibility to very practically get help for themselves – *fails in the battle against forced marriages*. (MP Grindel (CDU), 16/169: 17861, emphasis added)

In 2010, after a Left Party motion suggested abolishing the language requirement, MP Grindel (CDU) accordingly accused the party of refusing to help victims of forced marriages due to its "ideological blindness:"

> With their motion, the Left denies immigrating wives their right to defend themselves in any way against forced marriages. That should really be obvious to everyone: what good are the nicest consultancy offers and crisis lines if the affected women are not able, due to a lack of language skills, to even call the police for help, when they are subject to violence? (...) Due to their ideological blindness, the Left wants to leave women forced into marriage to fend for themselves." (MP Grindel (CDU), 17/43: 4372)

The suggestion that German skills can more easily be acquired in Germany, especially via the integration courses, was rebutted with reference to the issue of integration refusal. The CDU upheld the notion that since failure to participate in integration courses was not sanctioned (enough), individuals unwilling to integrate could still avoid attending an integration course and/or successfully prohibit women from taking part in the courses:

> The argument 'We also have the offer [to learn German] here in Germany in the integration courses' does not hold, because...we know that those families that need it the most, that until now have strongly kept clear of integration offers, in which German is not spoken, are exactly those that do not accept the offer of integration courses. That means that we do not see those in the courses that actually need it the most. (MP Grindel (CDU), 16/209: 22637)

> We wanted to empower women with German skills that they would acquire prior to their emigration to our country, so that they can get help and fight back against oppression and violence. That's why it is logical that these German skills need to be acquired prior to the migration; as women especially affected by forced marriages are not allowed to take part in the integration courses." (MP Grindel (CDU), 16/161: 16992)

The opposition's claim that the language requirement infringed ton the constitutional right to protection of marriage and family was also rebuffed by CDU MPs. They pointed out that Article 6 GG does not universally lead to a right to family migration, and that it is the "good right" of the German state to place certain conditions on migration. The possibility to restrict family migration was argued to be especially legitimate, even necessary, when the family and marriage patterns and norms involved are considered to be questionable. This was argued to be the case with forced (and arranged) marriages. The following statement made by MP Wolff of the FDP, after his party switched to the government bench in 2009, was an example of the family regulation approach in this respect:

> The fathers and mothers of the constitution never envisioned Article 6 as a carte blanche for uncontrolled and unconditional immigration into Germany. (...) Family reunification does not hold for the systematic marrying off of migrants or migrant children with partners from the countries of origin organised by extended family clans. This is also not compatible with the basic intention of Article 6 GG. (MP Wolff (FDP), 17/52: 5495)

The question whether the language requirement legally infringes the German constitution was also discussed, with CDU and government representatives citing legal experts who affirmed the compatibility with the constitution (16/143: 15132). However, there was a reflective acknowledgement that the issue was contested, with MP Mayer (CSU) responding to MP Dagdelen (Linke) citing independent opinions that attested the language requirement to be unconstitutional: "Esteemed Ms. Colleague Dagdelen, expertise exists in both directions. Constitutional doubts are nowadays always brought forward, when one rejects something politically or wants to move it in a different direction" (16/94: 9564). After the BVerwG had ruled in favour of the language requirement in March 2010, declaring it both constitutional and compatible with EU law,[222] CDU MPs cited this ruling in all further discussions as confirmation of their position (e.g. 17/43: 4372-4373).

Regarding the reproach of discrimination through differentiation, the notion of differentiated "integration need" was put forward, rather bluntly establishing a culturalised notion of integration capacities:

> From the viewpoint of integration policy, of course it makes an enormous difference whether a spouse lives in Germany permanently or only follows his/her spouse for a temporary job to Germany. It certainly also makes a difference whether a spouse speaks English or French fluently, or Turkish, Kurdish or Arabic instead. (MP Grindel (CDU), 17/43: 4373)

Concerning the practical difficulties, CDU MPs defended the language requirement by playing down the difficulty of the test, underlining the low level of language skills necessary, since A1 is "the very lowest of the six language levels possible. Language skills of this level enable you to

---

[222] See section 4.2.

buy a bottle of milk in a shop, nothing more." (MP Uhl (CSU), 16/103: 10588). This is an interesting view, since in other government arguments, the required language skills are portrayed as a crucial element of integration and of escaping forced marriages – therefore not low at all.[223] CDU MPs also emphasised that learning German lies within the personal responsibility of the incoming spouse (and his/her spouse in Germany) and that it can legitimately be expected of them:

> Before a person decides to relocate to Germany, in order to lead a marriage here, to have children and put them through school, one can expect that he/she makes the effort to acquire the simplest language skills in his/her home country in order to be able to include himself/herself linguistically into our German society. That is all we want. (MP Uhl (CSU), 16/103: 10587)

> The introduction of a hardship clause was categorically dismissed by the CDU since this would presumably lead to abuse of the process: "The entire residence law is characterised by the difficulty that wherever one opens a small crack for specific, difficult cases, many enter, some of whom are not wanted in the country" (MP Grindel (CDU), 16/209: 22636). In any case, despite all the sharp criticism, the CDU MPs proved rather unyielding in their framing of the language requirement, supporting it as an excellent measure in enhancing integration and preventing forced marriages.

6.1.4 The EU and other European states

References to the EU and to other European states also played a role in the discussion of spousal migration policies. The European Union was brought up in various respects: most obviously, the new spousal migration provisions bear a connection to the EU and EU law, since the revision of the *Zuwanderungsgesetz* was officially entitled, "Directive Implementation Act" (*"Richtlinienumsetzungsgesetz"*), referring to the transposition of 11 EU directives on migration and asylum into national law.

Early on in the debates – that is, in the discussions preceding the adoption of the new law in June 2007 – MPs of the CDU and Minister Schäuble referred to the EU and the need to negotiate the law as swiftly as possible, since Germany had been slow to act; other treaty violation proceedings against Germany had already been initiated by the Europe-

---

[223] The opposition also used the tactic of variously playing issues up or down, depending on the context. While the language tests' opponents generally underline the difficulties and hardships of acquiring German skills equivalent to A1, they sometimes also turned around their argument to claim 300 words of German to clearly not be enough to be able to truly integrate in Germany, e.g. to find employment (16/143: 15128).

an Commission (16/90: 9065; 16/94: 9564). This argument implies that responsibility for the new provisions was shifted upward, toward the EU level. This was also the opinion of the opposition, which denounced the references to the EU as hypocrisy, as in the words of Left MP Dagdelen: "The grand coalition has exploited the implementation of EU directives in order to establish further massive restrictions. This was not necessary." (16/94: 9559). However, in his first presentation of the bill in March 2007, Minister Schäuble explicitly stated (after a critical FDP inquiry on the exact extent of implementation of EU directives in the law) that the law did not only consist of EU requirements but was also informed by the evaluation of the *Zuwanderungsgesetz* 2005, along with other insights. He even agreed that the title could be changed, and he suggested calling it the "Law for the Promotion of Integration" (16/90: 9071).

Later in the discussions, especially after the *Metock* judgement in July 2008, and the manifestation of the privileging of intra-EU migrants, the references to the EU changed. For the opposition, the *Metock* judgement was an indication that the language requirement was not in line with EU law – and thus the reverse discrimination of German citizens emanating from it intolerable. They urged the government to abolish reverse discrimination and upgrade German citizens' spousal migration rights to those of SCNs (Green MP 16/209: 22640); also an SPD MP 16/184: 19730). CDU MPs, on the other hand, stated that the *Metock* judgement was unfortunate and portrayed the EU and the ECJ as meddling with national autonomy in this context. They suggested amending the Free Movement Directive in order to also be able to demand language skills from spouses of SCNs (16/209: 22640). This demand was even voiced by Minister Schäuble at a JHA Ministerial meeting in Brussels in February 2009 (16/209: 22640).

Regarding other national European models, CDU MPs on various occasions referred to the Netherlands and France as also having implemented similar requirements for spousal migration. Accordingly, Germany was cast as following a European trend (16/143: 15127; 16/143: 15132; 16/209: 22640). At other times, Germany was portrayed as a trendsetter, which other European states were following:

> In the meantime, we are setting an example for many countries in Europe. The provision to require language skills prior to family reunification is part of the asylum and migration package that has been presented by the French EU presidency. Also in other countries a consistent control [of migration] is advocated by now. The Spaniards for example have just implemented a comprehensive program on the repatriation of foreigners living illegally in their country. We are absolutely setting an example here. (MP Grindel (CDU), 16/169: 17863)

Both of these framings employed by the CDU MPs – Germany as both a policy-imitator and as a policy-trendsetter – were employed in order to enhance the overall legitimacy of restricting spousal migration; that is, German policies were posited squarely within a European trend. In contrast, the opposition also referred to other European states, although in the opposite direction: Germany was seen as being isolated within Europe due to the language requirement. For example, Green MP Wieland repeatedly spoke of the language policy, and especially the reverse discrimination emanating from it, as being an "errant German road," "absurd errant road" and even "German dead end road" *("deutscher Irrweg")* (16/209: 22640). By connecting this notion with the apparent suggestions of Minister Schäuble to change the Free Movement Directive, MP Wieland suggested that the government wanted to "oblige the other European states to follow this ridiculous errant road" (ibid.). This argument implied that not only was Germany isolating itself through its choice of a wrong policy but also wanted to force other European states into adopting similarly misguided policies.

6.1.5 Minister Schäuble's framing

The arguments brought forward by Interior Minister Wolfgang Schäuble (CDU) were somewhat distinctive. In only three instances (16/90, 16/94, 16/103) did Schäuble personally take a position in parliament vis-à-vis the law and explain the ministry's motives for placing further restrictions on spousal migration. The few statements he did make, therefore, provide valuable insights.

In the first government interrogation regarding the draft law in March 2007, Schäuble chose a very specific pattern of argument. Opposition MPs from the FDP, the Greens and the Left Party mainly criticised the draft law as being too restrictive and inhibiting integration. The proposed new provisions on spousal migration formed the single most contentious issue – with four interventions – but they were not the only topic to be mentioned. Other parliamentarian concerns included policies on asylum, "tolerated" individuals *(Geduldete)* and naturalisation. Schäuble's defence of the draft law hinged upon two interrelated arguments. First, he was highly concerned about possible abuses – "abuse" *(Missbrauch)* was mentioned seven times in the seven-page document – of the existing migration and residence provisions. He proclaimed that curbing abuses was one of the main goals of the new law:

> We wish to fight the possibilities for abuse, because combating the possibilities for abuse is a precondition for the circumstance that the majority society in this country continues to contribute to a climate of great openness and tolerance in Germany. (Minister Schäuble (CDU), 16/90: 9066)

He said he was convinced that real integration could only happen once abuse was effectively prevented, or as much as possible. This concern was also connected to his second main argument, that the toleration and acceptance of migration in the receiving German "majority [of] society" (*"Mehrheitsgesellschaft"*) could only be ensured if abuses were reduced to a minimum. Otherwise, his argument went, a breeding ground for right-wing extremist ideologies and xenophobia would be created, which he wanted to counter.

Schäuble implicitly constructed the argument that migrants display a high potential to abuse the generous immigration, residence and labour possibilities in Germany. This abuse would potentially lead the majority of society to oppose immigration and even react with xenophobia, amounting to a dual problem of 1) abuse of the system by migrants, and 2) xenophobia as a reaction among the society at large (diagnosis). This argument could be rejected as incoherent, since by continuously repeating the alleged abuse of German laws and the integration failure of migrants, Schäuble potentially further enhanced xenophobic tendencies instead of curbing them. To him, the logical response to counter this danger of xenophobia would be to reduce the possibilities of abuse to a minimum in order to ensure the continuation of an open and tolerant society. He implicitly accepted xenophobia, therefore, as a logical answer to the presence of (too) many foreigners, whom he believed were prone to abuse the system. As a policy solution (therapy) he suggested restrictions on immigration in order to boost integration and thus put a halt to right-wing tendencies:

> When making such a complex law, many aspects have to be kept in mind: the situation facing the affected [migrants] (...), but also the situation facing the other people living in this country, who, for example, are concerned because social benefits are cut down or because the labour market situation is problematic due to all kinds of developments. Sometimes we also deal with fighting extremism, left-wing extremism and right-wing extremism. In this context we can speak about what we can do in order to stifle xenophobic tendencies from the start. (Minister Schäuble (CDU), 16/90: 9067)

Here, Schäuble seems to juxtapose the interests of the "people living in this country" (i.e. the Germans) against the interests of migrants. By mentioning social benefit cuts and labour market difficulties, he refers to the notions of migrants weighing heavily on the social welfare system and taking away jobs. Immediately afterward, he brought up right- and left-wing extremism, which he wishes to squelch, thus implying that migrants' (perceived) activities within the social welfare system and labour market would be the cause for heightened xenophobia. This framing thus legitimised the newly restrictive immigration laws. When specifically addressing spousal migration policies, Schäuble also referred – just as his CDU parliamentary colleagues had done – to Article 6 GG as not inherently amounting to a universal right to family migration. In his mind, constraining some of the rights arising from Article 6 GG was constitutionally permissible, if "factual reasons" are present, such as the phenomenon of second and third generation migrants with Turkish origin marrying partners from abroad:

> We have carefully verified that it is compatible with Article 6 GG to say that you only receive the permit for spousal reunification if certain minimum conditions are fulfilled. There is a factual reason for [the language requirement] and I have mentioned this factual reason. It is that up to 50 per cent of the third generation of certain migrants[224] have spouses that did not grow up in Germany. This indicates that these are often arranged marriages; this is not even about forced marriages. This is an *abuse that inhibits integration*, which we have to fight precisely in the spirit of Article 6 of our constitution. (Minister Schäuble (CDU), 16/103: 10598, emphasis added)

Various aspects of Schäuble's argument become obvious here. First, the main reason for introducing the language requirement was the fact that a large part of the third generation of some ethnic groups married foreigners. Second, these marriages were considered to be arranged marriages. And third, these arranged marriages were classified to be both an abuse and an obstacle to integration. In this way, by repudiating arranged marriages and by classifying ethnic minorities marrying foreign spouses as a potential abuse and a phenomenon inhibiting integration, he connected the approach of regulating the family with that of regulating membership. In this way, he basically diminishes the ethnic minority individuals' right to rely on Article 6 GG.

---

[224] Note that while here, Schäuble speaks of "up to 50 per cent of the third generation of certain migrants", at the beginning of his speech, he states that "up to 50 per cent of the second and third generation of Turkish origin marr[y] partners from abroad." (16/103: 10594) It is thus obvious that with "certain migrants" he means those of Turkish origin.

6.2 Framing spousal migration in the legislative and the executive branches

In order to substantially broaden the scope of insight beyond just the parliamentary stage, the frames employed by members of Germany's legislative and executive branches involved in migration policies in the more intimate and spontaneous setting of interviews were analysed. Even though the MPs had already "been heard" via their speeches in parliament, I decided to interview them personally. I stated earlier that parliamentary debates can be considered as the epitome of political discourse, and surely, what is stated in parliament and how it is brought forward are highly relevant – especially when trying to understand what is specifically behind policy-making. However, apart from being made in public, the speeches are not overly spontaneous; rather, they are prepared by the MPs or their staffers and later read out in the parliament chamber. I hoped that setting up face-to-face interviews would generate more diverse (and possibly more honest) viewpoints, markedly different than what was heard during parliamentary debate.

Between October 2009 and March 2010, a total of 19 in-depth interviews with 25 individuals were held, with each interview lasting an average of 90 minutes. Fifteen of the interviews were single interviews; in the other four sessions, two or three colleagues participated. Eight of these interviews were with Members of Parliament, five were with former or current policy officers of federal institutions, three were with policy officers from the regional *(Länder)* authorities, and three were with administrative staff dealing with (spousal) migration at the municipal level. All the interviews were conducted in German in the interviewees' respective offices in Berlin, Düsseldorf, Frankfurt and Grevenbroich. All but two[225] interviews were taped, and later transcribed and partially translated by me. The semi-structured interviews were all based on interview guidelines with questions exploring the general views held by the interviewees on spousal migration, as well as their ideas on policies to control spousal migration and the role of institutions in the process.

With the MPs, a total of eight interviews were held, and these lasted 72 minutes on average. I sent out interview requests to all MPs who had spoken in parliament on the subject of spousal migration (n=18) in the 16th electoral term (2005-2009); presumably, to some degree, it

---

[225] In two interviews, both with policy officers working in federal institutions, I was not allowed to tape the interview. In these cases I took extensive notes during the interview which I transferred to a protocol immediately afterwards.

could be assumed that these MPs would be experts on the topic, and certainly were positioned to shape opinions and perceptions on spousal migration within their own parliamentary groups and parties, and perhaps in the public sphere as well. All but one of these 18 parliamentarians were either members or deputy members of the Permanent Committee on Internal Affairs *(Innenausschuss)*, which is the main parliamentary committee preparing decisions, discussing and deliberating on the field of migration and integration. Often, the MPs also held a position within their parliamentary group such as "spokesperson on migration issues." According to this selection of 18 parliamentarians, interview requests were sent out to five members of the SPD, four members of the Green Party and three members each of the CDU, the FDP and the Left Party. Members of all political parties represented in the parliament agreed to an interview – three from the SPD,[226] two from the Green Party and one each from the CDU, the FDP and the Left Party. These interviews are referred to as interviews 1a-1h in the following analysis.

The 12 policy officers of the federal and regional level interviewed all worked (or had worked, as I also spoke to two policy officers retired from their positions) in relevant positions dealing with migration, but their professional approaches to the topic were rather diverse. I spoke with policy officers working in the Federal Interior Ministry (BMI), in regional *Länder* interior ministries and the Foreign Office. Furthermore, civil servants from a regional ministry dealing with integration, and from the offices of the federal and regional commissioners for migration and integration issues, were interviewed. These interviews are labelled 2a-2h. At the municipal level, I spoke to three officials and one head of different aliens authorities *(Ausländerbehörden)*, and also to one officer of the municipal integration commission. The labels 3a-3c indicate these interviews. The annex provides a partly anonymised overview of the interviewees.

The analysis is organised into sections along the lines of "frame clusters," exploring the general problem frames (diagnosis) as well as the associated policy solutions (therapy) that were presented by the interviewees. The frame clusters are often interconnected, and some arguments are not easily assigned to only one frame cluster, thus some cross-references were added. Those frames that are rather similar to those detected within the parliamentary discussions are only briefly touched upon. References to all interviews are made via the above-mentioned labels:

---

[226] However, one SPD MP cancelled the interview and instead sent a member of his staff, who had been working extensively with him for an extended period, to speak to me.

1a-1h refer to interviews held with MPs, 2a-2h indicate interviews with civil servants at the federal or regional level, while 3a-3c relate to interviews with municipal civil servants.

6.2.1 *The protection of female victims*

The first frame cluster is concerned with the highly gendered framing of women within spousal migration and, more specifically, with females being potential victims within this process. Women victims within the spousal migration process are largely conceptualised in relation to human rights and gender equality, a situation that needs to be addressed through appropriate policies. The most important and frequent frame in this context is that of women as victims of forced marriages, either as incoming "import brides" or as sponsoring spouses, in which the residence permit that the incoming husband can gain through the marriage is essentially part of the dowry (3a). This framing alludes to (and is also explicitly connected with) Muslim families, mainly of Turkish or Arab origin. The perpetrators referred to are basically the relatives and/or the future husband of the victims, who, due to the patriarchal gender norms of their culture, oppress women, especially young women, and in the most extreme case force them into marriages. Many interviewees interpret forced marriages as being both a symptom of failing or failed integration and a practice that further inhibits integration; in other words, it is viewed as both a cause and an effect of integration deficits.

Another framing of female victims does not refer to Muslim women forced into marriage by larger family structures but rather to foreign women, especially those from Thailand and the former Soviet states, who marry (ethnic) German men. They are often referred to as "catalogue brides." The common image here is of (unattractive) German men, rather older than their intended wives; or as one civil servant put it, "those German men who have difficulties finding a German woman and specifically look abroad" (2c). A related idea is that the incoming wives will be completely dependent upon the husband and exposed to his possible caprices. Another, more general issue mentioned by various interviewees was the phenomenon of incoming wives falling victim to domestic violence at the hands of their husbands (1b). This topic is brought up in the context of forced marriages and catalogue brides, and also as a more general risk for incoming wives, who, due to their residential (and possibly economic) dependence on their husbands, can only break free with difficulty (1d).

These three framings display extreme situations of females as victims; but subtler kinds of victimisation of females can also be found within the frame cluster. For example, a common example invoked by interviewees speaking about marriages of convenience is that of the elderly German woman "fooled" into marriage by a young man from Africa or Latin-America (1b). In this scenario, even though she is the sponsoring spouse (thus formally in a more powerful position than the husband) and not exposed to any familial pressures, the female is framed as the abused victim of the situation.

Apart from these specific framings of female victims, generally all interviewees overwhelmingly focused on women as incoming spousal migrants – notwithstanding the fact that more than 30 per cent of spousal migrants entering Germany each year are male. This is a further point sustaining a framing of the woman as passive objects of the spousal migration process, without autonomous agency. Interestingly, the main area in which agency and responsibility were ascribed to female spousal migrants by quite a few interviewees was in raising children, thus conforming in its own respect to a somewhat archaic view of gender roles. Even when not explicitly referring to the extreme case of women being forced into marriages, the patriarchal gender norms supposedly present within ethnic minorities, especially Muslim ones, are often considered as oppressive to women. References are made to the phenomena of arranged marriages and the general hindering or obstructing of unfettered self-fulfilment *("freie Selbstentfaltung")* of women – for example, by inhibiting women from learning German, getting an education or holding a job (2g). These tendencies, which also were a concern for many interviewees, were seen to be sustained by ethnic minorities engaging in spousal migration and therefore refreshing the submissive elements among their communities by "importing" vulnerable wives who are presumably easy to oppress (see section 6.2.2 on parallel societies).

Framing women as victims of spousal migration can be classified as family regulating via quality, whether as "import brides" trapped in forced or arranged marriages in the Muslim context, as "catalogue brides" from Asia or the former Soviet Union, as romantically vulnerable elderly German women, or as victims of domestic violence. All these framings have the common effect of delegitimising the marriages of these women by implying that the women would certainly be better off outside the marriage than within it. Marriages that produce female victims were framed as conflicting with Western norms and thereby, measures aimed at "saving" female victims were justified.

Policy solutions (therapy) presented in order to protect women in the spousal migration process from oppression or abuse, and at the same time enhance their emancipation, were varied. A number of interviewees, mainly civil servants and the CDU MP, (1b, 2c, 2f, 2g, 2h, 3a) presented the language requirement as having an inhibiting effect on forced marriages. This dynamic was thought to work in a threefold way. First, the possibility was suggested (and sometimes reinforced with anecdotal evidence) that victims of forced marriages fail the German language test on purpose in order to resist familial pressure elegantly and without losing face (2f, 2h). Second, it was asserted that since learning a language would make females more educated, they would increasingly grow unattractive as potential wives – another method of preventing forced marriages. Third, if the first two mechanisms were to fail, German skills were seen as essential for the victim of a forced marriage to be able to find help through the police or social services. In this respect, however, a municipal civil servant admitted that, in practice, an increase of women breaking out of unwanted situations can instead be observed since the introduction of the integration courses in 2005, rather than after the language requirement was established (3a).

MP interviewees from the Left Party, the Greens, the FDP, and even one from the SPD (1a, 1c, 1d, 1f, 1g, 1h), dismissed this mechanism as implausible, some suggesting that this line of reasoning was simply a political tactic. But another more moderate framing was embraced by some civil servants as a sort of middle path: While not claiming outright that the language requirement would necessarily prevent forced marriages, they made the point that learning German abroad prior to immigration would have an emancipating effect on incoming wives. Emancipation would be established through the process of learning, because they "have fun" (2c), and because "it is an important step in the contemplation of the migration experience" (2h). Once in Germany, the newly acquired skills could help them to "move around freely in the country" (2e). This is similar to the framing concerning the integration courses, which, introduced in 2005, were also identified as aiding the emancipation of women by constituting their "own" activity, which sometimes had to be asserted vis-à-vis the male relatives; it also helped with the acquisition of German skills up to level B1 of the CEFR (2e).

The importance of incoming wives learning German was further framed as being especially important for the good of any children in the family, both in helping the children's own German skills and also facilitating the communication of the mothers with any relevant figures in the children's lives (teachers, doctors, etc.). However, one critical point also made by a few interviewees concerned the difficulty of reaching all those individuals who would need to go to integration courses and the practical difficulty of ensuring attendance. A number of interviewees felt the generous integration offer was all too often not embraced by those who "need it most," either due to their "unwillingness to integrate" (see section 6.2.2) or because they were not allowed to participate by their patriarchal or dominating familial network:

> The problem that you hear from all aliens authorities is that exactly those that would need it most, in the end don't turn up in the integration courses. For example, we cannot expel, or send home, or expressed neatly, readmit, Turkish nationals merely on the grounds that they refuse to participate in an integration course, due to EU law. This means that we have no sufficient instrument to also enforce they attend the integration course. (1b)

This somewhat tautological argument insists that migrants who do not attend integration courses are those who need it most, since their non-attendance exemplifies their integration need. The argument was brought up in order to justify the newly introduced language requirement. It can possibly be seen as a response to the criticism of the undue harshness of a requirement abroad if an integration course, arriving at level B1, is still obligatory after admission to Germany. Overall, the language requirement was far more controversial than the integration courses, which in turn were more or less accepted by all interviewees; only the Left MP (1f) criticised the possible sanctions in cases of non-attendance. To a lesser extent, a few interviewees (1e, 2c, 2e) mentioned the age requirement as another policy instrument that helped to prevent forced marriages.

While the abovementioned frames all referred to existing policies, interviewees also reflected on possible changes of laws and policies in order to protect or help female victims within the spousal migration process. Regarding forced marriages, many interviewees mentioned the possibility of introducing a "right of return" for TCN women forced into marriages abroad with a residence permit in Germany. Usually, a residence permit loses its validity after six months of stay abroad, and this law was considered to be very detrimental to those victims of forced marriage who are held abroad against their will. Apart from policy changes within migration and residence laws, interviewees also made suggestions to expand information campaigns, consultancy offers and shelter possibilities for forced marriage victims. The fact that the 2009 government coalition agreement contained the proposal to extend the probationary period *(Ehebestandszeit)* from two to three years was also mentioned and either criticised as counterproductive in the fight against forced marriages (1f) or, in another vein, it was defended as an important measure in the fight against marriages of convenience (2c).

6.2.2 Breaking up parallel societies

The second frame cluster revolves around the issue of failed integration that is symbolised by the notion of "parallel societies," referring to segregated communities of ethnic minorities characterised by little interaction with the majority society. While no clear-cut definition of parallel societies exists, certain common elements tended to recur in the interviews.

First, parallel societies were mostly discursively located in Turkish or Arab communities (1a, 1b, 2c, 2e, 2f, 3a), which were assumed to display very large cultural differences vis-à-vis the German/European culture (2c) – and thus less prone to rapid or successful integration. The most frequently cited challenge was the atavistic, patriarchal understanding of gender, which was seen to lead to the oppression of women and to leave little room for female emancipation (see section 6.2.1). These patriarchal gender norms were also assumed to influence marriage and family norms; seeking a submissive wife abroad was framed as a central motive to engage in spousal migration.

Another important aspect of parallel societies is the presumptive self-segregation, with members of parallel societies often being characterised as "unwilling" or "unable" to integrate. The interviewees referred mainly to a lack of interaction with the majority society, with the most frequent examples being missing language skills and an ensuing inability to communicate with Germans and "staying among themselves." Two interviewees presented anecdotes of "women, exclusively of Muslim faith, that have been living in Germany since the 1960s and don't speak a single word of German!" (3a, also 2c). Parallel societies were also framed as being generally characterised by a low education level *("bildungsfern")* and a high degree of unemployment, presumably or implicitly leading to welfare dependency and a concomitant bleak outlook for the next generation. This notion was further strengthened by an implicit juxtaposition of Muslim minorities with the highly-skilled, culturally segregated Japanese community. The Japanese "separateness" was considered unproblematic (see section 6.2.5 on differentiated migration management). Various interviewees explained the low social profile within parallel societies as stemming from the phenomenon of uneducated, rural guest workers bringing their similarly uneducated, rural family members into Germany by way of family migration:

> The profile of the immigrants reproduces itself. The trigger was the guest worker immigration that then lastly defined the profile of immigration, since it was the guest workers who reunited their families, and engaged in family reunification with their social network. (...) Spousal migration reproduces a certain profile of migration that is already here. (...) And the social profile of the Turkish migrants who came after the recruitment agreement in 1961 was made up of 73 per cent illiterates among the mothers [sic] of the labour migrants! (2f)

The vicious cycle of disintegration within parallel societies – with few possibilities for upward social mobility of children – was mentioned by some interviewees as being sustained through the continuous process of spousal migration. The importance of well-integrated, German-speaking spouses (especially wives) to the integration of the entire family (especially children) was emphasised. Likewise, poor integration of incoming wives was thought to be extremely detrimental for the future of their children.

Furthermore, parallel societies were discursively mainly located in urban surroundings. Interviewees made references to Berlin, and especially the district of Neukölln (2f), and Duisburg-Marxloh, both districts with a very high density of foreign inhabitants (2c). Even though a strong emphasis was put on the personal responsibility of the migrant to integrate, some degree of public responsibility for the present situation was acknowledged through interviewees making reference to the "mistakes of the past." Along this line, many interviewees agreed that German policy-makers for many years ignored the integration of immigrants, since the policy-makers assumed the guest workers would leave Germany again. Most interviewees saw this as both a mistake and one of the main reasons for the current integration problems (1a, 1c, 1h, 2e, 2g). However, it was also acknowledged that since 2005, especially with the introduction of the integration courses, a "paradigm change has taken place, with the realisation that migration and integration are two sides of the same coin" (2f).

Having explored the problem (diagnosis), the question arises as to what types of policy solutions (therapy) are suggested? First, many interviewees underscored the importance of an active integration policy, in which the state makes integration offers and the migrants are expected to make an effort as well, a concept subsumed under the headline "Demand and Assist" *("Fördern und Fordern")*. A few officials considered this especially important for spousal migrants in that their sojourn is widely believed to be permanent, rather than transitory, thus making successful integration into the host society all the more crucial (2c, 2f). The integration courses are basically the main integration offer made by the state, and many interviewees implicitly seemed to view the state's responsibility to "assist" *(Fördern)* to be fulfilled by the generous financing by the taxpayer of 280 million Euros each year (2f, 3a).

It therefore follows as *argumentum e contrario* that any failure to integrate can only be explained by a lack of effort on the part of the migrant; hence, the notion of "unwillingness to integrate." Further policy initiatives build, in turn, upon the "demanding" *("fordern")* element, including sanctions in cases of non-attendance of integration courses, and, more importantly for the case of spousal migration, the pre-entry language requirement. A civil servant from a regional Interior Ministry sums the problem up:

> In former times, [integration] was not taken care of, and the result was: there you had the Turkish worker, and he brought in his wife from Anatolia, and took her to Duisburg-Marxloh and there we had our parallel society. The wife could maybe go to the Turkish shop once in a while and buy Turkish products, and cook and clean at home, and if she was allowed to go outside, then only to the Mosque, where she had to sit upstairs on the tribune with the other women, and then home again. And this was her life, thus not a very self-determined life. So [the language requirement] is at least an attempt to break this cycle. (2c)

The integration-enhancing effect of the language requirement was underlined by many interviewees (1b, 1e, 2a, 2c, 2d, 2e, 2f), with one civil servant even making the point that the requirement has an effect on the choice of marriage partners: "…during the partner search emphasis is laid on the criterion of the potential partner being able to pass this minimum requirement" (2f). Even though lacking language skills are defined as only one problem of parallel societies, next to the issues of (youth) unemployment, welfare dependency and lack of education, all policy solutions concentrate on enhancing German language skills; German skills were frequently dubbed the "key" to integration. Only MPs from the left spectrum criticised this focus on language. They maintained that social and economic inclusion is what integration should achieve, and pointed to the insincerity of continually arguing that these issues could be solved merely by knowing German (1f, 1g). On a more theoretical level, the phenomena of parallel societies and integration deficits were mentioned as reasons to control and manage (family) migration, as exemplified by this BMI civil servant:

> Why are we having this integration debate? Because migration went so well, the past 20, 30 years? That's certainly not the case! But we are having the integration debate because we have social problems in the migrant population. And these social problems can easily be traced back to the fact that they have difficulties dealing with our education system, dealing with our labour market, finding employ-

ment, speaking the language, dealing with the norms and values of this society; these are the issues. And this is the paradigm change: How can I influence this? I can only influence this by influencing the type, the profile of migration. (2f)

As outlined in section 6.1.2, framing spousal migration as stemming from and leading to integration problems of minority groups ("parallel societies") and hereby justifying policy restrictions can be classified as a part of the government's regulation of membership. By suggesting that ethnic minorities marrying foreign spouses harm social cohesion, their full membership in the German community is called into question and curtailing their spousal migration rights is justified – an especially problematic situation since many of these ethnic minority sponsors are German citizens.

6.2.3 The "devaluation" of German citizenship

Nearly all interviewees commented in one way or another on the increasing ethnic diversification of the German citizenry and its significance for migration and integration policies. Just like the two above-described frame clusters, the prominence of frames relating to ethnic minority German citizens is also indicative of the fact that most interviewees' dominant preoccupation connected to spousal migration is related to ethnic minorities in Germany marrying spouses from the country of their ethnic origin (instead of worrying about "native" Germans marrying foreign partners). Contrary to the other two frame clusters, which were much discussed in parliament, the issue of German citizenship and its perceived devaluation was mentioned only in the interviews, thus making it a rather "backstage" policy issue.

Citizenship acquisition has been liberalised regarding naturalisation and *ius soli* provisions since 2000, and this has been perceived to have repercussions in the field of spousal migration. In earlier years, spousal migration could be relatively neatly sorted into the categories "reunification with Germans"/"reunification with foreigners" with the former enjoying more extensive rights than the latter. Recently, the increasing proportion of individuals with a migration background among the German citizenry – mainly *Aussiedler*, naturalised foreigners, and of late the first cohort of *ius soli* children – has started to blur the picture. More and more German citizens are now ethnic minorities – or, looking at it from a different perspective, more and more ethnic minorities are obtaining or being born into German citizenship – and this phenomenon was seen as influencing spousal migration policies by many of the interviewees. German citizens marrying foreigners are thus not necessarily "ethnic Germans" anymore, but also increasingly are Germans "with a migration background" (hereafter: ethnic minority Germans[227]). But the perspectives on this dynamic differ, with the Green MPs and an integration civil servant perceiving the problematisation of ethnic minority Germans to be a driving force behind conservative policy-making, and they criticising this outlook as discriminatory and racist (1a, 1g, 2b). They ironically described responsible policy-makers as having been influenced by the perception of "the naturalised Turk, who still isn't trusted to be clean. 'He's fooling us! He pretends to be integrated, gets naturalised and then, goes and gets another [relative] from Anatolia'" (2b).

Other interviewees described the phenomenon in a neutral fashion, stating that ethnic minority Germans are prone to marry partners from their (parents') country of origin (1e). However, the majority of the interviewees mentioning this topic explicitly connected policy restrictions for German sponsors with the increase of ethnic minority Germans, and they openly endorsed this reasoning (1b, 2c, 2e, 2f):

> [The decreasing rights of German sponsors] surely are also motivated by the increasing naturalisation rates, in the sense that 'reunification with Germans' often means that these Germans are former foreigners who have been naturalised, and then still nevertheless bring in their wife or husband from their original country of origin. This was surely an argument to have no reason to treat [German citizens] differently [from foreigners] in this context. (2e)

There were three main points that were mentioned as to why ethnic minority Germans sponsoring spousal migration are different (and implicitly thus, should be treated differently) than ethnic Germans. First, the heightened propensity of ethnic minority Germans to marry a spouse from their own ethnic background was brought up, either in a neutral fashion as a "natural" or "normal" phenomenon (1e, 2c), since "they have roots in other cultures and also foster them, and thus like to look for a partner from that culture" (1e). Alternatively, and this is the second point, this reference to transnational marriages among ethnic minorities is seen critically in that it is a symptom and a cause of reluctant integration (see frame on parallel societies). The interviewees reasoned that the

---

[227] Instead of the official term "Germans with a migration background," (Statistisches Bundesamt 2009a), I will hereafter employ the term "ethnic minority Germans." I conceptually include ethnic German resettlers from the former East Bloc into this definition, though aware that the term ethnic minority might be considered somewhat unfitting for this group, as it was just upon their (German) ethnicity that their admission and citizenship claim was based.

fact that someone has German citizenship in no way guaranteed his or her successful integration. On the contrary, German citizens could also live in parallel societies. This also connects to the third point, which was often presented as an argument as to why spouses of German sponsors need to fulfil the language requirement abroad: German citizens do not necessarily speak German well themselves and thus cannot be expected to ensure language acquisition of the incoming spouse. A CDU MP said:

> I would bet that the majority of German citizens joined by Turkish national spouses have a migration background. That is the point! The belief that German is spoken in all families where German citizens reunite with incoming spouses is a pious one. It would be nice if it was this way, but it's not! Instead many constellations exist, and this will only increase in the future through the option model,[228] where the male family members who bring in the Turkish women, *formally* are German citizens, but possibly live just as much in a parallel world as a Turkish citizen. (1b, emphasis added)

This CDU MP thus justified extending the language requirement to citizens by clearly positioning citizens with Turkish heritage outside the national German community ("formally Germans"). A civil servant (2f) also emphasised a German language deficiency among German citizens, especially within the *"Spätaussiedlermilieu"* and among those persons that were naturalised prior to the citizenship reform in 2000, when German skills were not a necessary precondition for naturalisation. Apparently, in the context of the integration course evaluation, a strong demand for integration courses among ethnic minority German citizens was detected. As a result, the courses were opened for German citizens with the change of the law in 2007. A more general wariness toward the new citizenship law, which facilitated citizenship acquisition since 2000, was expressed

---

[228] The "Optional Model" *(Optionsmodell)* was included into German citizenship law in 2000. It establishes *ius soli* for children born in Germany to two foreign parents, at least one of which has been residing legally in Germany for at least 8 years (§ 4 Abs. 3 *Staatsangehörigkeitsgesetz*, StAG). These children receive German citizenship at birth and in most cases also obtain one or more further citizenship(s) via descent from their parents, which they are entitled to hold alongside their German one until they turn 18. Between the ages of 18 and 23, these individuals must decide which citizenship they wish to retain and communicate their decision in writing to the German authorities (§ 29 StAG). In most cases, this means that they must renounce their other citizenship(s) in order to keep their German one. In case they opt for their foreign citizenship(s) or in case no decision is communicated to the authorities, the German citizenship is usually withdrawn. The constitutional compatibility of this rule, which includes the possibility of withdrawing a granted citizenship, is highly controversial among legal experts.

by a civil servant from a regional interior ministry. He perceived it as a devaluation of German citizenship:

> German citizenship has lost the significance it used to have. We recently had a case concerning the expulsion of a pregnant Nigerian prostitute, the child's father was also Nigerian and had a residence permit and been here longer than eight years. This child, born in Germany, will be German. Of two Nigerians! That is the new citizenship law. This is *ius soli*, of course, but the significance of citizenship has really been a bit relativised now. (2c)

It is interesting to note that the civil servant used the example of a child born to two Nigerian nationals, one of whom was presumably an irregular migrant and a prostitute, to underscore his point that German citizenship was "losing its significance." By choosing this example he hinted at the circumstance of a) the mother being in a morally and legally ambiguous position as an irregular migrant and a prostitute and, b) the child being black. Even though he did not explicitly make these points, he seemed indignant about the effects of the *ius soli* provisions.

The policy response (therapy) connected to this problem framing has basically been a decrease in some of the privileges German sponsors previously enjoyed or, in other words, the partial decreasing of German sponsors' rights, equating them partially with those of TCN sponsors.

First, the language requirement that was introduced would have to be fulfilled by spouses of TCN sponsors and Germans sponsors alike – not however, by spouses of SCNs or visa-free sponsors (see section 6.2.5). The arguments regarding forced marriages and integration were therefore thought to apply, at least partially, for German sponsors as well, mainly in cases of ethnic minority Germans.

The second pertinent policy solution is the income requirement, which prior to 2007 applied only to foreigners (and not to Germans) but was extended to German citizens in those cases where the relevant authorities deem it "reasonable" *(zumutbar)* that the marital life take place in the home country of the incoming spouse, primarily in cases of ethnic minority Germans (see chapter 4.2; this provision was overruled by a court decision in 2012). The interviewees were divided in their assessment of the relevance of this newly introduced provision. Some of them stated that the provision had mainly symbolic value and scant practical relevance (1e, 2e, 2g). However, some civil servant interviewees indeed confirmed that regular income checks for minority Germans have been installed since 2007, with *Aussiedler* being explicitly exempted from this category of minorities (3a). In the arguments defending the provision, mistrust was expressed vis-à-vis ethnic minority Germans and their right to lay claims to family migration as German citizens was also questioned.

Naturalised citizens, in particular, were implicitly not accepted as full German citizens:

> What is behind [the possible income requirement for Germans] is the fact that there are definitely cases where somebody is German, but has only been German for five years, and prior to that for 30 years was, let's say, a Serbian national. Why should he, if he wants to marry a Serbian woman, not *continue* to be married in Serbia with her? (2c, emphasis added).

> The constitutional principle states: the same things must be treated in the same way, and different things must be treated differently. And there is certainly a difference between dealing with an only-German, who has lived his entire life only in Germany, and dealing with somebody who has lived in Turkey for 30 years and now for eight years in Germany and *has managed* to be naturalised. (1b, emphasis added)

The suggestion by the first speaker quoted that a former Serb "continue" to live in Serbia, implies that he has stronger links to Serbia than to Germany, notwithstanding his German citizenship; the second interviewee described a Turk who "has managed" to obtain German citizenship, suggesting that there was a certain illegitimacy to the naturalisation (and thus, in the ensuing claiming of citizenship rights) in the eyes of the civil servant. Similar to the government's explanatory statement, the issue of "reasonability" regarding a relocation of the sponsor to the migrant spouse's country of origin was mentioned, and hinges particularly on language skills. This is illustrated by the following quote in which the local civil servant of an aliens authority repeatedly referred to ethnic minority Germans as foreigners. He also justified the "reasonability" of expecting second- or third-generation migrants to have their marriage and family in their (grand-)parents' home country while being able to use, naturally, their excellent language skills:

> [The income requirement] now also applies to Germans, if they are naturalised Germans, if the nationality of the incoming spouse and the nationality of the spouse living here [sic] coincide or are related. You cannot expect a Turkish national [sic] to lead a life in Morocco, but of a Tunisian [sic] you might. It is all a question of reasonability. (…) The idea is that for the German living here, who used to be a Turk, possibly Turkey is not an unknown place, particularly as he speaks the language. And this holds in the same way for the second generation. This even holds explicitly for the second generation! This widespread assertion, particularly among do-gooders *(Gutmenschen)*, that the foreigners [sic] of the second generation do not speak their language of origin, is simply a lie. This should be said frankly. It is a lie. Since then they would not be able to communicate at home. And anyone that ever walked with open ears through the city centre knows, that the foreigners [sic] of the third generation actually all speak their language of origin, even though they are all German. (3a)

According to one conservative MP, another idea behind this provision was to create an incentive for unemployed ethnic minority Germans to enter the labour market in order to sponsor their spousal migration:

> There are many naturalised Turks and Arabs, especially young ones, who have basically prepared themselves to live their entire life [on social welfare]. And here the question came up: how could we motivate them to actually get their act together concerning a job? That is the decisive issue, to say: 'If you want to have a family reunification, you have to get your act together and work!' This could be a soft way of forcing them to actually get a job. And that's why [the income requirement for minority Germans] is also an integration instrument, since they are now willing to actually (and) seriously make an effort to find employment, in order to then later be able to live with their wives in a marriage here. (1b)

Furthermore, another interviewee heading a municipal aliens authority bluntly stated that the idea behind this provision was the propensity of ethnic minority Germans to abuse family migration possibilities:

> That nowadays Germans with a migration background are treated differently from Germans, original Germans, very clearly has something to do with their systematic abuse of family reunification provisions. Very clearly. (3a)

In other words, in order to justify restricting spousal migration rights of ethnic minority Germans, government actors both framed them as prone to "abuse" family migration (and social welfare) provisions and pointed towards their transnational links to justify their possible emigration. This is an instance of membership regulating via quality. By creating the possibility to oblige ethnic minority Germans to fulfil the income requirement that "normal" German citizens are exempted from, a clear distinction is drawn between (formally equal) members of German society. That is, some citizens are classified as lesser members than others and thus are required, just as is the case for foreign sponsors, to prove they fulfil other conditions of "good membership," namely they have a regular and sufficient income. Most frames of government MPs and civil servants illustrated above confirmed this: They view ethnic minority Germans as members with less rights to spousal migration, and analogise their claims with those of foreigners rather than fellow citizens. Even though access to citizenship was substantially liberalized in 2000, ethnic conceptions of who can be a "real" German still prevail among many politicians and policymakers.

6.2.4 The protection of the public budget

The issue of the public budget, and here especially the welfare state, which is seen as being strained by spousal migration and which needs to be protected by corresponding policies, came up in the majority of interviews. In other words, the notion was rather widespread that preventing immigration into the welfare system *("Zuzug in die Sozialsysteme")* is one of the top priorities within migration policy-making. Most interviewees confirmed and accepted this rationale as their own (1c, 1d, 1e, 2c, 2e, 2f, 3a), while MPs from the left spectrum and an integration officer criticised this government logic (1f, 1g, 2d). Two ideas seemed implicit. The first was that the German welfare system is overall very generous and thus prone to abuse. The second was the notion that (spousal) migrants are quite likely abuse the system. The inherent injustice, vis-à-vis the German tax-payers which maintain the welfare system, was underlined as well:

> There is always this tension between constitutional law on the one hand, but also the state's legitimate interest to protect itself from immigration into the social welfare funds on the other hand. Abuse exists, in the sense that *they* want something, and that mostly is: money. The legislator thus expects that a so-called immigration into the welfare system should be prevented. That is the conception of the residence law. Try getting across to a German, who always paid his contributions and fed the welfare coffers, that somebody is coming in from outside, who never paid in anything, but immediately is maintained. (2c, emphasis added)

> One of the biggest political problems of all is: how can the financing of our social welfare system be secured? And if I then permanently organise fresh supply into the welfare system from outside, to put it that way, then this is an enormous political problem! For example, in the end all political camps supported the restrictions in the fields of ethnic resettlers and Jewish migration, because in the end 60, 70, 80 per cent of the late ethnic resettlers were landing in the welfare system, with very negative prospects of getting out again. (...) Other thoughts cede to play a role in situations like this. Politicians do not think about trifling things, they only see the big picture, and that is dominated by the financing of the welfare system and the federal budgetary situation, the debt situation of the budgets of the *Länder* and municipalities. I would put my hand into the fire to claim that all this is the main motivation of all political action of every MP of the German *Bundestag*. And if I have a phenomenon that is controllable, what is the justification to give them the right to immediately immigrate into our social security system? (2f)

The main policies protecting the welfare state are the income requirement for TCN sponsors, which has always been in place, as well as the income requirement for German sponsors introduced in 2007. This policy innovation in itself points towards the main target group policy makers are worried about in this context: Ethnic minorities, with and without German citizenship (see sections 6.2.2 and 6.2.3). As outlined above, an implicit notion seems to exist among some policy-makers that ethnic minority Germans can less legitimately lay claim to family migration rights. A similar and wholly interconnected notion exists regarding the perceived legitimacy of their right, and their families' right, to access the welfare state. Otherwise it is difficult to explain why the income requirement was not extended to all German citizen sponsors, regardless of ethnic origin. Such a policy would have surely been more sensible from the viewpoint of protecting the welfare state and the public budget from further burdens.

6.2.5 The differentiation of migration flows

This frame cluster deals with the discursive positioning of spousal migration within overall migration management, including the characteristics associated by the interviewees with spousal migration compared with other types of migration. The most important argument in this context, emphasised in different ways by the various interviewees, was that of family migration running contrary to an efficiently controlled and managed migration attracting desired migration flows. These desired inflows were mainly framed to be high-skilled migrants, who were assumed to be necessary and indispensable by many interviewees for economic and demographic reasons.

Family migrants, in contrast, were implicitly (and sometimes explicitly) assumed to be uneducated, thus economically undesirable and potentially a burden on the welfare state. One reason for this perception was the notion that family migration is a "reproduction of the present migrant profile" (2f). This "present migrant profile" mainly refers to former guest workers and their families. Occasionally, the interviewees even further differentiated, namely into the categories European vs. Muslim:

> I think you really have to differentiate among the guest workers. With the guest workers who came from Spain, Greece, from EU countries, this adaptation process took place rather quickly, since also in the home countries similar development occurred. And those guest workers that were sent for from the poor regions of Turkey, and also from Morocco, Tunisia, Algeria, there we really had very unqualified migration and now we have issues with their integration. (2c)

The juxtaposition of educated and economically valuable highly-skilled migrants with uneducated, welfare-dependent spousal migrants also has an integration component. Differentiations were made by some interviewees (1a, 1b, 1c, 2c, 2g) along the lines of integration necessity and willingness of migrants to integrate. Some migrants were seen to have an "integration need" *("Integrationsbedarf")* and others were not. Amongst those who would need to integrate, a further distinction was drawn between those willing and those unwilling to undertake an effort *("integrationswillig"/"integrationsunwillig")*. These differentiations along education level, as well as need and willingness to integrate, are further intermingled with notions of ethnicity and nationality. The example of Asian migrants as having more of an affinity for education as opposed to other, especially Turkish, migrants, was occasionally brought up (1a, 1d, 2d), as in this anecdote from a Green MP:

> It indeed is problematic with Turkish and also with Arab families. Because that's where we have the social problems. We don't have them with the Vietnamese. There we also have problems, illegal cigarette smuggling, Vehmic murders [sic], but we don't have the education problems. I come to different conclusions than Thilo Sarrazin, but of course I see it the same way. As a lawyer I used to sometimes go into a Chinese snack bar, and while I ate my lunch, the children of this snack bar sat at the next table doing their homework. The mother supervised them, sometimes she asked me whether I could help out. When I ate in the Turkish snack bar it was completely obvious, nobody knew where the boys were and it didn't occur to anybody to ask about the homework. That means, there are really very different cultural traditions and this idea: 'My child should one day be better off than me', is partly very strong, and partly completely lacking. And there you really need to intervene and control. (1a)

Along the same lines, Japanese businessmen and their families were variously mentioned as examples of an "unproblematic group," needing no integration (1c, 2c, 2e, 2f, 3a). For instance, an SPD MP referred to the Japanese immigrants as well-integrated "model migrants" who take care of their children's education and "always go to see Swan Lake and the Nutcracker at the opera" (1c), implying high levels of education and affluence. Other interviewees reflected more critically on the fact that this Japanese community also lives in a segregated fashion (2c, 2f), it was however not dubbed a "parallel society" but rather an "island within society" (2c). In addition, since this group is perceived of as being affluent, they were therefore considered unproblematic, or as one civil servant put it: "They are all economically so well-off, they don't need any integration" (2f). This did not only apply to Japanese migrants, even though this was the most common example. In general, migrants from the visa-free countries were considered to be educated and highly-skilled, and to be only staying temporarily. In any event they were conceptualised as not needing to be integrated:

> On the other hand we also want to be a modern country, attractive for highly-skilled individuals. If a professor from the USA comes here to do research, for two or three years, or a Japanese entrepreneur comes to Düsseldorf to live here for two, three years, then actually there is absolutely no integration need. (1b)

The interviewees did not reflect on the fact that spouses of highly-skilled migrants, researchers and entrepreneurs were in any case exempted from the language requirement. The majority of MPs and civil servants approaching this issue simply equated visa-free migrants (especially from Japan and the United States) with affluence and a high standard of education. Apart from (a high standard of) education and affluence as distinguishing features of certain migrants, "culture" was also brought up as a harbinger of integration or obstacle to it. Here, Western culture was associated with educated and urban foreigners who assimilate easily, who "do not stand out at all." These migrants were conceptualised to be distinct from those with a "completely different culture," indicating a rural and uneducated background, which presumably made it difficult for them to integrate:

> I think the cultural differences are really the decisive point. If it is really a completely different culture, then they really have a difficult time to gain a foothold here with us. If they themselves have already gotten to know a similar kind of life, and in some kind of way Western oriented life, then it usually works out quite well. That's why you really cannot only speak of 'the' country of origin. The typical example is really Turkey. There is Anatolia, Eastern Anatolia, with a truly very uneducated population coming here, and then there are Turks who are very educated, and very qualified, who do not stand out at all, who at most can be recognised as Turks because of their name! (2c)

Turkey was also explicitly associated with the two main "abuses" of spousal migration policies – forced marriages and marriages of convenience – by the CDU MP who recounted his personal visit to visa offices abroad:

> I regularly visit the visa offices, especially in Turkey, and ask the employees dealing with family reunification, which funnily enough are almost always women, what kind of constellations are we dealing with here? Through their practical work they have a pretty good impression of the situation and they tell us, at least in the case of the main country of origin, Turkey, it is split into thirds. They tell you very clearly: one third love, one third marriages of convenience, one third forced marriages. (1b)

In this context of differentiated migration management, the dilemma between the constitutional right to the protection of marriage and family on the one hand, and the sovereign state's right to control migration inflows on the other, was another prominent topic among interviewees. Opposition MPs of the Left and the Green Parties (1f, 1g) referred to the constitution in order to delegitimise the language requirement, which they claimed to be an infringement of the GG. Other MPs from the SPD and CDU also acknowledged the constitutional protection of marriage and family, but at the same time emphasised the state's right to migration control since "in the end, every state in the world decides for itself who is allowed to live in the country. And the mere fact that someone is married is in itself not a sufficient reason to open the doors for people from outside." (1e). Various interviewees went even further and, in a somewhat defensive fashion, strongly underlined that the constitutional protection of marriage and family in no way immediately leads to an unconditional right to family migration (1b, 2c):

> It has been confirmed by jurisdiction that norms protecting private and family life, such as Article 6 GG or Article 8 of the ECHR, do not immediately lead to a legal claim to come here as spouse or family member. Instead, [family reunification] needs to conform to national laws, and the national legislator has the right to set up the conditions for this. And in the framework of the national laws possibly these constitutional norms or also European law can be of relevance. But that is first of all the general approach; the state defines the general framework. (2c)

Parallel to the arguments mentioned above surrounding the income requirement for Germans, it was pointed out that if the conditions legitimately set up by the state could be fulfilled by the sponsor and the spouse, the family union could just as well be established abroad, especially since the legitimate interest of the state to enhance integration is weighed against the constitutional provisions (1b, 2c). Furthermore, some interviewees did not view the constitutional protection as a legitimate right of individuals that needs to be protected, as opposition MPs saw it, but rather as a cumbersome burden that inhibited effective policies. For example, the possibility of the Constitutional Court overruling the language requirement as an infringement of Article 6 GG was described by the CDU MP as a "risk" and a "problem" (1b), which, however, was consciously accepted in order to achieve the higher goal of appropriately dealing with integration. He praised the government for its activism ("We do something!") in the face of "overwhelming problems" and subtly condemned any critic as pedantic, saying:

> Since the problems are so overwhelming, there is really a disposition to do something, without checking into the very last detail one hundred per cent whether this is a thousand per cent constitutional. Instead we just do something, and also take a risk, a certain constitutional risk. I think this is fine. And if this in the end leads a young man to finally make an effort to find a job, then this is a great thing,

no? And if a woman comes into an environment where maybe at last the effort is made to speak German, then this is nothing terrible that we want to inflict upon them, but it is a gentle pressure to go the right way. And I think that is actually very permissible. (1b)

Civil servants of the *Länder* and at the municipal level also brought up the constitutional protection of marriage and family and the need to weigh different political objectives against one another (2c, 3a). It was mentioned that instances of prior criminality and expulsion of the incoming spouse could conflict with the constitutional protection and needed to be individually evaluated. Furthermore, the involvement of children in the family migration process was thought to complicate the state's possibility to control migration:

[When children are involved] the legislator is really on the side of the people and the children's well-being is always a top priority. When two adults engage in abuse, something can be done, the state is not powerless, and it is correct that we try to counteract such things. But as soon as children play a role, you cannot push through your principles as you wish. And what is sad is when children are only brought into the world for this reason. (2c)

FDP and Green MPs (1a, 1d, 1g) made the point that one of the reasons why such a large part of the total migration into Germany is spousal migration is the lack of alternative migration paths. This situation was also believed to make the institution of family migration, just as that of asylum, somewhat susceptible to abuse (1g). This argument was made in order to advocate the creation of more legal admission possibilities into Germany beyond family migration.

Various references were made to points-based migration systems. While the FDP MP strongly advocated it, arguing that Germany needs immigration for demographic and economic reasons and that this immigration in turn needs a "clear structure in order to have an economically rational character" (1d), the Left MP strongly rejected it as a "pure logic of exploitation" (1f). Several civil servants (2c, 2e, 2f) rather neutrally made reference to points-based migration management systems used in countries such as the United States, Canada and Australia; they contrasted it with the German migration policies, which according to them operate completely differently. The argument was made that these countries, with their highly selective migration policies, experienced much fewer integration problems than Germany. In Germany, without a points-based migration control, the main migration inflow consisted of family migrants from frequently uneducated backgrounds and that in turn led to problems with integration.

The policies (therapy) connected to these framings of spousal migration are varied. The language requirement functioning as a hurdle for uneducated spouses and raising the education level of the incoming spouses was one policy instrument mentioned. Furthermore, the exception from this language requirement for spouses of visa-free citizens was defended by three interconnected arguments. First, the visa-free citizens and also their spouses were considered to be educated and highly skilled – and thus caused few problems in the first place: "It would be crazy to tell the researcher who wants to come here: 'Your wife, who is fluent in English, French and Spanish, can only come if she learns German!'" (1b). Connected to this issue is the second notion of the desirability of these visa-free migrants. Most interviewees implicitly equated citizens from these countries with desired highly-skilled migrants. When asked about the government's reasons for installing the exception for visa-free migrants, the examples of businessmen from Japan or researchers from the United States were brought up – their migration into Germany should not be inhibited in any way. Therefore, also their spouses' migration should be facilitated, because a language requirement for these spouses would constitute "another hurdle in the fight for smart heads for Germany" (1b). In this constellation, the importance of marriage and family for personal well-being is thus accepted all around. Finally, the sojourn of visa-free citizens and their spouses in Germany was also considered to be only temporary and therefore not requiring integration (through German skills).

Various MPs (1d, 1f, 1g, 1h) openly criticised the visa-free exception as unfair, especially vis-à-vis German sponsors who were disadvantaged in their own home country; some spoke of "discrimination" (1h) and even "white racism" (1f). Those interviewees that in general supported the exception also acknowledged that it might be perceived as unjust (1b, 2g), but nevertheless defended it in order to achieve the goal of facilitating the desired immigration of high-skilled migrants. Regarding a possible infringement of the constitutional right to marriage, the argument was presented that the language requirement was "not so difficult" (1e, 2e, 2f) and not such a strong infringement. It was also argued that the requirement was permissible since the higher goals of integration and the prevention of forced marriages were achieved, and in any case, the family unity could also be established abroad.

6.2.6 Fighting abuse of spousal migration

The most common type of abuse mentioned by the interviewees was the phenomenon of marriages of convenience. Mirroring the near absence of the issue in parliamentary discussions, most MPs either did not talk about the issue at all (1h) or when pressed for a statement they said they regarded the issue as rather passé and outside the political spectrum or sufficiently monitored already (1a, 1c, 1d, 1e). Various MPs found it "overrated" (1d, 1e) and agreed that marriages of convenience were surely "not a mass phenomenon" (1e).

Civil servants, however, painted a very different picture. Many of them identified marriages of convenience as an intolerable evasion of the rule of law and thus a serious abuse of spousal migration provisions that they (or the authorities they deal with) are confronted with on a daily basis (1b, 2c, 2g, 2h, 3a, 3c). One especially problematic form of marriages of convenience was illustrated by two interviewees (1b, 2c), namely that of "creeping family reunification" *("schleichender Familiennachzug")*. This implies that a spouse from a marriage of convenience (either with a consenting or a fooled sponsor) is divorced after the probationary period, only to (re-) marry in the country of origin and subsequently sponsor the migration of this old/new spouse and possible children. Other types of abuse outside the classic consensual marriage of convenience were also mentioned and include marriages organised to facilitate human trafficking (2a), organ trade (3a), forced prostitution (3a) and the drug trade (3a).

In addition to this abuse of spousal migration via "fake" marriages, another form of "abuse" was mentioned by civil servants, especially those at the *Länder* and municipal levels (2c, 3a). They rather angrily report on the different ways in which authorities and institutions get "fooled" by sponsors and incoming spouses who try to circumvent parts of the regular admission procedure. For example, it is apparently not uncommon for sponsors to "dodge" the income requirement – that is, to falsify job contracts or income slips. Another abuse mentioned is circumvention of the German visa policy. Citizens of certain states – many Latin American countries, for example – can easily obtain a tourist visa for three months at the border when entering Germany. These are the so-called "positive states" *(Positivstaaten)*. On occasion, citizens from these states enter Germany on a tourist visa, then marry (also in Denmark, where marriage procedures are easier) and then immediately apply for family migration from within Germany, hereby trying to circumvent the language requirement abroad (3a). Another strategy mentioned, also applicable to citizens needing a visa even for a short stay, was that of obtaining a Schengen visa from another EU state, then entering Germany and applying for family migration. For instance, "very popular recently are the Baltic states, because they don't look so closely" (3a). All of these methods confront the German authorities with *faits accomplis* and are "circumventions of the visa procedure, which is the only effective instrument of control against unwanted migration" (3a).

The main policy solution to the issue of marriages of convenience has already been in place for years in the form of the intimacy inquiries executed by the representations abroad together with the local aliens authorities. As described in chapter 2, the intimacy inquiries try to assess the "quality" of the spousal relationship. This policy was criticised as discriminatory and invading privacy by various MPs of different parties (1a, 1e, 1f, 1g). Two MPs criticised instances of institutional discrimination they had heard of or experienced as lawyers, such as racist and sexist attitudes displayed by civil servants when dealing with white German women with African men (1e) or civil servants purposefully leading spouses to give false answers by phrasing the questions in confusing ways (1g). These negative attitudes towards intimacy inquiries are not surprising considering these MPs' assessments of the phenomenon of marriages of convenience being overrated in the first place. On the contrary, most civil servants supported and defended the intimacy inquiries as just being "in the spirit of the protection of marriage and family" (2b) and "actually in the interest of the couple to show that their marriage is serious" (2h). An interesting point is made by one civil servant who claimed that "if the inquiries were more lax, and this is what certain political camps are only waiting for, then overall family reunification would be put into question and become more restrictive" (2h).

Restricting spousal migration by pointing to the problems of abuse in the form of marriages of convenience is another classic instance of family regulating via quality. Marriages conducted for the sole purpose of gaining a residence permit do not fall under the constitutional protection of marriage and family; this is nothing new. However, as with forced marriages, those culpable of entering a marriage of convenience are unlikely to step forward and declare themselves guilty. Nonetheless, the intensity and intricacies of policies aimed at detecting and preventing such marriages can certainly function as instruments to restrict spousal migration. Chapter 7 goes into more detail on the consequences of marriages-of-convenience policies.

6.2.7 The role of Europe and other institutional dynamics

Europe came up in three contexts in the interviews. First, the EU 2003 Family Reunification Directive was mentioned extensively. Some interviewees claimed the directive had been a principal impetus for the restrictive law change, thus in a way searching for legitimacy from the EU level. Federal civil servants from the BMI rather openly revealed that German preferences in the field of spousal migration were successfully included at EU level during negotiations. Interviewees from the left spectrum instead claimed that the directive was interpreted in an overly restrictive way by the German government, strongly rejecting the notion of legitimacy from the EU level.

Second, the reverse discrimination of Germans vis-à-vis intra-EU migrants also was broached. This phenomenon was condemned by nearly all interviewees as unfair and unfortunate, although they differed on the proposed consequences. Opposition politicians suggested increasing German citizens' rights to the level of intra-EU migrants, while the CDU MP proposed decreasing intra-EU migrants' rights to the same as German citizens. Most interviewees however considered it utopian to change EU law in this respect and thus had no real suggestions to make.

Third, other European countries, mainly the Netherlands, France and Denmark, which have introduced similar restrictions in the field of spousal migration, were cited as examples and as instances of additional legitimacy.

> It is not completely wrong that the language requirement was also meant to be a hurdle, because we also looked at the Netherlands. When we decided upon the language requirement, the Dutch had already introduced this language requirement within spousal reunification, and of course the amount of spousal reunification declined, it was massively reduced. (2e)

In the second part of the interviews, I asked interviewees to reflect on the importance and preferences of their own institution and other important institutions in the field of migration policy-making. This second set of questions did not generate such fruitful answers as the first set, but certain patterns could be discerned.

Primarily, the Federal Ministry of the Interior (BMI) was recognised by most interviewees as fairly independent and a very powerful actor in the field of migration policy. The MPs mainly reflected on their party's position within the wider framework of the parliament and the political landscape in Germany, or they pointed out certain political compromises, such as the "deal" struck between the SPD and the CDU in the grand coalition mentioned above. The representatives of regional and lower administrations mainly pointed to their executive role. They claimed to receive orders and laws from above and fulfil them. In general it was observable that only the civil servants working in integration offices (2a, 2b, 2d) perceived of themselves as spokespeople of migrants and minorities and thus offered somewhat government-critical, pro-migrant attitudes. Meanwhile, all other civil servants from federal and *Länder* ministries and local aliens authorities by and large had very pro-governmental, "law and order" viewpoints, and supported and defended the government's restrictive stance on spousal migration.

Conclusions

After outlining the background and specifics of a recent legal and political restrictive turn regarding spousal migration in Germany in the previous chapters, the analysis presented in this chapter aimed at exploring why and how these (restrictive) shifts were initiated, discussed, concluded and implemented.

The main focus of the analysis was on individual actors as representatives of institutions. On the one hand, the issue was approached by way of parliamentary debates; in the first section the relevant framings presented by MPs of all parties in the German parliament from 2005-2010 on the issue of spousal migration were analysed. It was shown how in the *Bundestag* forced marriages and integration deficits are framed as pressing questions necessitating policy answers, especially by CDU MPs. By presenting the lack of language skills as a major reason inhibiting both integration and the possibility of escaping forced marriages, the language requirement can gain the status of a welcome legal instrument helping oppressed (Muslim) women and creating incentives for individuals unwilling to integrate instead of a restrictive barrier infringing on the human right to marriage and family in a discriminatory fashion, as the opposition in turn tends to frame it.

Returning to the approaches outlined in chapter 2.1, family regulating via quality happens by connecting forced marriages – a practice violating human rights and liberal Western norms – to spousal migration and thereby justifying restrictions within spousal migration policies. Put differently, restricting individual rights in one field can be justified with the goal of protecting them in another. At the same time, membership regulating occurs by framing spousal migration as the outcome and cause of integration deficits and "parallel societies" in order to justify restrictions. Here, the legitimate claim to both full membership in the polity and thus to the individual protection of marriage and family of the (ethnic minority) sponsor is put into question.

It is important to note the overwhelming discursive concentration on spousal migration from Turkish/Muslim communities. Since forced (and arranged) marriages and integration deficits are predominantly thought to be present in Turkish/Muslim communities, devising a policy to solve these specific issues forms part of a generalised spousal migration law that exemplifies the idea that spousal migration flows into Germany are also dominated by Turks/Muslims. In this way, both the problematic issues encountered within parts of a minority group are projected upon the entire minority group, and then generalised for an entire type of migration inflow (spousal migration). While the single largest group of spouses entering Germany are indeed from Turkey, the strong discursive concentration on forced marriages and integration deficits (both in turn implied to be issues mainly among Turkish/Muslim minorities) frames spousal migration as a phenomenon concerning only this group. However, a numerical dominance does not warrant a complete disregard of other constellations: in 2008, the second (Kosovo), third (Russian Federation) and fourth (India) largest national groups of spouses together also received about the same numbers of visas as the Turkish ones.[229]

A parallel observation can be made regarding gender. Notwithstanding the fact that around 30 per cent of incoming spouses are male, spousal migration is framed in parliament by MPs of all parties as a phenomenon mainly concerning incoming (implicitly meaning: oppressed) females. This view of the victimised bride "imported" (possibly against her will) by Turkish men who are themselves unwilling to integrate, fits squarely into notions of spousal migration leading to integration deficits, parallel societies and forced marriages and legitimises instruments such as the language requirement. That 30 per cent of incoming spouses are husbands sponsored by their wives in Germany fits less clearly into this imagery and is instead a story left untold. The following cynical quote of a CDU MP summarises this reduction of spousal migration to problematic Muslim minority behaviour:

> Someone who is able to arrange marriages, will arguably also be able to arrange German language skills. (MP Grindel (CDU), 16/94: 9555)

---

[229] Deutscher Bundestag, Drucksache 16/11997, p. 14.

The political opposition, especially MPs from the Green and Left parties, do not allow the frames and policies presented to go uncommented upon. By contrast, the government is continuously attacked for implementing a policy incompatible with the constitutional protection of marriage and family. The opposition is also highly critical of the justification presented by the government concerning the language requirement's alleged goals of preventing forced marriages and enhancing integration and denounces the justification as instrumental and hypocritical. Through the continuing minor interpellations of the Left Party regarding the implementation and evaluation of the language requirement, small victories are won for the migration-friendly left political spectrum. For instance, after being pressed by a Left MP about the relevance of the ECJ's *Toprak* decision establishing the incompatibility of "new restrictions" with association law, the government contended that the newly prolonged probationary period of three years was not applicable to Turkish spouses (Deutscher Bundestag, Drucksache 17/4623: 3).

The second section in turn presented the analysis of the series of in-depth interviews with MPs and civil servants formulating and implementing policies. An even more complex picture regarding the implicit and explicit goals of spousal migration policies emerges this analysis of the interviews, since civil servants' perspectives were included and the interview situation led to much less guarded statements. Generally, it can be observed that most interviewees saw spousal migration as a problem that needs to be controlled and, if possible, curtailed. How is the problem of spousal migration further differentiated? Just as in the parliamentary discussions, the issue of forced marriages was prominent but also positioned within a general framing of women as passive victims of the entire spousal migration process. These women are framed to be in need of protection and emancipation aid by the German state for their own good, for example through the language requirement.

Forced marriages are also connected to the second frame cluster, that of breaking up parallel societies, which is seen as the epitome of failed integration. Parallel societies are framed as consisting of unemployed, uneducated, culturally "backwards" (i.e. Muslim) minorities who have little interest in interacting with the German "majority society." The most important elements of the "backwards" culture in the context of spousal migration are certainly the patriarchal gender norms and the ensuing oppression of women. These parallel societies are depicted as being sustained through spousal migration, while at the same time the mere fact that a Turk/Muslim engages in spousal migration can be a sign that he is not sufficiently integrated – and is instead part of the odious parallel society. Spousal migration is thus an outcome *and* a cause of parallel societies. The idea of integration, while only really emerging on the mainstream political stage with the red-green government after 1998, has thus been completely adopted by conservative politicians and transformed into an argument for and instrument of migration control.

In a similar way to the phenomena of forced marriages and the oppression of women more generally, parallel societies also are implicitly located within Muslim/Turkish communities in Germany. It is interesting that within the German framing, which is notably different from similar discussions in the Netherlands, Islam as a religion or Muslim minorities' culture are seldom explicitly mentioned by politicians and policy-makers. Rather, criticism is uttered via discursive bridges of forced marriages, patriarchal gender norms or parallel societies, which immediately conjure up a certain image. An example of this intrinsic connection was revealed, for example, by one interviewee speaking of the Japanese community in Düsseldorf. He pointed out that this community was in no way culturally or politically integrated into Germany, thus formally fulfilling many of the features associated with parallel societies – and yet, it did not occur to him to call this group a "parallel society" or even to criticise it. Instead, he rather spoke of it as "an island in society." Yet, it is clear why: the Japanese community is considered to be affluent, highly-skilled and economically active. These highly-skilled migrants are often juxtaposed with typically Turkish, uneducated, economically inactive spousal migrants.

Apart from these two frames, which are fused together to function as the explanation for the newly introduced language requirement and were thus also very dominant in the parliamentary discussions, other frames proved to be salient in the interviews as well. First, it was noted that the German citizenry is growing increasingly ethnically diverse, which is perceived by some interviewees as a devaluation of German citizenship. This was also mentioned as the main incentive behind restricting the rules for spousal migration for German sponsors. Second, the burden on the public budget (and more specifically the welfare state) by poorly educated and economically inactive spousal migrants is also deemed to be an important problem. Third, spousal migration is framed as running contrary to efficient and rational migration management, which needs to be allowed due to the (cumbersome) constitutional protection of marriage and family. Finally, family migration provisions are generally considered to be prone to abuse, especially in the form of "marriages of convenience." Strict controls in this field are thus claimed to be both very common and necessary. Overall, the interviews thus revealed deeply classist imaginings of both migrants and ethnic minorities in Germany as uneducated and prone to (abuse) welfare provisions. These representations were largely absent from the plenary discussions, which were rather dominated by human rights discourses and arguments. This unsurprisingly points towards a much stronger liberal rights constraint at work in the official and public realm of parliament than behind policy-makers' closed doors.

7   The "other" side: Transnational couples' and migrant advocates' perspectives

Even though it is often classified as a single migration category, family-related migration is a highly heterogeneous phenomenon, which might account for part of the difficulties of coming to terms with it empirically. It includes minors, spouses and other relatives, who join citizens or foreign national residents who are either of the same or a different ethnicity as the incoming family members. It includes children of migrants as well as foreign parents of minor citizens. It includes second-generation migrants marrying spouses from their parents' country of origin as well as bi-national couples meeting abroad during work or holidays, but also meeting online, and deciding to settle in one of their home countries. It includes primary labour migrants, of both genders, both highly-skilled and low-skilled, being joined by their families after settling into a receiving polity.

At the junction between gendered family patterns and norms on the one side and migration dynamics and policies on the other, family migration is a multi-layered, complex phenomenon, which requires nuanced theorising beyond stereotypes and prejudices. However, as diverse and heterogeneous as the group of transnational families engaging in migration might be, the respective national policies controlling admission and residence usually confront all sponsors and their incoming family members. Of course, differentiated regulations can and often do apply, depending on specific characteristics of the sponsor and the incoming family members. It is nevertheless safe to say that in one way or another all individuals engaging in a family migration project inevitably are confronted with state policies on family migration. Therefore, exploring transnational couples' perspectives on family migration from the vantage point of the policies offered itself as a rewarding choice within the larger framework of this research.

While the previous chapters explored framings presented by institutional actors at different levels (national, regional, local) and in different branches of the state (executive, legislative), this chapter will thus focus on framings of transnational couples,[230] as well as their perspectives and strategies within the spousal migration process. Above, assuming migration policies to be instances of the "politics of belonging" (Yuval-Davis 2006), I have examined how differentiated notions of "membership" can influence policymakers and family migration policies. However, ideas of membership and the rights deriving from it also shape the ways in which individuals engaging in the process of spousal migration themselves, especially the native sponsors, react to restrictive policies. The main research questions to be answered here are: How do policies controlling spousal migration impact on individuals personally involved in a spousal migration project? What are the principal issues that emerge? How do transnational couples perceive their encounters with the institutional framework, both with polices and with the implementing administration, in the context of spousal migration? And what are their reactions?

As I interviewed individuals representing migrant interests (hereafter: migrant advocates) rather than speaking directly with transnational couples, a further research perspective emerged. While I had initially conceptualised migrant advocates as neutral sources of information ("experts"), in the course of the research I had to revise this notion. I realised that the migrant advocates themselves also must be perceived as embedded actors with their own strong preferences and goals concerning (spousal) migration. As occurred with the institutional actors investigated in chapter 6, migrant advocates (next to providing insights into transnational couples' viewpoints and practices) also frame the issues connected to spousal migration in their own ways, according to various policies they want to criticise or support, thus adding a further research question: How are spousal migration and the relevant policies framed by certain actors protecting migrant interests?

The present chapter will thus explore some of the issues that restrictive spousal migration policies have for transnational couples wishing to live

---

[230] I conceptualise transnational couples in this context as all couples engaging in the procedure of spousal migration, regardless of the sponsor spouse's nationality. The incoming partners applying for admission and residence as spouses of resident foreigners or citizens, are by default from outside of the EU, since they otherwise (as EU citizens have full free movement rights) would have no need to even apply for admission or residence. For the sake of simplicity, I will leave aside the special cases of EU citizens from the new Member States that temporarily do not enjoy a full set of EU citizenship rights, especially regarding access to employment.

in Germany. In this context, the migration policies explored are mainly immigration policies *sensu stricto*, that is, the conditions surrounding initial admission and residence. Clearly, migration policies in the broader sense are very important for transnational couples as well, such as provisions on integration measures, consolidation of residence status, access to education, the labour market, social benefits and naturalisation. Also, while this research project concentrates on the impact that political framings and subsequent policies have on transnational couples, I by no means wish to overstate the meaning of these dynamics. It is obvious that transnational migrant realities in the context of marriage are much more complex and include issues such as international marriage markets, ethnic marriage patterns, intercultural relationship dynamics, the consideration of which would go beyond this thesis. The focus of this chapter is, therefore, on the nexus between transnational couples and spousal migration policies. The chapter is structured into a first section (7.1) covering the perspectives of migrant advocates on spousal migration and German policies on the issue, and two further sections dealing with some of the main issues confronting transnational couples within the spousal migration process (7.2), as well as a range of couples' possible reactions to these issues (7.3).

As mentioned above, instead of conducting interviews with individuals affected by spousal migration policies, migrant advocates were interviewed. These migrant advocates professionally deal with couples wishing to engage in spousal migration. They worked for migrant organisations, consultancy services or law firms specialising in (family) migration law. This choice was made in order to gain a broader insight into the universe of cases of spousal migration in Germany. By virtue of their profession, migrant advocates are confronted with a plethora of transnational couples in their daily work. However, in order to also get a more direct grip on individual cases and explore transnational couples' own "voices," an analysis of a spousal migration case archive provided by the transnational family organisation IAF (*Verband binationaler Familien und Partnerschaften,* Association of Binational Families and Partnerships) was carried out as well. A general drawback of accessing the perspective of couples via migrant organisations that should be kept in mind is that most migrant advocates and their organisations have a bias toward dealing with "difficult" cases, as help from consultants or lawyers is mostly only required once problems occur.

I have titled this chapter "transnational couples' perspectives" instead of "migrants' perspectives" since one of the two partners involved in the spousal migration project is usually a resident and/or citizen of the receiving society and thus does not migrate. In the German case, this sponsor of spousal migration is either a German citizen or a foreign resident. In any case, in the course of the research this "domestic" element proved to be rather important, not only since the significant interests of an insider to the political community normatively and legally put strong weight on the admission claim of the spouse (see section 2.1.1 on the rationale of family migration), but also since it very practically opens up possibilities for agency and pressure (e.g. seeking consultancy, employing lawyers, creating media attention, exerting pressure on politicians as voters, etc.) that would not be possible in the same way in the case of an entirely external migration process. Analogously, not only the legal status of the sponsor, but also factors such as age, gender, ethnic background, socio-economic position, education and personal networks of the sponsors are likely to influence the possibilities and success prospects of the exercised agency. Indeed, the migrant advocates are mainly in touch with the sponsors since they are often the ones seeking help during the initial spousal migration project when the incoming spouse is usually still abroad. For example, in all the cases of the IAF archive, it is always the sponsor establishing the contact, explaining the issue and seeking the organisation's help with the admission procedure for the foreign spouse. Therefore, within this analysis of transnational couples' perspectives, a strong bias exists towards representing the sponsors' perspectives rather than those of the incoming migrants.

In total, five in-depth interviews, lasting an average of 81 minutes each, were held with migrant advocates between November 2009 and March 2010. Two of the interviewees were in charge of NGOs dealing specifically with aspects of spousal migration (4a, 4c), one other interviewee was the head of a traditional "ethnic" migrant organisation (4b), and two interviewees were lawyers in the field of migration, asylum and family law who often dealt with spousal migration cases (4d, 4e).[231]

---

[231] These labels (4a, 4b, 4c, 4d, 4e) are also employed to denote specific references in the following analysis, just as was done earlier in chapter 6.

The consulted archive documents single cases of individuals or couples engaging in a spousal migration project. It contains dossiers of assorted cases of couples (n=82) who either sought help and were supported by the organisation or simply chose to tell their story to the IAF immediately after the introduction of the language requirement from August 2007 to August 2008. This archive provides an insight into the issues encountered and reactions by transnational couples especially concerning, but not limited to, the language requirement. The dossiers contain the inquiries and accounts directed to the IAF, which are often supplemented and illustrated by written correspondence between the couples (or sometimes their lawyers) and state institutions. Some of the dossiers only contain a one-page letter or inquiry directed to the IAF, while others are made up of many different lengthy correspondences between the couples, the IAF, lawyers and various state institutions. Several correspondences are as long as 30 pages.

Of the 82 cases, half (n=41) are couples with a female sponsor; the other half concern couples sponsored by males in Germany. Only one of the sponsors was a foreigner, and all the others were German citizens, which is rather typical of the IAF's "clientele" – foreigners make use of their consultancy services much less often than citizens (4a). However, 13 sponsors (15 per cent) are citizens with a migration background, meaning they are either naturalised foreigners or have at least one foreign parent. The incoming spouses documented in the archive are third-country nationals (TCNs) from all across the globe; the countries of origin most represented are Thailand (n=8), Turkey (n=7), Egypt (n=5) and the Philippines (n=4). The anonymised case dossiers were numbered and coded with the qualitative data analysis software Atlas.Ti, when referring to individual cases in the following, the number of the case dossier (CD) will be indicated (e.g. CD 1).

7.1 Spousal migration framed by migrant advocates

7.1.1 General framing of spousal migration

The most important way migrant advocates frame spousal migration is by defining it as a basic right, derived from the constitutional protection of marriage and family (4a, 4b, 4e). While the ethnic migrant organisation president (4b) emphasises the fact that this right also holds for all foreigners legally residing in Germany, the migrant advocate working in the organisation traditionally dealing with bi-national couples with a German sponsor (4a) stresses that referring to constitutional rights is politically easier when it comes to German sponsors, possibly due to the majority of her clientele being made up of citizen sponsors:

> There's an obvious advantage when one partner is German; they are voters. Therefore the politicians listen to us entirely differently, and we can employ the constitution somewhat differently when Germans are immediately affected. You're really more likely to get an audience than if you come along with third-country nationals that want to have the same kinds of rights that exist here in this country; in those cases you're somewhat ignored legally and also politically. Then you have to rely on general human rights provisions and that can be politically tricky. Even with parties that start with a C [self-defining as Christian; CDU, CSU]. Or especially with those. (4a)

In addition, the relationship between spousal migration and other kinds of migration opportunities is a topic of concern. Here, the case is made that since so few other legal migration possibilities into Germany are available, family migration has developed into something of a bottleneck. One migrant advocate explicitly makes the point that this bottleneck situation influences the strategies of both aspiring migrants and the migration control strategies of the state. Not only do individuals wanting to gain admission into Germany perhaps partly view family migration outside of its intended context as an entry path, but also the state increasingly aims to exercise migration management "on the back" of family migration, where it does not belong, according to this migrant advocate:

> We actually still have a halt on recruitment, thus either you are skilled in a highly desired profession, or you only have the possibility to immigrate to Germany via marriage or family. This is also a point we discussed a lot with politicians again and again, that [family migration] has practically become a chokepoint and a lot is concentrated on family and marriage that does not really belong there. We would very much appreciate if there were other migration possibilities into Germany, since this would ease the burden on the area of spousal and family migration as a lot of people would not marry but try to enter Germany via the labour market. (…) We are confronted with the implementation of immigration rules and immigration control in the familial area, but we say: The two areas have nothing to do with one another. Family cannot be controlled this way. Families are formed and couples find each other according to completely different criteria, and thus cannot be subject to regulations that belong under labour market control. (…) Of course any sovereign state can introduce criteria for labour migration, but not within family migration, because it is bound by other parameters here, by human rights and also constitutional standards. (4a)

In this view, the abuse of family migration provisions exists, but is mainly due to the lack of alternative migration possibilities. The same migrant advocate also asserted that the government seems to have a misconception about global migration processes: "They assume that everyone wants to enter Germany and everyone will stay forever. This is just not realistic in the 21st century" (4a). It was also suggested that the logic of the state to introduce criteria prior to the admission of family migrants strongly correlates to the manifold possibilities to remain in Germany once inside and the legal and procedural difficulties of the authorities to remove these migrants (4d). Both lawyer migrant advocates brought up the phenomenon of "creeping family reunification" *("schleichender Familiennachzug")*, in which one spousal migration follows the next by remaining within one marriage just long enough to acquire an independent residence status and shortly thereafter sponsoring the migration of another spouse (possibly a previous partner). One of them mentioned it, in a rather neutral fashion, as an occasional phenomenon (4d). The other lawyer evaluated it politically by specifically terming this phenomenon "a thorn in the side" of the BMI, which the ministry seeks to combat with laws and administrative practices (4e).

Furthermore, all migrant advocates consider the protection of the welfare state to be one of the main driving forces behind restrictive immigration policy. For example, one migrant advocate questioned the dominant political framing of integration as the key issue and pointed toward the importance of the more covert goal of protecting the welfare state:

> I'm not even sure whether the crucial point here is really the integration of migrants or much rather this economic aspect, that the state is afraid of having to come to the rescue, while high-skilled people always find work and do not tap into the social welfare system. (4c)

7.1.2 Ethnic minority Germans

The issue of ethnic minority Germans – and especially their assumed role in the new spousal migration policies – arose at various occasions in the migrant advocate interviews. It was stressed that German citizens have a stronger position regarding the protection of their constitutional rights (4a, 4e), as mentioned above. But the new restrictions that also apply to spouses of German sponsors – notably the language requirement, and especially the possibility of demanding an income requirement of German citizens under certain circumstances (see section 4.2.2) – were criticised by the migrant advocates. The income requirement possibility, even though only one migrant advocate had heard of an actual application of the provision in practice (see section 7.2.1), was strongly opposed in principle. The migrant advocates variously interpreted it as "sending a very bad signal" and being "an integration policy no-go" (4a), as a clear case of ethnic discrimination creating "second-class Germans" (4b), and as an "indirect attack upon the citizenship law" (4e). In any case, all migrant advocates agreed that this new provision is clearly inspired by and directed towards ethnic minority Germans:

> Up until the Directive Implementation Act [2007] it was a core principle that those married to German citizens were privileged in family reunification, regarding the income requirement, but there were also no other conditions, except confirming the existence of a marriage. So this is really a watershed, also regarding the German language test. It is a conscious renunciation of earlier policies. And what is the reason for the turn against German citizens? Germans with a migration background! (4e)

7.1.3 Forced marriages

Forced marriages were mainly mentioned by the migrant advocates in reference to government discourses on the issue in the context of migration control policies (see also section 7.1.5 on the language requirement). They particularly criticised the government's justification of the language requirement with the prevention of forced marriages as an "instrumentalisation" of the issue, with one migrant advocate stating that "it is easier to sell restrictions to the public by claiming it helps victims" (4c). Another migrant advocate spoke of "fake and absurd arguments" that "by untrue statements and ridiculous regulations have curtailed the right of people to live together in Germany" (4b), while one of the lawyers termed it a "ridiculous" argument, especially in reference to women's rights: "All those lofty words that they even repeat all the time about female self-determination, they don't even believe it themselves!" (4e). The migrant advocates concurred with the opinion that the "real" goal behind this provision is the restriction of (family) migration. Two interviewees (4b, 4c) also made the point that while it "is very in vogue to speak of [forced marriages] at the moment" (4c), no reliable data on the number of forced marriages exist in Germany, suggesting a need for further research on the extent and exact mechanisms before devising (restrictive) policies.

Furthermore, various migrant advocates (4a, 4d, 4e) made the point that the local aliens authorities play no role in detecting or preventing forced marriages, which stands in contrast to their prominent role in the field of marriages of convenience (see section 7.2.3). It seems that while the issue of forced marriages has recently become important for the discursive legitimating of the language and age requirements, efforts going beyond these restrictive instruments play a minor role in practice. In the case of marriages of convenience, an opposite picture emerges. Within the political framing of spousal migration, increasingly less emphasis is placed on marriages of convenience, although their "prevention" plays a major role within administrative practices.

Instead, other kinds of policies to fight forced marriages, such as improving the infrastructure of support and consultation opportunities as well as awareness-raising campaigns are called for, especially by the migrant advocate working specifically with female migrants who are victims of violence (4c). In this context, almost all migrant advocates underline the fact that gaining an independent residence permit as a victim of domestic violence and/or forced marriage prior to the two-year probationary period is extremely rare and difficult to attain since the hardship situation must be proven to the authorities with medical certificates, etc. The plans expressed in the 2009 coalition agreement – and ultimately implemented – to increase the waiting period from two to three years is seen as potentially further aggravating the situation for individuals trapped in forced marriages (4a, 4c, 4d, 4e).

7.1.4 Integration

Perhaps unsurprisingly, the migrant advocates, being highly critical of the language requirement, criticised the predominant government framing of integration, since this is one of the official justifications of the language requirement. In this regard, the responsibility of the state to create integration opportunities for migrants is emphasised (4c, 4e), especially because "for five decades, nothing was done by the state in order to support integration" (4e), implying that integration difficulties are a domestically created problem that the state needs to address. The point is made that these state-run integration programmes have to take place in Germany once the migrants have settled, instead of abroad (4a, 4c). Furthermore, also hinting at the language requirement, the discursive equation of integration with German language skills is heavily criticised (4a, 4b, 4c).

The ethnic organisation migrant advocate, in particular, emphatically made the point that even with perfect German skills, structural and institutional discrimination make it difficult for individuals with a migrant background to find a job or a trainee position. According to him, *de facto* discrimination inhibits integration, as defined by equal participation opportunities within society and the labour market (4b). He further claimed that integration in Germany actually is meant to signify assimilation; since diversity is generally not accepted by large parts of society, his cynical "recommendation" is for migrants to change their name and hair colour in order to "truly integrate" (4b). Another migrant advocate made a similar point in a more moderate tone of voice. She claimed that in any immigration society there will always be individuals who are difficult or even impossible to fully integrate; thus if Germany seeks to be an immigration society, it must learn to accept this diversity (4a).

Finally, a point was made regarding the link between immigration and integration in Germany. Two migrant advocates (4b, 4e) claimed that the strain of German political discourse that often speaks of *"Zuwanderung"* instead of *"Einwanderung"* indicates the comparative closure of German society, making it very difficult for immigrants to integrate, even if they try.

7.1.5 Language requirement

Contrary to the newly introduced age requirement, which was only mentioned briefly once as playing a minor role (4a), the language requirement was an extremely "hot" topic for all migrant advocates. While the exact practical issues concerning the language requirement for transnational couples will be dealt with below, suffice it here to say that the general political considerations behind the language requirement were criticised as well. The arguments presented against the language requirement were made at the theoretical level, claiming it to be incompatible with EU law and the German constitution, as well as at the practical level, outlining the individual hardships stemming from the requirement. These two levels also intersect at times. As outlined above, the causal link between the introduction of the language requirement and the goal of fighting forced marriages was strongly criticised by all the migrant advocates. The most outspoken of all was the one migrant advocate working specifically in the field of violence against female migrants. She lamented an "instrumentalisation" of the issue of forced marriages and the ensuing stigmatisation of the Turkish community, both developments that she and her organisation strongly oppose (4c). For her, it is problematic that a measure such as the language requirement, which aims at one specific group, could be introduced "without evaluating in what relation this group stands to all those [individuals] that are affected by it" (4c).

Other migrant advocates were more moderate in their criticism of the government's objectives. According to one migrant advocate, the responsible politicians really did believe that the language requirement would help inhibit forced marriages, even though she is convinced that this is not the case, as the pressure on the victim only increases, and escaping a forced marriage needs more than just some knowledge of German (4a). Another migrant advocate partly accepted the government's logic by agreeing that the language requirement might indeed help forced marriage victims or "import brides" to escape unwanted situations, but he was still opposed to a general language requirement for all spousal migrants. He considered it problematic to deduce a generalised policy for this group to all spousal migrants, including those who have nothing to do with forced marriages, notably "from Mexico and Peru" (4d). He also questioned the link between integration and the language requirement: "Integration does not happen by listening to German radio in the Congo," he said, noting that it can only happen on-site, in Germany, aided by integration courses, thus making the language requirement obsolete in his view (4d).

Another topic of criticism in the context of the language requirement were the exceptions made for spouses of EU citizens and visa-free citizens, leading one migrant advocate to speak of "first-class foreigners" created by this exception (4e). Another migrant advocate interpreted this provision as aimed specifically against individuals with Turkish origins, based on a general "Turkophobia" in Germany (4b).

7.1.6 Marriage patterns and marriage norms

Apart from evaluating spousal migration policies, the migrant advocates also reflected upon general marriage patterns and marriage norms within spousal migration. The main points brought forward were a defence of network spousal migration and a criticism of the rigid marriage norms demanded of transnational couples. In both cases, the freedom to marry without state intervention was emphasised. The ethnic organisation migrant advocate, in line with his mission, admitted that networks are important for Turkish migration, but claimed that the phenomenon of marrying people "originating from similar family structures and the same village" is "good for social control" and "natural" (4b). He immediately connected this argument to marriage norms as well, since...

> ...it is the right of any person to marry and identify culturally in any way he/she sees fit, it cannot be the duty of the state to regulate that, but rather create [integration] opportunities for the incoming migrants here in Germany. (...) People marry anyway and I think it is their right to marry, no matter where they marry, whom they marry. I couldn't care less. (4b)

It becomes clear that he is highly conscious of the prevailing CDU discourse of "parallel societies" and "chain migration." He defended network spousal migration, implicitly that of second and third generation migrants, with the freedom to marry; he also rejected state intervention aimed at influencing marriage choices. At the same time he supported integration opportunities taking place in Germany, thus implicitly indeed accepting the likely integration difficulties of incoming spousal migrants. He thus argued in favour of marriage norms free of interventionist policies by the state that demand integration.

Another migrant advocate also criticised supposed governmental marriage norms, albeit with a different emphasis. She condemned an alleged double standard employed by the state. According to her, in the case of German-German marriages, the state has become gradually more liberal regarding marriage norms. Even with common children, there is increasingly less societal and legal pressure to marry. However, with transnational marriages the state seems to be much more worried: "The German Civil Code leaves [reasons for marriage] up to the individual, with good cause, but then in certain constellations the state suddenly cares." (4a). According to her, transnational couples have to fulfil a "marriage ideal from the past century" – namely, living together, having an "adequate" age structure and being able to "adequately" communicate. Furthermore, the couple's motivation to be together should be love and they should display the will and intention to stay together, "but all these notions that are relevant in this context are actually not codified anywhere and surpassed in many points by our societal realities already" (4a). The "scale" of this love and intentions are measured and evaluated by the responsible civil servants, which she found very problematic. In this framing, it becomes clear that this migrant advocate is very influenced by the intimacy inquiries and marriage-of-convenience suspicions with which her clients are confronted. She therefore advocated marriage norms free of state intervention, norms that would require "love." A lawyer migrant advocate knows these norms from his work as well, and admitted that the authorities seem to have very clear ideas on how a relationship "should" look and be structured, although, in his opinion these norms are due to a specific catalogue of criteria that the civil servants receive and are required to check (4d).

7.1.7 Institutional dynamics

Various migrant advocates clearly identified the Interior Ministry (BMI) as *the* main responsible institution when it comes to formulating spousal migration policies. One migrant advocate even denied that the parliament had much decision power at all: "The BMI decides and then the *Bundestag* rubberstamps it. (…) The government changes but the gentlemen in the BMI stay the same." (4e). Another migrant advocate voiced her frustration at most often dealing with the BMI rather than the family ministry when representing and defending transnational families and partnerships. To her, it is difficult to devise effective "family policies" when the basic conditions for "some families in this country" – that is, transnational families – are set by the BMI according to principles relating to security, law and order (4a). She also stated that her organisation was actively engaged in lobbying activities and tries to reach out to all political parties in parliament. An interesting dynamic regarding the interaction between migrant organisations and politicians was mentioned by the ethnic organisation migrant advocate. When speaking about the possible income requirements for (ethnic minority) Germans, the following dialogue emerged:

> 4b: "I will bring a motion into the *Bundestag* about this!"
> LB: "You are personally able to bring a motion into the *Bundestag*?"
> 4b: "No, but I can do it via an MP, via Sevim [Dagdelen, The Left], or via Memet Kilic [GRÜNE], or Aydan [Özoguz, SPD]. I write down the political things and they can formulate it and put forward the motion!"

This supposed direct cooperation between Members of Parliament (MPs) of Turkish origin of different political parties with ethnic migrant organisations implies that ethnic origin still continues to play a relevant role within (migration) policy-making that marginalises the importance of political parties.

Another way in which migrant advocates interact with authorities includes appearing as experts in legislative hearings. However, the one migrant advocate who mentioned this does not have a positive impression of the expert hearing process (nor the entire legislative process, for that matter). He was direct and pointed in his criticism:

> [The hearing] was really all a farce, but I'm used to that. In the last ten years all these hearings have been a complete farce. In a secretive process the ministry draft was discussed for one and a half years, the legislative proceedings had not been initiated, it was only the first draft from the Interior Ministry. So before it was submitted to parliament as an official law proposal where a public discourse can happen, it had been negotiated for one and a half years! Of course one could pick up via certain networks what was happening, but it was not a public discussion! It took one and a half years because of the *Altfallregelung*.[232] Various drafts were discussed, and then the government appeared before the public with a complete package, which was not changed at all anymore. Not a thing! And in this secretive process for the SPD the *Altfallregelung*, § 104a, was crucial, and they accepted everything else in order to get this regulation into the law. They accepted the German requirement and they accepted the possible income requirement for Germans, all rubber-stamped! (4e)

In addition to the *Bundestag* and the BMI, migrant advocates also mentioned the European Union as playing a role in policy formulation. The EU is gener-

---

[232] As elaborated in chapter 6, in the negotiations for the Zuwanderungsgesetz 2007, coalition partners SPD and CDU struck a deal. The CDU made its support for a provision enabling "tolerated" individuals to regularise their residence status (enshrined in § 104a AufenthG) dependent on the SPD agreeing to restrictions in the field of spousal migration.

ally seen as a liberal corrective for restrictive German tendencies. Two migrant advocates claimed that the language requirement was incompatible with the FR Directive, this alone being a legal reason to abolish it (4a, 4e). The ECJ was also mentioned as a liberal corrective. According to one lawyer migrant advocate (4e), the ECJ's *Chakroun* case[233] actually disabled the income requirement practice in Germany (which calculates the minimum income to include all social benefits an individual could possibly receive in an extreme situation). Nevertheless, he doubted that the consequences from *Chakroun* would be implemented but rather be met with a lot of resistance in Germany after "40 years of blockage politics" *("Betonpolitik")* (4e). So even though the EU institutions are seen as likely liberal correctives, the migrant advocates were pessimistic about the possibilities for change while also being frustrated over the continuation of restrictive German policies.

The migrant advocates did not naively view the EU as an exclusively liberal institution but were conscious of the dynamics of multi-level governance as well. In this regard, one migrant advocate recounted the lengthy and difficult negotiations of the national ministers on the FR Directive, while emphasising the "uploading" of national German preferences of then-Interior Minister Schily (SPD) to the EU arena. Schily apparently had strongly opposed the Commission's proposal to prohibit "reverse discrimination," due to the "specifically German issue" of ethnic German resettlers. According to her, Schily wanted to be uninhibited from restricting German resettlers' family migration (4a).

The German judiciary was also mentioned by migrant advocates as having an impact on spousal migration policies. On the one hand, high courts – especially the Federal Constitutional Court (BVerfG) – were referred to as a corrective instance for restrictive policies by defending the (constitutional) rights of the individuals. One example mentioned was the 1987 BVerfG case[234] (4a, 4e). A lawyer migrant advocate, while in principle questioning the constitutionality of the new restrictive spousal migration provisions and thus appreciating the possibility of fighting for one's rights by "going through the procedures," noted the difficulty for him as a lawyer of finding clients willing to pursue this route (4e). He mentioned that as a law suit

---

[233] ECJ, Case C-517/08, see section 5.1.2.
[234] BVerfG, 2 BvR 1226/83, 101, 313/84, judgement of 12 May 1987. See section 3.1.1.

costs a lot of time, energy and money – and the outcome is nevertheless uncertain – most transnational couples are more interested in finding a practical solution to their individual issues rather than fighting for the higher cause of overall justice.

In addition to being a corrective, the judiciary is also referred to as confirming restrictive policies in some cases. For example, two migrant advocates (4d, 4e) mentioned a recent decision of the BVerwG that has led to a different way of calculating the minimum income required to fulfil the income requirement, thus making spousal migration more difficult. The other restriction-confirming court decision that one migrant advocate mentioned and criticised – "Catastrophic!" he called it – was the BVerwG ruling of March 2010[235] that confirmed the constitutionality of the language requirement (4e) (This was the one person who I spoke to after the ruling was adopted). On a hopeful note, he pointed out that the decision only evaluated and confirmed the language requirement's compatibility with Article 6 GG, but with EU Law. He believed that bringing a case to court over the language requirement's compatibility with EU law was the last possible way to legally challenge the provision, although he worried that this might also fail, since all these lawsuits, because they challenge visa decisions, must in the first instance pass through the same court, the VG Berlin: "And if they don't want to do it," he said, "then you're stuck." (4e)

7.2 Transnational couples' difficulties

While the previous section examined the self-conception of migrant advocates and their framings of spousal migration and various respective policies, this section focuses on the transnational couples themselves. It explores the problematic issues encountered by these couples in their process of migration. This exploration is empirically sustained, on the one hand, by the information provided by the migrant advocates about their "clients," and on the other hand by the archive documenting individual cases brought to the attention of the IAF. As mentioned above, it should be kept in mind that a dual bias in the selection of cases exists. First, since support structures are

---

[235] BVerwG, 1 C 8.09, judgement of 30 March 2010. See section 4.2.

less likely to be consulted when spousal migration works swiftly, there is presumably a bias toward the more difficult and problematic cases. Secondly, mainly the perspective of the sponsoring spouse (rather than the incoming spouse) is presented, since it is usually the sponsor in Germany seeking the help of migrant organisations and/or lawyers.

7.2.1 Language requirement

First of all, the language requirement introduced in 2007 acts as a significant hurdle on various levels. For couples with few economic resources, the connected costs are a serious issue. The test leading to the certificate itself (to be taken at a Goethe-Institute or at one of three other providers[236]) must be paid for in all cases. Further potential costs are language instruction or courses (sometimes amounting to the equivalent of a month's income in the countries of origin – see CD 33), relevant language instruction material, transportation to classes, and possibly even a loss of income while the courses are undertaken. Next to the costs, the unavailability of language courses and test slots were often mentioned for instance when the migrant spouses live in regions (or even a country) without German language courses readily available. If those spouses find themselves unable to acquire the necessary skills without professional instruction at a language school or a Goethe-Institute, they sometimes even decide to relocate for the time period of the language course (at least three months, sometimes more) to a larger city where a course is held. In these cases, additional costs of rent, and especially lost income due to a complete suspension of gainful employment, weigh particularly heavily on the persons in question, as does the emotional hardship of having to tackle the task of learning German and preparing for migration outside of one's familiar environment. Private teachers – often return migrants from Germany – are sometimes resorted to as an alternative, although couples are also unsatisfied with the quality and the conditions of the language instruction (CD 36).

---

[236] Next to the Goethe-Institutes, certificates of the providers Telc GmbH, Österreichisches Sprachdiplom (ÖSD) and TestDAF are accepted.

Other problems mentioned were connected to the difficulty of learning German, with many incoming spouses struggling with the requirements, especially given sub-standard learning conditions, little prior experience with foreign languages or a generally low level of education. Additional logistical hurdles impeding swift language acquisition included unsettling conditions in some of the countries of origin – political or social unrest, difficult environmental or climate conditions, and inferior infrastructure. The archive also contains two cases of illiterate spouses who were unable to fulfil the language requirement. Finally, the possibility of individual hardships exists, particularly the impossibility of acquiring the necessary German skills due to illiteracy (CDs 24, 51) or other similar circumstances. In these cases, spousal migration is permanently inhibited (4c, 4d).

Another matter of concern are the practices of the Goethe-Institutes, where many spousal migrants take tests and courses. In various case dossiers, the test level was criticised as being much too stringent (CDs 31, 74, 78); other sponsors complained about the long waiting periods, high costs and incorrect information provided. Some spoke of the Goethe-Institutes as "abusing their monopoly position" (CD 36), and one sponsor even handed in a petition to the federal parliament on the practices and the monopoly position of the Goethe-Institute in Bangkok (CD 62).

Next to the costs and the logistical difficulties connected to the language requirement, the issue of separation time was important as well. Apart from the time required to learn German, many individuals reported further time delays in the process due to an unavailability of courses, and tests only being held at certain intervals. In addition, the usual visa procedure can sometimes take several months. Most embassies reportedly only start the visa procedure after the language certificate is provided, instead of allowing the certificate to be handed in later. In most cases the language requirement led to a significant increase in the duration of the overall spousal migration process. Two migrant advocates (4a, 4b) made the point that apart from the time, money and effort, the language requirement was rejected by many transnational couples due to the procedural difficulties of taking the test abroad and the large time gap between the language course and the actual entry into Germany. It was not, they noted, that the couples opposed the principle of learning German:

The people do not say: 'German isn't necessary.' It's undisputed that you need German in this country, and the couples believe that as well. Many of [the sponsors] even say: 'Oh, I don't think it is a bad idea that [the incoming spouse] gets to know the language before coming.' But fulfilling the requirement is what many of them oppose, because it is connected to a lot of additional costs and it would require much less effort and money to attend a course here. Also, the success would be much higher, in the case of learning in a German environment and being able to apply the new knowledge immediately, instead of forgetting it again abroad. That's actually one of the strongest points of criticism: 'If I learn a language and then have to wait for my visa for six months, I obviously forget everything again!'" (4a)

This is echoed in the case archive – many sponsors inquire about the possibility of completing the language requirement in Germany and argue that it would be much easier, cheaper and faster for their incoming spouses to follow a course in Germany and then take a test at a local language school. Furthermore, sponsors also criticised the language requirement as a strong psychological burden on their incoming spouses (CDs 33, 78). Since successful completion of the language test is one of the indispensable admission conditions, many incoming spouses feel rather pressured and anxious, which obviously makes learning German and passing the test even more difficult.

7.2.2 Marriage-of-convenience suspicions and intimacy inquiries

While the language requirement is a general, legally codified condition demanded of all transnational couples applying for spousal migration into Germany (unless they are exempted – see section 4.2), the second important array of difficulties only comes into play for some couples. Individuals considered "suspicious" of having a marriage of convenience are subject to "intimacy inquiries," as I dubbed them in chapter 2. Even though no data on the number of these inquiries exist, the migrant advocates suggest that they are indeed common. In any case, for those couples who came under these suspicions, the investigations were a significant burden.

The migrant advocates mentioned some of the "suspicion indicators" that authorities look out for, which are not legally codified. They include a large age difference between the spouses, especially when the wife is older; the absence of a common language of communication; a very short period of acquaintance, or the circumstance that the spouses never met prior to marriage (4a, 4d). Further circumstances likely to be considered "suspicious" are if one spouse has had a number of prior marriages (4d); if the incoming spouse is a rejected asylum seeker or otherwise has an (nearly) expired residence permit (4d), or if the sponsor spouse is considered to be a drug user (4a). Certain constellations of couples that are also often regarded as suspicious include German men with Thai or Eastern European women, as well as couples that met on vacation in Egypt or Tunisia (4a).

For same-sex unions, which are also legally entitled to spousal migration, marriage-of-convenience suspicions and ensuing intimacy inquiries apparently arise far less often, perhaps due to the fact that ideas regarding an "authentic" homosexual relationship are less rigid (4d). For instance, the case of a gay couple with a 60-year old sponsor and a 20-year old partner who was a rejected asylum seeker, and that of another gay couple where one of the partners was previously married to a woman, did not raise any suspicions for authorities. The migrant advocate who mentioned this was convinced that the same constellation in the case of a heterosexual couple would have surely been closely investigated by the authorities, while he assumes the civil servants follow the logic: "If they actually admit to be gay, it must be real" (4d).

The intimacy inquiry itself is not a legally codified procedure but is actually based on internal rules and includes various administrative practices that attempt to evaluate the character of the spousal relationship. One common practice includes the conducting of simultaneous interviews with both spouses, one abroad and the other in Germany. In these interviews, the spouses are quizzed about their partner and their relationship, focusing on details about relatives, employment and interests, as well as habits and history of their shared private life (For example, "Which side of the bed do you sleep on?" or "Where and how did you meet?") (4d, 4e). Unsurprisingly, it was reported that this situation is rather stressful for most couples and at times they are also tricked into inconsistencies by the civil servants (4d).If an intimacy inquiry ends negatively for a couple – that is, the authorities decide there is enough suspicion to not grant an entry visa – the only remaining legal possibility is to appeal this decision, initially through a so-called "remonstration," brought forward by a lawyer. But a remonstration is only a written legal appeal in which the presented data is re-checked; no new evidence is gathered, and most remonstrations on the basis of marriage-of-convenience suspicions are not successful. If the remonstration is refused, the couple's only recourse is to file a suit against the relevant authorities and try to persuade a court that their marriage is authentic and that they are worthy of being granted a visa. The relevant courts in all such cases are either the *Verwaltungsgericht Berlin* or the *Oberverwaltungsgericht Berlin-Brandenburg*, since the authority that is sued is the Foreign Office, seated in Berlin. In order to be granted a visa, during the court hearing the couple (and their lawyer) must explain any inconsistencies that might have arisen during the intimacy inquiries. They also must show how they have maintained contact via the internet, telephone, etc. The appeal process can take up to one year. According to the interviewed lawyers (4d, 4e), most cases brought to a court hearing are successful in the end, due in part to sensible judges who are able to take a more nuanced view of the situation:

> When you go to court, especially to the Administrative Court [*Verwaltungsgericht*], you actually come across very intelligent judges, and you get the feeling of not being forced to live up to all the clichés. They really take a much more differentiated look. (4d)

The fact that far more couples are regularly placed under suspicion and subjected to intimacy inquiries than the number of couples that actually turn out to be involved in "marriages of convenience" was also brought up. One migrant advocate pointed to a general dilemma of freedom vs. control, saying, "How many couples does the state need to put under suspicion with serious consequences for their privacy in order to prove how many to be guilty?" (4a).

7.2.3 Minimum income and required documents

Another of the main difficulties for such couples mentioned by the migrant advocates is the compliance with the requirement for a minimum income. Before 2007, this provision only applied to foreign sponsors, in practice meaning that foreigners receiving social welfare benefits generally could not sponsor spousal migration. From 2007 onwards, however, it could also be required of German citizens in special cases, mainly when a marriage abroad is deemed to be acceptable, as in the case of naturalised citizens. This provision was overruled in 2012, but it was in place when the interviews took place in 2009/2010, and was mentioned by the interviewees.

Even when a sponsor is gainfully employed, the income can be considered insufficient, especially since a recent BVerwG judgement held that all possible social welfare benefits the sponsor is theoretically entitled to (irrespective of the actual usage) must be included in the calculation of the minimum income. The lawyers (4d, 4e) were quick to point out that this recalculation effectively increased the minimum income that must be provided, making it much more difficult to fulfil the requirement, even for those gainfully employed. The administration may also examine the "employment history" of the sponsor – e.g. how long the sponsor has had the job, whether the sponsor has previously been unemployed, etc. If the aliens authority remains sceptical, it can postpone spousal migration by obliging the sponsor to further authenticate their employment situation. This is also substantiated by the experience that, in some cases, a job or even merely an employment contract is "created" for the purpose of the family migration application (4d). It seems, therefore, that while the income requirement plays a minor role within the political framing of spousal migration, in practice it is very important. This can be interpreted to be indicative of a more "backstage" motive of spousal migration policy – that is, a strong intention to protect the welfare state from an additional burden.

The expansion of the income requirement to include (ethnic minority) German citizens was seen as scandalous by the migrant advocates. It also apparently unnerved the affected ethnic minority sponsors:

> How do the people react? They are certainly rather shocked. Shocked that this happens to them and there is nothing they can so. In principle they have established themselves in Germany, and integrated in order to get citizenship and when they want to bring in their spouse, they are limited again. They have done so much, and it still isn't enough (4a).

While most migrant advocates (4a, 4d, 4e) had not yet encountered cases in their work where spousal migration was not granted to German citizens, one (4b) claimed to know of 25 cases in Berlin where authorities checked the income of German citizens and in five cases actually decided negatively, denying the spouse admission and saying that the marital life could also take place in the spouse's country of origin.

Difficulties arise in connection with the legal documents and certificates that must be presented in order to gain admission. First, many of the necessary documents must be translated and notarised – sometimes losing their validity while the couple waits for some other document (such as the language certificate) to be issued (CD 17). The ensuing reacquisition of the documents can extend the process even further. Even more difficult is the fact (as mentioned in chapter 3) that in some countries, especially in Sub-Saharan Africa and in Afghanistan, the validity of documents such as marriage and birth certificates is routinely questioned. As a consequence, such documents must be "legalised" – that is, checked and validated by a trusted lawyer *("Vertrauensanwalt")*, which requires added time and money (CDs 6, 51, 81). A visa application also may be completely denied if a spouse's identity cannot be authenticated due to an invalid birth certificate (as in CD 78).

7.2.4 Interaction with public authorities and procedural difficulties

The behaviour of public authorities during the spousal migration process, primarily the visa authorities abroad and the aliens authorities in Germany, is often a matter of concern and distress to transnational couples. It is repeatedly reported that civil servants, both abroad and in Germany, provide incorrect or incomplete information or even ask for documents they are not authorised to request, such as income documentation for German sponsors, even before 2007 (4a, 4d, CD 39). Shortly before and after the introduction of the language requirement, many sponsors complained that the visa authorities abroad had not mentioned the requirement in the couples' initial inquiries; the sponsors said that it was only later that the authorities added this information (CDs 17, 29, 31). One migrant advocate stated bluntly: "You really need to know your rights when dealing with the authorities!" (4a). Further, she said that in some cases a lawyer was indispensable in being able to deal effectively with the administration.

On the other hand, particularly in relation to representations abroad, having personal contacts or a good network – expatriates well-integrated into small German communities abroad, for example – can lead to swift proceedings (4d). It is also mentioned that some embassies and consulates were very cooperative after the introduction of the language requirement; some now accept spousal migration applications without the language certificate, which can be handed in at a later stage, in order to speed up the visa process (4d).

However, the general tone regarding the couples' interaction with authorities, and especially with the German visa authorities abroad, was very negative throughout many of the case dossiers. Communication difficulties, the unavailability of employees, long waiting periods for appointments and the dissemination of wrong information are all mentioned as common concerns. The archive contains one extreme case (CD 81) of harassment of a couple by a visa official. Though not the rule, this incident can be seen as an example of the chokepoint position that diplomatic staffers often find themselves in, particularly with few correctives from German supervisory institutions located thousands of kilometres away. After refusing a visitor visa to a German man's Vietnamese fiancée, the head of the visa section told the couple that they would "never get a visa" through him. In desperation, the couple married and applied for spousal migration, but the entry visa was still denied to them because they lacked a language certificate – despite the fact that the wife was now pregnant and thus exempt from the language requirement. The wife then took a German course and passed the language test, but again the head of the visa section denied the visa, citing a documentation situation whereby he demanded that the marriage certificate be legalised. After that had been taken care of and the couple handed in a renewed application, the official again denied the visa, this time on the grounds that there was suspicion of a marriage of convenience – somewhat absurd considering the pregnancy. The German sponsor, desperate, made repeated calls and inquiries to the embassy – until the head of the section was on vacation and the sponsor reached the man's substitute. After listening to the story of the applications and reading the case file, this staff member issued a visa to the wife that same day. Even though this is likely to have been an extreme case, it does illustrate the bureaucratic challenges of dealing with embassies and consulates abroad somewhat removed from immediate oversight.

Problematic interactions with local aliens authorities are also mentioned in the archives, albeit to a lesser extent. Here, especially the civil servants' "commitment" toward protecting the sponsors, came in for criticism. A 43-year old German sponsor was warned by an official at her local aliens authority that her husband, from Sri Lanka, was not serious about his relationship with her because she was supposedly too old to have his children and this amounted to a disgrace in Sri Lankan culture. Her husband's entry visa was denied on these grounds (CD 55). But it is not only women that the authorities feel the need to "protect." A male German sponsor also complained about repeated comments made by the aliens authority employees regarding his project to reunite with his Uzbek fiancée, her son and their common daughter. He said he was repeatedly told about the high divorce rates of bi-national couples and asked if he was sure about the responsibility of "saddling himself" with an entire family (CD 82).

The migrant advocates confirm this kind of behaviour, though here the point is made that overall, gender does have an impact on the treatment that sponsors receive. For instance, the tendency of civil servants (most of whom are men) to patronise and criticise German female sponsors was reported:

> German women are much more frequently asked questions that really go below the belt; men are simply treated a bit differently by the administration. (…) 'They are taking away our women!' It's especially men that say such things, this is really something we have observed in the course of our organisation's work. It is largely men that act against German women or ask very uncomfortable questions, because these German women have made a different choice, meaning they have made a choice against them: against German men as such. And this can include the civil servant sitting across the desk in the office, who then says things like: 'You're not that bad, you could've found someone else!' (4a)

According to this migrant advocate, not only are the authorities inclined to treat female sponsors more condescendingly, but also the attitudes displayed by the female and male sponsors themselves can differ. Men are inclined to act with more self-confidence, insisting on their rights and quickly feeling enraged and discriminated against, while women try to cooperate and find solutions:

> Men act completely differently. Men also feel discriminated against much faster, while women always try to solve everything on the relational dimension. They are very fast to say: 'Please, you can come over again and have a look!' Or quickly pull some photographs or emails out of their bag. Men react very differently, rather saying: 'What do you guys want from me?' You really do notice both different behaviour and different treatment, and this is also gender-specific. (4a)

Another example of differentiated treatment regarding ethnicity was mentioned by a migrant advocate who claimed that civil servants regard ethnic German-foreign couples as inclined towards marriages of convenience but rather scrutinise foreign-foreign or minority German-foreign couples for any signs of forced marriages (4a).

7.2.5 Emotional and relational difficulties

Finally, various dynamics stemming from state policies on spousal migration can lead to serious emotional difficulties for transnational couples, difficulties that can have an impact on their relationship. The first dynamic has been mentioned in chapter 2, where I dubbed it the "paradox of convenience", referring to the incentive to marry very early on in the relationship, with spousal migration being the only manner for the couple to be together due to a lack of alternative migration possibilities. This effect of "too strong a relationship too soon" can lead to serious partnership troubles since the spouses initially do not know each other that well and possibly are not fully conscious of "what they were getting into" (4a, 4d). The phenomenon is exacerbated by a highly restrictive visa policy, affecting at least those individuals from countries that need visas for tourist visits. In these cases, if the applicant has revealed to the authorities that a relationship exists with a potential sponsor, obtaining a (tourist or language course) visa is virtually impossible (4a). Also in the dossier, many sponsors report their, sometimes repeated, failed attempts to obtain a visitor visa for their fiancés or spouses (CDs 15, 16, 29, 47, 58, 61, 78). In all cases, the authorities denied a visa as they questioned the "willingness to return" *("Rückkehrbereitschaft")* of the spouses.[237] Thus, this rather paradoxical situation of being less able to obtain a visitor's visa when in a relationship leads many couples to marry prematurely and quickly initiate the formal family migration procedures. This strategy is apparently occasionally even recommended by the representatives abroad, telling couples, "Why don't you just marry?" (4a). This sudden marriage, "jumping into the deep end," can lead to relationship difficulties soon after the successful migration, even causing some sponsors to call the migrant advocates to ask, "How can I get rid of this person as soon as possible?" (4a).

Next to possible problems arising from a hasty marriage, long periods of separation – sometimes lasting a year or more, with the relationship essentially conducted over the internet and by telephone – can put the relationship under strain, just as the insecurity arising from the entire application situation, especially when there are intimacy inquiries or court hearings (4d).

---

[237] Courts have confirmed this practice of denying visitors' visas to individuals that allegedly lack a "willingness to return." See VG Berlin, 29 K 186.10 V, judgement of 23 June 2010.

This was echoed in numerous archive cases, with sponsors recounting the anxieties and stresses placed on both partners as a result. Some complain of depression or other health issues due to the separation, their loneliness and their worries about the future (CDs 71, 82). A description of these and similar emotional difficulties is also a widespread framing employed by the sponsors in their correspondence with authorities in order to gain sympathy for their cases. This will be further explored in the next section.

The asymmetric distribution of power between the spouses, since the incoming spouse depends on the sponsor for his/her residence status, can also turn problematic. In cases of any relationship difficulties arising, the sponsor can put the incoming spouse under pressure by threatening to divorce them before the three-year probationary period is up, which would lead the incoming spouse to lose their residence permit (4d). Even though it is theoretically possible for an incoming spouse to gain an independent residence permit prior to the three-year deadline in extreme cases, such as those involving domestic violence, the migrant advocates agreed that actually fulfilling the conditions is very difficult and rare (4a, 4c, 4d, 4e).

7.3 Transnational couples' reactions to restrictions

Transnational couples, in an attempt to overcome the difficulties they face during the spousal migration process, develop certain strategic forms of agency. Primarily, the couples try to fulfil all the formal requirements set by the law, although when faced with seemingly insurmountable difficulties they often resort to alternative forms of agency. The following section explores some of the different, often intersecting ways in which transnational couples, and especially the (mostly White German) sponsors, exert agency in their spousal migration project.

7.3.1 Transnational couples' agency: Creating pressure

When spousal migration plans do not work out, and one or more of the difficulties described above are encountered, transnational couples often exert agency to achieve their goal of spousal migration by creating civic or legal pressure. The most popular paths chosen by couples, as reported by the migrant advocates and as emerging from the case archive, are taking legal action, establishing contact with the local authorities, bringing cases to the attention of "influential" political figures, handing in a petition, and, lastly, contacting the press with their "story." Through these different types of agency, which are mainly initiated and executed by the sponsor spouse in Germany, the transnational couples typically have two aims. Primarily, of course, they want to increase their own chances of gaining a visa, but some also wish to fight against what they perceive to be generally unfair or detrimental policies.

Organisations such as the IAF and other welfare associations offer legal counselling and advisory services to couples in order to resolve the most general issues. But when things get serious, couples tend to prefer professional legal advice and representation. In cases involving suspicions of a marriage of convenience, a lawyer is nearly indispensable, since only they can appeal against a negative visa decision. If it comes to the point of a court hearing their case, most couples also feel safer having a lawyer by their side (4d, 4e). But legal advice and representation are also employed for other matters in the visa-application process, such as when admission is denied due to questionable identity documents (CD 6) or when an exemption to the language requirement is sought (CDs 6, 33, 38). In these cases, lawyers take over communication with the authorities. Another type of legal action, which came up especially in the context of the language requirement, is to file a constitutional suit. The language requirement was just recently introduced when the research was conducted and several sponsors inquired about the possibilities of filing a constitutional case against this specific policy instrument, also since it was publicly disputed whether the requirement was compatible with the constitutional protection of marriage and the family. However, the lawyer migrant advocates reported this approach to be rather cumbersome, and only one sponsor in the archive had actually handed in a constitutional remonstrance *(Verfassungsbeschwerde)* (CD 29). Further, employing an attorney and taking legal action can incur significant costs, which makes it unfeasible for many couples. One sponsor, when confronted with uncooperative embassy employees during the admission process for his wife (for whom legal representation might have been extremely helpful), stated bluntly: "I would really like to enforce my right by legal action, but I absolutely cannot pay a lawyer and the court fees!" (CD 81).

Another common exhibition of agency is for the sponsor to get in touch with the relevant civil servants handling the case, both at the local aliens authority and the German representation in the incoming spouse's home country. The archive contains various cases of sponsors accompanying the incoming spouse to appointments at an embassy or otherwise establishing personal contact with the diplomatic staff (e.g. CDs 33, 58, 78). Many sponsors also are pro-active in establishing contacts with their local aliens authorities in an attempt to influence the decision-makers, notably to speed up the process or grant exceptions (e.g. CDs 27, 29, 30, 82).

Reports of these experiences – and their results – varied from case to case in the dossier. For example, one sponsor (CD 51) recounted her aggressive establishment of contact with embassy officials and aliens authorities: "I wanted to show them that I was serious about the whole thing." She also noted that her efforts had a positive outcome: "In the end, they always did what I wanted them to do." However, others were extremely frustrated by the perceived lack of cooperation or empathy of the civil servants. One sponsor even handed in a disciplinary complaint *(Dienstaufsichtsbeschwerde)* against a staff member of the visa authority (CD 78). Still, a wish to "stay on good terms" with the local personnel was reported as well. While the IAF encouraged individuals to take a stronger stance and insist on their rights if there was misinformation or legally inadequate behaviour from the authorities, some couples preferred to keep quiet and merely comply, in an attempt to preserve a sympathetic stance vis-à-vis "their" officials (4a):

> I have not established any more direct contact to the German authorities, as I fear this will have a negative impact on the procedure. At the moment, everything lies within the discretion of the employees of the German embassy in Havana! (CD 29)

Another strategy among sponsors that emerged from the case archive was establishing contact with higher echelons of power in order to garner support. Letters or emails were sent not only to high-ranking civil servants within the BMI (responsible for foreigners in Germany) and the AA (responsible for the granting of visas abroad); communications were also made to such prominent figures as the Federal Chancellor, the Federal President *(Bundespräsident)*, the Federal Integration Commissioner or federal MPs, especially those from the sponsors' local electoral district. In these messages, the sponsors often described the difficulties of their individual cases while making a plea for support. While the migrant advocates did not mention this phenomenon at all, the archive displayed that in nearly 20 per cent of the documented cases (n=16 of 82), the sponsors had chosen to direct one or several of these kinds of letters to different officials. These records are a valuable source for the analysis of sponsors' perspectives on spousal migration policies; the rhetorical framings employed will be explored below.

Another more formalised possibility for civic agency is filing a petition to the petition committee of the *Bundestag*. In 2007 and 2008, several individual petitions were handed in against the BMI regarding the new language requirement. Personal petitions against refused visas actually formed the main focus of all petitions filed against the AA in 2007 and 2008, with most of the cases relating to family migration (Deutscher Bundestag 2008: 11-15; Deutscher Bundestag 2009: 13-15). The archive confirms this tendency, with almost 10 per cent of the examined cases having sponsors handing in petitions of their individual cases to the *Bundestag* petition committee (CDs 16, 17, 44, 61, 62, 81, 82). Interestingly, all of the petitioners were male German sponsors.

Finally, a few sponsors (CDs 16, 17, 30) tried to draw public attention to their cases by contacting the local media. Presumably this was an attempt to put pressure on the decision-makers, although a kind of moral obligation to inform the public of "bloodcurdling cases" affecting some transnational couples was also voiced:

> I repeatedly hear astonished and unbelieving reactions, even from lawyers and politicians. The majority of the population does not seem to know what is happening at the moment due to this new [language requirement]. This should change! (CD 30)
>
> I think the public has a right to learn more about [the language requirement]! (CD 16)

All these different instances of agency displayed by the sponsors – characterised by a high degree of personal involvement as well as inventive methods – is indicative of their strong motivation and will to achieve their goal, namely living together with their foreign spouses in Germany. The sponsors' ingenuity and dedication, to say the least, certainly indicate what an intensely personal and emotional project spousal migration is.

7.3.2 How do transnational couples frame their claims?

Perhaps the most valuable attribute of the IAF archive material is the insight it allows into the framings and discourses employed by sponsors when recounting their problems – primarily, but not limited to, the language requirement – in order to gain sympathy for their cause, that is the admission of their spouse into Germany. Both within the communication directed to the IAF as well as public authorities, political figures or the press, certain framings tend to return across cases.

One of the most common framings of sponsors is that of spousal migration as a human and/or a basic constitutional right that is being restricted or denied (e.g. CDs 16, 28, 29, 31, 33, 38, 44). Many sponsors refer to the constitution's Article, which they claim is incompatible with restrictive spousal migration policies, most notably the language requirement. This reasoning is surely inspired, at least in part, by arguments made by opposition parties and migrant organisations (See chapter 6 and section 7.1). The wording employed is in some cases rather sober: "Fully conscious that we have no legal claim to being granted an admission visa, we consider our human rights violated by your decision [to not grant the visa]" (CD 31). Other sponsors on the other hand, can be quite dramatic, whether referring to human rights in general or specifically to the constitution:

> This is a rape of human rights! (CD 44)

> This is mental cruelty through a watering down of the constitution! Our constitution does not have anything to do anymore with the will of the fathers of our constitution. Where is my right to family reunification, where is my right to being together? (CD 28)

In combination with this kind of rights framing, the sponsors often refer to their own German citizenship, in order to make their case even stronger:

> I am robbed of my basic rights in my own country! (CD 33)

> Why does the embassy claim I have no entitlement to be married in Germany? Am I German or not? This is a clear breach of the German constitution! (CD 44)

> I cannot accept that as a German citizen I must let myself be subordinated by these restrictions! (CD 61).

Some sponsors also make the case that ethnic Germans have an even stronger claim to family reunification than ethnic minorities: "I expect this absurd requirement of language skills for family reunification to be abolished immediately, *at least when one spouse has been German for generations!*" (CD 44, emphasis added). Noteworthy, too, is the framing employed by two sponsors (CDs 62, 78), who in letters to CDU MPs or members of government emphasise their common conservative ground and their position in society as politically active citizens:

> I am a member of the CDU as well, avowed and extremely conservative, but here, Prof. Dr. Maria Böhmer [Federal Integration Commissioner], something is going wrong, and it cannot go this way. This has nothing, absolutely nothing to do with integration, this is a policy contemptuous of marriages, inhuman and repulsive, that cannot even start to be explained by anything. (CD 78)

By emphasising their CDU membership or affinity, the sponsors cast themselves as politically conscious conservative citizens who are nevertheless being personally harmed by a conservative CDU policy, which in their eyes could not have been the original goal of the policy. At the same time, ethnic minority German sponsors also make reference to certain rights connected to their German citizenship (CD 58) or criticise the restrictive German policies:

> That really makes me ashamed to be German! (CD 36).

> It is always claimed that Germany is a democratic country. But the state wants to decide whom I marry! (CD 71).

Some sponsors also bring up the fact that spouses of EU citizens and visa-free foreigners are exempted from the language requirement (and thus privileged vis-à-vis Germans), which they see as outrageously unfair and discriminatory (CDs 44, 79). A very common framing is also that of the state intervening where it should not, and this notion is often paired with strong feelings of frustration and of impotence:

> I am powerlessly at the mercy of the authorities. (CD 41)

> I am disenfranchised! (CD 19)

> The government is keeping my husband from me! (CD 20)

> I am outraged about this new law, I feel incapacitated and my privacy is being violated. (CD 72)
>
> I'm not a small child anymore. (...) I am a German citizen and have the right to live together with my husband, but the state barges in and says no! This just can't be true! (CD 73)

All these framings are typically presented in a somewhat aggressive, outraged and demanding tone of voice. "This is a bottomless impertinence" (CD 47) and "I demand this absurd law to be changed immediately!" (CD 44) are representative of the enraged state of mind of the sponsors, and such comments also form part of their overall strategic framing in order to appear to be strong, self-confident individuals who know their rights and had better not be challenged.

In contrast to, but sometimes also combined with this aggressive kind of claims making, is a more modest and emotional framing. Here, the sponsors tend to describe, on the one hand, the joyous and loving relationship they sustain with their spouses; at the same time they also detail the hardships connected with fulfilling all the requirements for spousal migration and especially their separation from their spouses. This "playing on the heart strings" is a more consensual, harmonic strategy in order to win sympathy for the case, ultimately aimed at the same goal – accomplishing spousal migration.

> Can't you imagine what it is like to be married, to love one another, and still be forced to live separately? To be depressed every day, I really can't do it anymore. I don't know what to do anymore... (CD 71)
>
> It is very dissatisfying to look at your hand and see the wedding ring, but when you come home from work there is nobody to talk to and discuss the issues of the day. (CD 20)

Another recurring framing employed by some sponsors emphasises the special nature of both their marriage and their migrant spouse vis-à-vis other visa applicants, and distancing their own spousal migration project and their relationship from possibly "criminal" or otherwise problematic transnational couples:

> We have the impression that the normal and law-abiding citizens are lumped together with frauds and criminals. Criminal acts and attempts at fraud in the past and present throw their dark shadow upon those who are honest and sincere in their love and marriage. (CD 24)

> We understand the legitimate claim to impose German upon those living here in order to achieve a proper integration. However, this law [i.e. the language requirement] is now also being applied to people who do not fit into the pattern of those for whom it was created. (CD 58)

In order to depict themselves and their relationship in a positive light, sponsors place emphasis on the character of their relationships – "true love" (CD 38), "love at first sight" (CD 24) – while highlighting the potential role to be played by themselves, the sponsoring spouses. For instance, sponsors accentuate their presumed membership in academia or the upper social classes and being (true) Germans. While stressing the "authentic" character of the relationship is surely influenced by a potential or actual accusation of being in a marriage of convenience, highlighting the sponsors' "positive" attributes is connected to the incoming spouses' integration prospects. Thus, the sponsors take over and/or react to the government's framing of spousal migration as posing integration problems that need to be solved with the language requirement, by outlining why and how their spouse will not encounter integration problems:

> My personal situation as a German spouse is considered irrelevant [by the authorities]! My personal environment, e.g. German as a mother tongue, university degree, good job, my own apartment, supportive social surroundings, is not taken into consideration at all regarding a good and fast integration of my husband into Germany. (CD 24)

> I am a doctor and my parents are teachers, I thus consider it to be obvious that my wife has less need for integration. (CD 30)

One German sponsor, a medical doctor, made the case for an exception for his Cuban wife from the language requirement in a letter to the AA, saying that it would be in the best interest of the Federal Republic of Germany to keep him inside the country due to a general shortage of physicians. He tried to threaten the authorities with his emigration as a highly-skilled professional if his wife was not granted entry into Germany (CD 30).

Also, distancing their own spouses' ethnicity from other migrant groups was observed in some cases. The sponsor of a Peruvian wife accordingly claimed: "I think there are few Latin Americans who do not want to integrate in Germany; with other nationalities, such as Turks or Russians, I am not so sure..." (CD 44). The German husband of a Thai wife said: "Don't we have enough many radical Muslims, even with residence permits, in our country, who are being monitored by the authorities and according to the statistics commit far more than 30.000 crimes [sic]? I've never heard of such bothers from individuals from Buddhist environments." (CD 61)

A similar point was also brought up by the migrant advocate as she reflected upon the difficulty of creating in-group solidarity among the various individuals involved in spousal migration. According to her, transnational couples are mainly focused on achieving their own personal project and often are highly suspicious of other couples. She interpreted this to at least partly stem from the negative political framings of spousal migration that also influence German sponsors:

> There is this principle: 'divide and rule.' It seems as if the bi-national couples can decide whether they belong to the good ones, that fulfil all the categories, also the family norms, or not. So among bi-national couples you find people that say, to put it bluntly: 'Just because the others mess things up, we have to face the music!' That is what I mean with 'divide and rule', what the state or the politically responsible embody and demand, reaches everyone, also these people, whichever partner choice they might happen to make. Obviously no one wants to be part of the unpopular group, so they try to distinguish themselves from the others, with statements such as: 'Of course the state needs to investigate! He should investigate, since there is a lot of abuse!' This comes precisely from those that are affected! And I can only say: Aha, it has already worked so far, if the state tells the country and the population like a mantra: 'Migration is always accompanied by abuse and immigration into the welfare system and all migrants only want a piece of the economic cake here.' All these negative attributes are strongly internalised, even by those who marry bi-nationally! (4a)

While generally, as outlined above, the dossier echoes this tendency, contrasting cases of solidarity can also be found. One sponsor reflected on the language requirement saying that while she was lucky that her husband's business was going well enough to finance a language course and he is gifted at languages and will presumably master the test, she also was worried about other couples: "But what about the other men and women in the course? They are having a really difficult time learning German, especially since no German is spoken in their environment. I really wholeheartedly suffer along with these couples!" (CD 35). Another sponsor made a point of continuing to hand in his petition to the petition committee even after the successful admission of his wife: "For me, it was primarily about my wife, beyond that however [it is] about the principle of the matter as well" (CD 17).

One migrant advocate also made a point of differentiating between male and female sponsors in their reactions to state restrictions. She had the impression that men are generally more easily enraged and consider institutional restrictions as an unacceptable impertinence, possibly because they have had little prior experience of discrimination or being disadvantaged. Women and ethnic minority Germans, on the other hand, tend to approach the issue in a more sober and solution-oriented way, according to her:

> We notice that German men especially react vehemently to [the language requirement]. We concluded that this is obviously the first time that men in this country notice that they are being treated differently from their neighbour. Thus while women have necessarily also experienced discrimination earlier, it is the first time for many men. And it manifests itself in such remarks, for example on the telephone: 'Have you ever heard of something like this? They actually suggested that my wife...', 'This is outrageous!' and so on. They are so agitated about this that I sometimes even find it funny, because it spills over. They seem so incredulous as to what is being done to them as men in this country. And I think women just react differently, and Germans with a migrant background react differently altogether, because they tend to find it normal: 'OK, this is the way it seems to be, how can we best deal with the situation? And I thought the naturalisation would help me more.' (4a)

Certain tendencies supporting this kind of theorising can be found in the case archive. For example, as mentioned above, all of the sponsors who handed in a petition, which is a very formalised and serious way of bringing attention to perceived personal injustice or policy grievances, were male German sponsors. A hierarchy of membership might be said to exist: The more (ethnic) German, the more male, the whiter, the better educated, the higher socio-economic status a citizen has, the stronger the conception of citizenship rights he conceives of as being rightfully his. In this context, one interesting dossier included in the archive concerns a German soldier who served in Afghanistan and Uzbekistan and subsequently was involved in lengthy proceedings trying to acquire visas and residence permits for his Uzbek fiancée and their common daughter. In 2010, after three years of struggles with the authorities, the daughter and her mother were able to join him. The IAF, in a press release, subsequently chose exactly this case to draw media attention to their political cause and to specifically point out the hardships that some individuals suffer under the newly restricted policies (Verband binationaler Familien und Partnerschaften 2010). This shows that even migrant organisations are inclined to employ the logic of "hierarchies of membership" in order to raise public support for their cause. Put differently, the story of the white ethnic German male soldier who while nobly serving his country happens to meet a beautiful Central Asian woman and becomes romantically involved was expected to evoke more public sympathy than, say, a couple consisting of an unemployed naturalised woman of Turkish origin and her future husband from her parents' home village whom she had met through relatives.

Gender scholars have long pointed to the mechanisms of various layers of inequalities or disadvantages such as gender, age, ethnicity and socio-economic status intersecting with one another and exacerbating the discriminatory effects for the individual in question. On the other hand, a number of female sponsors also formulated highly outraged letters about their situations and some male sponsors also employed very emotional framing in their correspondences. The few cases involving ethnic minority German sponsors also exemplified rather aggressive and outraged framings, along with references to their rights and their German citizenship from both male and female sponsors, all of which made it difficult to draw an overall generalisation from the case archive.

7.3.3 What are the transnational couples' coping strategies?

While trying to create civic and legal pressure by way of the discursive framings described above, transnational couples only rarely actually manage to overcome the hurdles encountered within spousal migration policies. Therefore, this last section is dedicated to a short exploration – derived from the migrant advocate interviews and the IAF archive – of the available possibilities of dealing with the difficulties posed by restrictive spousal migration policies. What are the transnational couples' coping strategies?

Pregnancy/Childbearing

A pregnancy and the resulting parental responsibilities can relieve transnational couples from some of the above-described hurdles to spousal migration. Since the German state protects the child-parent bond to a greater extent than the spousal connection, no language skills and no minimum income are required for foreign parents of children born into German citizenship. This is the case if one of the parents is either a German citizen and the child acquires German citizenship by descent *(ius sanguinis)* or a foreigner with a) at least eight years of regular residence in Germany, b) an unlimited residence permit, and c) the child is born on German territory, which qualifies the child to acquire German citizenship via *ius soli*.[238] In these cases, the parent in Germany has the immediate right to be with his/her child, as does the migrating foreign parent; likewise, the German child has the right to be with both parents. As a result, the admission and residence rights of the incoming spouse/parent are now derived from the child under more favourable conditions, and most importantly no language certificate is demanded.[239]

Immediately after the introduction of the language requirement, it was unclear how to deal with future parents of German children, with aliens authorities in the southern part of Germany, in particular, denying admission until after the child had actually been born (2d). After one and a half years of legal struggles by couples in this situation, the administrative practice was established of granting future parents of German children a so-called anticipatory right *(Vorgriffsrecht)*, allowing them entry into Germany prior to the birth and without a language certificate. Future mothers are now regularly allowed to enter about six months prior to the birth date in order to spend the last phase of their pregnancy (and childbirth) in Germany. Future fathers are usually admitted about three months before the delivery in order to support their wives and be present at the birth (2d). Also, any marriage-of-convenience suspicions are usually overcome in the case of a pregnancy.[240]

Various migrant advocates mentioned examples of transnational couples that had "resolved" their difficulties by having a child together (4a,

---

[238] § 4 Abs. 3 Staatsangehörigkeitsgesetz (StAG).
[239] § 28 Abs. 1 Nr. 3 AufenthG.
[240] However, a parallel political discourse and also legal instruments exist regarding so-called "paternities of convenience." See Footnote 27.

4d), although it remained an open question whether this was the primary motivation for the pregnancy. When pressed to give a personal evaluation whether the pregnancies had been "tactical," the migrant advocates said they thought that pregnancies were probably not completely unwanted, although the timing of a number of pregnancies might have been accelerated to help gain a residence permit for the incoming spouse. This phenomenon might be interpreted as a more radical example of the "perverse effects" or the "paradox of convenience" mentioned earlier, in which restrictive migration policies induce transnational couples to marry at a very early stage in their relationship due to a lack of other possibilities to establish their relationship in Germany. This same mechanism might also here, with restrictive spousal migration policies creating an incentive for couples to have children early in their relationship or marriage in order to be able to actually live together. In chapter 4 it was also shown that the number of parents claiming family admission for a minor child has risen substantially since 2007.

Obviously, for many couples who do not wish or are unable to have children (at the moment of migration), overcoming hurdles via a pregnancy is not a viable option. Furthermore, a pregnancy does not always lead to an improvement in family migration rights – that is, to a reduction of the requirements to be fulfilled. For example, if the (future) child is not entitled to German citizenship because the sponsor is neither a German citizen nor meets the 8-year regular residence requirement, or if the child is born abroad, things can potentially get even more complicated because the sponsor can be required to provide an even higher income in order to take care of the entire family – including the child. In addition, doubts or complications about maternity or paternity can arise. The IAF chronicled the case of a German sponsor who had a child with an Uzbek woman who at the time of the birth was still married to another man (CD 82). According to Uzbek law, her first husband was the child's father. The ensuing negotiations with the different authorities in Uzbekistan and Germany were extremely difficult, and in the meantime the young family was separated. So, it can certainly not be concluded that childbearing might be described as an "easy way out."

Circumvention of restrictions with tricks or exceptions

Because the migrant advocates generally defended the interests and viewpoints of the transnational couples, they also tended to not reveal any illegal or semi-legal behaviour. The same also held true for the couples documenting their cases in the archive. However, as mentioned in section 6.2.6, the local civil servants (3a) reported that couples customarily tried to circumvent parts of the admission procedure – by entering Germany on a different visa, for example, and then applying for spousal admission from inside Germany. This is especially viable for citizens with immediate access to tourist visas (3a). However, the aliens authorities tend to be very strict regarding this kind of behaviour, which infringes on visa procedures, and work to inhibit it. Furthermore, the fact that the embassies abroad often find it necessary to check the authenticity of documents probably indicates that documents are indeed forged on occasion. In this context, the government has mentioned the problem of fraud in the context of the language certificate. Embassies reported a few cases of forged language certificates included with visa applications, and they reported, to an even larger extent, cases of identity fraud – i.e. individuals taking the exam claiming to be someone else (Deutscher Bundestag, Drucksache 17/3090: 29-30).

Other "tricks" mentioned were connected to faulty evidence regarding the minimum income, such as fake income slips or even the "creation" of a job on paper that in reality did not produce any income, which eventually led families to rely on social welfare (4d). Regarding the language requirement, it is possible for the incoming spouses to be exempted if they fulfil certain special conditions. As outlined in section 4.2, spouses unable to learn basic German due to a mental or physical impairment (which does not include illiteracy) and spouses who have "recognisably minor integration needs," also are exempted from the language requirement. But the migrant advocates knew of few cases where this exception had been applied.

The archive contained the dossier of a Moroccan-German couple that had great difficulties obtaining the language certificate and after intensive correspondences – *inter alia,* a seven-page letter to the Foreign Minister – had more or less coincidentally discovered the possibility of exemption with a university degree. When they presented the wife's Moroccan law degree she was granted admission without the language certificate (CD 38). More recent data show that some spouses, especially those from India and China, are regularly exempted from providing a language certificate (Deutscher Bundestag, Drucksache 17/1112: 8). In 2009, 39 per cent of all Indian applicants and 37 per cent of all Chinese applicants for spousal visas were exempted from having to provide a language certificate. However, it remains unclear how many exceptions were granted due to the spouses' university degrees and how many because they were joining highly-skilled migrants, foreign researchers or entrepreneurs, as these spouses are also exempted.

Emigration

Another possibility for transnational couples if spousal migration to Germany proves difficult is the temporary or permanent emigration of the sponsor spouse – that is, reversing the direction of the spousal migration, with the sponsors from Germany moving to the home country of their foreign spouses. Some couples already live together in the foreign spouse's home country and simply decide to remain there (CD 23). Alternatively, some (especially highly-skilled) sponsors or couples choose to emigrate to a country with more liberal family migration conditions than Germany, provided that at least one of them is able to acquire a primary residence (and work) permit. Both of these emigration decisions are often coloured by a certain disappointment regarding Germany, especially on the part of the sponsor. The feeling that the German state and bureaucracy are hostile is mentioned, as is an ensuing motivation to leave Germany:

> We are forced to raise loads of money in order to be granted our rights. THANK YOU GERMAN STATE. I would like best to s**t on Germany and move to Turkey. But I can't do that, because I have had my steady job here for more than 30 years and in Turkey I would be without work and income. (CD 73)

Another possibility exists due to the phenomenon of reverse discrimination mentioned earlier. If the German sponsor moves to another EU Member State and subsequently spousal admission is applied for there or upon returning to Germany, the sponsor is treated as a SCN. Accordingly, fewer conditions must be met, for instance, no language requirement is required.[241] A civil

---

[241] See section 5.1.3.

servant from an aliens authority reported that in the West German border region, sponsors moved to the Netherlands and subsequently applied to the Dutch authorities for their spouses' admission (3a). However, the archive also contained the dossier of a German woman who, in order to circumvent the language requirement, moved to Spain and initiated the spousal migration process for her Dominican husband from there. But Spanish authorities suspected a marriage of convenience and did not grant admission either (CD 19). Another sponsor with dual nationality (Greek and German) tried to convince the German authorities to recognise him as an intra-EU mover due to his Greek nationality and exempt his wife from the language requirement. The authorities refused to grant the exception and told him that his German citizenship was crucial. This led the sponsor to contemplate "giving back" his German passport, which he had acquired only a few years earlier via naturalisation (CD 18). Thus, even though in theory the (temporary and/or bogus) relocation to another EU Member State would seem to be an easy ploy to overcome the injustice allegedly posed by "reverse discrimination," in practice it does not always work so smoothly. Furthermore, for many sponsors, this strategy is simply unworkable due to financial, professional or social reasons. Not everyone is free (or able) to suddenly move to another EU country.

Abandonment of marital project

The ultimate way to deal with the various difficulties posed by restrictive legislation in the field of spousal migration is abandoning the entire common-life project altogether. Obviously, other factors will influence a couple's decision to separate or divorce, but the general difficulties posed by restrictive policies, including the often-exhausting struggle with the authorities, the insecurity regarding a common future and long periods of physical separation are reported by all migrant advocates as putting enormous (and occasionally fatal) strains on transnational relationships. The archive accordingly also contained the case of one couple that separated before the husband had come to Germany because, among other things, he "had not taken learning German seriously" (CD 27).

"Biting the bullet"

Apart from all these different possibilities of sidestepping at least some of the restrictive spousal migration policies (such as the language requirement), perhaps the most common response of all is a fulfilment of the increased requirements. Since spousal migration is such an intimately personal project, many couples are driven by a strong will and enduring commitment to eventually succeed, by also taking risks and enduring hardships over a long period of time. After an initial dip in numbers in 2007 and 2008 immediately after the introduction of the language requirement, spousal migration increased again in 2009 (see section 4.3). Although spousal migration is now connected with even higher costs and longer separation periods, transnational couples seem largely undeterred to achieve their goals.

Conclusions

This chapter helped to considerably widen the scope of the main research questions under scrutiny. While previous chapters mainly focused on spousal migration flows and policies from the viewpoint of the state and explored framings employed by institutional actors, the analysis of migrant advocate interviews and the IAF case archive gave a glimpse of the perspectives of both the individuals working in the representation of migrant interests as well as the transnational couples themselves, especially the sponsors.

The first section illustrated the perspectives and framings of the migrant advocates, who are strongly embedded actors within the arena of negotiating the ways in which spousal migration and resultant policies are framed, perceived and discussed in the political and public spheres. Similar to opposition politicians, their framings stand in marked contrast to the dominant state and government framings, with an emphasis on transnational couples' rights and their individual hardships connected to restrictive spousal migration policies. The next two sections looked more closely at the transnational couples themselves by exploring the most important issues and difficulties encountered during the spousal migration process, alongside the couples' reactions to restrictions, including a unique insight into the most widespread framings employed by the German sponsors in their communications with authorities.

Engaging in spousal migration into Germany is not an easy undertaking nowadays, but this chapter also made clear that this is not entirely new either. The new language requirement certainly constitutes an additional hardship, but hurdles such as the income requirement and intimacy inquiries are at least as burdensome for the couples – and these have been in place for years now. The migrant advocates' accounts and the case dossiers also certainly added some diversity to the inherent reduction of spousal migration flows to incoming young and vulnerable Muslim wives, as per the framings of many institutional interviewees. Instead, the phenomenon of spousal migration is a diverse one, with its own dynamics pertaining to age, educational background, ethnicity, gender and citizenship. The section on the couples' reactions revealed that the relationship between the couples and the state's institutions is obviously a highly asymmetric one, since the couples' possibilities to influence governmental and institutional decisions are close to zero: They must work within and around the restrictions. In this light, the ingenious displays of agency characterised by extraordinary perseverance and the strong will to "leave no stone unturned" is especially impressive. Finally, the couples' perspectives and their struggles are crucial to complete the picture and fully grasp what spousal migration is about. Beyond all the rhetoric of constitutional rights and infringements, it is a personal and very intimate issue that is intrinsically connected to individual well-being and satisfaction in life.

8   Conclusions

More than twenty years have passed since James Hollifield (1992) first hypothesised that Western democracies are constrained in their ability to restrict migration by their own commitment to liberal norms and individual rights. This research set out to reassess the implications of these "liberal constraints" by exploring the ways in which new restrictions upon spousal migration, a migration inflow based entirely upon individual rights, are approached by different actors within a European liberal democracy. Even though in the past decade family migration has been restricted all across Europe, rights-based liberalism continues to have an impact on migration policy.

First, at the risk of stating the obvious, liberal norms have a strong bearing on migration policies in the sense that at the most general level, family migration continues to be permitted. While restrictions have dominated policy development recently in many states, no European politician or policy-maker has seriously demanded to completely disallow or ban all family migration. Indeed, although increasingly subject to stricter conditions, family migration continues to be possibly the most accessible gateway into many European states and accordingly one of the main sources of migration. Furthermore, the option of spousal migration is at least theoretically open to nearly anyone with a sponsor spouse: It does not depend on elaborate skills (as in the case of specialised workers or highly-skilled migrants), substantial financial resources (as in the case of entrepreneurs) or specific living conditions in the country of origin (as in the case of asylum seekers).

Second, I proposed in chapter 2 that liberal norms are also important for the "fine-tuning" of family migration policies as a "liberal discursive constraint" influences the ways restrictive policy instruments are framed. As theorised earlier by scholars such as Lavenex (2001) for asylum policies, by discursively presenting inflows of foreigners as potential threats to internal security, instead of as an issue of human rights, restrictive policies can be better justified. In other words, framing matters. Instead of stating bluntly that the right to spousal migration will be limited because the inflows it produces are considered to be politically undesirable, restrictions are made via the approaches I termed "regulating membership" and "regulating family." Family migration is based on the individual right to the protection of family of members (citizens/foreign residents) of the polity in question. By instilling the contested concepts of "membership" and "family" with certain meanings in the context of family migration policies, restrictions can be justified. Put differently, by not putting the individual right as such into question, but regulating instead who can access this right and under what conditions, European governments can reconcile restricting humanitarian inflows – such as family migration – with their identity as liberal democracies committed to the protection of individual rights – such as the protection of marriage and family.

Intermingled with the approaches of membership regulation and family regulation are discursive strategies that frame spousal migration as leading to societal problems and human rights infringements in order to make a stronger case for restriction. For instance, excluding forced marriages from the right to family migration is an instance of family regulating – albeit one which by itself presumably would not have a great impact on policy practices due to the hidden nature of the phenomenon. Framing spousal migration as largely being composed of forced marriages and thereby justifying an age requirement for spouses as an adequate policy instrument is an instance of family regulating intermingled with strategic framing, which leads to more substantive policy changes. The fact that institutions, which could presumably act as liberal correctives to restrictive policies, such as courts, accept and adopt these government framings of spousal migration (e.g. the German Federal Administrative Court in its judgement of March 2010, see section 4.2), supports the conclusion that this is a successful strategy.

These different mechanisms were further explored by scrutinising the development of spousal migration policies in Germany. For the larger part of the post-war era, substantial amounts of family-related migration entered Germany without being federally regulated. In this phase, family migration policies were characterised by a large degree of administrative discretion, with large regional disparities across the *Länder* and a general political unwillingness to publicly accept the social reality of migration. While the admission of family members of the first generation of guest workers was more or less consensually viewed as an historical "moral" obligation among politicians, many viewed the rising tendency of second-generation minorities engaging in spousal migration very sceptically. Regional attempts to massively curtail these inflows via restrictive policies emerged. In this situation, German courts expansively interpreted foreigners' rights, including the protection of marriage and family. Several especially harsh family migration provisions were overruled by the Constitutional Court with reference to the importance that the German constitution's Article 6 guarantees for the protection of marriage and family, which was judged to apply to foreign residents of Germany as well. Germany's "activist judiciary" in that time period was, accordingly, the model case of a liberal constraint emerging from (constitutional) judicial review as theorised by Joppke (1998a) and Guiraudon (1998).

From 1990 onwards, a reformed *Ausländergesetz* finally enshrined family migration rights into the federal law. At the same time and dating from the mid-1980s, when it came to the subject of immigration, asylum inflows had already begun to attract attention. After the fall of the Iron Curtain, asylum dominated the political discussion for the next decade alongside the governance of massive inflows of ethnic German resettlers *(Aussiedler)* from Central Europe and the former Soviet Union. The asylum compromise of 1992 considerably altered the asylum procedure and, in the course of the 1990s, admission conditions for resettlers and their families grew stricter as well. Effectively, these previously rather substantial humanitarian inflows were largely reduced to a minimum by the end of the 2000s. Political attention slowly shifted back to the remaining substantial humanitarian inflow, family migration.

In a parallel process, negotiations for a common framework on family migration for third-country nationals at the EU level revealed the restrictive intentions in this field of various Member States such as Austria, Germany and the Netherlands. Instead of establishing a generous common standard for family migration as the European Commission had set out to do, the resulting 2003 directive granted domestic governments substantive possibilities to impose conditions on both sponsors and family migrants before being granted admission. The German government shifted to a conservative majority in 2005 and a law reform incorporating significant restrictive changes of spousal migration passed parliament and came into effect in mid-2007. The changes included a minimum age of 18 for incoming and sponsoring spouses and the possibility of making the admission of German citizens' spouses conditional upon a minimum income; this was previously only demanded of foreign sponsors. Most pertinently, a language requirement was introduced; basic German skills need to be proven by the applicants abroad before any admission visa to Germany is granted. This German restrictive shift in the field of spousal migration was not exceptional in Europe. During the same period, age requirements set at 18, 21, and even 24 were instituted in many other European states, income requirements were increased and similar integration conditions were introduced. Though differing in the exact details, to date, the Netherlands, France, Denmark, the UK and Austria oblige incoming spouses to fulfil an integration requirement in order to be granted a residence permit.

In what ways has this restrictive shift within spousal migration law been discursively reconciled with the "liberal constraint" to protect individual rights? Employing the epistemological approach of "policy frame analysis" (Verloo 2005), parliamentary plenary debates and a series of in-depth interviews held with German Members of Parliament (MPs) and civil servants were analysed. How do different political actors frame the issue of spousal migration (diagnosis)? Which policies are accordingly suggested (therapy) and how are they causally linked to the diagnosis?

Framing spousal migration

In the parliamentary stage of the *Bundestag*, the dominant way to make sense of spousal migration by conservative CDU MPs was by linking it to the problem-laden issues of forced marriages and integration deficits. Forced marriages, a practice violating liberal norms of gender equality and individual freedom of choice, are alleged to occur frequently within spousal migration processes. Spousal migration is causally linked to integration deficits among ethnic minorities, often referred to via the notion of "parallel societies," as marrying a foreign spouse is interpreted to be a sign of segregation. Since forced/arranged marriages and "parallel societies" are at the same time predominantly presented as problems involving the Turkish/Muslim communities, spousal migration is overwhelmingly associated with these groups as well. By defining forced marriages, and also the cultural norms dominant within mainly Turkish "parallel societies," as gender oppression, which is incompatible with liberal norms, the case for restricting spousal migration is made.

Apart from the fact that not all Turkish spouses are forced into marriages and that many individuals with a Turkish background are well integrated into German society, reducing spousal migration to a phenomenon only concerning Turkish communities is similarly inappropriate. While the single largest group of spouses entering Germany are indeed from Turkey, spouses from Kosovo, the Russian Federation and India together received about the same number of visas as Turkish spouses in 2008. A parallel observation can be made regarding gender. Notwithstanding the fact that around 30 per cent of incoming spouses are male, spousal migration is framed in parliament by MPs of all parties as a phenomenon concerning incoming females. This idea of the victimised bride, who is "imported" against her will by (Turkish) "macho men" who are unwilling to integrate, fits squarely into notions of spousal migration leading to integration deficits, parallel societies and forced marriages. The picture of incoming husbands sponsored by their wives in Germany fits less clearly into this imagery and is thus rather left untold.

By presenting insufficient German language skills as a major inhibition to both integration and the possibility of escaping from forced marriages, the newly introduced language requirement gains the status of a policy instrument, which helps oppressed women and creates incentives for individuals unwilling to integrate – instead of being an instrument of migration control infringing upon the individual right to marriage and family. In this way, the liberal constraints to protect individual rights emanating from the German constitution are alleviated by pointing to more pressing human rights violations such as forced marriages that are supposedly fought with the language requirement. In other words, restricting individual rights in one area is justified with the goal of protecting them in another. Family regulating thus occurs by connecting the problem of forced marriages – a practice violating human rights standards and liberal Western norms – to spousal migration and thereby justifying restrictions within spousal migration policies. At the same time, membership regulating occurs by framing spousal migration as an outcome and cause of integration deficits and "parallel societies" in order to justify restrictions. Basically, the legitimate claim to full membership and thus to the individual protection of marriage of the (ethnic minority) sponsor is called into question here.

The political opposition, mainly MPs from the Green and Left parties, contested these frames presented by conservative government MPs. They criticise the government for infringing on the constitutional protection of marriage and family, especially through the use of the language requirement. The opposition is also highly critical of the government's justification of the language requirement's goals as preventing forced marriages and enhancing integration; they largely denounce this justification as instrumental and hypocritical.

A more complex picture regarding factors underlying spousal migration policies emerges from the analysis of the interviews held with MPs and civil servants. Just as was the case in parliamentary discussions, the issue of forced marriages is positioned within a general framing of women as passive victims of the entire spousal migration process. These female victims need protection and help with emancipation by the German state for their own good; for example, through the language requirement. Forced marriages are also connected to parallel societies, which are seen as the epitome of failed integration. Parallel societies are framed as consisting of minorities who have little interest in interacting with the German majority society, mainly with a Turkish or Arab background. Members of parallel societies are further conceptualised to often be unemployed and dependent on social welfare, largely uneducated and most importantly, culturally very different from the majority society. The most important (negative) elements of the different culture in the context of spousal migration are patriarchal gender norms and the ensuing oppression of women. Spousal migration is depicted to further sustain these parallel societies, while the fact that a minority individual engages in spousal migration is interpreted as self-segregation. Spousal migration is thus framed to be an outcome and a cause of parallel societies at the same time. Just like the phenomena of forced marriages and oppression of women in general, parallel societies are also discursively located within Turkish/Arab communities in Germany. It is interesting that within the German framing, in contrast with similar discussions in the Dutch context, Islam as a religion or Muslim minorities' cultures are seldom explicitly mentioned to be an issue for politicians and policy-makers but rather criticised via discursive bridges of forced marriages, patriarchal gender norms or parallel societies, which conjure up certain associations.

Apart from these two frames, which were also very dominant in the parliamentary discussions, further frames proved to be salient in the interviews as well. First, it was noted that German citizens are increasingly ethnically diverse, which is perceived by some as a devaluation of German citizenship. This was also mentioned as the main incentive behind restricting the rules for spousal migration for German sponsors. Second, the burden on the public budget, and more specifically the welfare state, by poorly educated and economically inactive spousal migrants is perceived to be a real threat as well. Third, the constitutional protection of marriage and family is framed as a cumbersome obligation pressuring the state to allow spousal migration contrary to efficient migration management. Finally, family migration provisions are generally considered to be prone to abuse, especially in the form of "marriages of convenience." Overall, the interviews thus revealed deeply classist imaginings of both migrants and ethnic minorities in Germany as uneducated and prone to (abuse) welfare provisions. These representations were largely absent from the plenary discussions, which were rather dominated by human rights discourses and arguments. This unsurprisingly points towards a much stronger liberal rights constraint at work in the official and public realm of parliament than behind policy-makers' closed doors.

Additionally, the effects of spousal migration policies on affected transnational couples were explored by analysing in-depth interviews with migrant advocates and a dossier archive documenting individual cases. The focus of investigation here was the nexus between policies and affected couples. What effects do state policies have on transnational couples and in what ways do they deal with them? For the individual couples involved, spousal migration to Germany has recently grown more restrictive; although, as was pointed out, it was not all that simple before recent changes were introduced. The new language requirement certainly constitutes an additional hardship but hurdles such as the income requirement and intimacy inquiries aiming at detecting marriages of convenience are at least as burdensome for some couples and have already been institutionalised for years.

Exploring the interviews and the case archive added some diversity to the inherent reduction of spousal migration flows to incoming young and vulnerable Muslim wives, as in the framings of many institutional interviewees. Instead, it was shown that the universe of spousal migration is a diverse one, with its own dynamics pertaining to age, educational background, ethnicity, gender and citizenship of the spouses. The imaginative displays of agency characterised by extraordinary perseverance and strong willpower on the part of some couples is emblematic of how extremely personal the impact of spousal migration policies can be. Beyond all the rhetoric of constitutional rights and infringements, the success or failure of spousal migration is mostly an emotional and very intimate issue that can have a fundamental impact upon individual well-being.

Different actors and their positions

One of the main goals of this thesis was to pry open the "black box" of "the state" by presenting a more diverse picture of the positions of the various stakeholders involved. The most fundamental rift between actors can be discerned between government MPs, mainly those belonging to the CDU, and opposition MPs from the Greens and the Left Party. CDU MPs defend and justify the government's introduction of restrictive instruments with the arguments presented above, while the opposition endeavours to discredit the government and its policies. The main argument presented by the opposition is that the language requirement infringes too harshly on the protection of marriage and is thus unconstitutional, but they also critically reflect upon the government's framing and reject it as hypocritical.

Political power constellations are crucial in influencing the stance taken as well. Whilst part of the government from 2005-2009, Social Democratic MPs (SPD) tentatively supported the restrictions introduced by their senior coalition partner CDU but blatantly called for abolishing the language requirement once in opposition from 2009 onwards. Conversely, as an opposition party until 2009, the liberal democratic FDP criticised the language requirement and especially the provisions discriminating against German citizens, only to fully support the law after entering government in 2009.

When adding civil servants to the picture, further facets of differentiation emerge. First, while the MPs were predominantly concerned with the 2007 change in the law and focused mainly on arguments supporting or criticising the introduction of the language requirement, most civil servants had a much more complex view of the dynamics pertaining to spousal migration and its governance. For instance, while the problem of marriages of convenience was not mentioned by MPs during the plenary debates or in the interviews, nearly all civil servants emphasised the deep relevance this phenomenon and the corresponding measures (e.g. intimacy inquiries) have for the implementing authorities. This difference might be explained by the longstanding experience executive authorities have gained with spousal and family migration as a quantitatively very significant inflow over the years, while the topic is still rather novel at the legislative and political stage. Second, among the different civil servants, a distinction can be drawn between those working in "law and order" institutions, such as the federal and regional Ministries of the Interior, the Foreign Office and the local aliens authorities on the one hand and the civil servants associated with ministries and offices in charge of integration on the other. The former, according to their institutional profile, very strongly support the government's course of action, while the latter are much more critical of restriction since they often view themselves as defending migrants' interests.

The migrant advocates, who represent migrants' and transnational couples' interests, position themselves similarly to opposition politicians. Their framings strongly contest the dominant government framings, with an emphasis on transnational couples' rights and individual hardships connected to restrictive spousal migration policies. Contrary to Freeman's ideas (1995) on the influential role of interest groups in shaping (liberal) migration policies, these actors cannot be assessed to have any significant impact on the German government's choices. Although representatives of migrant NGOs and dedicated migrant lawyers are regularly invited to expert hearings regarding family migration, their demands remain largely ignored. Even the migrants advocates themselves evaluate these instances of civil society participation in the legislative process as a "farce" (see chapter 7).

What are the possible reasons for this failure of organised interests to influence policies? First, contrary to the labour migration inflows in Freeman's theory, which were demanded by employers' associations in order to sustain economic growth, family migration initially only serves the immediate interests of the individuals involved. Of course, protecting these individual rights can be considered as part of the state's duties, but apart from the general appeal to liberal rights and the fervent claims of those affected, few other organised interests are bound to lobby against restrictive family migration policies.

This is connected to the second factor, which concerns the relatively underdeveloped nature of migrant organisations, in general, and family migration NGOs, in particular, in Germany. Most migrant organisations are based around certain ethnic identities and are small and not well funded, often lacking a legal department. Accordingly, it is mainstream (partly Christian) welfare organisations, such as *Caritas*, *Diakonie* or the German Red Cross, academic institutions such as the German Institute for Human Rights, or international NGOs, such as Amnesty International and Terre des Femmes, that issue statements as input for the legislative process on family migration in Germany. The IAF is the only large NGO in Germany that specifically focuses on family migration. Since liberal changes in this field seem to emanate not from lobby work but from court judgements, NGOs such as the IAF could remodel their strategies of influencing policies by embracing the power of judicial review. Organisations such as GISTI in France and the Southall Black Sisters in the UK have supported individuals in challenging restrictive government policies in court or have themselves successfully pursued these policies. Therefore, contesting restrictive policies in court and providing material and ideational support for couples with the courage to take the long, windy road of litigation might be among the most successful ways for NGOs to actually have an impact in this field.

What direction could future research take?

The thesis results point towards various directions for possible future research. First, frame analysis has proven to be a very useful epistemological tool for analysing the evolution of migration policies, especially when dealing with specific fields such as spousal migration. Policies aimed at other specific flows such as high-skilled migration, ethnic kin migration, asylum or irregular migration could also be explored via policy frame analysis. Furthermore, for the analysis of related policies on integration or citizenship it is bound to be useful as well. Comparing frames across distinct migration policy fields, by contrasting the frames connected to high-skilled migration for example, with those linked to family migration, would surely lead to interesting results. By disentangling the arguments brought forward in the construction of related problems and solutions by different stakeholders in the policy field, one can trace how an issue is implicitly and explicitly given meaning. This way, a differentiated perspective on the factors and dynamics underlying policies governing migration emerges.

The existence of a "discursive liberal constraint," which I established for spousal migration, can be assumed to be of relevance for other humanitarian inflows as well. A certain pattern can possibly be discerned regarding the circumvention of liberal constraints via strategic framing. In the German case, the constitution devised in the aftermath of the Nazi experience, enshrined very strong individual rights for asylum seekers and ethnic German resettlers, just as it protected the individual right to marriage and family in its Article 6. But the resulting liberal policies were not exclusively due to humanitarian generosity but rooted in political considerations as well. During the Cold War, a subjective right of asylum for politically persecuted individuals from the East bloc and the inclusion of ethnic Germans into the German nation were crucial aspects of the Federal Republic's self-conception as a Western liberal democracy and the only legitimate German state. I suspect that once these inflows were perceived to be socially burdensome and politically no longer necessary, policy-makers embarked on a path of strategic framing. Individual rights, as such, were maintained in order to stay within the realm circumscribed by liberal constraints, and instead the individuals entering under these premises were placed under general suspicion for not really belonging to the self-declared category. Even though more research would be necessary in order to substantiate this hypothesis, it is known that in the late 1980s and early 1990s, asylum seekers were increasingly termed "bogus asylum seekers" ("*Scheinasylanten*") and "asylum frauds" ("*Asylbetrüger*") and were suspected of being economic migrants. In addition, asylum seekers were increasingly framed as threatening social cohesion and economic wellbeing. In this way, the alternative frame of granting asylum due to human rights obligations was crowded out. In the late 1990s in turn, resettlers and their families were increasingly obliged to "prove" their German heritage in order to come into consideration for the generous admission and citizenship provisions. Integration problems of resettlers began to attract greater attention. These developments continued in the 2000s in the realm of family migration, with transnational couples having to fulfil increasing requirements in order to prove their marriage and/or legitimate membership to the community in order to enjoy the right to have their family protected.

Certainly, this kind of frame analysis research could profit from cross-European comparisons. As illustrated in chapter 5, the trend towards family migration restriction is a European one and exploring the differences and similarities across countries is bound to generate important insights. For instance, Bonjour (2010) has compared parliamentary debates in France and Netherlands surrounding the introduction of the respective integration abroad requirements and has come up with insightful conclusions regarding the importance of judicial liberal constraints and of political opposition.

Next to these possibilities to advance the study of migration policy via frame analysis, the present thesis could also instigate further research concerning the specificities of family migration flows. As I have shown that stereotyped assumptions about spousal migration dominate the frames of conservative actors and are employed to justify restrictive policies, it is necessary to also assess the "authenticity" of some of these claims brought forward. For instance, one of the most widespread claims is that incoming spouses are a potential burden on the welfare state, but little evidence exists regarding their subsequent participation in the labour market. It would also be very useful to shed more light on the phenomena of forced marriages and marriages of convenience, as the supposed prevalence of these practices serve as the main justification for restrictive policies that include a language requirement and intimacy inquiries. However, the concealed and intimate nature of these criminalised activities is bound to make reliable research rather difficult.

Of special research interest would also be to scrutinise the interconnections between policies and practices of spousal migration in order to critically evaluate government policies. For instance, an area that could be explored is how successful intimacy inquiries are in detecting marriages of convenience or in what ways the language requirement really prevents forced marriages. While these connections are again bound to be difficult to uncover, a more reasonable research endeavour could however be an assessment of the integration potential of the language requirement: In what ways does the language requirement enhance integration? By comparing the "integration success" (e.g. by comparing integration course results or labour market participation) of spouses who fulfilled the language requirement with those who entered prior to 2007 and those who did not, results regarding the effectiveness of the language requirement could be obtained.

A glance into the future of spousal migration policies

Obviously, it is difficult to predict what direction family migration policies in Germany and Europe will take in the future. What seems certain is that the current dynamic nature of this unsettled policy field will continue for a while. In the four main years spent researching for this book (2008-2011), it was difficult to keep up with the many developments and changes taking place across Europe. Many governments' intentions to further restrict spousal migration still appear intact, but do not remain uncontested. Most importantly, various court judgements at domestic and European levels have overturned restrictive spousal migration provisions and will presumably continue to do so, confirming thus the ongoing importance of the "judicial liberal constraint."

The process is a complex one, with courts having ruled restrictive instruments to be incompatible with the European Convention of Human Rights (ECHR), the Family Reunification Directive and EU-Turkey association law. The European Commission has also played an important role in trying to defend family migration rights during European Court of Justice (ECJ) proceedings, for instance by issuing a statement in May 2011 declaring integration abroad requirements incompatible with the FR Directive. Furthermore, developments at different levels have a strong impact on one another, as ECJ judgements made in reference to the policies of one Member State are formally binding for other states as well, but the governments do not necessarily accept this liability by automatically applying all ECJ judgements into domestic law.

In contrast, just how much of an impact domestic judgements dealing with EU law have on other national spheres remains unclear. The German government has stated that the domestic Dutch court decision ruling the integration requirement incompatible with the standstill clause of association law, which subsequently led to an exemption of incoming Turkish spouses, has no impact on the German situation, and waited until a case came before the ECJ specifically dealing with the compatibility of the German policy with association law. In addition, governments can respond to judicial constraints with further restriction in other fields or by reducing rights. Shortly after the UK Supreme Court recently overruled the age requirement (that spouses must be 21 years old) as incompatible with the ECHR in 2011, the government's Migration Advisory Committee (MAC) recommended a substantial increase in the minimum income threshold for sponsors of spousal migration, which came into force in 2012. When the ECJ overruled the Dutch distinction between "family reunion" and "family formation" regarding minimum age and income in *Chakroun*, the age limit was increased to 21 years of age for all spouses.

Furthermore, it is important to keep in mind that the judicial liberal constraint does not work automatically. In order for any judge to overrule a restrictive law, legal action must be initiated, and mostly be fought through various courts. As outlined in chapter 7, this path is often long, expensive and the outcome uncertain. Substantive NGO support of the individual couples could perhaps make a crucial difference. Moreover, a strategy of selective lenience on the part of the government may also contribute to avoiding or at least forestalling policy-changing judgements. During a case brought to the Federal Administrative Court (BVerwG) in 2011 concerning the language requirement, for example, the Foreign Office relented and issued visas to the plaintiffs without German skills prior to the final hearing, even though the BVerwG had explicitly ruled the language requirement compatible with the directive as recently as March 2010. However, in light of the Commission statements concerning the incompatibility of mandatory integration requirements with the FR Directive, the Foreign Office could well have been worried that the BVerwG would refer the case to the ECJ (Rath 2011). The ECJ might then have overturned the German language requirement. Indeed, in its decision on the costs of the process, the BVerwG alluded to the Commission's statements and stated that the question of the language requirement's compatibility with EU law needed to be referred to the ECJ in the future. While extremely difficult to defend from a political and normative point of view, a possible covert strategy of selectively granting visas to the few cases per year that actually decide to initiate legal proceedings might be a temporarily viable strategy in order to defuse the judicial liberal constraint whilst continuing to require all other spouses to fulfil the language requirement. Finally, the possibility that reverse discrimination and European citizenship rights will have an effect for non-movers in the context of family migration remains unsettled. In *Zambrano*, the ECJ seemingly pointed to a very progressive direction, only to back-pedal on the issue in the *McCarthy* case. The ECJ's future stance is bound to be crucial, but still remains unclear.

This research has disclosed the some of the complexities surrounding policy-making on a highly controversial terrain. Actors with different interests struggle for the dominance to interpret complex matters to fit their ideological or instrumental needs in order to legitimise the policies they desire. In the case of spousal migration, the tension between protecting the individual rights of affected couples and dealing with the perceived strain on social cohesion, public funds and the rule of law potentially emanating from spousal migration inflows, strongly shapes the room of manoeuvre for discourse and policy. Behind all the political controversies and legal complexities, however, stand the lives of transnational couples and families. It is this intrinsically private and intimate nature that makes the matter so impossible to fairly or fully regulate for public authorities – and so vitally important to those involved.

Bibliography

Abrams, K. (2007). Immigration Law and the Regulation of Marriage. *Minnesota Law Review, 91*, 1625-1709.
Abu-Odeh, L. (1997). Comparatively Speaking: The "Honor" of the "East" and the "Passion" of the "West". *Utah Law Review, 1997*, 287-308.
Angenendt, S., & Kruse, I. (2004). Migrations- und Integrationspolitik in Deutschland 2002-2003. In K. J. Bade, M. Bommes & R. Münz (Eds.), *Migrationsreport 2004. Fakten – Analysen – Perspektiven* (pp. 175-202). Frankfurt/Main: Campus.
Ausländerbeauftragte. (2001). *Migrationsbericht der Ausländerbeauftragten im Auftrag der Bundesregierung*. [On-line].
http://www.bmi.bund.de/SharedDocs/Downloads/DE/Broschueren/2001/migration sbericht_2001.pdf;jsessionid=3E6AC8F33D67D760ED7D1384CFFEC2EC.2_cid231?__blob=publicationFile
Autant, C. (1995). La tradition au service des transitions: le mariage des jeunes turcs dans l'immigration. *Migrants-Formation, 101*, 168-179.
Bacchi, C. L. (1999). *Women, Policy and Politics. The Construction of Policy Problems*. London: Sage.
Bade, K. J., & Oltmer, J. (2004). *Normalfall Migration*. Bonn: Bundeszentrale für politische Bildung.
Ballard, R. (1990). Migration and kinship: the differential effect of marriage rules on the processes of Punjabi migration to Britain. In C. Clarke, C. Peach & S. Vertovec (Eds.), *South Asians overseas: migration and ethnicity* (pp. 219-249). Cambridge: Cambridge University Press.
Ballard, R. (2001). The impact of kinship on the economic dynamics of transnational networks: reflections on some South Asian developments. *Transnational Communities Working Papers WPTC-01-04*. Oxford: Oxford University.
Barbieri, W. A. (1998). *Ethics of citizenship: immigration and group rights in Germany*. Durham, NC: Duke University Press.
Bast, J. (2010). Rechtliche Rahmenbedingungen für staatliche Programme zirkulärer Migration. *Studie für den Sachverständigenrat deutscher Stiftungen für Integration und Migration (SVR)*. [On-line]. http://www.mpil.de/shared/data/pdf/bast_svr-studie_pzm.pdf
Bauböck, R. (Ed.). (2006). *Migration and Citizenship. Legal Status, Rights and Political Participation*. Amsterdam: Amsterdam University Press.
Bauböck, R. (2007). Why European Citizenship? Normative Approaches to Supranational Union. *Theoretical Inquiries in Law, 8*, 453-488.
Beck-Gernsheim, E. (2007). Transnational lives, transnational marriages: a review of the evidence from migrant communities in Europe. *Global Networks, 7*, 271-288.
Beikler, S. (2008). Hatuns Bruder will sich neuem Prozess doch nicht stellen. *Der Tagesspiegel*, January 20.
Bendix, J. (1990). *Importing foreign workers: A comparison of German and American policy*. New York: Peter Lang.
Besselink, L. F. M. (2009). Integration and immigration: the vicissitudes of Dutch 'Inburgering'. In E. Guild, K. Groenendijk & S. Carrera (Eds.), *Illiberal Liberal States. Immigration, Citizenship and Integration in the EU* (pp. 241-257). Surrey: Ashgate.

Bhabha, H. K. (1999). Liberalism's Sacred Cow. In J. Cohen, M. Howard & M. C. Nussbaum (Eds.), *Is Multiculturalism Bad for Women?* (pp. 79-84). Princeton: Princeton University Press.

Bielefeldt, H. (2005). *Zwangsheirat und multikulturelle Gesellschaft. Anmerkungen zur aktuellen Debatte*. Berlin: Deutsches Institut für Menschenrechte.

Bielefeldt, H., & Follmar-Otto, P. (2007). Zwangsverheiratung – ein Menschenrechtsthema in der innenpolitischen Kontroverse. In Deutsches Institut für Menschenrechte (Ed.), Zwangsverheiratung in Deutschland. Band 1. *Schriftenreihe des Bundesministeriums für Familie, Senioren, Frauen und Jugend* (pp. 13-25). Baden-Baden: Nomos Verlag.

Blinder, S., McNeil, R., Ruhs, M., & Varga-Silva, C. (2012). *Britain's "70 Million" debate: A primer on reducing immigration to manage population size* (Migration Observatory Report). Oxford, England: COMPAS, University of Oxford.

Block, L. & Bonjour, S. (2013). Fortress Europe or Europe of Rights? The Europeanisation of Family Migration Policies in France, Germany, and the Netherlands. *European Journal of Migration and Law, 15*, 203-224.

Blossfeld, H.-P., & Timm, A. (2004). Educational systems as marriage markets in modern societies: A conceptual framework. In H.-P. Blossfeld & A. Timm (Eds.), *Who marries whom? Educational systems as marriage markets in modern societies* (pp. 9-18). Dordrecht, Netherlands: Kluwer Academic.

Blumer, C. (2011). Ihre neue Aufgabe bleibt den Zivilstandsbeamten schleierhaft. *Tages-Anzeiger*, February 24. [On-line]. http://www.tagesanzeiger.ch/schweiz/standard/Ihre-neue-Aufgabe-bleibt-den-Zivilstandsbeamten-schleierhaft/story/18136619

Bonjour, S. (2009). *Gezin en grens. Beleidsvorming inzake gezinsmigratie in Nederland, 1955-2005*. Amsterdam: Aksant.

Bonjour, S. (2010). Between Integration Provision and Selection Mechanism. Party Politics, Judicial Constraints, and the Making of French and Dutch Policies of Civic Integration Abroad. *European Journal of Migration and Law, 12*, 299-318.

Bonjour, S. (2011). The Power and Morals of Policy Makers: Reassessing the Control Gap Debate. *International Migration Review, 45*, 89-122.

Bonjour, S., & de Hart, B. (2013). A proper wife, a proper marriage: Constructions of "us" and "them" in Dutch family migration policy. *European Journal of Women's Studies, 20*, 61-76.

Borevi, K. (2015). Family Migration Policies and Politics: Understanding the Swedish Exception. *Journal of Family Issues, 36*, 1490-1508.

Bosswick, W. (2000). Development of Asylum Policy in Germany. *Journal of Refugee Studies, 13*, 43-60.

Boswell, C. (2007). Theorizing Migration Policy: Is There a Third Way? *International Migration Review, 41*, 75-100.

Boswell, C., & Hough, D. (2008). Politicizing migration: opportunity or liability for the centre-right in Germany? *Journal of European Public Policy, 15*, 331-348.

Breitkreutz, K., Franßen-de la Cerda, B. & Hübner, C. (2007). Das Richtlinienumsetzungsgesetz und die Fortentwicklung des deutschen Aufenthaltsrechts – Fortsetzung. *Zeitschrift für Ausländerrecht und Ausländerpolitik, 27*, 381-389.

Brickner, I. (2011). Überraschende weitere Verschärfungen im Fremdenpaket. DER STANDARD, February 24.

Brubaker, R. (1992). *Citizenship and nationhood in France and Germany*. Cambridge, MA: Harvard University Press.

Brubaker, R. (1995). Comments on "Modes of Immigration Politics in Liberal Democratic States". *International Migration Review, 29,* 903-908.
Brubaker, R. (2010). Migration, membership, and the modern nation-state: Internal and external dimensions of the politics of belonging. *Journal of Interdisciplinary History, 41,* 61-78.
Bundesamt für Migration und Flüchtlinge (BAMF). (2007). *Migrationsbericht 2005.* Berlin: Bundesministerium des Innern.
Bundesamt für Migration und Flüchtlinge (BAMF). (2008). *Migrationsbericht 2006.* Berlin: Bundesministerium des Innern.
Bundesamt für Migration und Flüchtlinge (BAMF). (2009). *Migrationsbericht 2007.* Berlin: Bundesministerium des Innern.
Bundesamt für Migration und Flüchtlinge (BAMF). (2010). *Migrationsbericht 2008.* Berlin: Bundesministerium des Innern.
Bundesamt für Migration und Flüchtlinge (BAMF). (2011). *Migrationsbericht 2009.* Berlin: Bundesministerium des Innern.
Bundesministerium des Innern. (BMI). (2006a). Bericht zur Evaluierung des Gesetzes zur Steuerung und Begrenzung der Zuwanderung und zur Regelung des Aufenthalts und der Integration von Unionsbürgern und Ausländern (Zuwanderungsgesetz). July 24. [On-line].
http://www.bmi.bund.de/cln_145/SharedDocs/Standardartikel/DE/Themen/MigrationIntegration/Asyl/Evaluierungsbericht.html
Bundesministerium des Innern. (BMI). (2006b). Bericht zur Evaluierung des Gesetzes zur Steuerung und Begrenzung der Zuwanderung und zur Regelung des Aufenthalts und der Integration von Unionsbürgern und Ausländern (Zuwanderungsgesetz). Anlagenband I: Praktiker-Erfahrungsaustausch im Rahmen der Evaluierung des Zuwanderungsgesetzes am 30. und 31. März im Bundesministerium des Innern in Berlin. July 25. [On-line].
http://www.bmi.bund.de/cae/servlet/contentblob/151402/publicationFile/14875/Anlage_1_Evaluierungsbericht_Zuwanderungsgesetz.pdf
Bundesrat der Republik Österreich. (2011). Stenographisches Protokoll 796. Sitzung. May 12.
Bundesregierung. (2003). Entwurf eines Gesetzes zur Steuerung und Begrenzung der Zuwanderung und zur Regelung des Aufenthalts und der Integration von Unionsbürgern und Ausländern (Zuwanderungsgesetz). Drucksache 15/420. February 7.
Bundesregierung. (2007). Gesetzentwurf der Bundesregierung. Entwurf eines Gesetzes zur Umsetzung aufenthalts- und asylrechtlicher Richtlinien der Europäischen Union. Deutscher Bundestag, Drucksache 16/5065. April 23.
Bundesregierung. (2009). Allgemeine Verwaltungsvorschrift zum Aufenthaltsgesetz. Bundesrat Drucksache 669/09. July 27.
Bundesregierung. (2010). Entwurf eines Gesetzes zur Bekämpfung der Zwangsheirat und zum besseren Schutz der Opfer von Zwangsheirat sowie zur Änderung weiterer aufenthalts- und asylrechtlicher Vorschriften. [On-line].
http://www.bmi.bund.de/cln_156/SharedDocs/Gesetzestexte/_Gesetzesentwuerfe/zwangsheirat.html?nn=109632
Bündnis 90/Die Grünen. Bundestagsfraktion. (2008). *Pressemitteilung. EuGH stellt klar: Keine Deutschkurse vor der Einreise für Ehegatten von Unionsbürgern.* [On-line]. http://www.gruene-bundestag.de/cms/presse/dok/243/243494.html

Buzan, B., Waever, O. & de Wilde, J. (1998). *Security: A New Framework for Analysis*. Boulder, CO: Lynne Rienner.

Carens, J. H. (1987). Aliens and Citizens: The Case for Open Borders. *Review of Politics, 49*, 251-273.

Carens, J. H. (1992). Migration and Morality: A Liberal Egalitarian Perspective. In B. Barry & R. E. Goodin (Eds.), *Free Movement. Ethical issues in the transnational migration of people and of money* (pp. 25-47). London: Harvester Wheatsheaf.

Carens, J. H. (2001). The Philosopher and the Policy-Maker. Two Perspectives on the Ethics of migration with Special Attention to the Problem of Restricting Asylum. In K. Hailbronner, D. A. Martin & H. Motomura (Eds.), *Immigration Admissions. The Search for Workable Policies in Germany and the United States* (pp. 3-50). Oxford: Berghahn Books.

Carens, J. H. (2002). Citizenship and Civil Society. What rights for residents? In R. Hansen & P. Weil (Eds.), *Dual nationality, social rights and federal citizenship in the U.S. and Europe* (pp. 100-118). Oxford: Berghahn Books.

Carens, J. H. (2003). Who Should Get In? The Ethics of Immigration Admissions. *Ethics and International Affairs, 17*, 95-110.

Carrera, S., & Merlino, M. (2009). *State of the Art on the European Court of Justice and Enacting Citizenship*. Brussels: Centre for European Policy Studies. [On-line]. http://www.ceps.eu/ceps/download/1657

Carrera, S., & Wiesbrock, A. (2009). *Civic Integration of Third-Country Nationals. Nationalism versus Europeanisation in the Common EU Immigration Policy*. Brussels: Centre for European Policy Studies. [On-line]. http://www.ceps.be/ceps/download/217

Castles, S. (1985). The Guests Who Stayed - The Debate on "Foreigners Policy" in the German Federal Republic. *International Migration Review, 19*, 517-534.

CDU. (2000). Arbeitsgrundlage für die Zuwanderungs-Kommission der CDU Deutschlands. November 6. [On-line]. http://www.cdu.de/doc/pdfc/1100_arbeitsgrundlage.pdf

CDU. (2001). Zuwanderung steuern und begrenzen. Integration fördern. Beschluss des Bundesausschusses der CDU Deutschlands vom 7. Juni 2001 in Berlin. June 7. [On-line]. http://www.cdu.de/doc/pdfc/070601_zuwanderung_steuern.pdf

CDU, CSU & FDP. (2009). Wachstum. Bildung. Zusammenhalt. Der Koalitionsvertrag zwischen CDU, CSU und FDP. 17. Legislaturperiode. October 26. [On-line]. http://www.cdu.de/doc/pdfc/091026-koalitionsvertrag-cducsu-fdp.pdf

Charsley, K. (2005). Unhappy husbands: masculinity and migration in transnational Pakistani communities. *Journal of the Royal Anthropological Institute, 11*, 85-105.

Charsley, K., Storer-Church, B., Benson, M., & Van Hear, N. (2012). Marriage-related migration to the UK. *International Migration Review, 46*, 861-890.

Cholewinksi, R. (2002). Family Reunification and Conditions Placed on Family Members: Dismantling a Fundamental Human Right. *European Journal of Migration and Law, 4*, 271-290.

Constable, N. (2003a). *Romance on a global stage: pen pals, virtual ethnography, and "mail-order" marriages*. Berkeley & Los Angeles: University of California Press.

Constable, N. (2003b). A Transnational Perspective on Divorce and Marriage: Filipina Wives and Workers. *Identities, 10*, 163-180.

Constable, N. (Ed.). (2004a). *Cross-Border Marriages. Gender and Mobility in Transnational Asia*. Philadelphia: University of Pennsylvania Press.

Constable, N. (2004b). Introduction: Cross-Border Marriages, Gendered Mobility and Global Hypergamy. In N. Constable (Ed.), *Cross-Border Marriages. Gender and Mobility in Transnational Asia* (pp. 1-16). Philadelphia: University of Pennsylvania Press.
Constable, N. (2006). Brides, maids, and prostitutes: reflections on the study of 'trafficked' women. *PORTAL Journal of Multidisciplinary International Studies, 3.* [On-line]. http://epress.lib.uts.edu.au/journals/index.php/portal/article/view/164/274
Coontz, S. (2005). *Marriage, a History. From Obedience to Intimacy or How Love Conquered Marriage.* New York: Viking Penguin.
Cornelius, W. A. (1994). Japan – The Illusion of Immigration Control. In W. A. Cornelius, P. L. Martin & J. F. Hollifield (Eds.), *Controlling Immigration: A Global Perspective* (pp. 375-410). Stanford: Stanford University Press.
Cornelius, W. A., Martin, P. L. & Hollifield, J. F. (1994). Introduction: The Ambivalent Quest for Immigration Control. In W. A. Cornelius, P. L. Martin & J. F. Hollifield (Eds.), *Controlling Immigration: A Global Perspective* (pp. 3-41). Stanford: Stanford University Press.
Council of Ministers. (1997). Council Resolution of 4 December 1997 on measures to be adopted on the combating of marriages of convenience *Official Journal C 382, 16/12/1997*
Dagdelen, S. (2009). *Viele türkische Staatsangehörige können visumsfrei nach Deutschland einreisen. Presseerklärung.* March 19. [On-line]. http://www.sevimdagdelen.de/de/article/976.allgemeine_visumspflicht_fuer_tuerkische_staatsangehoerige_faellt.html
Danish Government. (2003). *The Government's Action Plan for 2003-2005 on Forced, Quasi-forced and Arranged Marriages.* August 15. [On-line]. http://www.nyidanmark.dk/NR/rdonlyres/05ED3816-8159-4899-9CBB-CDD2D7BF23AE/0/forced_marriages.pdf
Danish Immigration Service. (2015a). *New to Denmark. The attachment requirement.* [On-line]. http://www.nyidanmark.dk/en-us/coming_to_dk/familyreunification/spouses/attachment-requirement/attachment_requirement.htm
Danish Immigration Service. (2015b). *New to Denmark. The Danish spouse's attachment to Denmark.* [On-line]. http://www.nyidanmark.dk/en-us/coming_to_dk/familyreunification/spouses/attachment-requirement/danish-spouse-attachment.htm
Danish Immigration Service (2015c). *Test in Danish.* [On-line]. https://www.nyidanmark.dk/en-us/coming_to_dk/familyreunification/spouses/test_in_danish.htm
De Hart, B. (2000). De Goede Lobbes en de Onbezonnen Vrouw. Gemengde relaties en het schijnhuwelijk. *Migrantenstudies. Tijdschrift voor Migratie- en Etnische Studies, 16,* 246-259.
De Hart, B. (2001). Der herzensgute Kerl und die unbesonnene Frau. Scheinehenhysterie und die Bilder von Männern und Frauen in binationalen Partnerschaften – das Beispiel Niederlande. In Verband binationaler Familien und Partnerschaften, iaf e.V. (Ed.), *Fabienne: Familles et Couples Binationaux en Europe. Abschlussbericht* (pp. 18-27). Frankfurt/Main: Verband binationaler Familien und Partnerschaften, iaf e.V.
De Hart, B. (2003). Onbezonnen vrouwen - Gemengde relaties in het nationaliteitsrecht en het vreemdelingenrecht. *Nemesis, 19,* 54-62.
De Hart, B. (2006). Introduction: The Marriage of Convenience in European Immigration Law. *European Journal of Migration and Law, 8,* 251-262.

De Hart, B. (2009). Love thy neighbour: Family reunification and the rights of insiders. *European Journal of Migration and Law, 11*, 235-252.
Demleitner, N. V. (2003). How Much Do Western Democracies Value Family and Marriages?: Immigration Law's Conflicted Answers. *Hofstra Law Review, 32*, 273-311.
DER SPIEGEL. (1982). *Ausländerfeindlichkeit: Exodus erwünscht*. Nr. 18: 37-44. May 3.
DER SPIEGEL. (2006). *Rheinländer strebt Vaterschaft von tausend Kindern an*. May 7.
Deutscher Bundestag. (2008). *Bericht des Petitionsausschusses (2. Ausschuss). Bitten und Beschwerden an den Deutschen Bundestag. Die Tätigkeit des Petitionsausschusses des Deutschen Bundestages im Jahr 2007.* Bundestagsdrucksache 16/9500. June 17.
Deutscher Bundestag. (2009). *Bericht des Petitionsausschusses (2. Ausschuss). Bitten und Beschwerden an den Deutschen Bundestag. Die Tätigkeit des Petitionsausschusses des Deutschen Bundestages im Jahr 2008.* Bundestagsdrucksache 16/13200. June 17.
Deutscher Bundestag (2010). *Bericht über die Evaluierung des Nachweises einfacher Deutschkenntnisse beim Ehegattennachzug nach dem Aufenthaltsgesetz – Sprachlern- und Sprachtestangebote, Visumverfahren.* Bundestagsdrucksache 17/3090. September 24.
Deveaux, M. (2006). *Gender and Justice in Multicultural Liberal States*. Oxford: Oxford University Press.
Diez, T., & Squire, V. (2008). Traditions of citizenship and the securitization of migration in Germany and Britain. *Citizenship Studies, 12*, 565-581.
Digruber, D., & Messinger, I. (2006). Marriage of Residence in Austria. *European Journal of Migration and Law, 8*, 281-302.
Dienelt, K. (2008). *EuGH: Keine Deutschkurse vor der Einreise für Ehegatten von Unionsbürgern*. [On-line].
http://www.migrationsrecht.net/index2.php?option=com_content&do_pdf=1&id=1157
Drieschner, F. (2006). Ist Multikulti schuld? *Die ZEIT*, April 12.
Dustin, M., & Phillips, A. (2008). Whose agenda is it? Abuses of women and abuses of "culture" in Britain. *Ethnicities, 8*, 405-424.
ECRE (European Council on Refugees and Exiles). (1999). *Survey of provisions for refugee family reunion in the European Union*. [On-line].
http://www.ecre.org/component/downloads/downloads/201.html
Eeckhaut, M. C. W., Lievens, J., Van de Putte, B., & Lusyne, P. (2011). Partner Selection and Divorce in Ethnic Minorities: Distinguishing Between Two Types of Ethnic Homogamous Marriages. *International Migration Review, 45*, 269-296.
Eggebø, H. (2010). The Problem of Dependency: Immigration, Gender and the Welfare State. *Social Politics, 17*, 295-322.
Eisfeld, J. (2005). *Die Scheinehe in Deutschland im 19. und 20. Jahrhundert*. Tübingen: Mohr Siebeck.
Elger, K. (2008). Cousin und Cousine. *DER SPIEGEL, 45*. November 3. [On-line].
http://www.spiegel.de/spiegel/inhalt/0,1518,588067,00.html
Ersbøll, E. (2009). *Country Report: Denmark*. EUDO Citizenship Observatory. Florence: Robert Schuman Centre for Advanced Studies.
Ersbøll, E. (2010). On Trial in Denmark. In R. van Oers, E. Ersbøll & D. Kostakopoulou (Eds.), *A Re-definition of Belonging? Language and Integration Tests in Europe* (pp. 107-152). Leiden: Koninklijke Brill NV.
Ersbøll, E., & Gravesen, L. K. (2010). Country Report Denmark. *The INTEC Project: Integration and Naturalisation tests: the new way to European Citizenship*. Nijmegen: Centre for Migration Law Radboud University.

European Commission. DG Justice, Liberty and Security. (2006). *MIGRAPOL 144. Legal consequences of the use of fraud in migration and asylum procedures.*
European Commission. DG Justice, Freedom and Security. (2007). *MIGRAPOL 196. Legal consequences of the use of fraud in migration and asylum procedures.*
Faist, T. (1994). How to Define a Foreigner? The Symbolic Politics of Immigration in German Partisan Discourse, 1978–1992. In M. Baldwin-Edwards & M.A. Schain (Eds.), *The Politics of Immigration in Western Europe* (pp. 50-71). London: Frank Cass.
Fan, C. C., & Huang, Y. (1998). Waves of Rural Brides: Female Marriage Migration in China. *Annals of the Association of American Geographers, 88*, 227-251.
Fassin, E., Ferran, N., & Slama, S. (2009). "Mariages gris" et matins bruns. *Le Monde*, December 9.
Favell, A. (2001). Integration policy and integration research in Europe: A review and critique. In A. Aleinikoff & D. Klusmeyer (Eds.), *Citizenship today: Global perspectives and practices* (pp. 349-399). Washington, DC: Brookings Institution.
Fleischer, A. (2008). Marriage over time and space among male migrants from Cameroon to Germany. *MPIDR Working Paper WP 2008-006.* Rostock: Max-Planck-Institut für demografische Forschung.
Forced Marriage Unit. (2008). *What is a Forced Marriage?* London: Foreign and Commonwealth Office. [On-line]. http://www.fco.gov.uk/resources/en/pdf/foced-marriage-lgbt
Foreign and Commonwealth Office. (2004). *Young people & vulnerable adults facing forced marriage. Practice Guidance for Social Workers.* [On-line]. http://www.fco.gov.uk/resources/en/pdf/FM-Guidance-Social-Workers
Freeman, C. (2004). Marrying Up and Marrying Down: The Paradoxes of Marital Mobility for Chosonjok Brides in South Korea. In N. Constable (Ed.), *Cross-Border Marriages. Gender and Mobility in Transnational Asia* (pp. 80-100). Philadelphia: University of Pennsylvania Press.
Freeman, G. P. (1995). Modes of Immigration Politics in Liberal Democratic States. *International Migration Review, 29*, 881-902.
Freeman, G. P. (2004). Immigrant Incorporation in Western Democracies. *International Migration Review, 38*, 945-969.
Freudenberg, D. (2007). Verfangen im Netz des Aufenthaltsrechts. Aufenthaltsrechtliche Liberalisierungen als zentraler Bestandteil von Präventions- und Interventionsstrategien. In Deutsches Institut für Menschenrechte. (Ed.), Zwangsverheiratung in Deutschland. *Band 1. Schriftenreihe des Bundesministeriums für Familie, Senioren, Frauen und Jugend* (pp. 246-256). Baden-Baden: Nomos Verlag.
Gallo, E. (2006). Italy is not a good place for men: narratives of places, marriage and masculinity among Malayali migrants. *Global Networks, 6*, 357-372.
Gedalof, I. (2007). Unhomely homes: Women, family and belonging in UK discourses of migration and asylum. *Journal of Ethnic and Migration Studies, 33*, 77-94.
Gibney, M. (2004). *The Ethics and Politics of Asylum.* Cambridge: Cambridge University Press.
Giddens, A. (1992). *The Transformation of Intimacy. Sexuality, Love and Eroticism in Modern Societies.* Cambridge: Polity Press.
Glowsky, D. (2007). Staatsbürgerschaft als Ressource bei der Heirat ausländischer Frauen. Eine Analyse mit Daten des Sozio-oekonomischen Panel. *Zeitschrift für Soziologie, 36*, 282-301.
Göbel-Zimmermann, R. (2008). Verfassungswidrige Hürden für den Ehegattennachzug nach dem Richtlinienumsetzungsgesetz. *Zeitschrift für Ausländerrecht und Ausländerpolitik, 28*, 169-176.

González-Ferrer, A. (2006). Who Do Immigrants Marry? Partner Choice Among Single Immigrants in Germany. *European Sociological Review, 22*, 171-185.
González-Ferrer, A. (2007). The process of family reunification among original guest-workers in Germany. *Zeitschrift für Familienforschung, 19*, 10-33.
Green, S. (2004). *The politics of exclusion. Institutions and immigration policy in contemporary Germany*. Manchester: Manchester University Press.
Groenendijk, K. (2004). Legal Concepts of Integration in EU Migration Law. *European Journal of Migration and Law, 6*, 111-126.
Groenendijk, K. (2006). Family Reunification as a Right under Community Law. *European Journal of Migration and Law, 8*, 215-230.
Groenendijk, K. (2011). Pre-departure Integration Strategies in the European Union: Integration or Immigration Policy? *European Journal of Migration and Law, 13*, 1-30.
Groenendijk, K., Fernhout, R., van Dam, D., van Oers, R., & Strik, T. (2007). *The Family Reunification Directive in EU Member States; the First Year of Implementation*. Nijmegen: Wolf Legal Publishers.
Groenendijk, K., & Guild, E. (2010). Visa policy of Member States and the EU towards Turkish nationals after *Soysal*. *Economic Development Foundation Publications, No. 232*. Istanbul: Economic Development Foundation.
Guild, E., & Niessen, J. (1996). *The Developing Immigration and Asylum Policies of the European Union. Adopted Conventions, Resolutions, Recommendations and Conclusions*. The Hague: Kluwer Law International.
Guiraudon, V. (1998). Citizenship Rights for Non-Citizens: France, Germany and the Netherlands. In C. Joppke (Ed.), *Challenge to the Nation-State. Immigration in Western Europe and the United States* (pp. 272-318). Oxford: Oxford University Press.
Guiraudon, V. (2000a). European Integration and Migration Policy: Vertical Policy-Making as Venue Shopping. *Journal of Common Market Studies, 38*, 251-271.
Guiraudon, V. (2000b). European Courts and Foreigners' Rights: A Comparative Study of Norms Diffusion. *International Migration Review, 34*, 1088-1125.
Guiraudon, V. (2002). Including Foreigners in National Welfare States: Institutional Venues and Rules of the Game. In B. Rothstein & S. Steinmo (Eds.), *Restructuring the Welfare State. Political Institutions and Policy Change* (pp. 129-156). New York: Palgrave Macmillan.
Guiraudon, V., & Lahav, G. (2000). A Reappraisal of the State Sovereignty Debate: The Case of Migration Control. *Comparative Political Studies, 33*, 163-195.
Hailbronner, K., & Katsantonis, J. (1992). Non-EC Nationals in the European Community: The Need for a Coordinated Approach. *Duke Journal of Comparative and International Law, 3*, 49-88.
Hammar, T. (Ed.). (1985). *European Immigration Policy: A Comparative Study*. Cambridge: Cambridge University Press.
Hammar, T. (1990). *Democracy and the Nation State: aliens, denizens and citizens in a world of international migration*. Aldershot: Avebury.
Hansen, R. (1999). Migration, citizenship and race in Europe: Between incorporation and exclusion. *European Journal of Political Research, 35*, 415-444.
Hauschild, C. (2003). Neues europäisches Einwanderungsrecht: Das Recht auf Familienzusammenführung. *Zeitschrift für Ausländerrecht und Ausländerpolitik, 23*, 266-273.

Hensen, J. (2009). Zur Geschichte der Aussiedler- und Spätaussiedleraufnahme. In C. Bergner & M. Weber (Eds.), *Aussiedler- und Minderheitenpolitik in Deutschland* (pp. 47-61). München: R. Oldenbourg Verlag.

Herbert, U. (1986). *Geschichte der Ausländerbeschäftigung in Deutschland 1880 bis 1980*. Berlin: Dietz Verlag.

Hillgruber, C. (2006). Mindestalter und sprachliche Integrationsvorleistung – verfassungsgemäße Voraussetzungen des Ehegattennachzugs? *Zeitschrift für Ausländerrecht und Ausländerpolitik, 26*, 304-317.

Hofmann, R. M. (2008). Beobachtung der Europarechtstreue der Bundesrepublik. *Anwaltsnachrichten Ausländer- und Asylrecht, 4*, 26-37.

Hollifield, J. F. (1992). *Immigrants, Markets and States: The Political Economy of Postwar Europe*. Cambridge, MA: Harvard University Press.

Hollifield, J. F. (2004). The Emerging Migration State. *International Migration Review, 38*, 885-912.

Honohan, I. (2009). Reconsidering the Claim to Family Reunification in Migration. *Political Studies, 57*, 768-787.

Hooghiemstra, E. (2001). Migrants, partner selection and integration: crossing borders? *Journal of Comparative Family Studies, 32*, 601-26.

Howard, M. M. (2008). The Causes and Consequences of Germany's New Citizenship Law. *German Politics, 17*, 41-62.

Huddleston, T., & Niessen, J., with Chaoimh, E. N. & White, E. (2011). *Migrant Integration Policy Index*. Brussels: British Council and Migration Policy Group.

Hunn, K. (2005). *"Nächstes Jahr kehren wir zurück..." Die Geschichte der türkischen "Gastarbeiter" in der Bundesrepublik Deutschland*. Göttingen: Wallstein.

Huysmans, J. (2000). The European Union and the Securitization of Migration. *Journal of Common Market Studies, 38*, 751-777.

Ibrahim, M. (2005). The Securitization of Migration: A Racial Discourse. *International Migration, 43*, 163-187.

Jacobson, D. (1996). *Rights across borders: Immigration and the decline of citizenship*. Baltimore: Johns Hopkins University Press.

Jasso, G., & Rosenzweig, M. R. (1995). Do Immigrants Screened for Skills do Better Than Family Reunification Immigrants? *International Migration Review, 29*, 85-111.

Jelínková, M., & Szczepaniková, A. (2008). *Binational Marriages and Czech Immigration Policy: Sorting Truth from Fiction?* Prague: Multicultural Centre Prague. [On-line]. http://aa.ecn.cz/img_upload/6334c0c7298d6b396d213ccd19be5999/MJelinkovaASzczepanikova_Binational_marriages.pdf

Jesse, E., & Sturm, R. (Eds.). (2006). *Bilanz der Bundestagswahl 2005. Voraussetzungen, Ergebnisse, Folgen*. Wiesbaden: VS Verlag für Sozialwissenschaften.

Jobs, A. T. (2008). Beweismaß und Beweislast beim Ehegattennachzug. *Zeitschrift für Ausländerrecht und Ausländerpolitik, 9*, 295-298.

John, A. (2003). *Family Reunification for Migrants and Refugees: A Forgotten Human Right?* MA Thesis. Coimbra: Human Rights Centre, University of Coimbra. [On-line]. http://www.fd.uc.pt/igc/pdf/papers/arturojohn.pdf

Joppke, C. (1996). Multiculturalism and Immigration: A Comparison of the United States, Germany, and Great Britain. *Theory and Society, 25*, 449-500.

Joppke, C. (1998a). Why Liberal States Accept Unwanted Immigration. *World Politics, 50*, 266-293.

Joppke, C. (1998b). Asylum and State Sovereignty: A Comparison of the United States, Germany and Britain. In C. Joppke (Ed.), *Challenge to the Nation-State. Immigration in Western Europe and the United States.* (pp. 109-152). Oxford: Oxford University Press.

Joppke, C. (1999). *Immigration and the Nation-State: The United States, Germany, and Great Britain.* Oxford: Oxford University Press.

Joppke, C. (2001). The Legal-domestic Sources of Immigrant Rights: The United States, Germany, and the European Union. *Comparative Political Studies, 34,* 339-366.

Justizministerium Baden-Württemberg. Stabsstelle Integrationsbeauftragter der Landsregierung. (2006). *Stellungnahme zum Thema Zwangsheirat in der Anhörung des Bundestagsausschusses für Familie, Senioren, Frauen und Jugend am 19. Juni 2006 in Berlin.* Ausschuss für Familie, Senioren, Frauen und Jugend, Ausschussdrucksache 16(13)91i, June 14.

Kalthegener, R. (2007). Strafrechtliche Ahndung der Zwangsverheiratung: Rechtslage – Praxiserfahrungen – Reformdiskussion. In Deutsches Institut für Menschenrechte. (Ed.), Zwangsverheiratung in Deutschland. *Band 1. Schriftenreihe des Bundesministeriums für Familie, Senioren, Frauen und Jugend* (pp. 215-228). Baden-Baden: Nomos Verlag.

Keim, J. (2010). Scheingefecht um Eheschein. *Beobachter,* 18. September 1.

Kelek, N. (2005). *Die fremde Braut. Ein Bericht aus dem Inneren des türkischen Lebens in Deutschland.* Köln: Kiepenheuer & Witsch.

Klusmeyer, D. B., & Papademetriou, D. G. (2009). *Immigration Policy in the Federal Republic of Germany. Negotiating Membership and Remaking the Nation.* New York & Oxford: Berghahn Books.

Knop, K. (2008). Citizenship: Public and Private. *Law and Contemporary Problems, 71,* 309-341.

Knortz, H. (2008). *Diplomatische Tauschgeschäfte. "Gastarbeiter" in der westdeutschen Diplomatie und Beschäftigungspolitik 1953-1973.* Köln: Böhlau.

Kofman, E. (2004). Family-Related Migration: A Critical Review of European Studies. *Journal of Ethnic and Migration Studies, 30,* 243-262.

Kofman, E., & Meetoo, V. (2008). Family Migration. In International Organisation for Migration (Ed.), *World Migration Report 2008* (pp. 151-172). Geneva: IOM.

Kofman, E., Lukes, S., Meetoo, V., & Aaron, P. (2008). Family Migration to United Kingdom: Trends, Statistics and Policies. *NODE Policy Report.* Vienna: Bundesministerium für Wissenschaft und Forschung/International Centre for Migration Policy Development.

Kofman, E., Rogoz, M., & Lévy, F. (2010). Family Migration Policies in France. *NODE Policy Report.* Vienna: Bundesministerium für Wissenschaft und Forschung/International Centre for Migration Policy Development.

Kommission "Zuwanderung und Integration" der CDU Deutschlands. (2001). *Abschlussbericht.* April 28.

Kontos, M., & Sacaliuc, A. V. (2006). Analysis of Policy Formation and Policy Implementation. *Working Paper No. 1 - WP2, Integration of Female Immigrants in Labor Market and Society. Policy Assessment and Policy Recommendations. A Specific Targeted Research Project of the 6th Framework Programme of the European Commission.* Frankfurt/Main: Institut für Sozialforschung an der Johann Wolfgang Goethe-Universität Frankfurt.

Kostakopoulou, T. (2000). The 'Protective Union'; Change and Continuity in Migration Law and Policy in Post-Amsterdam Europe. *Journal of Common Market Studies, 38,* 497-518.

Kostakopoulou, T. (2002). Long-term resident third-country nationals in the European Union: normative expectations and institutional openings. *Journal of Ethnic and Migration Studies, 28,* 443-462.

Kostakopoulou, D. (2007). European Citizenship: Writing the Future. *European Law Journal, 13*, 623-646.
Kraler, A. (2010). *Civic Stratification, Gender and Family Migration Policies in Europe. Final Report.* Vienna: International Centre for Migration Policy Development.
Kreienbrink, A., & Rühl, S. (2007). Family Reunification in Germany. Small Scale Study IV in the Framework of the European Migration Network. *Working Paper 10 der Forschungsgruppe des Bundesamtes.* Nürnberg: Bundesamt für Migration und Flüchtlinge.
Kruse, I., Orren, H. E., & Angenendt, S. (2003). The failure of immigration reform in Germany, *German Politics, 12*, 129-145.
Krzyzanowski, M., & Wodak, R. (2009). *The Politics of Exclusion. Debating Migration in Austria.* New Brunswick: Transaction Publishers.
Kukathas, C. (2003). *The Liberal Archipelago: A Theory of Diversity and Freedom.* Oxford: Oxford University Press.
Kymlicka, W. (1995). *Multicultural Citizenship.* Oxford: Oxford University Press.
Lahav, G. (1997). International Versus National Constraints in Family-Reunification Migration Policy. *Global Governance, 3*, 349-272.
Lahav, G. (1998). Immigration and the state: The devolution and privatisation of immigration control in the EU. *Journal of Ethnic and Migration Studies, 24*, 675-694.
Lahav, G., & Guiraudon, V. (2006). Actors and venues in immigration control: Closing the gap between political demands and policy outcomes. *West European Politics, 29*, 201-223.
Lansbergen, A. (2009). Metock, implementation of the Citizens' Rights Directive and lessons for EU citizenship. *Journal of Social Welfare and Family Law, 31*, 285-297.
Lau, J. (2005). "Wie eine Deutsche". *Die ZEIT*, February 24.
Lauser, A. (2008). Philippine Women on the Move: Marriages across Borders. *International Migration, 46*, 85-110.
Lavenex, S. (2001). The Europeanisation of refugee policies: normative challenges and institutional legacies. *Journal of Common Market Studies, 39*, 851-874.
Lavenex, S. (2006a). Shifting up and out: The foreign policy of European immigration control. *West European Politics, 29*, 329-350.
Lavenex, S. (2006b). Towards the constitutionalization of aliens' rights in the European Union? *Journal of European Public Policy, 13*, 1284-1301.
Lievens, J. (1999). Family-forming migration from Turkey and Morocco to Belgium: the demand for marriage partners from the countries of origin. *International Migration Review, 33*, 717-744.
Lu, M. & Yang, W. (Eds.). (2010). *Asian cross-border marriage migration: demographic patterns and social issues.* Amsterdam: Amsterdam University Press.
Lumpp, S. (2007). *Die Scheineheproblematik in Gegenwart und Vergangenheit. Eine dogmatische Untersuchung des fehlenden Willens zur ehelichen Lebensgemeinschaft.* Berlin: Duncker & Humblot.
Maaßen, H. (2006). Zum Stand der Umsetzung von elf aufenthalts- und asylrechtlichen Richtlinien der Europäischen Union. *Zeitschrift für Ausländerrecht und Ausländerpolitik, 26*, 161-167.
Maaßen, H. (2007). *Ausländerrecht. Gesetze und Verordnungen mit einer erläuternden Einführung.* 18., überarbeitete Auflage. Stuttgart: Verlag W. Kohlhammer.
Markard, N., & Truchseß, N. (2007). Neuregelung des Ehegattennachzugs im Aufenthaltsgesetz. *Neue Zeitschrift für Verwaltungsrecht, 26*, 1025-1028.

Massey, D. S. (1999). International Migration at the Dawn of the Twenty-First Century: The Role of the State. *Population and Development Review*, 25, 303-322.
Mattes, M. (2005). *"Gastarbeiterinnen" in der Bundesrepublik. Anwerbepolitik, Migration und Geschlecht in der 50er bis 70er Jahren*. Frankfurt am Main: Campus.
Members of the Court. (Eds.). (1992). *Decisions of the Bundesverfassungsgericht – Federal Constitutional Court – Federal Republic of Germany*. Volume 1/Part II: International Law and Lawe of the European Communities 1952-1989. Baden-Baden: Nomos Verlagsgesellschaft.
Messina, A. M. (2007). *The Logics and Politics of Post-WWII Migration to Western Europe*. Cambridge: Cambridge University Press.
Michalowski, I. (2009). Liberal States – Privatised Integration Policies? In E. Guild, K. Groenendijk & S. Carrera (Eds.), *Illiberal Liberal States. Immigration, Citizenship and Integration in the EU* (pp. 259-275). Surrey: Ashgate.
Michalowski, I., & Walter, A. (2008). Family Reunification between EC Law and National Integration Policy. In A. Böcker, T. Havinga, P. Minderhoud, H. van de Put, L. de Groot-van Leeuwen, B. de Hart, A. Jettinghoff & K. Zwaan (Eds.), *Migratierecht en Rechtssociologie, gebundeld in Kees' studies* (pp. 103-120). Nijmegen: Wolf Legal Publishers.
Migration Advisory Committee. (2011). *Review of the minimum income requirement for sponsorship under the family migration route*. London: Migration Advisory Committee.
Migrationsrecht. (2010). *EuGH erleichtert den Zuzug türkischer Arbeitnehmern und ihrer Familienangehörigen - Wegfall der Sprachanforderungen beim Ehegattennachzug?* [On-line]. http://www.migrationsrecht.net/nachrichten-auslaenderrecht-europa-und-eu/1560-eugh-stillhalteklausel-standstillklausel-ehegattennachzug-sprachanforderungen-arb180-gebuehren.html
Mix, P. R., & Piper, N. (2003). Does marriage 'liberate' women from sex work? – Thai women in Germany. In N. Piper & M. Roces (Eds.), *Wife or Worker: Asian Women and Migration* (pp. 53-72). Lanham, MD: Rowman and Littlefield.
Münz, R., & Ulrich, R. (1997). Changing Patterns of Immigration to Germany, 1945-1955: Ethnic Origins, Demographic Structure, Future Prospects. In K.J. Bade & M. Weiner (Eds.), *Migration Past, Migration Future. Germany and the United States* (pp. 65-119). Providence & Oxford: Berghahn Books.
Muller Myrdahl, E. (2010). Legislating love: Norwegian family reunification law as a racial project. *Social & Cultural Geography*, 11, 103-116.
Murdock, T. R. (2008). Whose Child Is This?: Genetic Analysis and Family Reunification Immigration in France. *Vanderbilt Journal of Transnational Law*, 41, 1503-1534.
Mushaben, J. M. (2010). Rethinking Citizenship and Identity: "What it Means to be German" since the Fall of the Wall. *German Politics*, 19, 72-88.
Nauck, B. (2004). Familienbeziehungen und Sozialintegration von Migranten. In J. K. Bade & M. Bommes (Eds.), *Migration – Integration – Bildung. Grundfragen und Problembereiche* (pp. 83-194). Osnabrück: Institut für Migrationsforschung und Interkulturelle Studien.
Neue Zürcher Zeitung (NZZ). (2010). *Strengere Regeln gegen Scheinehen*. December 27. [On-line]. http://www.nzz.ch/nachrichten/politik/schweiz/strengere_regeln_gegen_scheinehen_1.8902862.html
Niessen, J., Huddleston, T. & Citron, L. in cooperation with Geddes, A. & Jacobs, D. (2007). *Migrant Integration Policy Index*. Brussels: British Council and Migration Policy Group.
OECD (Organisation for Economic Co-Operation and Development). (2008). *International Migration Outlook: SOPEMI 2008*. Paris: OECD Publishing.

OECD (Organisation for Economic Co-Operation and Development). (2011). *International Migration Outlook: SOPEMI 2011*. Paris: OECD Publishing.
Oestmann, C. (2008). Die Scheinehe im Visumsverfahren. *Informationsbrief Ausländerrecht, 30*, 17-22.
Okin, S. M. (1999). Is Multiculturalism Bad for Women? In J. Cohen, M. Howard & M. C. Nussbaum (Eds.), *Is Multiculturalism Bad for Women?* (pp. 8-24). Princeton: Princeton University Press.
ORF. (2010). *Zuwandererquote bleibt unverändert*. December 14. [On-line].
http://orf.at/stories/2030822/
Ortiz, V. (1996). Migration and Marriage among Puerto Rican Women. *International Migration Review, 30*, 460-484.
Pagenstecher, C. (1995). Die ungewollte Einwanderung. Rotationsprinzip und Rückkehrerwartung in der deutschen Ausländerpolitik. *Geschichte in Wissenschaft und Unterricht, 46*, 718-737.
Palriwala, R. & Uberoi, P. (Eds.). (2008). *Marriage, migration and gender*. New Dehli: Sage Publications.
Pascouau, Y., & Labayle, H. (2011). *Conditions for family reunification under strain. A comparative study in nine EU member states*. Brussels, Belgium: European Policy Centre. [On-line].
http://www.epc.eu/documents/uploads/pub_1369_conditions-forfamily.pdf
Pateman, C. (1988). *The Sexual Contract*. Cambridge: Polity Press.
Peers, S. (2003). Key Legislative Developments on Migration in the European Union. *European Journal of Migration and Law, 5*, 387-410.
Pellander S. (2015). "An Acceptable Marriage": Marriage Migration and Moral Gatekeeping in Finland. *Journal of Family Issues, 36*, 1473-1489.
Perlmutter, T. (1996). Bringing Parties Back In: Comments on "Modes of Immigration Politics in Liberal Democrat Societies". *International Migration Review, 30*, 375-388.
Pflugfelder, G. M. (1999). *Cartographies of Desire: Male-male Sexuality in Japanese Discourse, 1600-1950*. Berkeley: University of California Press.
Phillips, A., & Dustin, M. (2004). UK Initiatives on Forced Marriages: Regulation, Dialogue and Exit. *Political Studies, 52*, 531-551.
Phillips, A. (2007). *Multiculturalism without Culture*. Princeton: Princeton University Press.
Phillips, T., & Harding, L. (2006). Who's the daddy? *The Guardian*, June 15. [On-line].
http://www.guardian.co.uk/uk/2006/jun/15/immigration.germany
Piper, N. & Roces, M. (Eds.). (2003). *Wife or Worker? Asian Women and Migration*. Lanham, MD: Rowman & Littlefield.
Pressedienst des Parlaments. (2011a). Innenausschuss gibt grünes Licht für Fremdenrechtspaket 2011. Parlamentskorrespondenz Nr. 377. April 13. [On-line.]
http://www.parlament.gv.at/PAKT/PR/JAHR_2011/PK0377/
Pressedienst des Parlaments. (2011b). Fremdenrechtspaket passiert Bundesrat. Parlamentskorrespondenz Nr. 479. May 12. [On-line].
http://www.parlament.gv.at/PAKT/PR/JAHR_2011/PK0479/
Pressestelle des Bundesgerichtshofs. (2007). Bundesgerichtshof hebt Freisprüche im sogenannten Ehrenmordprozess auf. Pressemitteilung 117/2007. August 28.
Rath, C. (2011). Pflicht zum Deutsch-Test wackelt. die tageszeitung, November 8. [On-line].
http://www.taz.de/Beschluss-des-Bundesverwaltungsgerichts/!81517/

Razack, S. (2004). Imperilled Muslim Women, Dangerous Muslim Men and Civilised Europeans: Legal and Social Responses to Forced Marriages. *Feminist Legal Studies, 12*, 129-174.
Rein, M., & Schön, D. (1996). Frame-critical policy analysis and frame-reflective policy practice. *Knowledge and Policy, 9*, 88-90.
Reitman, O. (2005). On Exit. In D. Spinner-Halev & A. Eisenberg (Eds.), *Minorities within Minorities: Equality, Rights and Diversity* (pp. 189-208). Cambridge: Cambridge University Press.
Renner, G. (2005). Das Zuwanderungsgesetz – Ende des deutschen Ausländerrechts? *IMIS-Beiträge, 27*, 9-24.
Rijksoverheid. (2010). *Toelatingseisen gezinshereniging en gezinsvorming gelijkgetrokken.* Persbericht. March 12. [On-line].
http://www.rijksoverheid.nl/regering/ministerraad/persberichten/2010/03/12/toelatingseisen-gezinshereniging-en-gezinsvorming-gelijkgetrokken.html
Robinson, K. (2007). Marriage Migration, Gender Transformations, and Family Values in the 'Global Ecumene'. *Gender, Place & Culture, 14*, 483-497.
Rogers, N. (2000). *A Practitioners' Guide to the EC-Turkey Association Agreement.* The Hague: Kluwer Law International.
Roggeband, C., & Verloo, M. (2007). Dutch Women are Liberated, Migrant Women are a Problem: the Evolution of Policy Frames on Gender and Migration in the Netherlands, 1995-2005. *Social Policy & Administration, 41*, 271-288.
Roggeband, C., & Vliegenthart, R. (2007). Divergent Framing: The Public Debate on Migration in the Dutch Parliament and Media, 1995–2004. *West European Politics, 30*, 524-548.
Rostock, P., & Berghahn, S. (2008). The ambivalent role of gender in defining the German nation. *Ethnicities, 8*, 345-364.
Rubin, L. (2004). Love's Refugees. The effects of stringent Danish immigration policies on Danes and their Non-Danish spouses. *Connecticut Journal of International Law, 20*, 319-341.
Ruenkaew, P. (2003). *Heirat nach Deutschland. Motive und Hintergründe thailändisch-deutscher Eheschließungen.* Frankfurt/Main: Campus.
Ruggie, J. G. (1982). International Regimes, Transactions and Change: Embedded Liberalism in the Postwar Economic Order. *International Organizations, 36*, 379-415.
Russell, S. S. (1989). Politics and Ideology in Migration Policy Formulation: The Case of Kuwait. *International Migration Review, 23*, 24-47.
Ryan, B. (2009). The Integration Agenda in British Migration Law. In E. Guild, K. Groenendijk & S. Carrera (Eds.), *Illiberal Liberal States. Immigration, Citizenship and Integration in the EU* (pp. 277-298). Surrey: Ashgate.
Rytter, M. (2010). 'The Family of Denmark' and 'the Aliens': Kinship Images in Danish Integration Politics. *Ethnos, 75*, 301-322.
Sachdeva, S. (1993). *The Primary Purpose Rule in British Immigration Law.* Stoke-on-Trent: Trentham Books.
Samad, Y., & Eade, J. (2002). *Community Perceptions of Forced Marriages.* London: Community Liason Unit, Foreign and Commonwealth Office.
Sassen, S. (1999). Beyond Sovereignty: De-Facto Transnationalism in Immigration Policy. *European Journal of Migration and Law, 1*, 177-198.
Schiffauer, W. (2005). "Eine Lust am Schaudern". Interview von Heide Oestich und Sabine am Orde. *die tageszeitung*, October 17. [On-line].
http://www.taz.de/index.php?id=archivseite&dig=2005/10/17/a0186

Schmidt, G. (2011). Law and identity: Transnational arranged marriages and the boundaries of Danishness. *Journal of Ethnic and Migration Studies, 37,* 257-275.

Schöpp-Schilling, H. B. (2007). Zwangsverheiratung als Menschenrechtsverletzung: Die Bedeutung der internationalen Rechtsinstrumente. In Deutsches Institut für Menschenrechte. (Ed.), Zwangsverheiratung in Deutschland. *Band 1. Schriftenreihe des Bundesministeriums für Familie, Senioren, Frauen und Jugend* (pp. 201-214). Baden-Baden: Nomos Verlag

Schröder, B. (2011). Anwendungsbereiche und Auswirkungen der Stillhalteklausel im Assoziationsrecht der EU mit der Türkei. *Deutscher Bundestag, Wissenschaftliche Dienste. Ausarbeitung WD 3 -3000 -188/11.* June 21.

Schwerdtfeger, G. (1980). Welche rechtlichen Vorkehrungen empfehlen sich, um die Rechtsstellung von Ausländern in der Bundesrepublik Deutschland angemessen zu gestalten? Gutachten A zum 53. Deutschen Juristentag Berlin 1980. Munich: Beck.

Seol, D., & Skrenty, J. D. (2004). South Korea: Importing Undocumented Workers. In W. A. Cornelius, T. Tsuda, P. L. Martin & J. F. Hollifield (Eds.), *Controlling Immigration: A Global Perspective, 2nd Edition* (pp. 481-513). Stanford: Stanford University Press.

Serviço de Estrangeiros e Fronteiras (SEF). (2009). *Portugal. Annual Policy Report 2009. European Migration Network* [On-line]. http://rem.sef.pt/forms/content.aspx?MenuID=39&Publico=1

Shaw, A. (2001). Kinship, Cultural Preference and Immigration: Consanguineous Marriage among British Pakistanis. *Journal of the Royal Anthropological Institute, 7,* 315-334.

Snow, D. A., Rochford, E. B., Worden, S. K., & Benford, R.D. (1986). Frame Alignment Process, Micromobilization and Movement Participation. *American Sociological Review, 51,* 464-481.

Snow, D. A., & Benford, R. D. (1992). Master frames and cycles of protest. In A. D. Morris & C. M. Mueller (Eds.), *Frontiers in Social Movement Theory* (pp. 133-155). New Haven, CT: Yale University Press.

Soysal, Y. N. (1994). *Limits of Citizenship: Migrants and Postnational Membership in Europe.* Chicago and London: Chicago University Press.

Spijkerboer, T. (2009). Structural Instability: Strasbourg Case Law on Children's Family Reunion. *European Journal of Migration and Law, 11,* 271-293.

Steinert, J. (1995). *Migration und Politik. Westdeutschland – Europa – Übersee 1945-1961.* Osnabrück: Secolo Verlag.

Straßburger, G. (1999). „Er kann Deutsch und kennt sich hier aus". Zur Partnerwahl der zweiten Migrantengeneration türkischer Herkunft. In G. Jonker (Ed.), *Kern und Rand. Religiöse Minderheiten aus der Türkei in Deutschland* (pp. 147-167). Berlin: Verlag Das Arabische Buch.

Straßburger, G. (2003). *Heiratsverhalten und Partnerwahl im Einwanderungskontext: Eheschließungen der zweiten Migrantengeneration türkischer Herkunft.* Würzburg: Ergon.

Straßburger, G. (2007). Zwangsheirat und arrangierte Ehe – zur Schwierigkeit der Abgrenzung. In Deutsches Institut für Menschenrechte. (Ed.), Zwangsverheiratung in Deutschland. *Band 1. Schriftenreihe des Bundesministeriums für Familie, Senioren, Frauen und Jugend* (pp. 72-86). Baden-Baden: Nomos Verlag.

Statistisches Bundesamt. (2009a). *Bevölkerung mit Migrationshintergrund – Ergebnisse des Mikrozensus 2007 – Fachserie 1 Reihe 2.2.* Wiesbaden: Statistisches Bundesamt.

Statistisches Bundesamt. (2009b). *Wahlberechtigte, Wähler, Stimmabgabe und Sitzverteilung bei den Bundestagswahlen seit 1949 – Zweitstimmen.* Wiesbaden: Statistisches Bundesamt.

Stöcker-Zafari, H. (2006). In Bundesministerium des Innern (Ed.), *Praktiker-Erfahrungsaustausch im Rahmen der Evaluierung des Zuwanderungsgesetzes am 30. und 31. März 2006 im Bundesministerium des Innern in Berlin*, pp. 423-428.

Sterckx, L. (2015). Marrying "In" or "Out"? Scrutinizing the Link Between Integration and the Partner Choice of Young People of Turkish and Moroccan Origin in the Netherlands. *Journal of Family Issues, 36,* 1550-1570.

Strik, T., Luiten, M., & van Oers, R. (2010). Country Report The Netherlands. *The INTEC Project: Integration and Naturalisation tests: the new way to European Citizenship.* Nijmegen: Centre for Migration Law Radboud University.

Strik, T., de Hart, B., & Nissen, E. (2013). *Family reunification: A barrier or facilitator of integration? A comparative study.* Oisterwijk, Netherlands: Wolf Legal.

Strobl, R., & Lobermeier, O. (2007). Zwangsverheiratung: Risikofaktoren und Ansatzpunkte zur Intervention. In Deutsches Institut für Menschenrechte. (Ed.), *Zwangsverheiratung in Deutschland. Band 1. Schriftenreihe des Bundesministeriums für Familie, Senioren, Frauen und Jugend* (pp. 27-71). Baden-Baden: Nomos Verlag.

Stuttgarter Zeitung. (2011). Die Frischvermählten sind Nachbarn und Behörden suspekt. Lokalausgabe Kornwestheim und Kreis Ludwigsburg. April 1. [On-line]. http://www.stuttgarter-zeitung.de/inhalt.die-frischvermaehlten-sind-nachbarn-und-behoerden-suspekt.524c269f-70e5-4103-9a6d-6618c664db95.html

Taitz, J., Weekers, J. E. M., & Mosca, D. T. (2002). DNA and immigration: the ethical ramifications. *The Lancet, 359,* 794.

Ter Wal, J., de Munnik, S., & Andriessen, I. (2008). Turkish Marriage Migration to the Netherlands: Policy vs. Migrants' Perspectives. *Journal of Immigrant & Refugee Studies, 6,* 409-422.

Thadani, V. N., & Todaro, M. P. (1984). Female Migration: A Conceptual Framework. In J. T. Fawcett, S. Khoo & P. C. Smith (Eds.), *Women in the Cities of Asia: Migration and Urban Adaptation* (pp. 36-59). Boulder, CO: Westview Press.

Thai, H. C. (2003). Clashing Dreams: Highly Educated Overseas Brides and Low-Wage U.S. Husbands. In B. Ehrenreich & A. Russell Hochschild (Eds.), *Global Woman. Nannies, Maids and Sex Workers in the New Economy* (pp. 230-253). New York: Metropolitan Books.

Thiemann, A. (2007). Zwangsverheiratung im Kontext gleichgeschlechtlicher Lebensweisen. Erfahrungen aus der Beratungsarbeit. In Deutsches Institut für Menschenrechte. (Ed.), *Zwangsverheiratung in Deutschland. Band 1. Schriftenreihe des Bundesministeriums für Familie, Senioren, Frauen und Jugend* (pp. 187-200). Baden-Baden: Nomos Verlag

Thieme, M. (2009). Verwirrung bei Behörden. Freie Einreise für Türken? *Frankfurter Rundschau Online,* March 9. [On-line]. http://www.fr-online.de/in_und_ausland/politik/aktuell/?em_cnt=1687544&

Thierse, W. (2004). The German language and the Linguistic Diversity of Europe. In A. Gardt & B. Hüppauf (Eds.), *Globalization and the future of German* (pp. 187-196). Berlin: Walter de Gruyter.

Thym, D. (2008). Respect for private life and family life under Article 8 ECHR in immigration cases: A human right to regularize illegal stay? *International and Comparative Law Quarterly, 57,* 87-112.

Tietze, K. (2008). *Einwanderung und die deutschen Parteien. Akzeptanz und Abwehr von Migranten im Widerstreit in der Programmatik von SPD, FDP, den Grünen und CDU/CSU.* Münster: Lit Verlag.

Timmerman, C. (2008). Marriage in a 'Culture of Migration'. Emirdag Marrying into Flanders. *European Review, 16,* 585-594

Timmerman, C., & Wets, J. (2011). Marriage migration and the labour market. The case of migrants of Turkish descent in Belgium. *Nordic Journal of Migration Research, 1,* 69-79.

Triadafilopoulos, T., & Schönwälder, K. (2006). How the Federal Republic Became an Immigration Country. Norms, Politics and the Failure of West Germany's Guest Worker System. *German Politics and Society, 24,* 1-19.

Triandafyllidou, A., & Fotiou, A. (1998). Sustainability and Modernity in the European Union: A Frame Theory Approach to Policy-making. *Sociological Research Online, 3.* [On-line]. http://www.socresonline.org.uk/3/1/2.html

Turner, B. S. (2008). Citizenship, reproduction and the state: international marriage and human rights. *Citizenship Studies, 12,* 45-54.

UK Border Agency. (2010). *Information for applicants on the new English language requirement for partners.* [On-line]. http://www.ukba.homeoffice.gov.uk/sitecontent/documents/partners-other-family/guidance-for-applicants.pd

UK Border Agency. (2011). *Family Migration. A Consultation.* [On-line]. http://www.ukba.homeoffice.gov.uk/family-migration-consult

Unabhängige Kommission Zuwanderung. (2001). *Zuwanderung gestalten. Integration Fördern.* July 4. Available at http://www.bmi.bund.de/cae/servlet/contentblob/123148/publicationFile/9075/Zuwanderungsbericht_pdf.pdf

Van de Water, M. (2010). Court thwarts Dutch immigration policy. *NRC Handelsblad,* March 11. [On-line]. http://www.nrc.nl/international/article2501656.ece/Court_thwarts_Dutch_immigration_policy

Van Walsum, S. (2004). The Dynamics of Emancipation and Exclusion. Changing Family Norms and Dutch Family Migration Policies. *IMIS-Beiträge, 24,* 119-128

Van Walsum, S. (2008). *The Family and the Nation: Dutch Family Migration Policies in the Context of Changing Family Norms.* Newcastle upon Tyne: Cambridge Scholars Publishing.

Van Walsum, S. (2009). Against All Odds: How Single and Divorced Migrant Mothers were Eventually able to Claim their Right to Respect for Family Life. *European Journal of Migration and Law, 11,* 295-311.

Verband binationaler Familien und Partnerschaften, iaf e.V. (2001). *Fabienne: Familles et Couples Binationaux en Europe. Abschlussbericht.* [On-line]. www.verband-binationaler.de/europaeischevernetzung/AbschlussberichtD.pdf

Verband binationaler Familien und Partnerschaften, iaf e.V. (2008a). *"Haben Sie noch eine Idee?" Erfahrungen mit der Verschäfung beim Ehegattennachzug.* Frankfurt: Verband binationaler Familien und Partnerschaften, iaf e.V.

Verband binationaler Familien und Partnerschaften, iaf e.V. (2008b). Pressemitteilung. *Deutsche dürfen in ihrem Land nicht schlechter behandelt werden als Unionsbürger/-innen – der Sprachnachweis vor der Einreise muss gestrichen werden.* [On-line]. http://www.verband-binationaler.de/seiten/file/home/PM_Sprachnachweiss_Juli08.pdf

Verband binationaler Familien und Partnerschaften, iaf e.V. (2010). Presseinformation. *Ende einer Dienstfahrt. Bundeswehrsoldat muss nach einem Auslandseinsatz drei Jahre mit deutschen Behörden um seine Familie kämpfen.* [On-line]. http://www.verband-binationaler.de/fileadmin/user_upload/Bundesverband/Ende_einer_Dienstfahrt.pdf
Verloo, M. (2005). Mainstreaming Gender Equality in Europe. A Frame Analysis Approach. *The Greek Review of Social Research, 117 B'*, 11-34.
Verloo, M. (Ed.). (2007). *Multiple Meanings of Gender Equality. A critical frame analysis of gender policies in Europe.* Budapest: CEU Press.
Verloo, M., & Lombardo, E. (2007). Contested Gender Equality and Policy Variety in Europe: Introducing a Critical Frame Analysis Approach. In M. Verloo (Ed.), *Multiple Meanings of Gender Equality. A critical frame analysis of gender policies in Europe.* (pp. 21-50). Budapest: CEU Press.
Völker, M. (2010). Deutsch vor Zuwanderung: SPÖ stimmte zu. *DER STANDARD*, January 19.
Vogel, U. (1994). Marriage and the Boundaries of Citizenship. In B. van Steenbergen (Ed.), *The Condition of Citizenship* (pp. 76-89). London [etc]: Sage Publications.
Vogel, U. (2000). Private contract and public institution: The peculiar case of marriage. In M. Passerin d'Entrèves & U. Vogel (Eds.), *Public & Private. Legal, political and philosophical perspectives* (pp. 177-199). London: Routledge.
Volpp, L. (2001). Feminism versus Multiculturalism. *Columbia Law Review, 101,* 1181-1218.
Waever, O., Buzan, B., Kelstrup, M. & Lemaitre, P. (1993). (Eds.). *Identity, Migration and the New Security Agenda in Europe.* London: Pinter.
Waldis, B. (2006). Introduction: Marriage in an Era of Globalisation. In B. Waldis & R. Byron (Eds.), *Migration and Marriage: Heterogamy and Homogamy in a Changing World* (pp. 1-19). Münster: Lit.
Walter, A. (2008). *Reverse Discrimination and Family Reunification.* Nijmegen: Wolf Legal Publishers.
Walzer, M. (1983). *Spheres of Justice: A Defense of Pluralism and Equality.* New York: Basic Books.
Wang, H., & Chang, S. (2002). The Commodification of International Marriages: Cross-border Marriage Business in Taiwan and Viet Nam. *International Migration, 40,* 93-116.
Weil, P. (1991). *La France et ses etrangers. L'aventure d'une politique de l'immigration, 1938-1991.* Paris: Calmann-Lévy.
Weinzierl, R. (2007). Stellungnahme für die Anhörung „EU-Richtlinienumsetzungsgesetz" des Innenausschusses des Deutschen Bundestages am 21. Mai 2007 zu BT-Drs. 16/5065 und anderen Gesetzesentwürfen. *Innenausschuss. A-Drs. 16(4)209 J.* Berlin: Deutsches Institut für Menschenrechte.
Welte, H. (2009). *Familienzusammenführung und Familiennachzug: Praxishandbuch zum Zuwanderungsrecht.* Regensburg: Walhalla Fachverlag.
Westphal, V., & Stoppa, E. (2009). *Report Ausländer- und Europarecht Nr. 19. Februar 2009.* [On-line]. http://www.westphal-stoppa.de/O-Report/19ReportFebruar2009.pdf
Wodak, R., & van Dijk, T. A. (Eds.). (2000). *Racism at the Top. Parliamentary Discourses on Ethnic Issues in Six European States.* Klagenfurt: Drava Verlag.
Williams, C. J. (2002). ‚Honor killing' shakes up Sweden after man slays daughter who wouldn't wed. *Seattle Times*, March 8.
Williams, L. (2010). *Global Marriage. Cross-Border Marriage Migration in Global Context.* Hampshire: Palgrave Macmillan.

Woellert, F., Kröhnert, S., Sippel, L., & Klingholz, R. (2009). *Ungenutzte Potenziale. Zur Lage der Integration in Deutschland*. Berlin: Berlin-Institut für Bevölkerung und Entwicklung.
Wray, H. (2006). An Ideal Husband? Marriages of Convenience, Moral Gate-keeping and Immigration to the UK. *European Journal of Migration and Law, 8*, 303-320.
Wray, H. (2009). Moulding the migrant family. *Legal Studies, 29*, 592-618.
Wray, H. (2011). *Regulating Marriage Migration into the UK. A Stranger in the Home*. Farnham: Ashgate.
Wray, H. (2013). Regulating Spousal Migration in Denmark. *Immigration, Asylum and Nationality Law, 27*, 139-161.
Yuval-Davis, N. (2006). Belonging and the politics of belonging. *Patterns of Prejudice, 40*, 197-214.
Yuval-Davis, N. (2007). Intersectionality, citizenship and contemporary politics of belonging. Critical Review of International Social and Political Philosophy, 10, 561-574.
ZEIT online. (2007). *Gipfel-Boykott*. July 11. [On-line].
http://www.zeit.de/online/2007/28/integrationsgipfel-boykott
Zolberg, A. (2003). The Archeology of "Remote Control". In A. Farhmeir, O. Faron & P. Weil (Eds.), *Migration Control in the North Atlantic World* (pp. 195-222). New York: Berghahn Books.

Annex – Overview primary material

Parliament documents: plenary protocols (2005-2010)

Document	Date	Relevant pages
16/24	15.03.2006	1837-1839
16/62	08.11.2006	6058-6060; 6067
16/79	01.02.2007	7976-7981
16/84	07.03.2007	8458-8459
16/88	22.03.2007	8935-8943
16/90	28.03.2007	9065-9072
16/94	26.04.2007	9543-9567
16/103	14.06.2007	10584-10610
16/104	20.06.2007	10695-10696
16/107	04.07.2007	11011-11015
16/143	15.02.2008	15123-15134
16/144	20.02.2008	15187-15189
16/146	22.02.2008	15430-15452
16/159	07.05.2008	16797
16/161	09.05.2008	16977-16995
16/169	19.06.2008	17845-17865
16/179	25.09.2008	19006-19019
16/184	17.10.2008	19723-19731
16/188	25.11.2008	20296-20313
16/202	29.01.2009	21897-21904
16/209	06.03.2009	22633-22641
16/210	18.03.2009	22709
16/213	25.03.2009	23073-23075

16/214	26.03.2009	23340-23346
16/227	18.06.2009	25273-25278; 25333-25338
17/4	11.11.2009	200-217
17/7	26.11.2009	507-514
17/43	20.05.2010	4371-4378
17/51	01.07.2010	5426
17/52	02.07.2010	5490-5498
17/67	27.10.2010	7102-7111

Parliament Documents: Interpellations (2005-2010)

Party	Document	Date	Answer	Date
FDP	16/6856	24.10.2007	16/7259	22.11.2007
LINKE	16/6914	02.11.2007	16/7288	27.11.2007
LINKE	16/7953	29.01.2008	16/8175	18.02.2008
LINKE	16/8850	18.04.2008	16/9137	07.05.2008
GRÜNE	16/9496	03.06.2008	16/9722	24.06.2008
LINKE	16/9939	07.07.2008	16/10052	24.07.2008
LINKE	16/10113	13.08.2008	16/10198	02.09.2008
LINKE	16/10254	17.09.2008	16/10516	09.10.2008
LINKE	16/10564	13.10.2008	16/10732	29.10.2008
GRÜNE	16/10717	28.10.2008	16/10921	12.11.2008
LINKE	16/11811	28.01.2009	16/11997	16.02.2009
GRÜNE	16/11821	30.01.2009	16/12013	18.02.2009
LINKE	16/12764	20.04.2009	16/12979	08.05.2009
LINKE	16/13905	18.08.2009	16/13978	03.09.2009
LINKE	17/73	24.11.2009	17/194	11.12.2009
LINKE	17/946	05.03.2010	17/1112	18.03.2010
LINKE	17/2746	12.08.2010	17/2816	27.08.2010
LINKE	17/3268	06.10.2010	17/3393	26.10.2010
LINKE	17/4317	20.12.2010	17/4623	02.02.2011

Interviews

1. Members of Parliament
   a) Wolfgang Wieland (GRÜNE), 21.10.2009 – 68'
   b) Reinhard Grindel (CDU), 12.11.2009 – 79'
   c) Staff member of Rüdiger Veit (SPD), 19.11.2009 – 60'
   d) Sybille Laurischk (FDP), 23.11.2009 – 60'
   e) Dieter Wiefelspütz (SPD), 03.12.2009 – 47'
   f) Sevim Dagdelen (LINKE), 04.12.2009 – 139'
   g) Mehmet Kilic (GRÜNE), 21.01.2010 – 88'
   h) Sebastian Edathy (SPD), 04.03.2010 – 36'

2. Federal and Regional Executive
   a) Former Integration Commissioner Berlin (1981-2003), 26.10.2009 – 75'
   b) Head of Integration Section, Ministry for Intergenerational Affairs, Family, Women and Integration (*Ministerium für Generationen, Familie, Frauen und Integration*) North Rhine-Westphalia (NRW), 03.11.2009 – 115'
   c) Three policy officers, Unit Foreigners' Law, Interior Ministry NRW, 05.11.2009 – 145'
   d) Policy officer, Federal Integration Commissioner, 24.11.2009 – 90'
   e) Former Head of the Migration Department (1999-2009), BMI, 15.12.2009 – 90'
   f) Head of Unit Integration, BMI, 01.02.2010 – 105'
   g) Head of Unit Foreigners' Law, BMI, 16.02.2010 – 82'
   h) Two policy officers, AA, 16.04.2010 – 120'

3. Local Executive
   a) Head of Aliens Authority Rhein-Kreis Neuss, 04.11.2009 – 120'
   b) Civil servant, Integration Commissioner Berlin, 13.11.2009 – 46'
   c) Three civil servants, Aliens Authority Frankfurt/Main, 30.03.2010 – 80'

4. Migrant NGOs/Lawyers
   a) Head of the IAF (Verband binationaler Familien und Partnerschaften, iaf e.V.), 02.11.2009 – 150'

b) Head of the Turkish Community in Germany (*Türkische Gemeinde in Deutschland*), 13.11.2009 – 54'
c) Head of the KOK (Bundesweiter Koordinierungskreis gegen Frauenhandel und Gewalt an Frauen im Migrationsprozess e.V.), 27.11.2009 – 67'
d) Lawyer specialised in migration and family law, Berlin, 14.12.2009 – 92'
e) Lawyer specialised in migration and asylum law, Frankfurt/Main, referee in the *Bundestag*'s Committee on Internal Affairs (*Innenausschuss*), 31.03.2010 – 46'

Studien zur Migrations- und Integrationspolitik

Herausgegeben von Uwe Hunger, Roswitha Pioch und Stefan Rother

Bisher in dieser Reihe erschienen:

D. Softic
Migranten in der Politik
Eine empirische Studie zu Bundestagsabgeordneten
mit Migrationshintergrund
2016. XV, 380 S., Br. € 49,99
ISBN 978-3-658-11159-5

B. Nieswand · H. Drotbohm (Hrsg.)
Kultur, Gesellschaft, Migration.
Die reflexive Wende in der Migrationsforschung
2014. XIII, 346 S. Br. € 39,99
ISBN 978-3-658-03625-6

C. Ghaderi
Politische Identität-Ethnizität-Geschlecht
Selbstverortungen politisch aktiver MigrantInnen
2014. XX, 411 S., Geb. € 49,99
ISBN 978-3-658-05296-6

Der nächste Band der Reihe:

L. Block
Policy Frames on Spousal Migration in Germany
Regulating Membership, Regulating the Family

Stand: November 2015. Änderungen vorbehalten.
Erhältlich im Buchhandel oder beim Verlag.

Einfach portofrei bestellen:
leserservice@springer.com
tel +49 (0)6221 345-4301
springer.com

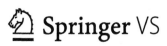

VS Forschung | VS Research
Neu im Programm Politik

Michaela Allgeier (Hrsg.)
Solidarität, Flexibilität, Selbsthilfe
Zur Modernität der Genossenschaftsidee
2011. 138 S. Br. EUR 39,95
ISBN 978-3-531-17598-0

Susanne von Hehl
Bildung, Betreuung und Erziehung als neue Aufgabe der Politik
Steuerungsaktivitäten in drei Bundesländern
2011. 406 S. (Familie und Familienwissenschaft) Br. EUR 49,95
ISBN 978-3-531-17850-9

Isabel Kneisler
Das italienische Parteiensystem im Wandel
2011. 289 S. Br. EUR 39,95
ISBN 978-3-531-17991-9

Frank Meerkamp
Die Quorenfrage im Volksgesetzgebungsverfahren
Bedeutung und Entwicklung
2011. 596 S. (Bürgergesellschaft und Demokratie Bd. 36) Br. EUR 39,95
ISBN 978-3-531-18064-9

Martin Schröder
Die Macht moralischer Argumente
Produktionsverlagerungen zwischen wirtschaftlichen Interessen und gesellschaftlicher Verantwortung
2011. 237 S. (Bürgergesellschaft und Demokratie Bd. 35) Br. EUR 39,95
ISBN 978-3-531-18058-8

Lilian Schwalb
Kreative Governance?
Public Private Partnerships in der lokalpolitischen Steuerung
2011. 301 S. (Bürgergesellschaft und Demokratie Bd. 37) Br. EUR 39,95
ISBN 978-3-531-18151-6

Kurt Beck / Jan Ziekow (Hrsg.)
Mehr Bürgerbeteiligung wagen
Wege zur Vitalisierung der Demokratie
2011. 214 S. Br. EUR 29,95
ISBN 978-3-531-17861-5

Erhältlich im Buchhandel oder beim Verlag.
Änderungen vorbehalten. Stand: Juli 2011.

Einfach bestellen:
SpringerDE-service@springer.com
tel +49 (0)6221 / 3 45 – 4301
springer-vs.de

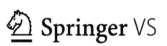 Springer VS

VS Forschung | VS Research
Neu im Programm Soziologie

Ina Findeisen
Hürdenlauf zur Exzellenz
Karrierestufen junger Wissenschaftlerinnen und Wissenschaftler
2011. 309 S. Br. EUR 39,95
ISBN 978-3-531-17919-3

David Glowsky
Globale Partnerwahl
Soziale Ungleichheit als Motor transnationaler Heiratsentscheidungen
2011. 246 S. Br. EUR 39,95
ISBN 978-3-531-17672-7

Grit Höppner
Alt und schön
Geschlecht und Körperbilder im Kontext neoliberaler Gesellschaften
2011. 130 S. Br. EUR 29,95
ISBN 978-3-531-17905-6

Andrea Lengerer
Partnerlosigkeit in Deutschland
Entwicklung und soziale Unterschiede
2011. 252 S. Br. EUR 29,95
ISBN 978-3-531-17792-2

Markus Ottersbach /
Claus-Ulrich Prölß (Hrsg.)
Flüchtlingsschutz als globale und lokale Herausforderung
2011. 195 S. (Beiträge zur Regional- und Migrationsforschung) Br. EUR 39,95
ISBN 978-3-531-17395-5

Tobias Schröder / Jana Huck / Gerhard de Haan
Transfer sozialer Innovationen
Eine zukunftsorientierte Fallstudie zur nachhaltigen Siedlungsentwicklung
2011. 199 S. Br. EUR 34,95
ISBN 978-3-531-18139-4

Anke Wahl
Die Sprache des Geldes
Finanzmarktengagement zwischen Klassenlage und Lebensstil
2011. 198 S. r. EUR 34,95
ISBN 978-3-531-18206-3

Tobias Wiß
Der Wandel der Alterssicherung in Deutschland
Die Rolle der Sozialpartner
2011. 300 S. Br. EUR 39,95
ISBN 978-3-531-18211-7

Erhältlich im Buchhandel oder beim Verlag.
Änderungen vorbehalten. Stand: Juli 2011.

Einfach bestellen:
SpringerDE-service@springer.com
tel +49(0)6221/345-4301
springer-vs.de

Printed by Printforce, the Netherlands